NATIVE VOICES

American Indian Identity and Resistance

Edited by Richard A. Grounds,
George E. Tinker,
and David E. Wilkins

University Press of Kansas

© 2003 by the University Press of Kansas

"The Psychology of Earth and Sky" and "There Is No Such Thing as a One-Way Land Bridge" © 2003 by Joy Harjo. First published in *A Map to the Next World: Poetry and Tales* (Norton, 2000).

Published by the University Press of Kansas (Lawrence, Kansas 66049), which was organized by the Kansas Board of Regents and is operated and funded by Emporia State University, Fort Hays State University, Kansas State University, Pittsburg State University, the University of Kansas, and Wichita State University

Library of Congress Cataloging-in-Publication Data

Native Voices : American Indian identity and resistance / edited by
Richard A. Grounds, George E. Tinker, and David E. Wilkins.
    p. cm.
Includes bibliographical references and index.
   ISBN 0-7006-1258-0 (cloth : alk. paper)—ISBN 0-7006-1259-9 (pbk.: alk. paper)
   1. Indians of North America—Ethnic identity. 2. Indians of North
America—Politics and government. 3. Indians of North America—Social
conditions. 4. Self-determination, National—United States. 5. Deloria,
Vine. I. Grounds, Richard A. II. Tinker, George E. III. Wilkins, David E.
(David Eugene), 1954–
   E98.E85.N38 2003
   305.897—dc21
                    2003005309

British Library Cataloguing in Publication Data is available.

Printed in the United States of America
10 9 8 7 6 5 4 3 2 1

The paper used in this publication meets the minimum requirements of the American National Standard for Permanence of Paper for Printed Library Materials Z39.48-1984.

Contents

Preface

"Native American studies" is a strange hybrid phenomenon of contemporary higher education, but it is also characteristic of the shifts in disciplinary arrangements of the past thirty years that have generated departments of ethnic studies generally. Traditional Euro-Western academics might complain that Native studies is hardly a discipline at all, that it does not fit into the discrete divisions of intellectual categories that have emerged in Western consciousness. Accordingly, they might argue that Native American studies has only an ephemeral place in the academy.[1]

The truth is that anyone engaged in the various aspects of Native American studies is necessarily involved in extensive cross-disciplinary exercises. Although our training may be in a particular university department, our teaching and research may cover multiple disciplinary territories. For example, it is inconceivable to many of us that an Indian scholar trained in Native religious traditions could meaningfully teach those traditions without paying close attention to the political history and contemporary sociological realities affecting them. Ultimately, the same scholar may find it necessary—simply out of intellectual self-defense—to engage the contemporary philosophical discourse of postmodernism. It goes without saying that a healthy engagement with political theory is quintessential to providing a deeper analysis of indigenous religious traditions. An understanding of the domestic history of federal Indian policy in the United States is an important starting point for almost any Indian scholar in any discipline. At the same time, the status of indigenous people generally in the global arena means that we also need an increasingly sophisticated understanding of international theory and international law. The practical demand for indigenous scholars with an interdisciplinary repertoire of analytical approaches is reflected in the authorial composition of this book. Several of the authors teach in law schools and cover aspects of "federal Indian law," but they have also developed expertise in such diverse fields as cultural analysis, church history, medieval canon law, and the natural sciences.

A striking example of the breadth represented by Native American studies is provided in the life's work of Vine Deloria, Jr., the current dean of all American Indian scholars. A "Coyote Old Man" figure, Deloria has always been a teacher, a wily man of the world who combines perspicuity, clear and convincing critical analysis, vision, and intuition with a sense of the ironic. Just as Coyote is the people's teacher in so many American Indian cultures and is committed to their well-being even in moments of feigned foolishness and individualism, Deloria is the consummate teacher whose remarkable intellectual gift to the Indian world inspires younger and older Indian intellectuals, even as it sometimes appears as unimaginable outrage to incredulous non-Indians.

Recently retired from his position as professor of history at the University of Colorado–Boulder, Deloria has accumulated a prolific list of accomplishments and publications. His work is widely renowned and highly regarded outside the Native American community as well as within it. Deloria's more philosophical or theological work, though especially pertinent to the development and articulation of Indian thinking, is not limited in its impact to Indian people but continues to be instructive to those who function largely within the Western intellectual tradition. His contribution to American Indian scholarship will become increasingly important to the academy as a whole and to the development and articulation of modern American Indian thought.

Four of his most recent volumes are illustrative of Deloria's striking intellectual breadth. His writing moves effortlessly from philosophy to the natural sciences, from law to religion, from political theory to archaeology, paleontology, and anthropology, speaking across a wide variety of academic disciplines. With his remarkable achievements as a legal theorist, theologian, historian, and political scientist, Deloria has influenced a whole generation of younger Indian scholars to be self-consciously indigenous thinkers—to reclaim an American Indian intellectual tradition, along with a political activism rooted in the oral traditions of our peoples and the wisdom of our elders and ancestors. Out of polemical and apologetic necessity, he has been a true polymathic educator.

Deloria's *Red Earth; White Lies* (1997) is a thorough dismantling of some of the most treasured white academic doctrines about the aboriginal peoples of the Americas—attacking, for instance, the Bering Strait theory head-on with the best evidence that modern earth science and traditional indigenous knowledge have to offer. *Spirit and Reason* (1999) includes an essay on the philosophy of science that affirms the radical edge of and moves beyond the work of Paul Feyerabend. In moving beyond Feyerabend, Deloria introduces notions that come directly out of Native cultures that pose their own critique of Western natural sciences. *Tribes, Treaties, and Constitutional Tribulations* (2000), coauthored with David Wilkins, describes the fictive nature of "federal Indian law." They go so far as to demonstrate that the entire corpus of federal Indian law is singularly unconstitutional and thus has no grounding in any rule of law other than the imagination of jurists and legislatures. As such, the volume implicitly challenges the cornerstone of Euro-Western civilization: the universal and constitutional affirmation of the "rule of law" as the organizing principle of Euro-Western societies. Certainly, it contests the validity of U.S. governmental control of Indian affairs. Finally, *Evolution, Creationism, and Other Modern Myths: A Critical Inquiry* (2002) analyzes the current state of evolutionary theory, religion, and science in a way that fundamentally challenges the comfort zones of both religious fundamentalists and evolutionists. Both these groups are steeped in the Western belief system and fail to accurately account for the rise of *Homo sapiens* or Earth's history in part because they disregard or undervalue indigenous and non-Western worldviews.

Perhaps Deloria's greatest contribution, however, is the extent to which he has been a role model to a generation of Indian scholars. Most important, his has not been an ivory tower intellectual life divorced from the realities of American Indian community existence. He has made countless visits to numerous reservation communities over the years. The guidance and support he provides to younger Indian scholars have been invaluable.

The chapters in this volume are not intended to glorify the work or life of Deloria. Rather, they are intended to honor him by presenting the original work of a variety of young (and middle-aged) scholars who have been deeply influenced by him. Nor is this book intended as an "introduction to Native America," but it is a collection of writings about Native America that critically assesses some of the fundamental issues facing American Indian people today—issues that have usually been clearly identified by Deloria either in his voluminous writings or in comments at one conference or another. The chapters cover a wide variety of topics— from religion to science, from law to politics and political science— reflecting again the interdisciplinary depth exercised by Deloria. They also represent a wide variety of methodological discourses—from law to religion, from anthropology and culture studies to science, from political science to general philosophical studies. As such, they are representative of the field called Native American studies that has emerged over the past thirty years in universities and colleges in North America.

This collection incorporates some works that clearly evoke the impact of Deloria's life and scholarship on Native scholars. Because his influence extends beyond the social sciences, law, and theology, we have included some shorter, more focused pieces that address similar themes but in a more creative style of evocative observations, ranging from poetry to shorter narrative commentaries relating to issues of indigenous resistance.

Since all the contributors are Native American scholars writing about Native America, they have an "insider's" perspective and keen experiential insight, drawing on their individual disciplinary expertise. To that extent, the chapters were written with a Native audience in mind, with the intent of extending the discourse among those who are already deeply involved in understanding the issues. At the same time, this book is readily accessible to readers new to Native American issues and the professional discourse of Indian scholars. We expect that these new readers will be introduced to key issues in such a way that they will find it easy to move on to other texts in the field. For the neophyte, this book will help build a base for a much deeper understanding of Indian peoples and their contemporary concerns.

At the time of its initial publication, Deloria's *God Is Red* (1973) presented us with an amazing systemization and articulation of general American Indian thought. As such, it continues to represent an important first for Native people. Both outrageous and important, it covered a huge intellectual waterfront, modeling a systematic, coherent Indian response to the fundamentals of Western, Amer-European historiography, philosophy, theology, social criticism, and political theory. As an interdisciplinary piece of writing, it portended Deloria's later writings in law, U.S. government Indian policy, education, religion, and natural science. Books such as *The Nations Within* and *American Indians: American Justice,* written with Clifford Lytle, became cutting-edge monographs in American Indian scholarship, dealing with U.S. Indian policy and federal Indian law.

Volumes such as *God Is Red* and *The Metaphysics of Modern Existence* were much more than a systematized introduction to American Indian thinking. In large part, they were critical reflections on Euro-Western thought and culture. Deloria's writings have been, if you will, American Indian ethnographies of Amer-European intellectual and religious lifeways. As a result, the greatest contribution of his work is that it seriously "stirs the pot" and provokes a rethinking of established and accepted academic doctrines. Again and again, Deloria demonstrates the inadequacy of various Western modes of discourse, offering stunningly fruitful new ways of understanding the evidence. At the same time, he demonstrates that his own hermeneutical reflections, infused with indigenous values yet uniquely his own, firmly and empirically refute the generally accepted solutions offered in Western scientific and social scientific explanations of the world. Deloria exposes the inherent contradictions of the leading conventional theories for various phenomena in both history and science. More important, Deloria's challenges to these conventions of history and science reveal the political purpose that has been served by these popular fictions, especially how they have been used to signify American Indian existence in terms controlled and controllable by the colonialist settler population in North America. Deloria's suppositious argumentation serves as a powerful and useful challenge.

More to the point, Deloria engages in this dialogue with minimal concession to explicit categories of cognition common to those Western traditions. Instead, he models the existence and articulation of enduring natural categories of Indian cultures that are foundational for tribal existence and for tribal intellectual, social, political, and religious traditions. Thus his writings continue to be a forceful challenge to the presumed inherent hegemony of the Western intellectual tradition. It is in this very exercise that Deloria's writings instruct many bright Indian youth—a future generation of Indian scholars—in the validity of their own cultures and the resources, categories of knowledge, and modes of discourse already at their disposal for reasoned, analytical thought. A singular achievement in *God is Red*, advanced significantly in *Metaphysics*, is its systematic and consistent analysis of the distinction between spatiality and temporality as culturally discrete ways of being in the world. In a sense, nearly every Indian person had already noticed this important difference between tribal Native American peoples and the Amer-European settler population, yet it was little discussed in the literature until Deloria finally and irrevocably named it. Likewise, Deloria spelled out in critical argumentation the communitarian-individualist difference between Indian and Amer-European cultures. These category distinctions have since become foundational for a genuine, analytical understanding of any particular Indian culture and for Indian intellectual thought in general. Thus, Deloria has articulated what might be called a "metascience," that is, a critique of Euro-Western science from the perspective of indigenous knowledge systems. His is an Indian intellectual mind at work. Anyone genuinely interested in the lifeways of American Indian peoples should carefully ponder Deloria's work. More to the point, this is a fine intellect at work. Those of us genuinely interested in the health and well-being of our world community need to pay close attention to the issues and ideas raised by Deloria.

We believe that this volume has real merit. It provides evidence, as if any were still needed, of the vast and nuanced manner in which Deloria's work has influenced a number of individual Indian scholars, tribal nations, and academic disciplines. It provides a set of indigenous perspectives on topics that typically are treated by non-Indians. Finally, it provides discussion and analysis of substantive topics of vital interest to indigenous communities.

Indigenous nations face a future of great uncertainty because of their unstable political, legal, and economic position in the United States; environmental degradation, which is continuing and worsening; and internal problems of language loss, rising crime rates, and tribal governments that are still struggling to sort out their place within and without tribal society. Fortunately, Deloria has produced a bevy of interdisciplinary and behavior-modifying works that Indian nations in general and Indian academics in particular can draw on for inspiration, guidance, and support as we prepare to face the unpredictable years ahead.

The chapters that follow detail a small cross section of the indigenous scholarship that Deloria has influenced and that situates the various arenas of ongoing indigenous resistance. The book has been divided into four parts. Part I, "Cultures of Resistance," is introduced by a short piece from Joy Harjo, who evokes the alternative cultural stance, the contrary perspective harbored within indigenous communities. Her remarks fittingly suggest the largely ignored promise that is bound up within our indigenous understandings of human life as a vital part of the larger, living cosmos. Her poetic reflection evokes the intergenerational persistence of our cultural heritages. It is the same intergenerational theme with which Deloria concludes this volume. The chapters included here articulate specific aspects of indigenous societies as the embodiment of cultures of resistance and demonstrate the rich and long-embattled alternative cultures of indigenous nations. The first chapter points to the stars as a frame for understanding that indigenous nations are oriented around fundamentally different axes than those notions that frame European patterns of living in the world. The second chapter covers the conflicted reactions within Seneca society to the prominent role of women as it reshaped itself historically in order to conserve its traditional understanding of itself. The third discusses the ongoing struggle of Native nations to preserve and promote their unique understandings of the world through indigenous literatures.

Part II, "Resistance, Politics, Colonization, and the Law," showcases Deloria's influence in the critical arena of legal resistance to long histories of Western oppression against indigenous nations. His importance as a career and legal training model, as a protean legal theorist, and as a practical influence in the area of Native American legal matters is hard to overestimate. As M. A. Jaimes-Guerrero's introduction underscores, the entire corpus of legal doctine, its development and application, needs to be questioned. Even the notion of the "rule of law" itself must be interrogated as an accomplice in the deep history of colonial rationales for domination. The chapters included here reflect the directions of resistance within the legal arena, ranging from revealing the intricacies of underlying legal doctrines to laying out the trend toward extending international law to protect the legal rights of indigenous peoples.

The narrative introduction to Part III, "Native American Religious Traditions and Resistance," by Cecil Corbett recalls those moving times when Deloria's intellect first articulated for a bewildered national audience the sharp concerns of Native Americans that were being raised by activists across the land, times when Custer died and God became red. Deloria was embroiled in a substantive way in both the practical shifts in personnel, strategy, and funding and the ideological, theological, and philosophical changes that were stirring. These chapters cover the special distinctions among indigenous nations in their celebration and understanding of land and their struggle for it, the specific disciplinary efforts to decolonize religious studies, and the naming of particular and insidious patterns of intrusion into contemporary Native religious practices.

The final part, "Indian Intellectual Culture and Resistance," opens with the haunting counterreflections of Joy Harjo on the Amer-European pet themes of extinction and late-arriving Native peoples as she points to the linkages between European intellectual traditions and the political and moral justifications that have characterized the multifarious processes of dispossession. The chapters here range from the further pursuit of the foibles found within the academy, such as questioning the evidentiary basis for the notion of the land bridge, to the predilection of academics to fall into the little-considered assumptions of the larger colonial-based society in their thinking about the claimed "extinctions" of Native populations.

Deloria's powerful closing essay, "The Passage of Generations," reminds us of our responsibilities and obligations to one another and to the before and after generations. Indigenous self-determination begins with individual self-determination. It is the hope of the editors that this volume will provide readers with useful insights into Deloria's profound life and ongoing career and will introduce and detail some of the critical issues confronting Native nations.

NOTE

1. There has been a dazzling array of new disciplines added to the modern university during the past century. The original European university, dating to the late European Middle Ages, consisted of only four departments: theology, philosophy, law, and medicine. Today, of course, a school of medicine alone can consist of a couple dozen different departments, and universities can have scores of departments and programs leading to undergraduate degrees (nearly 300 are listed on the web page of the University of California–Berkeley). Often, each department is divided even further into a variety of discrete discourses and specialties. In a political science department, for example, a degree in political theory is considerably different from a degree in comparative politics.

PART I: CULTURES OF RESISTANCE

The Psychology of Earth and Sky

Joy Harjo (Mvskoke)

It is just before dawn. The mango tree responds to the wind's fierce jostling. A rooster stridently marks the emerging light. We are alerted, and our spirits trek back through night and the stars to awaken here in this place known as Honolulu. Clouds harboring rain travel fast over the city, and now a trash truck beeps as it backs up for collection. And dawn arrives, no matter the struggle of the night and how endless that night might be.

We are part of an old story, and involved in it are migrations of winds, of ocean currents, of seeds, songs, and generations of nations.

In this life it seems like I am always leaving, flying over this earth that harbors many lives. I was born Indian, female, and artist in the Creek Nation. It is still gray out as I follow the outline of memory. Over there is my teenage self getting out of a car, still a little drunk, waving good-bye to friends. We've been up all night, singing into the dark, joining the stars out on the mesa west of the Indian town, Albuquerque.

"When the dance is over, sweetheart, I will take you home in my one-eyed Ford. Wey-yo-hey-ya. Hey-yah-hah. Hey-yah-hah."

That song was destined to become a classic.

The shutting of the car door echoes and echoes and leads to here. I always hear that door when I return to that memory. It's a holographic echo, turning over and over into itself. I am leaving. I am returning.

I turned to walk to my apartment in the back. All of us lived in the back of somewhere in that city where we were defining what it meant to be Indian in a system of massive colonization. It was a standing joke. A backdoor joke. The world was suddenly condensed by the shutting of the door, the sweet purr of the engine as the car drove off, and the perfect near silence of the pause in the morning scramble of sparrows, the oohhing of doves. I can still breathe it, that awareness of being alive part of the ceremony for the rising of the sun. I often lived for this moment of reconciliation, where night and morning met. It didn't matter that I didn't quite know how I was going to piece together what I needed for tuition, rent, groceries, books, and child care; how I was going to make sense of a past that threatened to destroy me during those times when I doubted that I deserved a place in the world. The songs we sang all night together filled me with promise, hope, the belief in a community that understood that the world was more than a contract between buyer and seller.

And that morning, just as the dawn was arriving and I was coming home, I knew that the sun needed us, needed my own little song made of the whirr push of the blood through my lungs and heart. Inside that bloodstream was born my son, my daughter. I was born of parents who would greet the dawn often in their courtship with their amazing passion driven by love, and later heartbreak. Dawn was also the time my father often came home after he and my mother were married, had four children, dropped off by his friends, reeking of smoke, beer, and strange perfume. And I am his daughter. How much do we have to say in the path our feet will take? Is it ordained by the curve of a strand of DNA? Mixed with the urge to love, to take flight? My family survived, even continues to thrive, which works against the myth of Indian defeat and disappearance.

CHAPTER ONE

Ethnoastronomy as the Key to Human Intellectual Development and Social Organization
Clara Sue Kidwell (Choctaw/Ojibwe)

In the Bighorn Mountains of Wyoming, a medicine wheel sits at an altitude of approximately 7,500 feet on a bluff offering a spectacular view of the land below and of the eastern horizon. The wheel is built with twenty-eight radiating spokes, a central stone cairn, and six stone cairns positioned at irregular intervals around its perimeter. The spokes and cairns define a number of sight lines across the horizon. At sunrise on the day of the summer solstice, the line from one of the perimeter cairns across the central one of the wheel points directly to the rising sun. Other cairns and spokes align with the first yearly rising immediately before dawn of the bright stars Rigal, Aldabaran, and Sirius. Carbon dating places its construction at about A.D. 1500. Contemporary tribal people in the region—Crow and Shoshone—do not know who built the wheel (Eddy, 1035–43).

Snow often covers the ground in June when the solstice occurs at the medicine wheel. It is not near any sites of permanent occupation. Why did people come to this particular site to construct this wheel to mark celestial events? The answer lies, I think, in the nature of human intellectual endeavor to understand and deal with the physical world. The work of creating the wheel must represent the efforts not of a single individual but of several generations. Although the summer solstice is an important event, it is not totally apparent on a single day. The term *solstice* literally means that the sun appears to sit in one place for several days before it begins to move back across the horizon. The heliacal appearance of the bright stars is much less dramatic than the solstice sunrise, since it appears against the backdrop of the other fixed stars in the sky.

Ethnoastronomy provides insight into the worldviews of indigenous people in the Americas. The medicine wheel is evidence of the practice of science, which begins first with systematic observation of events in nature. To identify the first appearance of the sun and stars on the horizon required systematic observation for considerable lengths of time. It required that observers passed on their knowledge to others, and that they left a permanent record of results.

American Indians are generally the object of scientific study rather than being considered scientists in their own right. Their stories of their origins and relationships with the natural world around them are folk-lore, not cosmology. Because their knowledge came from oral traditions rather than written language, and they subsisted by their own human labor rather than by domesticating animals and using mechanical devices such as plows, Europeans considered them primitive, although some scholars have given them credit for practicality. G. Stresser-Péan maintains, "Though it would be misleading to call the religious systems and technical achievement of these people 'scientific,' even the most primitive among them made practical contributions that no historian of science can ignore" (293).

In both Europe and the Americas, however, astronomy and mathematics were serious intellectual endeavors, the beginning of scientific practice (Neugebauer, 1–2; Lounsbury, 759–818). According to Francis LaFlesche, the Osage Indians "kept together for protection and moved about without tribal or clan organization, a condition which they termed 'ga-ni'-tha,' which may be freely translated as without law or order." It was, however, "in those days that a group of men fell into the habit of gathering together . . . to exchange ideas concerning the actions of the sun, moon, and stars which they observed move within the sky with marvelous precision, each in its own given path." They observed that the stars "move from one side of the sky to the other without making any disturbances in their relative positions, and that with the great movements four changes take place in the vegetal life of the earth, which they agreed was affected by the actions of some of the heavenly travelers." From these observations they derived the notion that there was a "procreative relationship" between the earth and celestial bodies. They concluded that a silent, invisible creative power pervades the sun, moon, stars, and earth; gives them life; and keeps them eternally in motion and in perfect order. This creative power, which to their minds was the source of life, they named Wa-kon-da (Mysterious Power) and sometimes E-a'wa-won a-ka (Causer of Our Being) (LaFlesche, 29–30).

This attention to the cycles of nature becomes the organizing principle of intellectual inquiry and social organization in American Indian cultures. Ceremonies are timed by the stars, sun, and moon. The study of cosmology, ultimate explanations of the nature of the world, is important to both science and religion and is the area in which we can examine the intersection of observation and faith. Celestial phenomena are the most obvious source of repetition in human experience. The movements of heavenly bodies become the organizing principles of social groups. Easter is, after all, timed by the appearance of the first full moon after the spring equinox. The Hopi Soyal ceremony is timed by the winter solstice

(Titiev, 142–46). The Inca and Mayan people had calendar systems that governed transitions in political leadership in their communities (Zuidema, 231; Farriss, 566–93). The Pawnee organized their villages with reference to the patterns of stars in the sky (Chamberlain, 22–23).

The relationship between human social organization and celestial bodies represents a common human concern, useful for the needs of people who depended on knowledge of changing seasons to manage agricultural and hunting activities, but inspired, perhaps, by both the remoteness and the immediacy of celestial phenomena. The sophistication of knowledge systems concerning the movement of stars and their relation to human activities indicates the importance of the stars in elaborating human culture. As Vincent Malmstrom notes for pre-Columbian Mesoamerica, "bound up with the calendar are many if not all of the more sophisticated aspects of the region's early intellectual life: the awareness of a cyclicity in the movement of celestial bodies, the evolution of mathematical skills by which they could manipulate the numbers derived from those cycles, and the development of a system of hieroglyphics for recording the results" (Malmstrom, 14).

The practice of ethnoastronomy constitutes a basic principle in Native American societies—that time is a function of place and space. Seasonal cycles repeat themselves in endless time and space. The year is marked not only by cycles but also by the movements of heavenly bodies both overhead and in relation to the horizon. Measurement of movement of bodies in space constitutes a measurement of time.

But the conjunctions of star movements are extraordinarily complex, and some cycles, such as eclipses, recur at seemingly irregular intervals. Knowledge of the stars is thus the work not of a single individual observing over a lifetime but of generations of accumulated experience, passed from one generation to another. The record, oral or in permanent form, of the movement of heavenly bodies is thus the earliest form of human science—systematic observation and recognition of recurrent patterns in nature. Stonehenges, woodhenges, medicine wheels, and alignment of structures constitute records of observation.

The sun, moon, and stars are also associated, however, with the emotional aspects of life—the association of the sun's generative powers with human sexuality, the fear of events that celestial events presage. Origin stories in Indian tribes are replete with accounts of young women who married star husbands and lived in the world above this one. An Ojibwe story tells about two foolish girls who slept outside every night, even in winter. They decided that they wanted to marry two stars. When they awoke, they were in the star world, and the white star that one wanted was a white-haired old man, while the red star that the other had admired was a red-headed young man. The girls lived with their star husbands until they became homesick. An old woman told them to make long ropes out of roots, and the star people lowered the girls back to earth in a basket, which stuck, however, in the top of a very tall tree from which they had to be rescued by Wolverine, who made them his wives (Thompson, 126–27).

Everyone in an Indian community has access to a certain level of knowledge about the stars. This access is important for the social organization of Indian societies. In an intellectual sense, there are two sources of knowledge—esoteric and individual knowledge, available only through dreams, visions, or initiation; and common knowledge, available to all people through everyday experience. The knowledge of spiritual beings is personal, the emotional experience of dreams and visions. Black Elk described the vision quest as a time of self-sacrifice—fasting, prayer, sleeplessness, the ultimate offering of human suffering to the spirits to seek their pity (*Black Elk Speaks,* 117).

Initiation rites are another source of esoteric knowledge. Don Talayesva, a Hopi, was initiated into the Kachina society during the Powamu ceremony, which begins on the day after the new moon in February. Hopi children learned that the Kachina dancers who appeared in their villages after the first snowfall were spirits who came from the San Francisco Mountains to bring seeds, protect the villages, and discipline unruly children. When they appeared in dances on the village plazas, they were objects of fear and awe. In the ceremonies in kivas, where Hopi children were initiated into the various secret societies, they unmasked themselves and revealed that they were the fathers, uncles, and other male relatives of the village. Talayesva described his sense of shock and disillusionment at this revelation, but he also came to a deeper understanding of the nature of the Kachinas' significance in Hopi life (*Sun Chief,* 83–84).

Although Indians cultures are deeply spiritual, they are also pragmatic. Knowledge is individual, and Native languages make careful distinctions between what people know from personal experience and what they know only because they have heard it from other people. Origin stories become common knowledge because they are passed from one generation to the next, but they are always acknowledged as such, beginning with "They say that" (Wyman, 109; Kilpatrick, 372–76).

Because knowledge of spiritual beings is personal, much of the intellectual life of Native people is grounded in emotional experiences. Dreams and visions are sources of personal knowledge. Initiation rites are sources of esoteric knowledge, generally gained through experiences that involve physical pain to inspire a different emotional understanding of events.

Knowledge of the stars, however, is available to all people. The Navajo person who goes outdoors to offer a pinch of cornmeal and a prayer to the rising sun acknowledges the importance of the celestial cycle in Navajo life. Although certain individuals may be given responsibility for watching the path of the sun and alerting community members to begin ceremonial preparations, people in the communities can observe the stars to anticipate that these events will happen. Pragmatic knowledge and community knowledge merge in ceremonies based on the movements of the sun, moon, and stars.

Patterns in the stars have their explanations. A Navajo story recorded by Berard Haile tells how Black God was patiently placing the stars in patterns on the roof of his hogan. He kept the stars in a deerskin bag. Coyote came along to ask Black God what he was doing. Black God said, "See for yourself what we have done," and started to seat himself on the floor of the hogan. Coyote, mischievous as ever, snatched the bag and blew all the stars up onto the roof of the hogan. The stars that Black God had placed are the recognizable groups such as Cassiopeia *(ba'á.di)* and the Big Dipper *(náxo.kos bᵃka')*, while Coyote's wild toss created the random pattern of stars against which these stars stand out (Haile, 4–5).

Randomness explains one aspect of the heavens, but uniformity is more important. The cluster of seven stars known as the Pleiades is significantly associated with planting seasons in the Western Hemisphere. North American tribes that observed the Pleiades include the Cheyenne, Paviotso, Kiowa, Cherokee, Shasta, Tewa, Zuni, Hopi, PaiPai, and Inuit. The Pleiades appears to move along the same path as the sun's. Depending on the latitude of the observer, it appears on the eastern horizon shortly after sunset in the fall and remains in the sky, rising progressively higher each night, through the winter. At the latitude of the Seneca villages, approximately 42 degrees north latitude, the Pleiades is in the sky from about 15 October to 15 May, a time that correlates with historical records of first and last killing frosts (Cesi, 304–5).

For the Seneca communities in upstate New York, the timing of the midwinter ceremony is determined by the conjunction of the new moon with the appearance of the Pleiades directly overhead at dusk. The ceremony begins following this moon, and the Pleiades appears directly over the smoke holes of the longhouses at midnight during the ceremony (Cesi, 308; Tooker, 39–40).

The Lakota origin story of the Pleiades tells of Fallen Star, son of a Lakota woman and a star, who came to the aid of a band camped near Harney Peak in the Black Hills. Every day for seven days an eagle carried a young girl from the band to the top of a mountain and killed her. Fallen Star arrived, killed the eagle, and placed the spirits of the seven girls in the sky. Today the Pleiades is known as *wicincala sakowin,* Seven Little Girls.

The constellations recognized by the Lakota are associated with events that happen on earth. They are important in a ceremonial sense, in that a small group of Lakota makes an annual spring journey through the

Black Hills in the three-month period from the spring equinox to the summer solstice. They time their stops at certain places to coincide with the appearance of three specific constellations, thus affirming the relationship between human beings and the sun (Goodman, 3–11).

The Aztec calendar system was derived from the earlier Mayan system, developed during the great intellectual flowering of that civilization from about A.D. 300 to 900. The Mayan system comprises two separate elements. One is the 365-day solar year, although the Mayans did not correct for the additional quarter of a day that the earth requires to complete its circuit around the sun. The calendar consisted of eighteen months with twenty named days. An additional five days were added as a ceremonial period after the months. Some scholars have postulated that the twenty named days of the Aztec ceremonial calendar corresponded with parts of the human body. This idea is based on an illustration in the codex *Vaticanus Latinus* 3738, but other sources do not support this system (Guerra, 323–24; Ortiz de Montellano, 135–39).

A more explicit connection between the stars and human society is in the 260-day ceremonial calendar, the *tzolkin,* which has twenty named days repeating through thirteen numbers, similar to the month in the Gregorian calendar. This calendar results in a sequence of 260 uniquely named and numbered days. Malmstrom postulates that this calendar derives from the 260-day interval between the zenith transits of the sun over the ruins of the Olmec city of Izapa on the coast of southern Mexico (Malmstrom, 4–5).

The import of the calendar is analogous to modern astrology in that personality traits are associated with the day on which a person is born (Tedlock, 107–31). Specially trained individuals can interpret events in a person's life and cure illnesses based on their knowledge of this calendar. Midwives use it to predict the due date for pregnant women. The moon controls menstruation, and the day on which a woman's flow does not begin with the moon is the same name day on which the child will be born (Earle, 160–61).

The individual is the focus of the 260-day calendar, but the uniformity of its operation also indicates the deterministic features of governance. The Aztec empire, with its extensive and complex relationships with subject peoples, had an emperor, but transitions of leadership followed the calendar. Cycles of celestial events determined the ascension of new leaders. The day carriers of the calendar, glyphs associated with the transition from one month to the next, imply the importance of human leadership. By remembering past transitions, people will know what the future holds (Farriss, 566–93).

This idea of remembering and anticipating is a powerful construct. For people living in a subsistence society, depending on the cycles of nature for their survival, repetition of events in nature is essential. Whorf describes the Hopi sense of time as "anticipation" in the heart. Rather than past, present, and future, the Hopi speak of that which has manifested itself (the present) and that which waits to be manifested. The sense of time is bound with remembering and expecting, and the act of thinking about the future, expecting its arrival, is what makes things happen (Whorf, 57–64).

The Hopi anticipated the future actions of the sun because they knew what he had done in the past, but the very nature of their language gave their thoughts a causal power—that is, their thoughts and the ensuing actions caused things to happen. The performance of ceremony maintained the Hopi world. They were keenly aware of the regularity of celestial patterns, but that regularity was not a purely mechanistic function of the movements of heavenly bodies. The sun was perceived as a spirit who moved across the sky from his southern to his northern home and back again. The solstice points on the horizon were where his homes were located, and he rested in each one. Specially designated sun watchers observed the horizon before dawn for a month before the solstice to note the rising points of the sun. Because they knew the markers of the sun's progress across the horizon, they could alert ceremonial leaders when to begin the Soyal (winter solstice) and Niman Kachina (summer solstice) ceremonies (McCluskey, 31–57).

The villagers of San Juan Pueblo followed an elaborate cycle of ceremonies throughout the year. There were two moieties, Summer People and Winter People. Leadership of the Pueblo was exchanged on a regular basis between the Summer chief and the Winter chief. Social organization included three categories of people—the Dry Food people, the Towa e, and the Made People (members of eight secret societies). The societies carried out their ceremonies in a sequence, and each one occupied about a month. The ceremonial cycle throughout the year assured that crops would grow and harvests would be successful. The ceremonies of Lessening the Cold, Bringing the Buds to Life, and Bringing the Leaves to Life presaged the occurrence of events in nature (Ortiz, 98–103).

In the Inca empire in Peru, a highly developed administrative structure exercised control over a widespread group of people in an extraordinary terrain. Through the mountainous spine of the South American continent, Native people built communities such as Machu Picchu, which had an elaborate system of terraced dwellings to control the sparse rainfall at its high desert elevation of approximately 13,000 feet (Bingham, 1, 41–42, 58, 80). An elaborate system of roads linked towns with the central capital at Cuzco.

The technology of the Inca empire rested on cloth, not metal, and fiber provided a medium for making permanent records. Padded garments served as armor, woven slingshots as weapons, and fabric bags as storage. Quipus, series of knotted strings tied to a cord, served to store information. Although it is assumed that they were used to record the contents of central storehouses or land areas, their interpretation is still subject to speculation (Ascher and Ascher, 2–3). In this respect, Inca culture differed from European technology and suffered at its hands. Within Inca society, however, weaving constituted meaning. The hair of llama, alpaca, and vicuna was different in texture and produced different kinds of wool for weaving. The llama was the utilitarian beast of burden, and its hair was used to make cloth for peasant clothing and bags for carrying and storage. Alpaca wool was softer and produced a better grade of cloth, and vicuna, like cashmere, produced the finest and softest fabrics worn by those of high rank (Gayton, 114–19).

The quipu, as a device for recording information, has been used to explain the political organization of leadership in Cuzco. The city was surrounded by 328 *huacas,* or shrines. These were aligned along *ceques,* forty-one lines radiating out from the Temple of the Sun and reaching to the horizon. In most cases, eight shrines stretched along each *ceque.* The shrines were analogous to a quipu laid out over the city, its strings radiating from a central knot, and the *huacas* were like the knots on each string, their pattern constituting a special meaning and the arc between them defining a discrete sector of the horizon. This arc then divided time into units, because the arc of distance on the horizon between any two lines was traversed in a set time. This system could work as a calendar to organize the space around the city into political units whose residents had special ceremonial responsibilities during the time the sun passed the arc of the horizon that included their homes (Zuidema, 231).

If the image of the quipu defined the horizon, the numbers of *ceques* and *huacas* may have correlated with certain aspects of the lunar year. Cuzco is 23 degrees latitude from the equator, and the sun crosses a range of sky only 46 degrees wide. The change in its aspect is much less than that of the moon, whose waxing and waning make lunar calendars as important as solar ones, if not more so. The evidence for a lunar calendar comes from two pieces of cloth. Each piece has ten rows of thirty-six circles, and the diagonal rows of circles across the piece are of different colors. The diagonal arrangement of elements in the fabric divides the circles into groups that add up to 365, the approximate number of days in a solar year. The second fabric has rectangles in patterns that can be summed to the number 28, which is close to the average number of days (29.5) in a lunar month, that is, the time it takes for the moon to return to its original position with regard to the stars, regardless of its phase (Zuidema, 220–25).

The phases of the moon move in complex patterns with regard to the sun, the earth, and the fixed stars, but the regular waxing and waning of the moon are the basis for most Indian calendar systems because they correlate with seasonal changes. For instance, the Tewa of San Ildefonso month names translate as ice month, wind month, month when leaves break forth, month when leaves open, corn planting month, St. John month, St. James month (a concession to Catholic influence), wheat cutting month, month when syrup is made, month of falling leaves, month when all is gathered in, and ashes fire month (Cope, 149–67).

The moon is usually associated with the feminine. The Wichita believed that Man-Who-Never-Was-on-Earth created the sun and moon as a man and a woman who taught human men to hunt and women to raise corn (Dorsey, 25–29). The story is explicit about the association between the moon's phases and the female menstrual cycle, an association that was obvious physiologically. The power of the cycle was one that men had no control over, and as a result, they feared it. The association of women with farming and life giving also associates them with the cycles of the moon.

Three unusual archaeological sites in what is now central Kansas are marked by circular depressions surrounding low, central mounds on which log houses were built. Three sites were aligned in a manner that constituted a sight line to the point of winter solstice sunrise on the eastern horizon, and from historical evidence, we know that lodges had their entrances aligned toward the east to view the rising sun. The alignment may also have allowed villagers to time ceremonies, and bones in the sites suggest the possibility of human sacrifice (Wedel, 54–65).

The great mound complex at Cahokia, in eastern Illinois, includes a circle of postholes that has been compared to Stonehenge in England (Wittry, 102–7). This complex encompassed an area of about 50,000 acres and a number of outlying villages below the central mound site. The central area served as both a ceremonial and an administrative center. The chief could stand on Monk's Mound, the great earthen pyramid that centered the complex, and look out across a circle of wooden posts to observe solstices and send word out to the villagers below so they could time their activities.

The Pawnee people of Nebraska had one of the most elaborate systems of star knowledge and cultural practices of any of the Native peoples of North America. Their cosmology was based on the mating of Morning Star and Evening Star. Morning Star in the east represented thought and planning, and Evening Star in the west represented fulfillment. The appearance of bright stars in the sky and their conjunctions are basic to Pawnee cosmology. The origin tradition recorded by James Murie tells of the journey of Morning Star through the sky to the west, how he encounters and vanquishes Evening Star's other suitors, and their union, which produced the first human child, a woman (Curtis, 99–104; Chamberlain, 22–23).

Based on analysis of real-time celestial events, the morning star can be either Mars or Venus. Venus appears in the morning sky for part of the year and in the evening sky for the other part. The Morning Star Ceremony of the Pawnee was their great sacrifice to the spirit world. A young girl, captured from a neighboring tribe, was killed with arrows, and her body was buried on the prairie. Although the timing of the ceremony depended on the dreams of a warrior, it seems to have always occurred after Mars had completed its orbit around the sun. Because Mars exhibits retrograde motion—that is, it appears to reverse its course in the sky and move from west to east for a part of each orbit—an awareness of when it has completed its orbit indicates a sophisticated understanding of its movement. Their earth lodges were also aligned with east-facing doorways that would allow observation of the stars (Weltfish, 79).

The relationship of stars and humans is ongoing. An Apache man sings the songs that help shape the future of the young woman whose first menstrual cycle is the occasion for the puberty ceremony, which reenacts the ceremony held for the deity Changing Woman. The girl goes through a series of ceremonial events, and the quality of her performance will determine her health and long life. The songs that are sung during the ceremony are timed by the movements of the stars as observed through the smoke hole of the tepee, and they end just as the sun appears above the horizon. Thus the singer has the power to pull the sun over the horizon, and the girl's future is inextricably woven into the processes of the world (Farrer, 128–72).

Seasons provide the great metaphors of cosmology and a key to understanding different cultural worldviews. Human and natural cycles are inextricably linked in patterns of life, death, and rebirth. The commonality of human experience allows for learning by analogy, which involves the comparison of the unknown and the known. Learning by analogy is probably the most common way individuals learn on a daily basis. Metaphors, however, depend on cultural knowledge, on associations based on accepted understandings of symbols. Apache people use metaphors of hunting in telling stories that relate human behavior to physical places, what Keith Basso calls "stalking with stories." A person who behaves in an inappropriate way hears a story of similar behavior associated with a particular place in the region. The person who passes that place on a regular basis is continually reminded of how he or she behaved and what he or she should have done (Basso, 58–70).

The analogy between seasonal change and Indian stories is dramatically demonstrated in the Navajo story of Changing Woman. One of the deities, she was found as an infant by First Man and First Woman, who took her into their home to raise her. In four days she reached puberty, in four more days she was a mature woman, and after four more days she was old. But in four more days she became young again (Reichard, 21). As a culturally understood metaphor for the Navajo, Changing Woman's powers are part of the association between her sexuality and seasonal and human changes. Changing Woman's puberty is celebrated with the first Kinaaldá ceremony, and Navajo girls go through the same ceremony. They are molded and strengthened for their future lives. The ceremony affects the girl's health and that of the children she is being prepared to bear. The levels of meaning in the story of Changing Woman imbue the movements of heavenly bodies and the changing of the seasons with meaning that affects major aspects of Navajo life (Frisbie, 10–11).

The Cherokee story of Selu, the Corn Mother, demonstrates the power of metaphor in a different culture. Although not explicitly related to star lore, it relates human beings to the seasonal cycles. Selu lived with her husband Kana'ti, the hunter, and her two sons. She fed her sons a delicious food, but it was a mystery where she got it. Her sons decided to find out her secret, and they followed her one day to a small shed behind the cabin, where they saw her rubbing skin from her body into a basket. They were fearful because they saw her action as evidence of strong magic, but when she discovered that they knew her secret, she told them that they must kill her and drag her body around the field behind the house seven times, covering all the ground with her blood. They slew her and began to drag her body, but they grew tired and circled the field only twice and did not cover all the ground. The next spring, they found corn plants growing from the places her body had touched. But because they had circled the field only twice, corn can be harvested only twice a year, and because they did not cover the ground with blood, corn grows only in certain places (Mooney, 244–45).

Ethnoastronomy is the most accessible form of general knowledge. Although specialists such as sun watchers are trained, and although secret societies may operate on esoteric knowledge to perform ceremonies that cause seasonal changes, the general population can observe and experience the power of heavenly bodies. World renewal ceremonies can involve all members of the community. Origin stories involve human interaction with stars. The processes of the human world are inextricably linked with—indeed, are causal—in the star world.

Indians have been the object of curiosity and the subject of scientific study since Europeans first encountered them. Europeans have been as curious to Indians, but their time for inquiry into European behavior was limited. Technology based on metals, infectious diseases, and domesticated animals gave a materialistic advantage to Europeans in their conquest of a new environment. These materialistic elements are easily explained.

The intellectual impact of Indians on the mind-set of Europeans in their colonizing efforts is much more complex. How did the way Europeans understood their world lead them to perceive Indians, and how did Indians account for the behavior of the strange people who invaded their land? How did differing worldviews and systems of knowledge encounter each other and change as a result?

As Krupp notes, "If careful observation of the world around us counts as science, then there is no doubt that our ancient and prehistoric ancestors were scientists. They would not have survived without a detailed knowledge of the environment" (Krupp, 1). Their observations of the heavens were indeed remarkable achievements in the systematic gathering of information that revealed, predicted, and explained the cyclical patterns of the natural environment. But the cycles did not happen by themselves. Human energy in the form of ceremonial activity gave the stars the energy and incentive to continue their motions. Human thought was a causal agent in the processes of the environment. Ongoing relationships between humans and the spirit world, including the sun, moon, and stars, were necessary for the world to continue.

American Indians observed the world around them with keen and scientific interest. They explained their relationship with that world in personal terms, and they saw themselves as agents in the processes in the environment. In this regard, they differed from the Christian world of Europeans, where the spiritual supremacy of God was absolute, and the political supremacy of European rulers rested on their representation of God's will.

American Indians lived with their environments, while early Christians largely rejected the physical world as a sinful place and turned their attention to the heavenly paradise that Christian redemption promised. This rejection plunged Europe into the so-called Dark Ages, from the fifth through the thirteenth centuries. While Pueblo cultures in the American Southwest and Mayan communities in Mesoamerica were developing sophisticated systems of astronomical observation, intellectual inquiry in Europe retreated to theological matters. Not until the Christian crusades of the eleventh and twelfth centuries exposed Europe to Arabic scientific knowledge did the idea of science emerge as a driving force in the European Renaissance.

As major European cities emerged in those centuries, urban centers such as Cahokia and Moundville in North America flourished. In Europe, however, desire for new knowledge went hand in hand with the desire for material wealth. Christopher Columbus arrived on the shores of Hispaniola convinced that he would discover untold wealth. Instead, he encountered Native people who, he declared, would easily become Christians because they had no religion of their own (Jane, 8). Although European colonizers such as Bishop Landa would subsequently attempt to destroy Native knowledge (Todorov, 200), the works of Sahagun and

Hernández and the Mayan codices that escaped the mass destruction wreaked by Landa in Yucatán in 1562 preserved some of the knowledge of the stars that was an integral part of their social organization and government.

Observation of the heavens is a universal human phenomenon. In North America, archaeological sites show distinct astronomical orientations. Ethnographic studies reveal the intertwining of human activities and celestial ones. Plains cultures, particularly, with their views of the sky uninterrupted by physical terrain or vegetation, saw the sun, stars, and moon as guardians of and intervenors in human life. Solstice markers are found in cultures as diverse as Pueblo agriculturalists in the Southwest and the hunters who constructed the Bighorn medicine wheel.

Space and time, past and future, cycles of life and death, all are integrated by the movements of the stars in the sky. For Indian people, as for Europeans, the heavens are a metaphor for life on earth. The sun, the moon, and the stars, in their processions, both influence and replicate the processes of human life. European science ultimately objectified the sun, moon, and stars as simple matter, subject to physical laws of behavior. In Native traditions, they are living beings, interacting with humans and influenced by human behavior in ceremony and song.

The phenomena of the stars in the sky are still accessible to all people. How they understand them both comes from and shapes culture. For many Americans, daily horoscopes influence their lives. For the Mayan people in Guatemala, the Mayan calendar is the dominant influence in their lives. Although the two systems of knowledge are based in different cultural beliefs, their basis is still knowledge from the skies. Indians and Europeans, despite the cultural differences that prevented their mutual understanding, were pursuing similar ways of knowing.

REFERENCES

Ascher, Marcia, and Robert Ascher. *Code of the Quipu: A Study in Media, Mathematics and Culture.* Ann Arbor: University of Michigan Press, 1980.
Basso, Keith. *Wisdom Sits in Places: Landscape and Language among the Western Apache.* Albuquerque: University of New Mexico Press, 1996.
Bingham, Hiram. *Machu Picchu: A Citadel of the Incas.* New York: Hacker Art Books, 1979.
Black Elk Speaks, Being the Life Story of a Holy Man of the Oglala Sioux, as told through John G. Neihardt. Lincoln: University of Nebraska Press, 1961.
Cesi, Lynn. "Watchers of the Pleiades: Ethnoastronomy among Native Cultivators in Northeastern North America." *Ethnohistory,* vol. 25, no. 4 (fall 1978), 306–8.
Chamberlain, Von Del. *When the Stars Came Down to Earth: Cosmology of the Skidi Pawnee Indians of North America.* Los Altos, Calif.: Ballena Press, 1982.
Cope, Leona. *Calendars of the Indians North of Mexico.* University of California Pub-

lications in American Archaeology and Ethnology, vol. 16, no. 4. Berkeley: University of California Press, 1919.

Curtis, Natalie, ed. *The Indians' Book: Authentic Native American Legends, Lore & Music.* New York: Bonanza Books, 1987.

Dorsey, George A. *The Mythology of the Wichita.* Norman: University of Oklahoma Press, 1995 [1904].

Earle, Duncan M. "The Metaphor of the Day in Quiche: Notes on the Nature of Everyday Life." In *Symbol and Meaning beyond the Closed Community: Essays in Mesoamerican Ideas,* ed. Gary H. Gossen. Albany, N.Y.: Institute for Mesoamerican Studies, University of Albany, State University of New York, 1986.

Eddy, John A. "Astronomical Alignment of the Big Horn Medicine Wheel." *Science,* vol. 184 (1974), 1035–43.

Farrer, Claire R. *Living Life's Circle; Mescalero Apache Cosmovision.* Albuquerque: University of New Mexico Press, 1991.

Farriss, Nancy. "Remembering the Future, Anticipating the Past: History, Time, and Cosmology among the Maya of Yucatan." *Journal for Comparative Study of Society and History,* vol. 29, no. 3 (1987), 566–93.

Frisbie, Charlotte Johnson. *Kinaaldá: A Study of the Navaho Girl's Puberty Ceremony.* Middletown, Conn.: Wesleyan University Press, 1967.

Gayton, A. H. "The Cultural Significance of Peruvian Textiles: Production, Function, Aesthetics." *Kroeber Anthropological Society Papers,* no. 25 (1961), 114–19.

Goodman, Ronald. *Lakota Star Knowledge: Studies in Lakota Stellar Theology,* 2nd ed. Rosebud, S.D.: Sinte Gleska University, 1992.

Guerra, Francisco. "Aztec Medicine." *Medical History,* vol. 10 (1966), 315–38.

Haile, Berard. *Starlore among the Navaho.* Santa Fe, N.M.: Museum of Navajo Ceremonial Art, 1947.

Hernandez, Francisco. *De antiquitatibus Novae Hispaniae autore Francisco Hernando, medico et historico Philippi II et Indiarum omnium redico primario codice de la Real Acadamia de la historia en Madrid.* Edicion facsimilar. Mexico: Talleres graficos del Museo nacional de arqueologia, historia y ethografia, 1926.

Jane, Cecil, trans. and ed. *The Four Voyages of Columbus.* 2 vols. New York: Dover, 1988.

Kilpatrick, Jack Frederick. "Verbs Are Kings at Panther Place: The Cherokee Tongue versus 'English.'" *Southwest Review* (autumn 1965), 372–76.

Krupp, E. C., ed. *Archaeoastronomy and the Roots of Science.* Boulder, Colo.: Westview Press, for the American Association for the Advancement of Science, 1984.

LaFlesche, Francis. "The Osage Tribe: Two Versions of the Child Naming Rite." In *Forty-third Annual Report of the Bureau of American Ethnology (1925–26).* Washington, D.C.

Lounsbury, Floyd G. "Maya Numeration, Computation and Calendrical Astronomy." In *Dictionary of Scientific Biography,* ed. Charles C. Gillispie. 16 vols. New York: Scribners, 1970–1980, 15: 759–818.

Malmstrom, Vincent H. *Cycles of the Sun, Mysteries of the Moon.* Austin: University of Texas Press, 1997.

McCluskey, Stephen C. "Historical Archaeoastronomy: The Hopi Example." In *Archaeoastronomy in the New World: American Primitive Astronomy,* ed. A. F. Aveni. Cambridge: Cambridge University Press, 1982.

Mooney, James. *Myths of the Cherokee and Sacred Formulas of the Cherokees.* Nashville, Tenn.: Charles and Randy Elder, 1982.

Neugebauer, O. *The Exact Sciences in Antiquity,* 2nd ed. New York: Harper and Brothers, 1962.

Ortiz, Alfonso. *The Tewa World: Space, Time, Being and Becoming in a Pueblo Society.* Chicago: University of Chicago Press, 1969.

Ortiz, Alfonso, and Richard Erdoes. *American Indian Myths and Legends.* New York: Pantheon Books, 1984.

Ortiz de Montellano, Bernard R. *Aztec Medicine, Health, and Nutrition.* New Brunswick, N.J.: Rutgers University Press, 1990.

Reichard, Gladys. *Navaho Religion: A Study of Symbolism.* Tucson: University of Arizona Press, 1983.

Sahagun, Bernardino de. *General History of the Things of New Spain,* trans. Charles E. Dibble and Arthur J. Q. Anderson. Monographs of the School of American Research and the Museum of New Mexico. 13 parts. Santa Fe, N.M.: School of American Research, 1950–1965.

Stresser-Péan, G. "Science in Pre-Columbian America." In *History of Science,* ed. Renè Taton, trans. A. J. Pomerans. Vol. 1, *Ancient and Medieval Science.* New York: Basic Books, 1963.

Sun Chief, the Autobiography of a Hopi Indian, ed. Leo W. Simmons. New Haven, Conn.: Yale University Press, 1942.

Tedlock, Barbara. *Time and the Highland Maya.* Albuquerque: University of New Mexico Press, 1982.

Thompson, Stith. *Tales of the North American Indians.* Bloomington: Indiana University Press, 1966.

Titiev, Mischa. *Old Oraibi: A Study of the Hopi Indians of Third Mesa.* Albuquerque: University of New Mexico Press, 1992.

Todorov, Tzvetan. *The Conquest of America,* trans. Richard Howard. New York: HarperCollins, 1985.

Tooker, Elisabeth. *The Iroquois Ceremonial of Midwinter.* Syracuse, N.Y.: Syracuse University Press, 1970.

Waters, Frank. *Book of the Hopi.* New York: Ballantine Books, 1963.

Wedel, Waldo B. "The Council Circles of Central Kansas: Were They Solstice Registers." *American Antiquity,* vol. 32, no. 1 (January 1967), 54–63.

Weltfish, Gene. *The Lost Universe.* New York: Basic Books, 1965.

Whorf, Benjamin. "An American Indian Model of the Universe." In *Language, Thought, and Reality.* Cambridge: Massachusetts Institute of Technology Press, 1970.

Wittry, W. L. "An American Woodhenge." *Cranbrook Institute of Science Newsletter,* vol. 33, no. 9 (1964), 102–7.

Wyman, Leland C. *Blessingway.* Tucson: University of Arizona Press, 1970.

Zuidema, R. T. "The Inca Calendar." In *Native American Astronomy,* ed. Anthony F. Aveni. Austin: University of Texas Press, 1977.

CHAPTER TWO

The Power of Seneca Women and the Legacy of Handsome Lake

John Mohawk (Seneca)

Three books appeared between 1986 and 1995 that discuss the role of Seneca prophet Handsome Lake (1730–1815) in the decline of power among Seneca women and the presumed rise of patriarchy in Seneca culture. Each accepts the thesis that ancient Iroquois society was characterized by a hierarchy in which women exercised political power and that women's power was undermined by males led by Handsome Lake and his followers, who commanded the Seneca to abandon the ancient communal longhouse dwellings of their ancestors and establish nuclear families in households headed by males. The clear indication of each of the authors is that this radical transformation of Seneca society was contrived as a strategy to subordinate women to men.

Scholars have generally supported a view that Iroquois women in traditional society enjoyed more power relative to men than did European or Euro-American women of the same period. The privileged status of Iroquois women in their own society[1] has generally been consistent within contemporary feminist scholarship. It is also agreed by scholars that Seneca society underwent a radical transformation between 1784 and 1819, a period that saw the end of the American Revolution, the loss of most Seneca land in land cessions, the visions and prophecies of Handsome Lake, the War of 1812, and the arrival of Christian missionaries among the Seneca. Paula Gunn Allen describes the existence of women's power in Iroquois society and its subsequent decline in *The Sacred Hoop: Recovering the Feminine in American Indian Traditions*: "The Iroquoian peoples, including the Cherokee, had another custom that bespoke the existence of their 'petticoat government,' their gynocracy. They set the penalty for killing a woman of the tribe at double that for killing a man. . . . The Iroquois story is currently one of the best chronicles of the overthrow of gynocracy."[2]

The argument that many Indian tribes practiced customs that defined women's societal roles dramatically differently from their roles in European and Euro-American societies of the same period is widely

20

acknowledged, if somewhat open to a variety of culturally specific interpretations. Allen continues: "The Seneca prophet Handsome Lake did not
appreciate 'petticoat government.' . . . When his code became the standard for Iroquois practice in the early nineteenth century, power shifted
from the hands of the 'meddling old women,' as he characterized them,
to men."[3] The passage goes on to interpret Iroquois customs in broad
terms, arguing that Seneca customs contained a "mother-right" that was
undermined when Handsome Lake advocated that young women
"cleave" to their husbands rather than to their mothers and that they
abandon the clan mother–controlled longhouse in favor of a patriarchal,
nuclear family arrangement.[4]

Furthermore, Allen notes that until Handsome Lake's time, the
chiefs of the Iroquois Confederacy who composed the Grand Council
were subject to impeachment by the matrons should they prove inadequate or derelict in carrying out their duties as envisioned by the matrons
and set forth in the Great Law of Peace: "The women were to be considered the progenitors of the nation, owning the land and the soil."[5] She
then states that Handsome Lake encouraged a shift from a woman-centered to a patriarchal society.

M. Annette Jaimes, in *The State of Native America: Genocide, Colonization, and Resistance,* quotes Allen and joins her in asserting that Handsome
Lake replaced the "petticoat government" with a male-centered one more
acceptable to the colonizers.[6] Joy Bilharz, in an article in *Women and Power
in Native North America,* is specific in asserting Handsome Lake's role in
attacking the Iroquois matriarchy: "it is clear that the Quakers were successful in prevailing on the Seneca to adopt single-family log and shingle
fenced farmsteads in place of the matrilineage longhouses."[7]

These three books constitute a significant part of the work on Seneca
social history, Handsome Lake, and the role of women in traditional
Seneca society published since 1986. Numerous articles have subsequently incorporated their assertions about the shift away from the Iroquois "gynocracy." These assertions raise two questions that call for
further investigation: (1) Did Handsome Lake or his followers urge, command, or otherwise cause the Seneca to abandon their ancient communal
longhouses and therefore the woman-centered way of life represented by
the longhouse communal way of life? (2) What was the nature of the
power of women in ancient Seneca society?

Handsome Lake was born around 1730 in the Genesee Valley. His
half brother was the Seneca war chief Cornplanter, also known as John
O'Bail, and his nephew was Governor Blacksnake, both of whom played
significant roles as warriors during the American Revolution. *Ganeodiyo,*
or Handsome Lake, is one of the title names on the roll call of chiefs, or
sachems, who sit as government and council of the Six Nations Confed-

eracy, and the prophet Handsome Lake was one of eight representatives from the Seneca Nation to that body.

The American Revolution proved a turning point in Iroquois history. Although the Six Nations Council adopted an official policy of neutrality, both the British and the Americans tried to recruit mercenaries and whole nations to their cause. Eventually, most of the Oneida and many Tuscarora went over to the American cause, the Onondaga tried valiantly for a time to remain neutral, and Seneca and Cayuga warriors were recruited by the British. During meetings prior to the siege of Fort Stanwix in 1777, the British invited the warriors and women of the Confederacy, especially the Seneca Nation, to war councils at which presents were offered and speeches made urging participation against the Americans.[8]

Iroquois participation in these meetings followed Iroquois conventions whereby the women and warriors represented themselves and not the Confederacy. It would prove to be a major theme during the Revolution that the warriors and women of the Confederacy acted in diplomatic roles that tradition and custom had ascribed to the sachems of the Grand Council. At the end of the war, warriors and not sachems would sign a 1783 treaty at Fort Stanwix that ceded significant Six Nations territories. The treaty was so unpopular that the Confederacy Council was moved to reject it.[9] The nations were internally divided, and many were deeply critical of the role warrior leaders such as Cornplanter had played.

At the end of the war, the exuberant United States assumed the posture that Britain's capitulation amounted to a conquest of all its Indian allies, a point of view that was both factually incorrect and inconsistent with standards of international law of the day. American representatives dealt harshly with the Seneca and other Iroquois warriors during the period, and American officials sought to seize Indian lands to repay debts incurred during the fighting. The most contentious conflict involved lands in Ohio described in the Northwest Ordinance of 1787, because the U.S. government disposed of the lands before obtaining ownership from the Shawnee and allied Indians who owned it.[10] War ensued, and at first the Shawnee Indians and their allies were successful in repelling American forces. President George Washington enlisted the help of Cornplanter, who tried unsuccessfully to intervene and urge a compromise. The 1790 Non-intercourse Act and the 1794 Canandaigua Treaty emerged from this period as efforts by the U.S. government, as part of an inconsistent and politically contested policy, to practice fair treatment of Indian nations when acts of fraud and dispossession were giving rise to wars that the federal treasury could ill afford.

In 1797 the Seneca ceded most of their remaining lands to U.S. interests at the Big Tree Treaty. The Seneca women and warriors played central roles in this land cession. Significant individuals had been bribed,[11] including Cornplanter. The Seneca Nation, which had not been defeated on the battlefield, had been completely outflanked when warriors acted as the diplomatic corps and the collective interest of the nation was subordinated to that of the possessive individualism of the warriors. The ancient form of government headed by sachems who were appointed by women had been subverted, albeit temporarily, at a critical moment by the warriors and by the women who supported them.[12] A mass psychological depression among the Seneca reportedly occurred at this time, and increasingly heavy use of alcohol and the adoption of a variety of other bad habits from the frontiersmen were infecting Iroquois country, especially the Seneca towns in western New York. Impoverished, depressed, and plagued by vices introduced by white settlers, some Seneca thought they would not survive as a people.[13]

Two strategies to accomplish Indian acculturation were tried during this period. One involved identifying young, willing, and able individuals among the Indians and recruiting them to attend schools among the whites. This strategy evoked opposition from both Indians and whites, who found that the marginalized Indians this strategy produced were suited for neither the white nor the Indian world. They were likely to suffer an identity crisis that rendered them susceptible to a variety of degenerate behaviors, including alcohol abuse and an inability to function in Indian society. Timothy Pickering, the secretary of state who had negotiated the Canandaigua Treaty, favored bringing Western technology to the Indians, and President Washington supported his efforts.[14] By 1796, a significant effort to bring tools and Western agricultural practices to the Indians of the Northeast was under way, and Pickering was enthusiastically urging the Onondaga to accept help of this type from the Quakers. The latter arrived at Cornplanter's town on the Allegany River in Seneca country in 1798, and from that time on, Quaker efforts were concentrated there. Similar projects were under way among other Iroquois communities and other Indian nations. The arguments for receiving Western agriculture carried both pragmatic and ideological trappings.

White settlement was slow to arrive and thrive in northwestern Pennsylvania in the vicinity of the Cornplanter settlement, and white farmers were, for a considerable period, unsuccessful in the surrounding areas. Meanwhile, the Seneca were experiencing a decline in available game animals, and the traditional military occupations within their own system were no longer possible. The conservative Seneca were faced with what appeared to be two options: poverty or plowshares. The Seneca would combine Western agricultural technology with traditional Iroquois food crops and horticultural practices to produce what would become a prosperous hybrid agriculture, and the roles of women in Seneca society would be impacted. At the same moment, in an arc from New England to western Pennsylvania (and strongly represented in central and western New York), a new form of Christian evangelism was being invented among the Americans. This was characterized by the camp revival meeting and the phenomenon of individuals lapsing into trancelike states from which they emerged to give testimony to a spiritual enlightenment.[15]

In the spring of 1799 Handsome Lake departed from Cornplanter's village at Burnt House near the Pennsylvania–New York border with a party of hunters. They eventually arrived at white settlements on the Allegheny River in Pennsylvania to trade hides and other forest products, and they returned with barrels of whiskey. Days of drunkenness and violence followed, during which the children and women reportedly fled to the forest to hide. At the end of this episode, Handsome Lake was found in an incapacitated condition and lapsed into a coma. When he awoke and recovered, he called an assembly at the council house and announced that he had experienced a vision while unconscious. The memory of that vision and subsequent ones was preserved by his followers beginning a few years after his death at Onondaga in 1815 and has come to be called the Code of Handsome Lake.[16]

Handsome Lake's public career as a prophet occurred at a moment of tremendous and rapid change in Seneca culture and history, but the Seneca had been undergoing relatively profound changes for more than a century before his first vision. Among other things, there had been a change in Seneca housing patterns, such that by 1799, "gone were the communal longhouses and the large, densely populated hilltop palisaded villages of the previous century. The newer single-family houses might be of traditional pole and elm-bark construction like the longhouses they replaced, but log cabins were found with increasing frequency through the eighteenth century."[17]

Iroquois social and political life was centered at the village level.[18] It was here that work parties were formed and the basic day-to-day interactions took place, and it was at the village level that men functioned in their everyday lives and women undertook their community roles. There were civil chiefs and what I call here war chiefs,[19] but our understanding of their respective roles is imperfect. Some warriors displayed special talents for organizing and leading military expeditions. Such men might be designated "war" or "warrior" chiefs and were chosen for leadership by the fighting men who were willing to follow them into harm's way. The Seneca Nation, in addition, had two formal "war chiefs" who reported to the Six Nations Council, the confederacy government.

The Seneca organizational chart for governance had more than one kind of civil chief. There were village chiefs and confederacy chiefs, or sachems, as they have come to be called. The village chiefs represented the clans and were in charge of the daily affairs of the village. They sometimes maintained a virtually continuous open council and, among other things, paid attention to issues involving village tranquillity. In the seventeenth century, these village chiefs or council of elders initially decided whether individual captives would be turned over to mourning women as slaves or potential adoptees or, occasionally, tortured and killed. They usually facilitated the town meetings, which were the true government of the settlements. The Seneca sachems of the confederacy numbered eight members, and each town may have had one or two of these chiefs. The sachems, along with their counterparts from the other nations of the Iroquois Confederacy, were in charge of negotiating peaceful settlements of military and other matters among nations.

It is likely that some of these sachems sometimes served as village chiefs and even as war chiefs, depending on their talents and the needs of the moment. By custom, if a sachem took up the warpath, he was required to set aside his sachem title until he had put away his weapons. The fact that an individual might occupy more than one office at a time or different offices at different times, and the fact that there were different kinds of chiefs for different purposes, caused considerable confusion among the European witnesses of the day. In some ways, the Grand Council of Chiefs was a larger version of the local council of elders, but the scope of authority of the former was national in nature, and its mission was the peaceful settlement of disputes among nations, although it appears to have been less egalitarian than the village council of elders.

Seneca chiefs had no coercive powers and no apparatus of state government to implement their will. They facilitated thinking at town meetings but had no enforcement powers other than public support. Women participated equally with men in public meetings. In this closely knit society, behaviors were modified so effectively by fear of public scorn or ridicule that the Seneca and other Indians of the woodlands were internally peaceful and successful societies. With regard to the French reaction to the Huron, an Iroquoian nation similar to the Seneca, anthropologist Bruce Trigger observed, "the French were at first puzzled, then intrigued, to see a government maintaining law and order among many thousands of people without the aid of a police force, imprisonment, or capital punishment, all of which were regarded as essential in their own society."[20]

Although some individuals might tell others what to do, no one could mobilize state force to implement his or her will on an unwilling Seneca, except through force of persuasion at a town meeting or through long-established common practice and right of custom. There was, in effect, no practical hierarchy as that term is understood, and therefore no patriarchy or, for that matter, any meaningful matriarchy. To the extent tyranny existed in Seneca country, it was entirely the product of customs, but such customs were powerful and did much to shape Seneca life.

During the mid-seventeenth century, diseases such as smallpox were introduced to Iroquoia, with devastating effect. It is estimated that during the decade 1640 to 1650, half or more of the population died of European-introduced diseases to which the Seneca had no immunity. Such deaths caused intense mourning and sorrow in Seneca towns. Custom held that women could call on their male relatives to replace their lost loved ones with captives from other nations. The dramatic loss of population led women to demand mourning wars and inspired young men to seize even more captives to requicken the dead.[21]

It has been noted that the purpose of organized armed force, throughout history, has been plunder. Among the Iroquois, women participated as equals in public political life, but they also had power to make demands: "Women of the mourning household could demand the ultimate socially sustained release for their violent impulse: a raid to seek captives who, it was hoped, would ease their pain."[22] Women could plead for or even demand such captives.[23] Lucien Carr, speaking of the Iroquoian people generally, believed that the power of the chief matron over the fate of captives was absolute. Once the council of elders had sent a captive to her, she could save and adopt him; if she refused to receive him and "threw him into the fire," as it was termed, he was invariably burned. "There was no power in the tribe that could save a prisoner whom she had condemned, nor condemn one whom she had decided to save."[24]

This absolute power over the fate of a prisoner brought about the ruin of the Erie Nation, a people closely related to the Seneca. In 1654 an Onondaga chief, Annenraes, was captured by the Eries. A powerful body of Onondaga warriors was joined by Senecas to seek his rescue. The Erie chiefs offered Annenraes to the sister of a slain warrior, expecting her to adopt him. Instead, she ordered his death. Although they pleaded with her to spare him, her orders were eventually carried out. Annenraes was killed, the outraged Onondaga and Seneca attacked, and the Erie Nation was destroyed,[25] although most of the Erie people survived and were absorbed by the Seneca.

The seventeenth century brought dramatic changes to the Seneca and other Iroquois nations. Europeans arrived in 1609 in the St. Lawrence valley, and by midcentury, the Iroquois had already experienced expanding trade, the arrival of devastating European diseases that killed half their people, firearms, and an expanding condition of warfare. During most of the seventeenth century, Seneca housing patterns tended toward amalgamation of settlements into larger and larger towns. By 1687, the Seneca were living in four large towns located on hilltops near the Genesee River. Palisades were present, indicating the need for defense against armed aggression from enemies intent on revenge and plunder, but Indian palisades were no match for cannon. That year, the Seneca were attacked by a combined French and Indian force of some 3,000 combatants. Most of the able-bodied Seneca warriors were absent from the towns, out on raiding expeditions against Indian allies of the French in the west, when this force arrived. After a short battle, the French and allied Indians sacked and burned the towns and set about destroying the orchards and cornfields while the Seneca elders, women, and children fled for their lives to Cayuga country.

Following this event, known to history as the Denonville Campaign, the Seneca did not rebuild their large towns: "The tightly packed, palisaded villages of the seventeenth century were to be seen no more. The Seneca spilled off their hilltop fortresses and into the valleys. The longhouse fell into comparative disuse, replaced by single family dwellings."[26] A trend toward single-family housing had been taking place among all the Iroquois during this period, and the Seneca were no exception: "By 1750 most Senecas seem to have been living in single-family cabins built in a European-style that often included such European features as roughly finished attics. The only major structural characteristic that set them apart from the homes of many contemporary Euro-Americans was their preference for a central open hearth and smoke hole in the roof rather than a fireplace and chimney."[27]

At midcentury, only some Cayuga were known to be living in multifamily longhouse dwellings. Single-family housing, however, did not mean the same thing in matrilineal Iroquois society that it did in patriarchal Euro-American communities. It seems clear that the intense communal interaction among members of an *ohwichira* characteristic of earlier generations had loosened in fundamental experiential ways.[28]

WOMEN IN TRADITIONAL SENECA SOCIETY

Child abuse and wife beating were rare in seventeenth-century Iroquois society. There is little testimony from the Seneca or other Iroquois about daily life in the period of the classic longhouses, and even less from Seneca women. Seneca women did not write and, for the most part, did not converse with the chroniclers among them. Despite this, we do know with certainty some things about Seneca life and thought that shed light on their lives.

A Seneca town was a collection of communal longhouses in a compact space, often but not always enclosed by a palisade. The society was matrilineal, which in this case meant that, upon marriage, men usually but not always moved into the house of the woman.[29] The house was therefore the abode of an extended family descended from (theoretically) a woman and represented a segment of a Seneca clan. The process by which an adult male came to leave the family of his birth and move into a longhouse with his wife is informative. Ideally, marriage was arranged by the elder women of the two families. It was initiated by the young woman's female clan elder, who negotiated the affair and, to seal the offer, left twenty-four wedding bread loaves at the door of the longhouse of the female clan elder of the intended bridegroom.[30] The grandmother (in Seneca terms, "grandmother" might refer to a female clan elder who is not necessarily the biological mother of the intended groom's mother) tasted the bread and then informed the young man's mother that a marriage had been proposed. Unless the prospective bridegroom's mother had valid objections to the union, the grandmother then made twenty-four cakes to send to the clan elder of the proposed bride's household. Upon receipt, the young woman was informed of the arrangement.

According to this arrangement, an elder woman of a clan initiated the marriage of her granddaughter to a young man of a separate clan, and elder women were the primary agents of negotiation throughout the process.[31] During the seventeenth century, most cultures of the world practiced some form of arranged marriages, and Seneca custom allocated to women privileges that most traditional European societies reserved to men.

WOMEN AND POWER IN SENECA SOCIETY

Young men who wished to marry were well-advised to cultivate the good graces of older women of clans other than their own who would be looking for good hunters, potential statesmen, and successful warriors as husbands for their young women. A lazy or shiftless husband was often forced to leave the household.[32] If laziness was not tolerated, wife beating and child abuse were even less so, although apparently they were not unknown.[33] But such instances were rare enough among the Indians of the Northeast woodlands that Jesuits complained that the children were undisciplined, and they met resistance when they urged Indian men to use physical force to control recalcitrant wives and daughters.[34] What is described here is an elder-centered as well as woman-centered society. The rights of individual young men and women were clearly subordinated to the perceived needs of the group by custom, and in this case, the defined group was the extended female family occupying the longhouse of the wife.[35] In this egalitarian society, custom was restrained from undue tyranny, and a woman retained control over her person. Divorce was easily accomplished, and the arranged marriage underwent a one-year trial, following which the couple was free to continue the arrangement or not. Such marriages were reported to be relatively stable.

The communal longhouse provided the metaphor for the social origins of the Seneca and was the analogy on which the league was built. The Iroquois referred to themselves as the people of the longhouse. The figurative longhouse of the league was divided into geographic compartments, each occupied by a nation. It is probable that this analogy helped to consolidate the considerable political power of the Iroquois matrons.[36]

It is predictable that women's power declined in some ways with the gradual abandonment of the communal household in which communities of women held considerable control over the produce of the gardens, housing arrangements, whether warriors would or would not go to war, and final disposition of captives. Women also selected the sachem and village chiefs and participated as full members of the assembly at town meetings. The communal longhouse provided the foundation of women's powers, and although significant elements of power survived the longhouse's demise, most of these powers were diminished with its disappearance. Richter cited several possible reasons for this abandonment of the traditional longhouse: heavily fortified towns were little defense against European armies, and hostile Indian neighbors had been largely dispersed; decimated populations may have had no need for large towns; political quarrels that had created intense factions several decades earlier may have diminished the preference for close-quarter living in large numbers; and a century of participation in a capitalist, market-driven economy may have given rise to individualism and thus a desire for private housing. Another compelling reason for the changes in housing and town patterns was that liquor had become increasingly available to the Iroquois as the century continued, resulting in numerous deaths in drunken brawls and the appearance in some towns of drunken gangs. Even one or two drunken people would have been chaotic in a communal longhouse situation.[37] Despite these signs of change, Seneca practices continued to favor collective ownership of land along clan lines, and Seneca customs of hospitality remained healthy.[38]

Although women probably continued some of the customs of arranged marriages, the absence of the extended family of women in physical proximity to the married couple would have altered basic power relationships between the genders. Husbands would no longer be as dependent on the goodwill of their wives' female relatives. In addition, under the traditional longhouse arrangement, the man was considerably less essential economically, because he was one of a number of men providing for the household. In addition, the relationships—economic and otherwise—between a man and his children and his wife's children by other men would now be more significant. No longer were the children exclusively the children of the household or the clan.[39] Paternity took on a different definition than it had under the old system. The Seneca were a long way from the kind of tyrannical claim to ownership of women and children expressed by some Euro-Americans of the day, and there was certainly no rule of thumb encouraging physical abuse of women and children, but fundamental changes were under way.

HANDSOME LAKE AND THE DEMISE OF THE COMMUNAL LONGHOUSE

Handsome Lake and his followers could not have been guilty of destroying the Seneca "gynocracy" by urging or commanding the abandonment of woman-centered housing because the communal longhouses no longer existed in 1799, the earliest possible date necessary to sustain this assertion. The longhouse as a dwelling had disappeared at midcentury, some two generations before Handsome Lake began his career as prophet. The housing pattern that emerged involved log cabins and bark houses inhabited by six to twenty people. These were not exactly nuclear households (some Seneca did not adopt nuclear households until the beginning of the twentieth century), but they were a distinct step in that direction.

The new housing patterns intensified behavioral problems, which had been rare in Seneca culture. Prior to Handsome Lake's first vision, Cornplanter and other Seneca complained about white men who fathered children among Seneca women and then left without providing for the support of those children. Handsome Lake condemned child and wife beating, a clear indication that such things happened at that time.

WOMEN IN SENECA POLITICAL LIFE AND THE LEGACY OF HANDSOME LAKE

During the seventeenth century, Iroquois men responded to the demands for captives by women in mourning by attacking those groups that might prove most profitable in that regard. As the seventeenth century progressed, the purpose of warfare appears to have transformed from retaliation for past wrongs to replacement of loved ones lost to disease or warfare and desire for plunder in the form of furs to be traded for weapons and other goods of European manufacture.

The confederacy chiefs were sometimes cast in the position of mediators between the warriors and women on the one hand and the external nation on the other. Because their only truly effective tool was the power of persuasion, they tended toward a tradition of oratory, which was noted by witnesses of their day. But the keepers of the Great Law of Peace, an oral tradition that served as a kind of constitution of the confederacy, had a mission that was clearly different from that of the warriors and women who demanded captives and the spoils of war. Thus we find the sachems often apologizing for being unable to control the warriors.

What they could do was to take offers between foreign nations and the warriors and women and try to arrange some accommodation that would end the hostilities. During much of the seventeenth century, the sachems were fully occupied with such tasks. It was part of the genius of Iroquois culture that an aggressive military tradition existed alongside one of elders earnestly seeking peace. The sachems could be effective negotiators precisely because they were not the warriors and could represent themselves as a party of interest whose primary desire was peaceful resolution. The Iroquois realized that they could not sustain endless warfare, partly because they were surrounded by more numerous nations and could not fight them all at once. The system of chiefs seeking peace offered a solution to a dilemma; had it not been present, the result would have been exhaustive retributions and endless struggles that they had no chance of winning in the long run. At the end of the American Revolution, the warriors abandoned this system of elder-diplomats that had worked so well for at least a century and a half, and possibly much longer, and pushed the chiefs aside to confront the Americans directly. The results were disastrous for the Seneca.

Seneca social life was centered at the village level.[40] It was also at the village level that the political life of the Seneca was played out. Seneca political life was, by all accounts, egalitarian, and women played a role equal to that of men at the town meetings, where major decisions were made. In 1687 women participated fully in the town meetings, which took place as Denonville's army approached, and some women took part in the fighting that followed. Even at the time of the American Revolution, the British took pains to ply the Seneca women with gifts. A Mohawk woman, Mary Brant, made a stirring speech at a Six Nations Council meeting at Onondaga, urging the confederacy to remain loyal to the late Sir William Johnson. That speech is said to have swayed the assembly in her favor not long before the fateful battle at Oriskany, where many Seneca leaders were killed and where Oneida and other confederacy warriors met as enemies on the battlefield. The powers of women had declined somewhat since the disappearance of the communal household, but through the Revolution, women remained a powerful force in Seneca society.

Following the Revolution, the Iroquois never again went into battle as a united people, and the role of the Iroquois warrior, as such, was at an end. Women had partnered with the warriors in their many and varied enterprises, and as the role of warriors declined, some of the power of the women who supported them also declined. Although they would not go to war after 1784, the Seneca were not finished as a people. With the exception of powers and privileges relating to war and to the privileges of women in communal households, traditional Seneca society remained remarkably conservative in the decades following the American Revolution and the rise of Handsome Lake. The most significant threat to the Seneca, and to Seneca women, was the rise of American imperialism and the dawn of a century that would bring wave after wave of threats to extinguish the Seneca as a people forever.

Among the Iroquois, only those who professed to follow the memory of the vision of Handsome Lake retained the ancient practices. They carried on the old ceremonies, built ceremonial longhouses, called themselves longhouse people, and generally preserved what they could of the culture of their ancestors. By 1900, the terms *longhouse* and *Handsome Lake religion* had become synonymous. Although the legacy of Handsome Lake and the issue of the power of Seneca women are complex issues with mixed results, the fact that he initiated a movement that preserved significant parts of Seneca culture intact cannot be overlooked. All Iroquois communities that rejected the Handsome Lake movement had been Christianized, and few of the ancient traditions survived among the Christian Iroquois. Of those practices that remained as reflections of the powers of women, including the power to nominate sachems, most were found only among the traditionalists in the longhouses, where the walking song of Handsome Lake and the recital of orally transmitted memory of his teaching survived.

NOTES

1. In 1799 the Iroquois Confederacy was composed of Six Nations: Mohawk, Oneida, Onondaga, Cayuga, Tuscarora, and Seneca.

2. Paula Gunn Allen, *The Sacred Hoop: Recovering the Feminine in American Indian Traditions* (Boston: Beacon Press, 1986), 32.

3. Ibid., 32–33.

4. Ibid., 32.

5. Ibid., 33.

6. M. Annette Jaimes, *The State of Native America: Genocide, Colonization, and Resistance* (Boston: South End, 1992), 320.

7. Joy Bilharz, "First among Equals? The Changing Status of Seneca Women," in *Women and Power in Native North America*, ed. Laura F. Klein and Lillian A. Ackerman (Norman: University of Oklahoma Press, 1995), 108.

8. This story is recalled in some detail in Barbara Graymount, *The Iroquois in the American Revolution* (Syracuse, N.Y.: Syracuse University Press, 1972), 104–28.

9. The issue of dissatisfaction with the Fort Stanwix Treaty would be raised at the Canandaigua Treaty of 1794. Anthony F. C. Wallace, *The Death and Rebirth of the Seneca* (New York: Knopf, 1970), 173.

10. An account of the wars in Ohio, in the context of the birth of the U.S.

Army, is found in Wiley Sword, *President Washington's Indian War: The Struggle for the Old Northwest, 1790–1795* (Norman: University of Oklahoma Press, 1985). The U.S government passed legislation disposing of Indian land prior to purchasing it from the Indians (see 45–59). When the Indians refused to sell and violence broke out, the federal government embarked on a campaign to use military force to obtain Indian land. This marked the birth of American imperialism and a series of Indian wars that would last until 1890.

11. "But bribery had done its work too well; a deliberate plot to subvert the decision of the chiefs had been in the making for months. . . . Cornplanter informed Thomas Morris . . . that he had called 'a general Meeting . . . at which no sachem was to be present, that his Intention was to induce the Warriors to insist upon a division of the property and to sell their proportion of it.'" See also R. Morris to T. Morris, August 1, 1797, in Wallace, *Death and Rebirth of the Seneca.*

12. This conflict in Seneca culture between those who supported the continued existence of the Seneca Nation and those who would put the financial interests of the individual warriors or politicians ahead of the collective interests of the Nation would become a signifier of Seneca factionalism to the present. Although it is arguable that such tensions had existed earlier, the period following the American Revolution saw the rise of an unmistakable practice of possessive individualism.

13. Wallace, *Death and Rebirth of the Seneca,* 196–98.

14. Ibid., 199–221.

15. Ibid., 216.

16. Ibid., 332, 368.

17. Thomas S. Abler, *Chainbreaker: The Revolutionary War Memoirs of Governor Blacksnake as Told to Benjamin Williams* (Lincoln: University of Nebraska Press, 1989), 22.

18. See William N. Fenton, "Locality as a Basic Factor in the Development of Iroquois Social Structure," *Bureau of American Ethnology Bulletin,* vol. 149 (1951), 35–54.

19. Similar social organization is noted among the Huron. Bruce G. Trigger, *The Huron: Farmers of the North* (New York: Holt, Rinehart and Winston, 1969), p. 69.

20. Ibid., 71.

21. Daniel Richter, *The Ordeal of the Longhouse: The Peoples of the Iroquois League in the Era of European Colonization* (Chapel Hill: University of North Carolina Press, 1992), 60.

22. Ibid., 33.

23. Carr argued that the Iroquois matron possessed power over men, "sending him out on . . . an expedition whenever she pleased." Lucien Carr, "On the Social and Political Position of Woman among the Huron-Iroquois Tribes," in *16th and 17th Annual Reports of the Trustees of the Peabody Museum,* vol. 3, no. 3–4, p. 223; reprinted in W. G. Spittal, ed., *Iroquois Women: An Anthology* (Ohsweken, Ontario: Iroqrafts, 1990), 25.

24. Ibid., 29. Carr also cites Lafitau and La Hontan.

25. William M. Beauchamp, "Iroquois Women," *Journal of American Folk-Lore,* vol. 13, no. 49 (1900), 89; reprinted in Spittal, *Iroquois Women,* 47.

26. Thomas S. Abler, "Factional Dispute and Party Conflict in the Political System of the Seneca Nation (1845–1895)" (Ph.D. thesis, University of Toronto, 1969), 79; Fenton, "Locality as a Basic Factor."

27. Richter, *The Ordeal of the Longhouse,* 261.

28. Ibid., 261–62.

29. Sometimes young men brought their wives into their mothers' long-houses. Lewis Henry Morgan, *Housing and House-life of the American Aborigines* (Chicago: University of Chicago Press, 1965), 65–66; quoted in Judith K. Brown, "Economic Organization and the Position of Women among the Iroquois," in Spittal, *Iroquois Women,* 151–67.

30. William N. Fenton, ed., *Parker on the Iroquois: Iroquois Uses of Maize and Other Food Plants, the Code of Handsome Lake, the Seneca Prophet, the Constitution of the Five Nations* (Syracuse, N.Y.: Syracuse University Press, 1968), 72.

31. Fenton describes an origin myth for the ancient marriage ceremonies of the Seneca that tells the story of a man who resisted arranged marriage by absent-ing himself at the appropriate time of year. On one occasion, he met a woman deep in the forest who invited him to live with her "people." Her "people" turned out not to be people at all, and the man returned to human society with a vow to subject himself to the tradition of arranged marriage. The story and the elaborate tradition of music and ceremony that survived into the twentieth century confirm that at some point the Seneca ideal included marriages arranged by women according to the needs of the *ohwichira,* or clan segment. See the pamphlet with the identical title accompanying the recording: William N. Fenton, "Seneca Songs from Coldspring Longhouse by Chauncey Johnny John and Albert Jones" (Wash-ington, D.C.: Library of Congress, 1949), 11–12.

32. "Woe to the husband or lover who was too shiftless to do his share of the providing . . . he might at any time be ordered to pick up his blanket and budge; and after such an order it would not be healthful for him to disobey; the house would be too hot for him." Morgan, *Housing and House-life,* 65–66.

33. It is noted that abused women and children might resort to suicide. Beauchamp, 47.

34. An excellent discussion of contemporary European views of this topic is found in Karen Anderson, *Chain Her by One Foot: The Subjugation of Women in Sev-enteenth Century New France* (London: Routledge, 1991).

35. Contemporary North Americans would see choice of marriage partners as a right of individuals. Most traditional societies considered young people too inexperienced to make such important decisions without their elders' assistance.

36. Brown, "Economic Organization and the Position of Women," 187.

37. Richter, *The Ordeal of the Longhouse,* 266–67.

38. See ibid., 262–65.

39. A revealing discussion of Iroquois blood-kinship patterns is provided by Hewitt: "It must be remembered that the English rendering of a majority of these native kinship terms can not be considered satisfactory." It is probably equally true that whatever the term *paternity* means in English, or whatever it meant in the seventeenth century, there was no Seneca equivalent. J. N. B. Hewitt, "Status of Women in Iroquois Polity before 1784," in Spittal, *Iroquois Women,* 55; originally published in *Annual Report of the Board of Regents of the Smithsonian Institution* for the year ending June 30, 1932, p. 477.

40. See Fenton, "Locality as a Basic Factor."

CHAPTER THREE

The Power of Native Languages and the Performance of Indigenous Autonomy: The Case of Mexico

Inés Hernández-Ávila (Nez Percé/Chicana)

Sé que hemos sufrido, llorado, padecido, pero con nuestro trabajo y presencia y lucha cotidiana, tenemos que superar esas etapas de dificultades para encontrar un camino seguramente no desprovisto de dificultades, pero sí acceder a los beneficios de la humanidad porque formamos parte de ella y somos actores y protagonistas de su desarrollo.

[I know we've suffered, cried, gone through very hard times, but with our work, our presence, and our daily struggle, we have to go beyond these stages of difficulty to find a path surely not completely free of difficulty, but yes, to have access to the benefits of humanity because we are part of humanity and we're actors and protagonists of its development.]

Apolonio Bartolo Ronquillo[1]

Si algo señala y marca el fin de siglo mexicano, en medio de los desconciertos, transiciones y desastres, es el renacimiento (o como llamarlo?) de los pueblos indígenas, de sus culturas, sus luchas, sus lenguas. Hoy nadie escapa al debate sobre sus derechos. Sus cosmovisiones y formas de organización comunal han ganado el reconocimiento ora si que ontológico que se es negó siempre. . . . La década reciente ha sido el tiempo de su "aparición" en el escenario. No solo migran, sobreviven y resisten. También se subleven, y su ya basta conmueve y mueve a la solidaridad y la simpatía entre la población no india del país, y en muchos países del mundo.

[If something signals and marks the end of the Mexican century, in the middle of the disorders, transitions, and disasters, it is the renaissance (or what should we call it?) of indigenous peoples, of their cultures, their struggles, their languages. Today no one escapes the debate over their rights. Their cosmovisions and forms of organization have won them the very ontological recognition that has always been denied them. . . . The recent decade has been the time of their "apparition" on the stage. They don't just migrate, they survive and resist. They also rise up, and their "Enough!" affects and moves to solidarity and sympathy the non-Indian population of the country, and in many parts of the world.]

Hermann Bellinghausen[2]

Iquino yolqui yancuic cuicatl	That is how the new song was created
iquino chamanqui masehaulcuicatl	That is how the Indian song was revived;
huehca caquistic inintlahtol	Their voices resounded in the distances
nochi tepeme tlananquilique.	All of the mountains responded.
Ayoc aca quicotonas ni tlahtoli	Now no one can stop these words
ayoc aca quicotonas ni cuicatl:	Now no one can interrupt this song:
yancuic cuicatl, yancuic tlacatl.	New song, new human.

Natalio Hernandez[3]

In *Red Earth, White Lies: Native Americans and the Myth of Scientific Fact,* Vine Deloria, Jr., calls for "a more respectful climate" in which Native elders can share their wisdom and knowledge of the land, of this hemisphere, and of the planet. In a time when many are calling for "new languages," I offer this chapter as a climate in which the old indigenous languages of the elders, the old words, the big words that contain those ancient understandings, can be recognized and revitalized, and I offer this essay to Vine Deloria, Jr., for his life's work.

Escritores en Lenguas Indigenas, A.C. (Writers in Indigenous Languages, Civil Association), or ELIAC, is a national association of Mexico formally established on 27 November 1993; in November 1996 the national office of ELIAC was opened in Mexico City, with the name Casa de los Escritores en Lenguas Indígenas (House of Writers in Indigenous Languages). Using compelling creative and critical strategies, these Native writers, initially working in isolation from one another, evolved into a national movement now being recognized in Mexico, this hemisphere, and Europe. Through literary and song recitals; local, regional, national, and international conferences and literary gatherings; writers' workshops in urban and rural areas; the awarding of strategic (and strategically named) prizes; the publication of works by Native writers writing in their languages; and a recent initiative to pass a federal law on behalf of indigenous language rights, the members of ELIAC are occupying crucial spaces in the national political map and creating in those spaces the opportunity for the articulation of their particular communities' identities and needs.

As they manifest the plurilingual, multicultural reality that is Mexico, they are demanding that the nation do the same, not only rhetorically, but in a formally and socially realized way. In this context, the creative use of language through literary production and performance and language advocacy serves as an organizing performative strategy and a weapon for political transformation.[4] This movement has immediate relevance in the United States to Native language revitalization as a concrete, land-related expression of autonomy[5] and to the current discourse on multiculturalism and multilingualism. It also has relevance to the potential dialogue (called for by Deloria) between tribal peoples and Western science; in fact, indigenous languages represent the key to the questions of authority he raises about indigenous self-representation and systems of knowledge.

The late distinguished Mexican anthropologist Guillermo Bonfil Batalla, in his seminal 1987 work *México profundo: una civilización negada* [Profound Mexico: a civilization denied], presaged (with acute sensibility) the drama that is unfolding in Mexico today, of which ELIAC is a part. In *México profundo*, Bonfil Batalla posits that the (neocolonial) narrative of nation promoted by the state, by the elites, by those in power, is an "imaginary Mexico," one that is, in effect, an illusion, albeit one rigorously enforced and insisted on by all the institutional, political, economic, and military machinery of the state. As Hermann Bellinghausen has said, *"La persecución y el asesinato impune eran la regla con ellos. Estaban condenados a desaparecer, incorporados a la mítica unidad nacional que se inventó el sistema para prevalecer. Te integras o te mueres, era el mensaje implícito."* [Persecution and unpunished assassination were the rule with them. (Indigenous people) were condemned to disappear, incorporated into the mythical national unity that the system invented to prevail. Either you integrate or you die, was the implicit message] (2). The actual Mexico is the *México profundo*,[6] the rest of the nation, Native peoples, and what Bonfil Batalla calls "the 'de-Indianized' rural communities, and large sectors of the urban poor, many of them recent immigrants to the cities"(vii). *México profundo*, which is the majority population, represents the Mesoamerican civilizational model, in constant tension since the so-called conquest with the imaginary Mexico, the Western civilizational model, intent on erasing all real vestiges of *México profundo* through any means of "cultural control" necessary (except what can be distorted and exploited to serve the interests of a voracious consumer-tourist capitalism).[7]

The intensely exclusionary politics of imaginary Mexico has perpetuated a state of conflict and opposition through both wars of independence up to the present; decolonization has never been achieved. Yet, "the peoples of *México profundo* continually create and re-create their culture, adjust it to changing pressures, and reinforce their own, private sphere of control. They take foreign cultural elements and put them at their service; they cyclically perform the collective acts that are a way of expressing and renewing their own identity. They remain silent or they rebel, according to strategies refined by centuries of resistance" (Bonfil Batalla, xvii).[8]

Feliciano Sanchez Chan (Maya/Yucateco), one of the founding members of ELIAC, speaks of the "zones of refuge" in indigenous communities, wherein knowledge has historically been guarded, exercised, and sustained (interview). These zones of refuge represent the safe (physical and psychological) spaces where Mesoamerican cultural matrices continue to find expression, even as the advocates of imaginary Mexico persist in their obstinate project of erasure and substitution.

Sanchez Chan has actually transformed the term *zona de refugio* or *región de refugio* originally introduced by the late founder of modern *indigenismo*, Gonzalo Aguirre Beltrán, in his *Regiones de Refugio: El Desarrollo de la Comunidad y el Proceso Dominical en Mestizo América* [Regions of refuge: the development of the community and the dominical process in Mestizo America]. Aguirre Beltrán's perspective was that these regions were unviable, isolated, obsolete places sorely in need of complete modernization and integration, since nothing from the indigenous cultures was worth preserving (33–44).[9] Sanchez Chan, in contrast, says of contemporary indigenous literature:

> No sé si podíamos hablar de un "resurgimiento" porque hay una continuidad, nada mas que a veces se guarda en las cuevas, se refugia en los pueblos. Yo he escuchado de repente gente, cuando voy al monte, que mientras está trabajando, está cantando una canción en Maya, entonces digo ahí es donde se encuentra sus zonas de refugio y que ahora estamos solamente proponiendo una nueva forma de presentarlo ante los ojos del mundo, que es la escritura que antes existía también aunque en formas distintas en el pueblo Maya, pero ahora estamos usando una herramienta que prácticamente toda la humanidad domina que es el alfabeto . . . para poder escribir en nuestra lengua a partir de nuestros propios conceptos culturales y de nuestra propia cosmogonía y de cómo esta cosmogonía se fisiona y camina de manera paralela con la vida nacional y universal.
>
> [I don't know if we can speak of a "resurgence" because there is continuity, it's just that sometimes it's guarded in the caves, it seeks refuge in the pueblos. I've heard when I go to the countryside, people, who while they're working, suddenly singing a song in Maya, then I say that's where you can find the zones of refuge and now we're only proposing a new way to present it before the eyes of the world, and that's through written literature, which existed before just in different forms among the Maya, but now we're using a tool that practically all of humanity masters, which is the alphabet . . . to write

in our language starting from our own cultural concepts and our own cosmogony and how this cosmogony fuses and goes in a parallel manner with the life of the nation and the universe.] (interview)

Pertinent to Sanchez Chan's reinterpretation of the concept of zones of refuge is Stefano Varese's agreement with Bonfil Batalla regarding precisely how Native societies make external cultural elements their own. Varese says, "a process . . . of allomorphism" occurs wherein the original is "socially imagined" in such a way that the ethnic-indigenous form, in effect, supplants the initial element (or concept), which becomes "indianized" (Militant Utopians, 4). It is crucial to recognize the agency exercised by indigenous peoples even under the most repressive conditions. In spite of intense efforts to control them, the absolute notion that they have been simply acted upon, and that they have responded with passivity, belies their actual expressions, over the centuries, of cultural strength and continuity (often tacitly and tactically disguised or relegated to clandestinity).

Bonfil Batalla's point is that Mexico will realize itself fully as a nation only when it adopts a pluralist project, embracing both the achievements of the West and the heart of *México profundo,* the diversity of cultures whose roots go back to ancient meso-American civilizations.[10] Then, he says, "in affirming our differences, to ourselves and to outsiders, we will be radically denying the would-be hegemony of the West, which rests on the supposition that difference implies inequality and that what is different is by nature inferior" (176). In concrete terms, what Bonfil Batalla suggests is the restoring of cultural (and therefore, in my estimation, creative) authority and political autonomy to indigenous communities in Mexico, "pick[ing] up the thread of history that was temporarily broken by colonial domination," with the goal being nothing less than the reconstitution of the nation itself (174). He affirms, "It is imperative that we let *México profundo* speak, and that we listen to its words" (174), a goal to which he dedicated himself rigorously.

Bonfil Batalla reflected a praxis between his thinking and his daily work as an anthropologist and public intellectual. A lifelong advocate for indigenous rights and autonomy, he organized Mexico's first National Congress of Indigenous Peoples in 1975; he worked with like-minded colleagues such as Salomón Nahmad and Stefano Varese (whom he recruited to Mexico from Peru in 1975); he founded and directed the National Museum of Popular Culture, during which time he met and began to collaborate with Natalio Hernández (Nahuatl), clearly the major figure and founding member of ELIAC; and he established the program in ethnolinguistics that was so crucial in preparing many of the founding members of ELIAC, including Juan Gregorio Regino (Mazatec), past president of

ELIAC and currently president of the advisory board to the association. His work has impacted the lives of Native intellectuals and activists throughout Mexico in multiple ways, and his vision of the collapse of the old (neo)colonial nation and its replacement by the new but really old and deeply rooted multicultural Mexico resonates in diverse sites of struggle for indigenous autonomy, one of which is ELIAC.

In a similar manner, Stefano Varese's work, specifically in Peru and Mexico, has borne witness and contributed to indigenous movements in these countries. In the early 1970s, during the "risk-taking" administration of Peruvian president Juan Velasco Alvarado, Varese was responsible for implementing agrarian reform in the Amazon area, ensuring not only territorial control for indigenous communities but also their jurisdiction over their cultural, linguistic, and other resources. In 1975, a military countercoup toppled Velasco Alvarado's government, expelling the intellectuals who had been working with him. It was at this point that Bonfil Batalla, with whom Varese had already been corresponding, invited him to Mexico.[11] It is important to acknowledge Varese's work in the context of this discussion of ELIAC, because in some of his first writing on arriving in Mexico, he immediately began to defend the political and cultural-linguistic autonomy of Mexican indigenous peoples, even suggesting (in the late 1970s) the need for legislation very similar to what ELIAC is now promoting (Dialéctica Negada, 151). With Varese, Bonfil Batalla brought to Mexico a crucial ally who would also manifest a consistent and deep commitment to working with and acknowledging the agency of Native peoples.

THE HISTORY

Since 1990, the writers who would become the founders of ELIAC, guided by Natalio Hernández and working with Bonfil Batalla, began organizing regional and national conferences focusing on indigenous languages and the creation of a contemporary indigenous literature; their goal was to attest to the living presence of indigenous peoples in Mexico and to contest the anthropological and folkloric stereotypes of *indios* commonly held in wide sectors of Mexican society (Hernández, *In tlahtoli*, 139). One of the first spaces where the writers got to know one another was through a multicultural (newsprint) supplement *Nuestra Palabra* [Our word] that Bonfil Batalla suggested and supported while he was director of Popular Cultures (Hernández interview, 1998). The publication had impact not only because the contributors found themselves suddenly in a community of Native writers (on the pages) but also because, as Hernández explains, he *"quería acabar con esa discusión de muchos años de los lingüistas que si del alfabeto tal, que si se escribe, que si no se escribe, que si es dialecto, toda esa discusión que nos había llevado todo el 70. Dijimos 'se escribe,' y vamos a demostrar que el chontal, que el huasteco, que el maya se escribe"* [wanted to finish once and for all with the discussion among many linguists about whether this alphabet existed, was it written, was it not written, was it a dialect, all the issues which had been raised since the 70s. So we said, 'It's written,' and we're going to show it, in Chontal, in Huasteco, in Maya] (interview, 1998). In a democratizing gesture, the publication also accepted submissions *"Con el alfabeto que sea, del lingüístico de verano, del colegio de no se qué, o de la academia. Simplemente nos llegaba un texto en huichól y en español y se publicaba"* [in whatever alphabet, from the summer linguistics institute, from whichever college, or from the university. To put it simply, if a text in Huichol and Spanish came to us, we published it] (interview, 1998). This factor of inclusivity is crucial and points to the principles that were guiding both Bonfil Batalla and Hernández.

Nuestra Palabra had special issues on the regions and corresponding indigenous peoples of Mexico, such as the highlands and lowlands of the Mazatecs; the Coras, Huicholes, and Tepehuanos of Nayarit; and the Mayo, Yaqui, T'ohono O'otham, and Pima of Sonora, in each case including profiles of the region (often through a focus on sacred places), traditional stories and teachings, a news section, and sometimes contemporary poetry from each of the groups. The supplement also had editions addressing such themes as traditional medicine, ecological questions and concerns, the relation of indigenous people to the earth, children's art and literature, narrative forms (of the Nahuatl and the Zapotec, for example), indigenous women, the African cultural heritage of Mexico, and indigenous cosmovisions.[12]

In October 1990 the first national gathering of writers in indigenous languages was held in Mexico City; this was a turning point for what would become the association. Many of the writers had never seen the others in person, but they did know of one another's writing. Each individual was doing his or her work through Popular Cultures, which had regional offices in all the states (a consequence of Bonfil Batalla's directorial contribution to decentralization).[13] Hernández, working at the national level, was keeping abreast of the writers from the different regions. According to Huichol writer (and founding member of ELIAC) Gabriel Pacheco, Hernández was very important because he would get the list of grant winners and invite them to national gatherings.[14] The 17 December 1993 issue of *Nuestra Palabra* announced the official establishment of ELIAC and published the principles, objectives, and plans of action of the association. In the same issue, the national, annual, federally funded Premio Nezahualcoyotl for literature written in indigenous languages was announced, the prize taking its name from an indigenous ancestor famous for his wisdom and his poetry, the philosopher and *tlatoani* (leader) of Texcoco, Nezahualcoyotl (Fasting Coyote), who lived before the time of invasion.[15]

Conscious of the need to work in a more consistent and systematic manner, the fledgling group of writers had two more national meetings, in the states of Chiapas and Michoacán, before they formally established themselves in 1993 as ELIAC. Their formally stated guiding principles were unity and fraternity, to be achieved by reaching deep into the roots of their peoples to know how to work with one another in spite of possible ideological differences; hard work, because their people taught them that communitarian work dignifies people and earns the respect of the community; the art of the word (written and oral) as the fundamental tool for their work, to communicate and to express their spirits, with the help and teachings of their elders; and the validation of the ancient scientific, humanistic, and philosophical knowledge of their communities, as a base of inspiration for their own work.

One of their first dreams, according to Hernández, was to have a physical space, a house with a library, auditorium, and meeting rooms, because they "were writing and doing the association's business on street corners, in cafés" (interview). With the help of distinguished Mexican scholars and intellectuals such as Miguel León-Portilla, Carlos Montemayor, and Rodolfo Stavenhagen, who knew them well, they were able to secure the support of the secretary of public education and the United Nations Educational, Scientific, and Cultural Organization. So, the House of Writers in Indigenous Languages was born in November 1996; Hernández says, *"Es una niña chiquita"* [the space is like a baby girl]. Even though the movement in favor of contemporary indigenous literature has been ongoing for over a century, it had been unarticulated. *"Lo que hace la Asociación de Escritores en Lenguas Indígenas es de alguna manera articular este movimiento. Lo que hace la casa es crear un espacio de encuentro, de intercambio, de reflexión. Eso sería la historia"* [What our association has done is in some form to articulate this movement. What the House does is to create a space of gathering, of interchange, of reflection. This is our history] (interview, 1998).

THE CONTEXT

ELIAC's timing coincided with certain pivotal moments well known in Indian country, including the hemispheric indigenous protests of the quincentennial; Rigoberta Menchú winning the Nobel Peace Prize in 1992; the Zapatista uprising that burst forth on the international scene from Chiapas, Mexico, on 1 January 1994; and the United Nations declaring 1995 to 2004 as the Decade of the World's Indigenous Peoples (on 9 December 1994). It is important to acknowledge the history of struggle of indigenous peoples, as well as the horrific context of violence of the 1970s and 1980s in Guatemala and El Salvador. Since the early 1970s, indigenous peoples have made their presence felt consistently in global arenas, through local and national movements, and through advocacy and solidarity work at the level of the United Nations, the World Court, and the IV Russell Tribunal. The quincentennial commemorations provided an especially dramatic opportunity for sustained public critiques of the historical effects of colonialism and for the ardent demands for social, political, and economic justice for indigenous peoples. In July 1990 a hemispheric gathering called "500 Years of Indigenous Resistance" took place in Quito, Ecuador, attended by representatives from 120 indigenous nations. The major demands of the conference were *"recuperación y control territorial, autodeterminación, autonomía económico-política y autogobierno indio"* [territorial recuperation and control, self-determination, economic and political autonomy, and Native self-government] (Varese, Dioses, 454).[16]

Natalio Hernández writes of the quincentennial, *"El llanto, el dolor y el coraje contenido por siglos explotó y trascendió hacia los diferentes rumbos del continente para empezar a construir una nueva esperanza, un nuevo porvenir"* [The tears, the pain, and the rage contained for centuries exploded and extended to the different directions of the hemisphere to begin to construct a new hope, a new future] (*In tlahtoli*, 137).[17] He considers 1992 the beginning of a new stage of the indigenous movement, and Rigoberta Menchú is its symbol and main protagonist at the international level. Referring to the "dramatic pages" of her book as the life of a people exploited, discriminated against, and without hope for the future, he emphasized how the story is representative of the larger drama in which indigenous peoples of the Americas and of the world are engaged at the end of the twentieth and beginning of the twenty-first century. Her life, including the winning of the Nobel Prize, represents for Hernández the awakening of consciousness, after which indigenous peoples decide to more vigorously assume their own history, to rewrite it, and to take on their roles as the principal actors and shapers of their communities' destinies. Another related and important development that contributes to this reinvigorated setting is the fact that early in the 1980s human rights activists began to travel regularly to Central America, to Nicaragua, El Salvador, and Guatemala to bear witness to the violence and to elections and peace processes; the presence of witnesses from other countries was critical to the communities engaged in struggle. With Menchú's acknowledged presence on the international scene, and with indigenous peoples' awareness that their audience is suddenly (relative to the centuries of domination) the global community, the stage is set for new scripts to be written and performed, in different arenas and often simultaneously.[18]

On 27 November 1993, ELIAC was formally constituted as a national association. On 1 January 1994, in the highlands of Chiapas, the Ejército Zapatista de Liberación Nacional (Zapatista Army of National Liberation), mostly Mayan men and women, stunned the world by rising up in armed struggle against the Mexican government, against the caciques and landowners, against the North American Free Trade Agreement (NAFTA), saying *"Basta!"* (Enough!) to the centuries of bloodshed and suffering.[19] In his essay "La Literatura Indígena en tiempos de guerra en Chiapas" [Indigenous literature in times of war in Chiapas], Natalio Hernández points out that the armed conflict in Chiapas shattered the illusion that Mexico was ready to enter the First World of development and power. Instead, Mexico showed its other face, *"el rostro negado, oculto, producto del proceso colonial y de las políticas indigenistas paternales del presente siglo; de la actitud excluyente y racista de la burguesía nacional"* [the face denied, hidden, a product of the colonial process and of the paternalistic indigenist politics of the current century; of the elitist and racist attitude of the national bourgeousie] (*In tlahtoli*, 143).

As the world knows, the Zapatistas made their voices heard, first with weapons in their hands (some of which were wooden replicas of rifles, as well as stones and sticks). For public appearances, as a protective and ironically destabilizing strategy, they have kept their faces covered with bandannas or ski masks (consequently, Zapatistas do indeed "all look alike"), choosing to reveal only their eyes, which have always seen and understood the causes of the centuries of suffering. But they raise their voices, and in the words of Subcomandante Marcos, *"Cuando bajamos de las montañas cargando nuestras mochilas, a nuestros muertos y nuestra historia, venimos a la ciudad a buscar la patria"* [When we came down from the mountains carrying our backpacks, our dead, and our history, we came to the city to look for our country] (*In tlahtoli*, 142–43). The dialogue they have initiated and sustained has opened paths like no other in contemporary times; indigenous America will never be the same. In a conscious performance of autonomy, the writers of ELIAC join their voices, poetically and polemically, with those of the Zapatistas in this national struggle over the present and future of Mexico. One thing is certain, as Ronquillo says, *"México nunca ha sido de un rostro uniforme sino de un rostro diverso en todo, linguístico, cultural, económico, político, etc., por lo cual esos modelos uniformes, homogéneos que quieren encajonar en las conciencias no tienen futuro"* [Mexico has never had a uniform face, but rather a face diverse in everything, linguistically, culturally, economically, politically, etc. That's why those uniform models, the homogeneous ones that some would like to engrave on our consciousnesses, have no future] (interview).

In "Yo Jñá' a Jñatrjo"[20] [Indian Voices], dedicated to all those who have fought for their ideals, Mazahua poet Fausto Guadarrama (founding member of ELIAC) tells the story of how in the silence of the night the always-hidden yesterday burst forth powerfully and, with machete swings, destroyed the old myths. Women and men were born whose faces remind Native people of their own common origins, while those with privilege feel as if these unknown voices are tearing at their hearts. In the Native communities, fires are roaring; the grandparents are incensing with copal; the mountains, no longer silent, are now crying with the wind; and the feet of Native women are bleeding from the knife-sharp rocks that want to punish them for singing. The poet says this *México profundo*, old as the sun, comprises the Indian voices that history denied, and they will never again be silent. They will express themselves with their own words, think with their own thoughts, smile with their own laughter, and write their own history. Never again hiding, grandparents, men, women, and children go out contented to work the earth, willing to give their lives, joining with one another to find the world that was stolen from them and to which they promised one day to return[21] (*"Pa joduji nu xoñijomu nu o ponb'uji / Jango o mamuji, k'u ru nzhoguji!"*). He ends the poem with the declaration, *"Yo jñaa jñatrjo! Ri b'ub'ujmeba!"* [Indian voices! We are standing up!] (58–59),[22] a direct reference to Emiliano Zapata's famous statement, "It's better to die standing than to live on your knees."

In the poem "Bidao Nhólh Yadslhaa Llíw—Ke yell Chiap"[23] [The girl-child freedom—for Chiapas], Zapotec poet Mario Molina Cruz (founding member of ELIAC) calls Chiapas the cradle for the baby girl Freedom and announces her birth as a message of hope for the *"Bene'ki chhen le' yéj"*[24] [heirs of the rocky hills], who have been marginalized for centuries. *"Yel'bajachiee, chhao nhú lu'yay, / yel'bajachiee chha'luill tu llios kuéll, / na' bzulhao chhayeb' aké yel'win"*[25] [Tired of eating roots / of beseeching a deaf God / [they] vomited their rage], and the girl-child Freedom was born. She is adored by those who live in the huts, and under their care, she will grow to womanhood. The poet says, *"Dillen ne'bé, dillen llwe'bé, / duxhén yell'liu chhejnhielen"*[26] [she speaks only one language / that the continents understand] (72–73). This language crystallizes the struggle of indigenous peoples, synthesized, according to Hernández, in the words "Democracy, Justice, and Freedom" (*In tlahtoli*, 143). Native peoples in Mexico are employing multiple strategies to achieve their goals, yet language is central in each setting; it is not an accident that the poets' and subcomandantes' (inter)mediations through the word find resonance in each other, even when articulated in multiple languages, because the cultural signals are similar from one indigenous nation to another. They have to do with heart.

In the Nahuatl language, for instance, the term *in xochitl in cuicatl* (flower and song) means poetry, and in that tradition, poetry is the closest way to arrive at the root of the truth, poetry inspired by the internal dialogue of the heart with Ometeotl (the dual god, male-female), through which a human being becomes a "deified heart" (León-Portilla, 141–43).[27] According to Juan Julian Caballero (Mixtec; current president of ELIAC), *"Para el mundo Mixteco cuando alguien le pregunta a alguien 'que tienes,' 'estoy enfermo y está enfermo mi corazón' y cuando la gente señala que es el centro del pecho, no está señalando el corazón físicamente sino el centro del ser humano, el centro de la humanidad, el centro del universo. . . . Dicen 'es que no piensa mi corazón'* [In the Mixtec world when someone asks "What's bothering you?" [and the answer is] "I'm sick and my heart is sick," and they point to the center of their chest, it's not just the physical heart, but the center of the human being, the center of humanity, the center of the universe. They say, "It's that my heart is not thinking"] (interview). Even in the North, the Sioux have the expression *cante ista,* which means to "see with the eye of the heart," and Jeannette Armstrong (Okanagan) writes about her language, "We never ask a person, 'What do you think?' Instead we ask, 'What is your heart on this matter?'" (Keepers, 321). In California, Advocates for Indigenous California Language Survival (AICLS), in referring to the first language-immersion preschool now in place in the Wukchumne community, write, "The dawn has come and out of the morning fog arises a new home for language. This house will provide shelter against the elements and safety from the distractions of a demanding society. This place at this time doesn't have a name, but it does have a heart. . . . That heart can be felt in the parents and grandparents who see this as a chance to give to their children more than what was available for themselves. This heart is a house of language" (*The Advocate,* 1997).

The late linguist William Elmendorf wrote (in his field notes) that the Nez Percé (my people on my mother's side) consider the "center of thinking" to be the heart; "thought and feeling are both from *timíne*/heart" (4). To say *timínehihínaq'iya* means "he's made up his mind, literally, he's gotten ready his heart" (4). It might be said that those indigenous people who realize the powerful connection between their original languages and their struggles for autonomy and sovereignty have gotten ready their hearts.

THE PERFORMANCE OF AUTONOMY

On 3 October 1997, directing itself from Mexico City to "the national and international society, . . . the government of the Republic, . . . the media, . . . governmental and non-governmental institutions, and . . . the political parties," ELIAC proclaimed its "Declaración de los Escritores en

Lenguas Indígenas en torno a la Diversidad Etnica, Linguística, y Cultural de Mexico" [Declaration regarding the ethnic, linguistic, and cultural diversity of Mexico]. Calling on "the most profound consciousness of Mexican society" to consider its proposals related to the ethnic, linguistic, and cultural diversity of the nation, it said:

> En el umbral del siglo XXI, llegamos excluidos del mundo moderno; pese a ello, estamos aquí con nuestros pensamientos y nuestra historia como pueblos; hablamos desde el corazón de la tierra que nos vio nacer y nos preguntamos quién puede decretar la muerte de una lengua? qué pensamiento racional es capaz de borrar una cultura?
>
> [In the threshold of the twenty-first century, we arrive excluded from the modern world; despite that, we are here with our thoughts and our histories as peoples; we speak from the heart of the earth who witnessed our birth and we ask ourselves: Who can decree the death of a language? What rational thinking is capable of erasing a culture?] ("Declaración," 4)[28]

Citing Article 4 of the Mexican national constitution, wherein Mexico defines itself as a pluricultural and thereby plurilingual country, based on the ancestral presence of Native peoples, the declaration affirms that the law mandates the protection and promotion of indigenous languages, cultures, customs, resources, and specific forms of social organization, as well as guaranteeing to indigenous peoples effective access to the services of the state. This particular article was officially expanded on 28 January 1992, to specifically address indigenous concerns, constituting a significant revision of the Mexican constitution, one that would serve as the door by which ELIAC would subsequently push for its national legislative initiative.

In the October 1997 declaration, ELIAC called on the nation to elaborate a linguistic politics that reflects the reality of the country, affirming the indigenous languages *"que nos dan identidad, presencia, cohesión y dignidad"* [which give us our identity, our presence, our cohesion, and our dignity] (4). It asks for a national educational system that recognizes indigenous peoples' humanity as citizens of Mexico and the globe and *"que tome en cuenta nuestro acervo étnico, linguístico y cultural"* [takes into account our ethnic, linguistic, and cultural perspectives], saying,

> pensamos que no puede haber igualdad mientras nuestras lenguas y culturas sigan subordinadas; no puede haber verdad mientras se siga negando nuestra existencia, no puede haber razón mientras no comprendamos que la diversidad es riqueza, no puede haber equidad mientras se privilegie una cultura y se someta a las otras. No puede haber respeto mientras la dis-

criminación persista y no puede haber justicia mientras el flagelo de la mar-
ginación social, económica y cultural forme parte de la vida cotidiana de
nuestros pueblos.
[we believe that there cannot be equality while our languages and
cultures are subordinated; there cannot be truth as long as our existence is denied, there can be no reason unless we all understand that
diversity is richness, there can be no equity as long as one culture is
privileged and others are subdued. There can be no respect while
discrimination persists and there can be no justice as long as the
scourge of social, economic, and cultural marginalization forms part
of the daily life of our peoples.] (5)

Cognizant of the "exceptional moment of humanity" in which they
are acting, the members of ELIAC, echoing Bonfil Batalla and the Zapatistas, emphasize the richness and living presence of their cultures and
languages as the patrimony of Mexico and of humanity (5). They affirm
their will to live and participate fully in society and "to open new paths
towards human development," peace, and justice, ending the long history of oppression and domination (5). Declaring their will to fight for
their rights, they call on the federal government to honor the 1996 agreements of San Andrés (between the Zapatistas and the federal government), which call for a recognition of indigenous autonomy and set the
stage for a transformed relationship between indigenous peoples and the
nation.[29] With their minds and hearts open, they call for solidarity and
hermandad, ending the declaration with the statement, *"Hoy como ayer con-*
vocamos a toda la sociedad mexicana a unirnos, a recocijarnos de nuestras
lenguas y culturas, como dice el Chilam Balam: 'Que no seamos ni uno, ni dos,
ni tres, que todos se levanten, que nadie se quede atrás'" [Today like yesterday
we urge all of Mexican society to join us, to rejoice in our languages and
cultures, as the Chilam Balam says, "Let there not be only one, or two, or
three, let everyone rise up, let no one be left behind."][30]
    Because the ostensible guarantees in Article 4 of the Mexican consti-
tution are actually ineffective, in April 1999 the association sent to the
national House of Representatives a "Legislative Initiative on the Recognition of the Linguistic Rights of Indigenous Peoples and Communities of
Mexico," in which they proposed the following: to help and promote the
preservation and development of the indigenous languages of Mexico; to
define a linguistic politics that guarantees that the languages of each
indigenous people and community become official within and outside of
their territories; to articulate the linguistic and cultural projects of indigenous peoples and communities as part of the project of nation; to transcend the present linguistic inequity as a means of assisting in the
reconstruction of indigenous peoples and communities (Presentan).

According to Juan Gregorio Regino (Mazatec, past president of the association and current president of the advisory board of ELIAC), this initiative implies a radical revision of the concept of nation-state that prevails in Mexico today, as well as a revision of the content of practically all the laws of the nation (Haw). To ensure that there is a broad-based consensus for the initiative, the association is circulating the document among indigenous organizations, academic specialists, and especially indigenous communities, through regional workshops dedicated to the careful reading and analysis of the initiative's contents.

In the article "Analizan escritores indígenas la problemática de su lengua" [Native writers analyze the problematics of their languages], Dora Luz Haw describes Regino's position: *"A pesar de las políticas etnocidas, del paternalismo, la discriminación y de la 'absurda idea de homogenización del País', las lenguas indígenas persisten y son una realidad inevitable que debe considerarse como sustancial para la consolidación del Estado nacional"* [In spite of the ethnocidal politics, the paternalism, the discrimination and the "absurd idea of the homogenization of the country," indigenous languages persist and they are an inevitable reality that should be considered substantial for the consolidation of the national state]. For Regino and the members of ELIAC, the state's insistence on Spanish as the only language, resulting in the denial of other languages in the media and the educational system, is blatantly discriminatory. The strengthening of Article 4 of the constitution, so that Native languages are practiced and respected at regional levels, is, according to Regino, a *"planteamiento totalmente viable que se acomoda en esta labor de decentralización que se está impulsando en el País"* [a proposal totally viable in relation to the work of decentralization that is being promoted in the country] (Haw). ELIAC members realize that their objective implies a dramatic cultural shift, a social transformation whereby everyone accepts substantive diversity, and the major impulse for this shift has to come from indigenous communities themselves, validating their languages and cultures. Regino adds, *"La diversidad no implica ruptura en el Estado nacional, eso lo provocan las grandes potencias, la intervención de otros países. . . . En cambio las lenguas implican una inyección de identidad"* [Diversity doesn't imply a rupture with the nation-state; that is what the great powers provoke, the intervention of other countries. . . . In contrast, the issue of languages implies an injection of identity] by and for Native people and, ultimately, for the nation (Haw). Although the legislative initiative is a legal way of achieving recognition of indigenous languages and peoples, Hernández reflects, *"Pero no un respeto formal, sino un respeto humano, que va mas allá de las leyes y de los derechos estipulados en la constitución. El derecho es un respeto que nosotros traemos desde chicos, el respetar la planta, la hormiga, la mariposa, el colibrí. Es algo muy profundo que rebasa estos códigos legales"* [What we

need is a respect as humans that goes beyond the laws and the rights stip-
ulated in the constitution. The right of respect that we have from when
we're small, to respect the plant, the ant, the butterfly, the hummingbird.
It is something very profound that goes beyond these legal codes] (interview, 1998).

According to its own formal acknowledgment, ELIAC supports the
initiative (as well as its foundational principles) by drawing on the statements on behalf of linguistic rights in the following international declarations and pacts: the Universal Declaration of Human Rights (1948); the
International Pact on Civil and Political Rights (1966); the International
Pact on Economic, Social, and Cultural Rights (1966); the Declaration of
Recife, Brazil (1987); Convention 169 of the International Labour Organi-
zation (1989); the Universal Declaration of the Collective Rights of Peo-
ples (1990); the Final Declaration of the General Assembly of the
International Assembly of Professors of Living Languages (1991); the
Declaration on the Rights of Persons Belonging to National or Ethnic,
Religious, and Linguistic Minorities (1992); the European Charter on
Regional or Minority Languages (1992); the Declaration of the European
Council (1993); the Declaration of Santiago de Compostela of the Inter-
national Pen Club (1993); the Marco Pact for the Protection of National
Minorities (1994); the Interamerican Draft Declaration of Human Rights
on the Rights of Indigenous Peoples (1995); and the Universal Declara-
tion of Linguistic Rights (1996).[31]

The legislative initiative is a bold move on the part of this relatively
young but representative association. According to the Secretaria de Edu-
cación Pública (Department of Education) and the Fondo Nacional para
la Cultura y las Artes (National Foundation of Culture and the Arts),
Mexico has 6.7 million speakers of Native languages; 1.2 million are children less than four years of age (there are another 4 million Native people who do not speak their languages). Of the 170 distinct languages alive
before colonization, there are 62 indigenous languages spoken in the
country today, 24 of which are in danger of extinction. The largest indigenous populations include the Nahuatl (2,563,000); the Maya (1,490,000),
the Zapotec or diidzaj (785,000), the Mixtec or ñuu savi (764,000), the
Otomí or ñahñú (566,000), the Tzeltal or k'op (547,000), and the Tzotzil or
batzil k'op (514,000). This official count, however, according to scholars
working in Mexico, is low.[32] Hector Díaz Polanco describes what he calls
the ethnocidal strategies (etnófaga) of the integrationist model, "[que] urge
borrar cuanto antes a los pueblos indios del paisaje nacional y hasta de las
estadísticas y los censos" [which urgently intend to erase indigenous peoples as quickly as possible from the national landscape and even from the
statistics and censuses] (Ligorred Perramon, 5). He criticizes the pretension that intentionally dismisses indigenous peoples "mientras se esfuman

en el crepúsculo de la modernidad, que en mala hora, los engendró" [while their fragile outlines are shaded over in the twilight of modernity, which in a bad hour, engendered them] (ibid.). That is, indigenous peoples were made over into the image the colonizers had of them and, in effect, were created to be ignored.

Diana Taylor, in her study *Theater of Crisis: Drama and Politics in Latin America,* declares, "African playwrights have an option that Latin Americans no longer have—that of using their native languages in a step toward cultural decolonization." She notes that Kenyan novelist-dramatist Ngugi wa Thiong'o now writes only in Gikuyu, which is a "significant political rather than symbolic gesture in several respects" (34). In sweeping statements, Taylor continues:

> In Latin America . . . most playwrights have no "native" languages to turn to; they would have to learn them, and even then they could address only minuscule populations, such as the Mayan-speaking peoples of the Yucatan or the Andean Quechua speakers. . . . Ngugi's return to a vital autochthonous language like Gikuyu fights against further marginalization of his fellow African writers, but a similar move on the part of the Latin American dramatists would only further marginalize them. The fact that Latin America was colonized three centuries earlier than Africa explains the differences to a large degree. . . . A revival of indigenous languages, then, seems problematic and unlikely—yet the dominant language itself continues to function as an instrument of exclusion. . . . The problems posed by the virtual loss of autochthonous languages also hold true in regard to native dramatic traditions. . . . There is no question, again unlike the case in Africa, of returning to a native drama. (34–35)[33]

Her analysis is faulty on several counts. There are obviously strong Native languages in Mexico (as there are in much of Latin America), and the minuscule populations she refers to actually number in the millions.[34] Regarding the Maya of the Yucatán, Francesc Ligorred Perramon, writing in *Unicornio,* says, *"No debe olvidarse . . . que cuando hablamos de la lengua maya-yukatek no nos estamos refiriendo a una lengua* minoritaria, *sino en todo caso a una lengua* menos favorecida y minorizada *que se encuentra, eso sí, ante una* lengua expansiva y mayorizada *como es el castellano"* [It should not be forgotten that when we speak of the Maya-Yucatek language, we are not referring to a *minority* language, but in fact to a *disfavored and minoritized* language that finds itself faced with an *expansive(ist) and majoritized* language, Spanish] (3). The power relations that favor the dominant language notwithstanding, Mayan languages continue to persist in Mexico.[35]

Taylor relegates indigenous peoples in colonial times to passive, silent observers, acted upon, co-opted, easily deceived and manipulated, until "the appropriation of spectacle and images to convey a very different world view gradually eroded the beliefs, the memories (conserved through oral traditions) and the language of the indigenous people and unraveled their world from the inside out"; implicit in her analysis is a corollary fatalism regarding indigenous peoples in the present (28). In contrast to Taylor's view, Varese has written in reference to Mexico and Latin America that consistently *"dioses y héroes culturales indígenas asesinados y desmembrados, escondidos en el mundo subterráneo o subacuático, consagrados a un lento, difícil y secular proceso de recomposición"* [indigenous gods and cultural heroes, assassinated and dismembered, lost in worlds below earth or below water, consecrated to a slow, difficult, and secular process of *recomposition* (emphasis mine)] symbolize the historical-cultural response to the experience of invasion and subsequent European and national colonialism (Dioses, 436). These symbols, Varese says, allow for points of unity and cohesion of vision in relation to both the devastation brought on by the colonial project and the utopian hope of an indigenous political rebirth *"fundado sobre principios éticos propios, autónomos, radicalmente separados de la moral colonialista"* [based on Native peoples' own autonomous ethical principles, radically separated from colonialist morals] (Dioses, 437).[36]

As Dakota scholar, novelist, poet, and editor Elizabeth Cook-Lynn has said, "The presence of the [sovereign] Indian nation as cultural force [must] be a matter of principle" in the "critical discourse that functions in the name of the people" (85). She also speaks of the moral view that Native people can offer humanity. Implicit in indigenous notions of autonomy (and sovereignty in the North) is the idea of the profound respect for difference. Closely related to the respect for difference between indigenous nations and individuals is the affirmation of creativity and the right to name. Exclusion, hegemony, and linguistic barriers are intimately related facets of the same dialectic of domination and control. Nothing less than creation is the issue, because the creative act rejects control and expresses, performs, insists on autonomy at the individual and collective levels; it is a claiming and a taking of power. Cook-Lynn, writing about "what it means to claim the power to narrate, and how crucial it is to block dissenting narratives from audience," says, "Who gets to tell the stories is a major issue of our time" (64).

How the stories are told is another major issue. Liggorred Perramon, calling for the Maya to derive new strategies of resistance in defense of their languages, insists that bilingualism inevitably leads to a process of linguistic substitution, or the "muerte *de una lengua*" [*death* of a language] (3). He also criticizes the position articulated in the March 1998 issue of the journal *Navegaciones Sur,* wherein the work of indigenous writers of the Yucatán appears bilingually, as does the work of other non-Indian Yucatecos whose work is translated into Maya; he characterizes as "confused" the editors' statements that speak to an *"voluntad integradora que, en el conocimiento recíproco, busca la mutua aceptación"* [integrative will that, in reciprocal recognition, seeks mutual acceptance] and their hope for the future for all peoples of the nation (5). Emphasizing that *"lo que se integra se desintegra"* [what is integrated disintegrates] (5), he challenges the editors to say how often such publications will appear, since he doubts that non-Indian writers will suddenly choose to learn and write in Maya, and he asks if bilingualism is then the obligation of only Mayan writers and not "the colonials" (6). In contrast, Natalio Hernández has said that indigenous languages *"deben de convertirse realmente, en el caso de México, lenguas mexicanas. . . . Que la sociedad las haga suyas, que no digan que es de los indios nada mas, que las incorpore a su proyecto de vida"* [must become truly, in the case of Mexico, Mexican languages. . . . Society should make them hers, they shouldn't be thought of only as Indian languages, they should be incorporated into the life of the nation] (interview). The writers of ELIAC have consciously chosen to publish their works bilingually, in their respective indigenous languages and Spanish, and in effect, for them, these bilingual publications affirm the coexistence they are proposing (and manifesting). It is an expression of the coexistence of diversity within the individual as well, since these writers are, indeed, fluent in both languages.

THE ACTORS AND STORYTELLERS

The Native intellectuals of ELIAC, men and women, grounded in their languages and communities, are poets, novelists, singers, essayists, storytellers, playwrights; many of them are also actively engaged in the political and social struggles of their peoples. While they have common trajectories not only as writers but also as bilingual teachers, community activists, cultural workers, and ethnolinguists, there is one individual, Natalio Hernández, who emerges as the key figure of the movement. Among the founding members of the association, Hernández is named most often as the person who brought them all together.[37] In 1998 Hernández won the Bartolomé de las Casas award from Spain for his literary and leadership achievements on behalf of indigenous peoples of Mexico.[38] He is clearly one of the major sources of the history of ELIAC, as is Juan Gregorio Regino. Regino serves as the institutional memory for the association, because he drafted all its major documents, based on fertile discussions of the group. When the organization became a civil association, he was the one who coordinated the work of elaborating the statutes, the objectives, the structure.

For those members of ELIAC who began as bilingual teachers, the process resulted in an awakening of consciousness, for several reasons: the way they were trained; the way they were treated; the way their training put them in diametric opposition to their esteem for their communities, precipitating a return to the validation of their own cultures and languages.[39] Hernández describes the poor and unsystematic, rapid and circumstantial, training that many of them received as bilingual teachers, a training that, he says, *"era olvidar, negar, rechazar lo propio"* [consisted of forgetting, denying, rejecting what was ours] (interview, 1998). Recalling the inadequacy of the training, he notes, *"Los maestros no sabían que habían lenguas distintas, culturas distintas, o si sabían, no les importaban"* [Our teachers didn't know that there were different languages, distinct cultures, and if they knew it, they didn't care] (interview, 1998). Regino speaks of the training he received as a bilingual teacher: *"Lo que me enseñaron ahí fue a ser un agente de aculturación, un agente de cambio, un agente que llevara a la comunidad el español, que llevara un conocimiento de la sociedad no indígena y que desplazara todo lo que había de indígena."* [What I was taught was to be an agent of acculturation, an agent of change, an agent who would take Spanish to the community, who would take the knowledge of the non-indigenous society [to them], displacing everything indigenous] (interview). He notes how difficult it was for him to carry out this charge with his own people, a factor that contributed to his awakening.

Reflecting on the extremely adverse experiences shared by many ELIAC members, Hernández says:

> *Fuimos muy golpeados como maestros bilingües, la sociedad nos señaló, en algunos casos, y esto lo he dicho incluso en algún poema, a los perros les llamaron bilingües, para degradarnos como maestros. De alguna manera son cicatrices que uno tiene en algún momento de su vida. Son heridas que uno tiene en buena parte de su vida pero que hay que cicatrizar esas heridas. Yo estoy convencido que el futuro no tiene que ser por la vía de la confrontación permanente entre culturas, incluso la confrontación interior. Eso que sale afuera, que unos son indios, los otros son mestizos y que los indios son buenos y que los mestizos son los malos. Eso tiene que acabar. El mundo, nuestras sociedades tienen que reconciliarse, pero la reconciliación es interior, si uno no se reconcilia con uno mismo, es difícil que uno se reconcilie con el otro, con el vecino, con su pueblo, con su país.*
>
> [We were very beaten (mistreated) as bilingual teachers, society often looked down on us, and I've even said this in a poem, they would call dogs bilingual, to degrade us as teachers. These are scars that a person gets in his or her life. . . . I am convinced that the future does-

n't have to be along the path of permanent confrontation between cultures, including internal confrontation. What's said often, that some are Indian, some are mestizos, and that Indians are good and mestizos are bad, that has to stop. Our world, our societies, must reconcile, but the reconciliation is internal, if a person doesn't reconcile with him or herself, it's difficult to reconcile with someone else, with one's neighbor, with the community, with the nation.] (interview, 1998)[40]

The reconciliation that came for many of ELIAC's members was a coming to terms with the distorting integrationist politics governing their training. For Regino, self-realization came during his pursuit of a higher degree in ethnolinguistics. This path allowed him more intellectual theoretical exploration and led him to the contradictions and manipulations of (colonialist) history. He says, *"Y empecé a darme cuenta como éramos vistos nosotros en esa historia. Entonces fue despertar, fue darme cuenta"* [And then I began to realize how we were seen in that history. That's when I woke up, that's when I understood] (interview). He radically exchanged his role as an agent of acculturation to a promoter of his own language and culture, and he now writes and thinks in his language.

Those members of ELIAC who went on to become ethnolinguists have contributed to the writing of dictionaries and grammars for their communities, often standardizing the alphabets of their regions. Gabriel Pacheco, who is now one of a group of seven Huichol ethnolinguists working at the University of Guadalajara, says the dictionary and grammar they are working on are *"dedicado a los maestros bilingues, es otra aportación que estamos haciendo para nuestra comunidad, . . . en algún tiempo fuimos maestros, tenemos la obligación de donar los materiales o herramientas de los que ellos puedan valerse para que también enseñen su lengua, su escritura"* [dedicated to the bilingual teachers, it's another contribution we're doing for the community. . . . We were once teachers, so it's our obligation to give whatever materials or tools we can to those who will appreciate their worth in the teaching of our language and writing] (interview). Regino standardized the Mazatec alphabet, then promoted it by holding workshops and disseminating it throughout the community. Anna Aguilar-Amat has noted, *"Cuando una lengua ha estado sometida a condicionamientos históricos represivos, es preciso defender aquellas opciones que enriquecen y choesionan el sistema, razón por la cual la normalización del léxico y la terminología son una pieza clave"* [When a language has been submitted historically to repressive conditions, it is necessary to defend those options that enrich the system and make it coherent, which is why the normalization of the lexicon and terminology are a key piece] (Ligorred Perramon, 4). This particular work has been painstaking, necessitating diplomacy, tact, and

other strategic community organizing skills to bring the differing interpretations of the distinct languages into a negotiating(ed) space whereby
consensus can be reached.

Clearly cognizant of the repressive conditions their communities and
languages have faced, the members of ELIAC articulate a transformative
agenda that is dignifying, validating and ensuring the continuance of
their peoples' languages and cultures. Juan Julian Caballero, ELIAC's second president,[41] says that the association represents a collective commitment to the advancement of their communities. In the case of his people,
the Mixtecs (from Oaxaca), he says that even though they are not all in the
same region, they still identify as the Mixtec nation, and the work they
are doing with the Mixtec language is about much more than simply language revitalization. One of their goals is to have Mixtec educational
institutions at all levels, an objective they have begun to concretize by
establishing the Academy of the Mixtec Language in 1997, thus creating
a space for investigating such areas as Mixtec history (through a study of
the codices as well as oral history); Mixtec healing traditions (including
the sweat house); and Mixtec literature, music, and games. The Mixtec
language is at the center of all this work (interview).

ELIAC faces a multiplicity of challenges. Caballero emphasizes that
their work is harder because there is much less institutional support for
projects that do not favor integration (interview). He also strongly criticizes the individuals who write only for personal gain and prestige,
insisting that the communities must be socialized to see themselves as
creators and receptors of contemporary indigenous literature. He says,
*"Esto es una política cultural, esto es un política lingüística. . . . No basta con
que yo escriba sino que debo contagiar a los demás. Debo formar a los lectores
para que consuman mis textos, porque a lo mejor si escribo en otra lengua, es a
otro público que está dirigido"* [This is a cultural politics, a linguistic politics. . . . It's not enough that I write, I must inspire others to do the same.
I must form the readers for my works, because otherwise if I write in
another language, then my work is directed to another public] (interview). Caballero does not agree with works being translated into Spanish; he says when the work is a creative piece, such as poetry, much is lost
in the translation. The other issue, he says, is that when a work is bilingual, even Native people prefer to read the Spanish version, because it is
familiar to them; thus there is an urgent need for workshops in reading
and writing in indigenous languages.

Gabriel Pacheco (Huichol), besides being an ethnolinguist, is an
award-winning fiction writer, excelling in the genre of the short story; in
1999 he won the Premio Nezahualcoyotl, a national award given annually to a writer in indigenous languages. His collection of fiction *Tatei
Yurienaka y otros cuentros huicholes* is being used as a text in a secondary

school established and directed by Huichol teachers in a town called San Miguel to serve several Huichol communities. Reflecting on the impact of his book, he says, *"La gente se sorprendió cuando por primera vez conoció una obra escrita en su lengua. Siento yo que ese impacto que tuvieron los ancianos o comuneros de mi región, despertó bastante interés"* [The people were surprised when they saw a work written in their own language for the first time. I feel that the impact it had on the elders and the community people of my region awakened much interest] (interview). Recognizing the solitary nature of his work as a Huichol writer, he longs for the day when he will have others from his own community with whom he can speak about literary creation and share suggestions for their works. He teaches classes in writing in Huichol, hoping that out of those classes future writers will emerge. His first book of stories focused on the realities and hardships the Huichol people experience, but now he says he would like to pursue his people's spiritual traditions, to understand them and write about them creatively. He says, *"Es un reto . . . es muy difícil penetrar para uno que es parte de esa cultura, y yo ya no pongo en discusión a gente extraña que llegue queriendo conocer de un momento a otro todo lo que hay allí porque es difícil realmente"* [It's a challenge . . . it's very difficult to penetrate even for someone who is from that culture, and I won't even mention other foreign people who arrive wanting to know from one moment to the next everything there is, it's really difficult] (interview). In his reflections, as in Caballero's, there is the germination of a model for indigenous studies, Huichol studies, Mixtec studies, again with language at the center.

Perhaps one of the greatest challenges facing ELIAC is the involvement of more women at the national level. Women are very active at the local and regional levels, and some organizations, such as FOMMA (Fortaleza de la Mujer Maya), a women's center and theater group from San Cristobal de las Casas, Chiapas, have gained international recognition as well. Run by a collective of Mayan women (mostly Tzetzal and Tzotzil) native to the villages surrounding San Cristobal, the center has a twofold orientation: a teaching strategy of self-sufficiency, and an emphasis on the creative arts, particularly theater, as a powerful vehicle to transform violence. Because of their workload, the codirectors of FOMMA, Petrona de la Cruz and Isabel Juarez, take turns participating in the national meetings of ELIAC. One of the most active and vocal women at this level is María Roselia Jiménez Perez (Tojolobal Maya), past secretary of finance for the national office, essayist, writer of children's stories (published bilingually), and powerful singer and songwriter. In her essay "El futuro de la palabra" [The future of the word], she sends a message to the association regarding women's roles within this movement. She emphasizes the need to recognize women's contributions and capacities, calling for mutual respect and collaboration, and she suggests that the association focus formally in its meetings on the theme of women as social and cultural subjects. She points out that

> *Históricamente el aporte y la participación social de las mujeres no se reconoce, porque también promueve un cambio social y presta atención a problemas considerados como privados y propios de la vida cotidiana que no merecen un tratamiento político y social. Si existe comprensión y se hace a un lado el egoísmo podemos superar las barreras y caminar alimentando nuestro futuro, de nosotros depende.*
> [historically the contribution and social participation of women is not recognized, because it also promotes a social change and calls attention to problems considered private and pertaining to everyday life which (presumably) do not deserve a political and social treatment. If there is comprehension and ego is put aside we can go beyond the barriers and walk together nourishing our future. It's up to us.] (8)

In her larger message in the essay, she stresses women's need to devote themselves to the craft of writing; to the creation of a readership through the organization and support of literacy workshops for children, young people, and adults, dedicated to the analysis of literary production; and to reading out loud, because reading *"abre espacios de cuestionamiento y de meditación, en suma, de libertad"* [opens spaces for questioning and meditation, in sum, freedom] (8). It is clear that her commitment to the overall movement is strong. Her essay ends with a passage from the noted Mexican writer Rosario Castellanos, which is a prayer of invocation dedicated to women. More of the women's stories of this movement remain to be told.

WHAT IS AT STAKE

The actual revitalization of indigenous languages and the promotion of creativity in those languages are admittedly not without linguistic complications. The members of ELIAC (such as Feliciano Sanchez Chan and Juan Gregorio Regino) are aware of the vast difference between the everyday language and the more specialized language that encodes the ancient systems of knowledge. Sanchez Chan points out that Mayan people often speak Maya employing Spanish structures and ample word borrowings; he has made a deliberate effort, working with the elders of his community, to return to Mayan grammar, syntax, and vocabulary. Because he is recognized for his talent as an emcee (as well as a poet and thinker), he impresses Mayan communities with the performance of his responsibilities, at once recalling for them an articulation of identity that goes beyond surface or remnant expression, taking them beyond (or back to) a more dignified presence as distinct people. He says:

> *Eso implicó otro reto . . . en el '96–'97 [tuve] un acercamiento no solamente con los ancianos de mi pueblo sino con los señores que tienen el conocimiento y el poder para oficiar las ceremonias y los rituales de las comunidades y que tienen un lenguaje hermosísimo y profundo. Recopilo algunas oraciones en boca de ellos que yo incluyo en un material que se publicó en Mérida mimeografiado que tiene que ver con la medicina tradicional donde expongo que no basta solamente las plantas sino que las palabras tienen mucho que ver para la posibilidad de una sanación. Entonces yo trabajé varios años con estas gentes.*
>
> [It represented another challenge . . . in '96–'97, I was able to work not only with the elders from my community but with the spiritual leaders who perform the ceremonies and rituals in the communities; they have a beautiful and profound language. I was able to collect some prayers from the mouth of one of them, and I included it in a mimeograph publication that came out in Merida—it had to do with traditional medicine. In the piece I say that it's not enough to know the plants but also the words have a lot to do with the possibility of a healing. So I worked many years with these persons.] (interview)

Regino, working as *"un poco etnólogo de mi propia cultura"* [something of an ethnologist of [his] own culture], says he recuperates old words and understandings, situating them in a new context. These old words are sometimes not in use, having been substituted by borrowings. So, he says, *"Cuando encuentro ese tipo de palabras, trato de darle un realce, de empezar incluso mi poesía por esa palabra para que la gente sepa, "Ah, y esto qué quiere decir." Incluso la propia gente Mazateca dice "Y esto qué quiere decir?"* [When I find these words I try to give them an embossing, including beginning my poetry with the word so that the people will respond, "Ah, and what does this mean?" Even Mazatec people say, "And what does this mean?"] (interview) Thus, the new language is the old language not only recalled but also reinserted in human vocabulary, and reinscribed on the land and from the land.

Bonfil Batalla writes that Mexicans who do not speak an indigenous language have lost the ability to understand the meaning of the land, yet even after five centuries, "many of the old names remain" (12). He calls them "a stubborn reserve of knowledge and testimony that will be within reach of the majority of Mexicans only when our relationship with indigenous languages changes substantially" (13). He claims that indigenous languages are richer than Spanish, because their classifications contain "precise knowledge of the botanical characteristics" of plants native to the Mexican land; what is implicit in his assertion is that within the indigenous languages are the more intimate understandings of the specific land base of each people, expressed through what Jeannette Armstrong would call "land language," and revealing, as Bonfil Batalla says, that "our geography is also our history" (14). If indigenous languages are richer than Spanish, however, it is because indigenous languages pertain to this hemisphere, and so represent a longevity of experience, unlike languages foreign to the hemisphere. "In-depth study of these vocabularies [according to Bonfil Batalla] will provide information of singular importance about the diverse principles and codes that Mesoamerican peoples have employed to classify and understand the natural world in which they live and of which they form a part" (14). Deloria, in speaking to the link between storytelling, or the oral tradition, and Indian languages, also attests to the precision of words having to do with the "various states of human emotion, the intensity of human physical efforts, and the serenity of the land itself" (52–53); he reminds us that often "elders functioned . . . as scientists do today," working with the specialized languages of the land.

Bai-Mass Taal, from the United Nations Environmental Program on Biodiversity, has called attention to the immense overlap between "the world's areas of biological megadiversity and areas of high cultural and linguistic diversity."[42] He indicates that approximately 300 million indigenous peoples throughout seventy nations live in environmental hot spots threatened by exploitation of resources and habitat destruction. "The loss of linguistic diversity represents a huge loss in intellectual resources," as indigenous epistemologies, including unique ways of "synthesizing the world" and problem solving, disappear along with languages.[43] The destruction of forests and other ecosystems results in the forced relocation or migration of indigenous peoples to urban areas, where they are coerced into assimilation modes. Anna Aguilar-Amat echoes Bai-Mass Taal, acknowledging each language as inimitably distinct not only linguistically but also because it instructs the speaker about the perception of the world and the way of being as an individual and as a collective. "In the same way there are biological species that are eliminated from the earth, a language that disappears takes valuable information which helps explain the culture and the evolution of human beings" (Ligorred Perramon, 4).[44] Russell Lawrence Barsh, in "How Do You Patent a Landscape" describes indigenous ancestral land bases as "embedded landscapes" that are, in effect, "book[s] of human history and ecological science" layered with "linguistic, social, spiritual, and ecological knowledge and meaning" (18).[45] The text changes over time in a fluid way through the familiar, "patient observation of changes in the ecosystems which each landmark anchors in mental space" (18). At the same time, the cultural ceremonial life of the people reflects in story and performance the detailed record of these readings. The old languages represent the archives of knowledge and wisdom of indigenous peoples.

IMPLICATIONS FOR THE NORTH

ELIAC's movement represents a critical challenge to Native writers in the United States, given that most of us write in English, the other colonizer's language (after having made it our own at the often high price of losing our Native languages). Louise Erdrich offers the perspective that "the omnivorous nature of a colonial language is the writer's gift"; English, she says, is a "mongrel feast" (B2). Nevertheless, Native writers in Mexico have articulated the position that actual indigenous identity is linked to the ability to speak one's language.[46] The test of Native literature is in the (textual-contextual) performance, the delivery in the Native language, with the corresponding translation into (in their case) Spanish being secondary. It is not enough to point to the distinct colonial experiences of devastation that Native peoples in the United States underwent (and undergo) in contrast to Native people in Mexico with regard to language. Mexican indigenous writers argue that colonial particularities of experience notwithstanding, the charge for the millennium for Native communities hemispherically is to restore and re-create ourselves through the original languages, thus resuscitating the profundity of our understandings, which are the keys to our autonomy and originality, including our practice of performance-manifestation in its many forms. Native writers in Mexico are in the vanguard of indigenous language revitalization in their country, and according to Hermann Bellinghausen, *"algunos de ellos se cuentan entre los mejores escritores mexicanos vivos"* [some of them are among the best living Mexican writers]. They have framed their articulation as an issue of autonomy, one that dignifies and protects not only the ethnic, linguistic, and cultural differences but especially the ancient and contemporary intelligence encoded in the languages of indigenous peoples.

The Native writers in Mexico are not without their counterparts in the United States and Canada, although the extent to which the latter Native writers address indigenous language issues is minuscule in comparison, especially in relation to political (or cultural) sovereignty. One of the major voices is Jeannette Armstrong (Okanagan), poet, novelist, essayist, and major figure with the En'owkin Centre in Canada. Armstrong writes that in Okanagan, the "word for 'our place on the land' and 'our language' is the same" (Keepers, 323); human beings are a part of the "land language" (Land, 178). The land teaches the language: "It is said in Okanagan that the land constantly speaks. It is constantly communicating. Not to learn its language is to die. . . . It is the land that speaks N'silx-chn through the generations of our ancestors to us. It is N'silxchn, the old land/mother spirit of Okanagan people, which surrounds me in its primal wordless state" (Land, 176).[47]

In a similar manner, Apache scholar Bernadette Adley-SantaMaria, who is engaged in Apache language revitalization, remembers the words of her grandmother: "If you do not sing the songs—if you do not tell the stories and if you do not speak the language—you will cease to exist as 'Ndee' (Apache)" (19). Navajo writer Esther Belin remembers the instructions she received as a child: "Know your clan. Know your language because someday only Indians who know their language will be recognized. Learn the ways of the *bilagáana* but don't forget where you came from" (52). This is the coexistence that Mexican indigenous writers are cultivating.

This notion of one's origins is directly related to the cultural principles (and protocols), relationships, ways of being, seeing, knowing, and speaking emanating from the land (base) of each distinct indigenous people. Elizabeth Cook-Lynn writes, "The indigenous view of the world, . . . the very origins of a people are specifically tribal (nationalistic) and rooted in a specific geography (place), . . . mythology (soul) and geography (land) are inseparable, . . . even language is rooted in a specific place" (88). Erdrich says that once she realized that the Ojibwe "word for stone, asin, is animate, . . . [she] started to wonder whether [she] was picking up a stone or it was putting itself into [her] hand" (B2). She speaks of the "intellectual states and the fine points of moral responsibility" encoded in the Ojibwe language. One of these fine points has to do with the reciprocal relationship between the people and the land; Russell Barsh states that he was told by a Kalahari San elder, "if the people are removed, 'the land will die'" (19). In the 1996 Declaración de Valladolid, the following position was articulated: "*Máh unaj chéjsa'al mayathaanih, tumen ichil may-athaan ku tsolik u tuukul mayawínik. Bix tún kin beytal u kustal mayaka'aj wa'ma'atan u ch'abal u tsolik u tuukul ichil u thaan?*" [The Mayan language must not be exterminated, because in this language the Mayan person organizes his/her thoughts. How can the Mayan people live if they are not permitted to order their thoughts in their own language?][48] (Ligorred Perramon, 4). The implicit corollary question is How can the land live without the people, and without the sacralized science of the languages of the people, who are original to it?

In the United States, the Native American Languages Act of 1992 (102 Public Law 524, 106 Stat. 3434) declares as U.S. policy the protection of "the rights of Native Americans to use and develop their languages, as well as prohibiting restriction of the right of Native Americans to express themselves in their native language during any public proceeding,

including publicly supported education programs."[49] This act further recognizes the right of Native American governing bodies to use their languages for instruction in schools funded by the Bureau of Indian Affairs
and "the right of Native American governing bodies to give official status to Native American languages for conducting their own business." It
"establishes as U.S. policy the encouragement of elementary, secondary,
and higher education institutions to include Native American languages
in their curricula as foreign languages." Through this law, grant money
has been made available for federally recognized tribes to engage in projects of language revitalization.[50]

What could ELIAC contribute to the conversations being generated
at these conferences? Precisely the link its members have articulated (and
promoted) between originality and creativity; original languages, cultures, and belief systems and their expressions and manifestations; and,
perhaps most important, the self-conscious role they have undertaken, as
Native writers, to act as protagonists of their (and, by extension, their
communities') destinies. At the same time, they are working with their
communities, and as Regino has said:

> Entonces es toda una lucha, es todo un movimiento de reivindicación.
> Porque no es solamente la literatura, son muchas otras cosas mas que se
> tiene que integrar para que efectivamente pueda plantearse una lucha mas
> fuerte. Creo que la literatura coadyuva, pero no sólo la literatura va a poder
> hacer eso, también hace falta integrarnos a lo que están planteando los
> campesinos organizados, lo que están planteando los artesanos, las mujeres,
> todos los grupos indígenas que están organizados ya y que están planteando
> sus demandas, y sobre todo creo que lo más importante es que tengamos un
> proyecto de nación, nosotros, la nacionalidad mazateca. Pero necesitamos
> tener nuestro propio proyecto como nación mazateca.
> [So it's an entire struggle, it's a movement of revindication. Because
> it's not only literature, many other things must be integrated so that
> a struggle more deeply rooted can be established. I think literature
> helps, but by itself, it can't do everything, we must also integrate
> ourselves into what the agricultural [farm] workers are proposing,
> what's being proposed by the artisans, the women, all the indige-
> nous groups who are organized and who are establishing their
> demands, and above all, I believe the most important thing is that we
> have a national project, we, the Mazatec nation. We need to have our
> own project as a Mazatec nation] (interview).

Native nations, Native languages, Native articulation (written and oral),
and Native autonomy coexisting on a par with the Mexican nation: this is
ELIAC's goal. The outstanding feature of ELIAC's movement is the plac-

ing of indigenous languages at the center of communities' struggles for political and cultural autonomy. It is this factor that distinguishes its members from, for example, Native peoples in the United States.

ELIAC is organizing (and seeking governmental support) for workshops in creative writing for their communities (for all ages), with the intent of producing bilingual material in indigenous languages and Spanish for use in the national educational system and to attest to the richness of linguistic and cultural diversity in the country. Members are also insisting that the Mexican mass media support the recognition of literature written in indigenous languages, thereby contributing to the construction of consciousness of the profound diversity in the national society. Native writers in Mexico are revealing to the (indigenous) world a powerful and promising strategy for linguistic, cultural, and political revindication. In the 12 October 1998 issue of *Ojarasca*, which features thirteen writers from ELIAC, Hermann Bellinghausen says, *"Los indios mexicanos ingresaron al nuevo milenio por la puerta mas grand. Y esto sólo un sistema de dominación decrépito y pasmado puede vivirlo como una amenaza. En realidad, es un privilegio para los mexicanos. La sencilla sabiduría ancestral de los otros Mexicos hace algo más que sobrevivir. Se instala en la modernidad.* Su *modernidad. Ni el país, ni el mundo, podrán hacerse los indiferentes"* [Mexican Indian peoples entered the new millennium by the biggest door, and only a decrepit and stupefied system of domination could take this as a threat. In reality, it is a privilege for Mexicans. The simple ancestral wisdom of the other Mexicos does more than survive. It installs itself in modernity, its *own* modernity. Neither the country, nor the world, can pretend to be indifferent] (2). His own stereotypical view of the "simplicity" of indigenous ancestral wisdom notwithstanding, Bellinghausen's words are worth noting, even though the implications for those of us in the North can seem staggering.

For many Native writers who have lost much of their Native languages, the yearning is there, the consciousness of the endangered richness is clear. Liz Woody, in her poem "The English in the Daughter of a Wasco/Sahaptin Woman, Spoken in the Absence of Her Mother's True Language," says, "This Mother-tongue, the Queen's language, is lonely, / singular, bereft of the relationships to Blood-kin, / medicine, or tradition. This utterance should regenerate / or adequately resonate with the intention of helical essence" (107). Esther Belin, in her essay "In the Cycle of the Whirl," writes of the "tribal language . . . scrambled within [her]," which is the price she (and many of us) has paid to be fluent in English; yet the old language is there, she says, "In my blood silently circulating. In my back pocket squashed incomprehensible. The color of my skin. The rhythm, ba-bum, the ticking, ba-bum, leading me home" (51). For many of us, the path to language retrieval is an arduous one, but at the same time a potentially joyous one. It seems the time has come.

In 1996 the Linguistic Society of America issued a "Statement on Language Rights"[51] expressing and urging a strong continuing support of the Native American Languages Act. Admitting the historical and "deliberate government policy" of eradication, and echoing the UN Declaration,[52] the Linguistic Society urged the government and people of the United States "to enable indigenous peoples to retain their languages and cultures" through legislation, funding, and monitoring (Sollors, 190). Recognizing the benefits of multilingualism to the practical ends of business, diplomacy, national defense, and language teaching itself, as well as to the development of "the sense of international community" crucial for competition in the global economy, the statement also supports "the presence of diverse languages" for the expression of art and culture of the United States (Sollors, 390). The statement then offers the following slate of linguistic rights that should be protected, promoted, and guaranteed to all people of the United States:

A. To be allowed to express themselves, publicly or privately, in the language of their choice.
B. To maintain their native language and, should they so desire, to pass it on to their children.
C. When their facility in English is inadequate, to be provided a qualified interpreter in any proceeding in which the government endeavors to deprive them of life, liberty, or property. Moreover, where there is a substantial linguistic minority in a community, interpretation ought to be provided by courts and other state agencies in any matter that significantly affects the public.
D. To have their children educated in a manner that affirmatively acknowledges their native language abilities as well as ensures their acquisition of English. Children can learn only when they understand their teachers. As a consequence, some use of children's native language in the classroom is often desirable if they are to be educated successfully.
E To conduct business in the language of their choice.
F. To use their preferred language for private conversation in the workplace.
G. To have the opportunity to learn to speak, read, and write English. (Sollors, 390–91)

These proposed rights have some resonance with the national legislative initiative ELIAC is currently promoting, although that initiative is much more comprehensive and speaks to the creativity of indigenous peoples as well as putting forward specific organizing strategies for the achievement of their goals. Yet the fact that the Linguistic Society of America has taken this stand is a positive sign, especially in the "English only" climate currently permeating the United States.

Escritores en Lenguas Indígenas is fast achieving recognition locally, regionally, nationally, and even internationally. In fact, ELIAC has assumed a leadership position hemispherically, generating international meetings in Mexico, Chile, Venezuela, Nicaragua, and in fall 2000 once again in Mexico (in Quintana Roo). Central to the work its members are doing is a clear understanding of their role as protagonists (enacting autonomy) in the restoring, re-creating, and empowering of community identities, cultures, and histories through their written and spoken words. In her poem "Ja jk'umaltiki" [Our word], Jiménez Perez says the voices emerge because the old ones cause them to return. Cook-Lynn confirms "the memories of the grandmothers who were witnesses to outrage have informed the present story" (75). And Armstrong declares, "I will emphasize the significance that original Native languages and their connection to our lands have in compelling the reinvention of the enemy's language for our perspectives as indigenous writers" (Land, 175). Bellinghausen says, *"Los efectos políticos de este surgimiento múltiple aún están por verse. Por lo pronto, la suya ya no será la visión de los vencidos"* [The political effects of this multiple rising are yet to be seen. For now, their vision will no longer be the one of the vanquished].

In the broader context of human and civil rights, the story of this movement demonstrates that Mexico as a nation is clearly in the lead (in contrast to the United States) in the recognition of and move toward a pluricultural and multilingual society.[53] This is so in spite of the other more repressive, violent actions by the Mexican government toward indigenous communities. The key factor to understanding this apparent contradiction, however, is the agency that indigenous communities have enacted to precisely occupy and articulate those spaces in the narrative of nation. As in the United States, the advances made in Mexico on behalf of indigenous communities have come about through the organizing strategies of those communities themselves and through the efforts of the writers of those communities who clearly understand their role as subjects in the history of their country.

NOTES

I want to thank ELIAC for welcoming me as a colleague and for giving me permission to attend national assembly meetings and regional workshops, as well as honoring me by asking me to be one of the jurors for the first hemispheric Premio Canto de America (Song of America Prize). I am thankful, also, for the generous support I received for this research project from UC MEXUS (University of California–Riverside), as well as the University of California–Davis Office of Research and the Davis Humanities Institute.

1. Interview with Apolonio Bartolo Ronquillo. Here and elsewhere, when the written source or interview is in Spanish, the English translation is mine.
2. Hermann Bellinghausen, "Umbral," *Ojarasca en La Jornada,* 12 octubre 1998, 2.
3. Natalio Hernández, *Canto nuevo de Anahuac,* 38–39 (the volume is bilingual, Nahuatl/Spanish). Throughout this chapter, for works published in bilingual editions, I include the original indigenous language in the text, followed by my English translation; the author's Spanish translation appears in the note. In this case, the lines read, *"Así crearon el canto nuevo / así revivieron el canto indio; / sus voces resonaron en las distancias / todos los cerros respondieron. / Ya nadie podrá detener estas palabras / ya nadie podrá interrumpir este canto: / canto nuevo, hombre nuevo."*
4. I want to acknowledge Diana Taylor's assertion, in *Negotiating Performance,* that "performance has claimed its autonomy both from the dramatic text and its representations to constitute itself in various antitheatrical forms—among them performance art, public art, and what we might call public performance" (11), as well as her understanding that "the concept of performance made it not only possible, but necessary, for us to place 'roles' within a larger socioeconomic system of representations."
5. I use the term *autonomy* because that is how indigenous struggles are cast in Mexico, whereas in the North, Native peoples are more familiar with the term *sovereignty.*
6. I use the Spanish *México profundo* because it is a widely recognized term in Mexico and is immediately understood in intellectual circles as representing Bonfil Batalla's perspective.
7. On the surface, Bonfil Batalla's analysis seems to be a polarizing essentialism, but his discussion addresses precisely the area in between as the path for the future, although he clearly foregrounds the significance of the Mexico that has been denied.
8. Bonfil Batalla's perspective, and his validation of the agency of Native people, is in stark contrast to Diane Taylor's limited observation in *Theater of Crisis:* "Throughout the centuries the inhabitants of the Americas, both the indigenous peoples and the Criollos, witnessed the display of foreign power as passive and silent observers—as audience" (31). I reiterate, with Phillip Dennis, the importance of translating major works by Mexican scholars, such as *México profundo* (translator's foreword, viii), in order to demonstrate (in this case) indigenous peoples' actual agency.
9. Aguirre Beltrán's work is a major statement against indigenous identity, community, and autonomy. His analysis is replete with condemnations of indigenous knowledge systems and rights to land base. He assumes a tremendous ideological distance between what he calls the magical-religious interpretation of the world and the scientific cosmovision of industrial civilization, a distance that can be traversed only through a high cost to indigenous peoples. The high cost explains, for him, their weak representation in the culture of the nation (87).
10. There is a significant distinction between the concepts of "pluralism," "diversity," and "multiculturalism" as they are employed in Mexico and in the United States. In the United States, the terms have obfuscated historical and cultural factors of difference, diffusing, if not altogether dispelling, the very analysis that would lead the United States out of the "imaginary" into the "profound" (to

follow Bonfil Batalla's lead). In Mexico, the terms suggest the possibility of co-existence of different projects within the same nation-state and the full development of all the cultural potential of each group. In fact, in Mexico, discussion is often centered around the term *interculturalism,* highlighting the actual dynamic nature and possibility of (inter)cultural exchange. Furthermore, in Mexico, *interculturalidad* is tied to plurilingualism, and the articulation of support for Native languages is a core element related to the political autonomy of indigenous peoples, many of whom are referring to themselves collectively as nations.

11. My source for this information is a telephone interview with Stefano Varese, 13 May 2000.

12. In the 27 August 1991 issue of *Nuestra Palabra,* Zapotec writer Victor de la Cruz and Natalio Hernández pay their deep respects to Guillermo Bonfil Batalla, who died in a car accident in July of that year. Hernández says of him, *"Su palabra y sus textos conservan esa espontaneidad y esa frescura que caracterizan a nuestros pueblos . . . fue un rebelde permanente ante las injusticias"* [His words and books preserved the spontaneity and freshness that characterizes our peoples. . . . He was a permanent rebel against . . . injustices].

13. Apolonio Bartolo Ronquillo remembers, for example, that this conference allowed him to meet other people who were creating and promoting the Mazatec alphabet, which was a strengthening process for all of them (interview). Ronquillo is one of the members who chose the path of elective office, having served a term as presidente municipal in Temazcal, Oaxaca. He used his poetic and songwriting skills in his campaign and conducted much of it in his language. One of the first projects he introduced in his community was a poetry workshop, with poets from his region as well as from other parts of the country.

14. In fact, Hernández was named over and over again, in the interviews I conducted, as the person responsible for bringing them all together.

15. The Nezahualcoyotl Prize was instituted and is funded by the Dirección General de Culturas Populares (which Bonfil Batalla previously headed) and the Fondo Nacional para la Cultura y las Artes.

16. In the multilingual collection in which this essay by Stefano Varese appears, each essay appears in Spanish and is also translated into one of the indigenous languages of Chiapas. Varese's contribution was translated into Tzotzil.

17. Hernández made this comment in July 1995 at the Encuentro entre Artistas e Intelectuales Amerindios y Españoles, held in Madrid. From his perspective, since 1992, the indigenous movements in each country took on an international and global dimension, impacting the indigenist politics of the governments of the different countries of America (*In tlahtoli,* 137).

18. I choose not to give space to David Stoll's attack on Menchú. Stefano Varese and I discussed this issue in "Indigenous Intellectual Sovereignties," 83–84. I do want to acknowledge, however, that Menchú continues to hold a place of high esteem in Native communities throughout the Americas, and in Guatemala, she is greatly respected and considered one of many leaders in the Mayan communities of the nation.

19. Chiapas is one of the poorest states in Mexico, home to more than a million Mayan people from several Mayan communities, including the Tzeltal, Tzotzil, Tojolobal, and Chol. The rebellion in Chiapas surfaced not only as a result of centuries of oppression but also specifically in response to NAFTA and to the repeal of Article 27 of the Mexican constitution (under President Carlos Salinas de Gortari), "ending federal protection for the *ejido* lands held by local communities"

(Dennis, translator's foreword in Bonfil Batalla, viii).

20. "Voces Indias" is the title of the poem in Spanish in the bilingual (Mazahua/Spanish) edition: Fausto Guadarrama López, *Male Albina/Ne Male Bina* (Mexico City: CONACULTA, 1998), 57, 59.

21. This is my English paraphrase of the poem, which is published in a Mazahua/Spanish edition.

22. *"Las voces indias! Estamos de pie!"*

23. "La Niña Libertad" is the title of the poem in Spanish, from the bilingual (Zapotec/Spanish) collection (72–73).

24. *"Los herederos del peñasco."*

25. *"Cansados de comer raíces, / de clamar a un Diós sordo / vomitaron su coraje."*

26. *"Habla una sola lengua / que los continentes entienden."*

27. In the Aztec tradition, as in any indigenous tradition, the concept of Supreme Being is intricately complex; for the Aztecs, this entity is referred to by the term *Ometeotl*, or the "dual god" (male-female), although this only begins to explain the concept.

28. All passages from this declaration are found in *La Palabra Florida* and are my translations of the Spanish original.

29. "The Accords also included other required modifications of constitutional, federal, state, and local laws, dealing with the remunicipalization of indigenous regions of the country, the 'free determination' of indigenous peoples, the promotion and protection of indigenous cultures and customs, the use of natural resources on indigenous lands, the promotion of bilingual and culturally-aware education in indigenous communities, and the right of indigenous women to hold positions of authority equal to men at all levels of government and in the development of their communities" (Paulson, 19).

30. ELIAC's declaration also addresses the projects elaborated and the limited institutional support received.

31. This information comes from the article "Presentan Escritores en Lenguas Indígenas A.C. Iniciativa de Ley."

32. According to Stefano Varese, the numbers are much higher than these official state records, which, he says, "from a demographic view, are notoriously biased" (telephone interview, 13 May 2000). Indigenous organizations, he says, have counted 12 million to 17 million Native peoples in Mexico.

33. Taylor also makes the statement, "Unlike the hundreds of national languages and dialects that actively survive in many African countries, the indigenous languages still spoken in Latin America, such as Quechua and Guaraní, are alien to most Latin Americans" (34). The fact is, Guaraní is actually recognized as an official state language of Paraguay, along with Spanish; almost 80 percent of the population speaks Guaraní. In 1982, Tadeo Zarratea of Paraguay wrote a novel in Guaraní, which was published bilingually in Guaraní and Spanish, and won national awards.

34. In "Militant Utopians," Varese cites a 1979 study by the Interamerican Institute of Indian Affairs that says, "there are in Latin America 28.5 million indigenous people, divided in [sic] more than 400 ethnolinguistic groups" (1). In comparison, the population of Native people (of all Native nations combined) in the United States numbered approximately 2 million in the 1990 census.

35. It is apparent that Taylor accepts with facility the myth of integration and *mestizaje* (i.e., that Native peoples have all but vanished and all that's left are the cultural remnants of ancient civilizations, which are so marginalized that they would be a detriment to the dramatists who might consider them a potential

audience). Her simple explanation that Africa's later colonization is largely responsible for the survival of indigenous African languages does not hold true when one considers the colonial experience in the United States, which is also more recent, yet the impact on Native languages has been catastrophic. The determining factor of difference is not only the distinct colonial experience, which is much more complex than (but obviously includes) the time period, but also the particular nature of the (inter)mediation between the colonizer and the colonized. In effect, it seems that Taylor has fallen prey to what Varese calls the indifference of academicians to the "unusual phenomenon" of the "growing ethnopolitical mobilization of indigenous people in Latin America" (Militant Utopians, 1).

36. What Varese is describing is not like the "drama of liberation" that Taylor elaborates later, "the revolution [which creates] a sense of national and international identity mediated through an image" (*Theater*, 47). Even though Taylor's discussion refers to a drama (specifically the Cuban revolution) wherein Latin America discovers a possibility of seeing itself (in terms similar to Varese's) "as a united, coherent entity, a producer (rather than importer) of cultural images" (*Theater*, 47), her critique of the "drama of revolution, both onstage and off" (50), is that its main goal is the promotion of a particular ideology. The key difference between the two perspectives has to do with autonomy (or sovereignty) and solidarity and the recognition among Native nations that even though they might share similarities of culture and history, their autonomy lies in their distinction, and vice versa.

37. There were clearly regional expressions and early organizing efforts, for example, in central Mexico and Oaxaca. Hernández recalls a core group of individuals active in the initial stages who were "mostly Nahuatl" (interview, 1999). Regino recalls a similar core, all of whom were from Oaxaca (interview).

38. Fernando Villalonga, who presided over the jury that selected Hernández, noted that the prize represents *"una llamada de atención a la conciencia internacional para que los pueblos indígenas iberoamericanos sean respetados"* [a call to international consciousness for Iberoamerican indigenous peoples to be respected] (http://dulenega.nativeweb.org/congreso.html). In the awarding of the prize, Hernández was referred to as a *"pionero de un movimiento cultural que fomenta el entendimiento y la comprensión de culturas indígenas y la sociedad e instituciones no indígenas"* [pioneer of a cultural movement that is fomenting an understanding and comprehension between indigenous cultures and nonindigenous society and institutions].

39. According to Varese, bilingual teachers are among the most militant, politicized members of the Independent Teachers Union in Mexico (telephone interview).

40. Hernández speaks of the crisis in his life when he became conscious of the value of his own culture. He says, *"Yo me muevo en este mundo, pero al rato salgo y yo llego a mi pueblo amaneciendo y camino descalzo, y voy a traer leña, y lo disfruto. Es MI vida, MI yo interior, que eso no lo tenía hace 10–15 años"* [Now, I move in this world, then after a while I leave and arrive at my community with the dawn, I walk barefoot, I go for wood, and I'm happy. It's MY life, and MY internal "I," which is something I didn't have ten to fifteen years ago] (interview, 1998).

41. The president of ELIAC, as of this writing, is Fausto Guadarrama; former presidents include Juan Gregorio Regino, Juan Julian Caballero, and Agustín Jiménez García.

42. *allAfrica.com*, "Environmental Destruction a Threat to Languages," *The Nation* (Nairobi), 26 August 1999, http://allafrica.com/stories/printable/199908260090html.

43. Ibid.

44. Aguilar-Amat takes a misdirected perspective, however, in her statement, "We cannot defend diversity and at the same time forget the most defenseless languages and the peoples who find threatened the continuance of their values ancestrally rooted in a collective psychology and who react, sometimes with aggression, to the attempts at diffusion of a presumed standard culture that destroys their traditional forms" (Ligorred Perramon, 4). The "aggression" in the case of Chiapas, for example, has something to do with the destruction of their traditional forms but much more to do with the dire poverty, violence, and degradation in which they are forced to live. *Aggression,* also, is a charged term, considering that, from a Native perspective, even though the Zapatistas, for example, began in armed struggle (and even though their weapons were sometimes nothing more than wood carvings of rifles), they have always wanted to achieve peace through formal negotiations with the Mexican government.

45. Barsh notes how seafaring people similarly embed oceanscapes and skyscapes (18).

46. In an interview with Zapotec writer Javier Castellanos, he takes the exceptional position that being indigenous is more than the language; it is a different way of being, of (critical and creative) thinking, a distinct way of social organization. Castellanos recognizes that a person or community could ostensibly speak the Native language yet be completely Westernized (and, for example, Catholicized). This is also a point I have brought up in my interactions with ELIAC.

47. Armstrong also notes, "I have been surprised by how unfamiliar sounds in those languages [related to her own] resemble and resonate closely with the physical differences between their land and mine. The language lets me feel the points where our past was one and lets me 'recognize' teaching sites of our common ancestry" (Land, 179).

48. *"No debe exterminarse la lengua maya, porque en esta lengua organiza su pensamiento el hombre maya. Cómo puede vivir el pueblo maya si no se le permite ordenar su pensamiento en su propia lengua?"*

49. This act expresses some of the intent of the 1992 UN Declaration on the Rights of Persons Belonging to National or Ethnic, Religious, and Linguistic Minorities.

50. Indigenous language activists are currently working on an expansion of the parameters of the law. In his article "To Promote, Protect, and Preserve," Jon Reyhner states that the U.S. government funded two Native language conferences (1994–1995) at Northern Arizona University "to bring together language activists and experts to discuss how indigenous languages could be revitalized" (32). The seventh such conference took place in May 2000 in Toronto, Canada; one of the major themes was "best practices" (33) for indigenous language revitalization.

51. The membership of the society consists of about 7,000 persons and institutions. It was "founded in 1924 to advance the scientific study of language" (Sollors, 389). The members are experts on language, with expertise in bilingualism and multiculturalism. In their statement, they acknowledge that "many past and present members of the society have devoted their professional lives to documenting and analyzing the native languages of the US" (ibid.). The statement was "prepared by the Committee on Social and Political Concerns, approved by the Executive Committee, and ratified in June 1996 by the membership" (ibid.).

52. From the UN Declaration on the Rights of Persons Belonging to National or Ethnic, Religious, and Linguistic Minorities (1992).

53. In a highly articulate rendering of federal support by the director of the center for the arts in Toluca (August 1997), he acknowledged the indigenous languages of Mexico, and the cultures and peoples they represent, as national treasures. This acknowledgment was even more profound because he also admitted the "grievous errors" of the colonial and modernization projects, whereby every attempt was made to exterminate indigenous languages and to "save the human by killing the Indian," to paraphrase the well-known saying from the U.S. boarding-school ideology.

REFERENCES

Adley-SantaMaria, Bernadette. "Interrupting White Mountain Apache Language Shift: An Insider's View." *Practicing Anthropology*, vol. 20, no. 2 (spring 1999), 16–19.

The Advocate (newsletter of Advocates for Indigenous California Language Survival), vol. 10, no. 3 (spring 1997), 32.

Aguirre Beltrán, Gonzalo. *Regiones de Refugio*. Mexico City: INI, 1967.

Armstrong, Jeannette. "Keepers of the Earth." In *Ecopsychology: Restoring the Earth/Healing the Mind*, ed. Theodore Roszak et al. San Francisco: Sierra Club Books, 1995.

———. "Land Speaking." In *Speaking for the Generations: Native Writers on Writing*, ed. Simon Ortíz. Tucson: University of Arizona Press, 1998.

"Asociación de Escritores en Lenguas Indígenas." *Nuestra Palabra*, Año IV, Número 12 , 17 diciembre 1993, 4.

Barsh, Russel Lawrence. "How Do You Patent a Landscape? The Perils of Dichotomizing Cultural and Intellectual Property." *International Journal of Cultural Property*, vol. 8, no. 1 (1999), 14–47.

Belin, Esther. "In the Cycle of the Whirl." In *Speaking for the Generations: Native Writers on Writing*, ed. Simon Ortíz. Tucson: University of Arizona Press, 1998.

Bellinghausen, Hermann. "Umbral." *Ojarasca en La Jornada: Suplemento Mensual*, 12 octubre 1998, 2.

Bonfil Batalla, Guillermo. *Mexico Profundo: Reclaiming a Civilization*, trans. Philip A. Dennis. Austin: University of Texas Press, 1996.

Caballero, Juan Julian. Interview with author, September 1999.

Castellanos, Javier. Interview with author, September 1999.

"Conclusiones del Coloquio sobre Lenguas y Literaturas Indígenas." *La Palabra Florida*, Año II, Número 4 (Invierno 1997), 8–13.

Congressional Information Service Index. Native American Languages Act, 90 PL 101–477.

Cook-Lynn, Elizabeth. *Why I Can't Read Wallace Stegner and Other Essays: A Tribal Voice*. Madison: University of Wisconsin Press, 1996.

"Declaración de los Escritores en Lenguas Indígenas." *La Palabra Florida*, Año II, Número 4 (Invierno 1997), 4–6.

Diskin, Martin, Thomas Bossert, Salomon Nahmad, and Stefano Varese. *Peace and Autonomy on the Atlantic Coast of Nicaragua: A Report of the LASA Task Force on Human Rights and Academic Freedom*. Pittsburgh, Pa.: University of Pittsburgh, 1986.

Dominguez Michael, Christopher. "Lengua Nonata o Lengua Muerta? Literatura Indígena Actual." *Vuelta*, Año XX, Número 232 (Marzo de 1996), 43–47.

Elmendorf, William. [Field] Notes on Nez Perce Semantic Structure and Social Behavior. Ms. collected 1962–1965.

"Environmental Destruction a Threat to Languages." *The Nation* (Nairobi), 26 August 1999, http://allafrica.com/stories/printable/199908260090.html.

Erdrich, Louise. "Two Languages in Mind, but Just One in the Heart." *New York Times,* 22 May 2000, B1.

Guadarrama López, Fausto. *Male Albina/Ne Male Bina.* Mexico City: CONACULTA, 1998.

Haw, Dora Luz. "Analizan escritores indígenas la problemática de su lengua." *Reforma,* 19 agosto 1997, 3C+.

Hernández, Natalio. Interviews with author, 1998, 1999.

———. *Canto nuevo de Anahuac: Yancuic Anahuac Cuicatl.* Mexico, D.F.: Editorial Diana, 1994.

———. *In tlahtoli, in ohtli/la palabra, el camino: Memoria y destino de los pueblos indígenas.* Mexico, D.F.: Plaza y Valdez Editores, 1998.

Hernández-Avila, Inés, "Mexico: Native Writers in Defense of Indigenous Languages." *American Language Review,* vol. 4, no. 3 (May/June 2000), 57–59.

Hernández-Avila, Inés, and Stefano Varese. "Indigenous Intellectual Sovereignties: A Hemispheric Convocation." *Wicazo Sa Review,* vol. 14, no. 2 (fall 1999), 77–91.

Jimenez Perez, María Roselia, "El Futuro de la Palabra." *La Palabra Florida,* Año I, Número 1 (Invierno 1996), 5–9.

———. "Ja jk'umaltiki." *La Palabra Florida,* Año II, Número 6 (Otoño 1998), 10.

———. *Jna'jeltik: Vivencias Tojolabales.* Chiapas: Colección Letras Maya Contemporáneas, 1996.

León-Portilla, Miguel. *Aztec Thought and Culture,* trans. Jack Emory Davis. Norman: University of Oklahoma Press, 1990.

Ligorred Perramon, Francesc. "De hablar y de crear en lengua maya-yukateka." *Unicornio,* 23 agosto 1998, 3–8.

Linguistic Society of America. "Statement on Language Rights." In *Multilingual America: Transnationalism, Ethnicity, and the Languages of American Literature,* ed. Werner Sollors. New York: New York University Press, 1998.

Molina Cruz, Mario. *Volcán de Pétalos/Ya'byalhje xtak yejé.* Mexico City: CONACULTA, 1996.

Pacheco, Gabriel. Interview with author, December 1999.

———. *Tatei Yurienaka y otros cuentros huicholes.* Mexico, D.F.: Editorial Diana, 1994.

"Palabras Para Amanecer: Literatura indígena contemporanea de México." *Ojarasca en La Jornada: Suplemento Mensual,* 12 octubre 1998, 1–12.

Paulson, Joshua, "Special Report: The San Andrés Accords: Two Years Later (February 1, 1996–February 1, 1998." *Fourth World Bulletin: Issues in Indigenous Law and Politics,* vol. 6 (summer 1998), 19–22.

"Presentan Escritores en Lenguas Indígenas A.C. Iniciativa de Ley, JYASU." n.d.

"El Príncipe Entrega Premio Bartolomé de las Casas." http://dulenega.nativeweb.org/congreso.html.

Regino, Juan Gregorio. Interview with author, 1998.

———. *No es eterna la muerte: Tatsjejin nga kjabuya.* Mexico, D.F.: Editorial Diana, 1994.

———. "Otra parte de nuestra identidad: Literatura Indígena." *Ojarasca en La Jornada: Suplemento Mensual,* 12 octubre 1998, 3–4.

Reyhner, Jon. "To Promote, Protect and Preserve." *American Language Review,* vol. 3, no. 6 (November/December 1999), 32–33.

————. "Te Kohanga Reo." *American Language Review,* vol. 4, no. 1 (January/February 2000), 29–30.

Ronquillo, Apolonio Bartolo. Interview with author, December 1999.

Sanchez Chan, Feliciano. Interview with author, December 1999.

Sollors, Werner, ed. *Multilingual America: Transnationalism, Ethnicity, and the Languages of American Literature.* New York: New York University Press, 1998.

"Soy un aprendiz que intenta aproximarse a la palabra y cultivarla, dice Juan Gregorio Regino." *La Jornada,* 12 octubre 1999, 31.

Taylor, Diana. *Theater of Crisis: Drama and Politics in Latin America.* Lexington: University Press of Kentucky, 1991.

————, ed. *Negotiating Performance: Gender, Sexuality, and Theatricality in Latin/o America.* Durham, N.C.: Duke University Press, 1994.

United Nations. "Declaration on the Rights of Persons Belonging to National or Ethnic, Religious, and Linguistic Minorities." Adopted by the General Assembly at its 47th session, 92nd plenary meeting, New York, 18 December 1992.

Varese, Stefano. Telephone interview with author, 13 May 2000.

————. "Los dioses enterrados: el uso político de la resistencia cultural indígena." *El arreglo de los pueblos indios: la incansable tarea de reconstitución,* ed. Jacinto Arias Perez. Chiapas: SEP/Gobierno del Estado de Chiapas y Instituto Chiapaneca de Cultura, 1994, 433–462.

————. "Militant Utopians: Notes on the Indian Political Movements in Latin America." Paper presented at the Summer Institute on Colonial Indian Literature, sponsored by the National Endowment for the Humanities, Brown University, 26 July 1990.

————. "Una dialéctica negada: Notas sobre la multietnicidad mexicana." In *En Torno a la Cultura Nacional,* 2nd ed., ed. Héctor Aguilar Camín et al. Mexico: INI, 1989.

Woody, Liz. *Luminaries of the Humble.* Tucson: University of Arizona, 1994.

Zimmerman, Klaus. "La 'modernización' de las lenguas amerindias como estrategia de supervivencia." *Société suisse des Américanistes/Shcwizerische Amerikanisten-Gesellschaft,* Bulletin 59–60 (1995–1996), 189–96.

PART II: RESISTANCE, POLITICS, COLONIZATION, AND THE LAW

The Metaphysics of Federal Indian Law and U.S. Colonialism of American Indians

M. A. Jaimes-Guerrero (Juaneño/Yaqui)

American Indians, as individuals or tribal nations, are not only survivors of U.S. colonialism but, more importantly, practitioners and holders of indigenous knowledge in many fields of study. This introduction touches on several subjects that Vine Deloria, Jr., emphasized early in his career and continues to work in: indigenous nationalism; political, legal, and institutional analysis of Western law and its impact on tribal cultures, identities, and nationhood; and the need for Native scholars to construct critical responses to the legal domination, craft indigenous understandings, and resurrect and refurbish tribal-based systems of law and governance that still hold the United States accountable for its treaty and trust-based obligations to Native nations.

From the very beginning, Deloria's work had both domestic and international dimensions. The chapters by Glenn T. Morris and S. James Anaya both speak to the important international aspect of indigenous legal and political status by emphasizing the moral legitimacy of First Nations and their quest for political autonomy. David E. Wilkins's chapter focuses on one of the central legal doctrines of U.S. domestic law— reserved rights—that has provided Native peoples with a measure of protection for their natural resources, treaty rights, and remaining properties.

Deloria deserves significant credit for creating the spiritual-strategic framework for a comprehensive understanding of the federal-Indian relationship since the birth of the American Republic. This dominant-subordinate construction has unfortunately established a codependency between Indian nations and the federal government, as well as creating in many Native individuals a perspective not of Indian nationalism and self-governance but of ethnic-minority status because of the ongoing effects of racism, dependency, and internal colonialism.

One area that concerns all Native legal and political theorists is the state of tribal repatriation presently being played out in the controversy over "Kennewick Man," whose remains were found on the banks of the Columbia River in Washington State. In response to the charge that Deloria was a "Native creationist," he made this satiric statement: "American Indians are defending the rights of all people to have their relatives and ancestors lie buried in peace rather than stretched out on some science lab where people can play with them. How long are people going to sit by and allow a select group of self-proclaimed experts scream 'science, science, science' and disrupt their lives and beliefs? NAGPRA [the Native American Graves Protection and Repatriation Act] has set the limits, and it is up to people to follow the law, particularly since that law was approved by the mass of professional archaeologists. They overreach themselves on behalf of their own publicity, and they need to be stopped and made law-abiding citizens" (*Denver Post: Online Opinion*, 30 November 1998).

Living in both worlds himself, Deloria has always been able to see between and within the two realities of indigenous peoples and non-Indians. Since his statement, *Discover* magazine has seen fit, "in the name of science," to feature an article by a novice that seeks to contradict the controversial but conventional Bering Strait theory of indigenous origins by proposing that ancient Europeans may have been the "First Americans" (Wright, 53–62). This Western, Eurocentric view is just the latest in a burgeoning Euro-American backlash that seeks to claim preeminence in the Americas at the expense of Native peoples and their ancient cultures and origin beliefs.

Such specious claims insult Native peoples' origin accounts, creation stories, and cosmologies. A cosmological theory among today's Native peoples suggests that this hemisphere was the "cradle of civilization." This historical understanding is particularly strong among the Pueblo peoples of the Southwest. In this vein, Deloria has always been a spokesman who challenged Western science, and he has been the leading voice supporting indigenous assertions of a "Native genesis" in the Americas.

Beyond this, Deloria has influenced others by his writings and teachings and through his remarkable achievements as a theologian, historian, legal theorist, and political activist. His example has inspired others, among countless Native sons and daughters, to envision a cultural renaissance among a Native intelligentsia who would be expected to produce a body of scholarship and yet still engage in grassroots activism when conditions warranted such work. His work in this arena also lends itself to what I call a "metascience," which was espoused in his powerful study *Metaphysics of Modern Existence* (1979). In 1973, he contributed a stunning comparative study on indigenous-Western religion, *God Is Red* (revised in 1994).

Such an orientation can also be contextualized in what could be thought of as an "indigenous dialectics" for Native decision making and problem solving. It is in today's hypermodernist contemporary context that Native peoples can find visibility only through tourism, gaming, and other forms of economic exploitation, rather than through genuine respect and recognition of traditionally based indigenous economic systems and cultural values that include reciprocity with the natural environment. As the most distinguished indigenous thinker of the past century, Deloria counters these colonialist agendas with his more recent work on Native geomythology and environmental ethics in the pathbreaking book *Red Earth, White Lies* (1996). This text highlights the obfuscation and subterfuge that Eurocentric scientists and others employ to disguise their hidden agendas as "scientific "knowledge" and "intellectual discovery." Such alleged "expertise" is almost always wielded in a fashion that reduces the sovereignty or rights of Native peoples.

Finally, we can conclude that the United States, as a duplicitous, sociopolitically engineered, and globalizing society, mimics the notion of a genuine culture in its parasitic appropriation of indigenous peoples' knowledge for commercial enterprises. Such enterprises are also motivated by the profit motive that is commodifying indigenous peoples at the expense of our greater humanity. The only alternative to this pathological anti–American Indian scheme is an emerging transnational indigenous movement in these postnationalist times. This is critical in order to assert precolonialist cultural, human, and sacred rights in the restoration of a Native America that may also serve as a model for non-Natives to follow—a Native America that exhibited a profound respect for the earth as a living being.

Deloria's political, legal, and cultural analyses anticipated many of the problems Native peoples have encountered, but his stunning insights also forewarned the larger society about educational, technological, and moral crises caused by its Eurocentric decision makers. And it is his written body of work, along with his many speeches to a variety of audiences, as well as his leadership in managing and creating organizations to combat these crises, that will enable Native peoples in the United States and aboriginal peoples in other parts of the world to find ways to cope and still evolve.

As a Native intellectual and philosopher, Deloria continues to leave his Sartrean mark in an enduring legacy that sustains an indigenous and human rights movement for all committed people. He has most significantly provided us with an alternative vision for the twenty-first century, and he envisions a Native America that is inclusive of non-Natives as well. This is his blueprint for what he has called and contextualized as "the metaphysics of modern existence" (1979), and it also provides us with a manifesto of concepts and ideals in the context of our traditional cultures and histories that sustains an indigenous worldview so that the people may live.

REFERENCES

Deloria, Vine Jr. *God Is Red*. New York: Grosset and Dunlap, 1973. Second rev. ed. Golden, Colo.: Fulcrum Publishing, 1994.
———. *The Metaphysics of Modern Existence*. New York: Harper and Row, 1979.
———. *Red Earth, White Lies*. New York: Scribner, 1996.
Denver Post: Online Opinion, http://www.denverpost.com.opinion/deloria/229.htm.
Wright, Karen. "First Amendment." *Discover,* February 1999, 53–62.

CHAPTER FOUR

From Time Immemorial: The Origin and Import of the Reserved Rights Doctrine
David E. Wilkins (Lumbee)

This chapter addresses what is generally regarded as one of the most important legal doctrines undergirding the treaty and trust rights of indigenous nations—reserved rights. On its face, it is less problematic than doctrines such as plenary power, discovery, trust, or good faith, since the word *reserve* is the root of the *reservations* that constitute a fundamental aspect of the Indian-U.S. relationship. At the present time there are 278 reservations in thirty-two states formally recognized by the federal government.

Broadly, reservations are tracts of land expressly set aside or reserved for Indian nations by some federal action, typically with the concurrence of a tribe or group of tribes. Many Indian reservations were created during the treaty era, when tribes were often persuaded or coerced to cede a majority of their original homelands, reserving a much smaller portion of their territory as a specific reservation. Other Indian reservations were created by presidential executive orders in the latter part of the nineteenth and early twentieth centuries. Still others have been created by congressional acts, and since the 1934 Indian Reorganization Act, the secretary of the interior has been empowered to establish, expand, or restore Indian reservations.[1]

Many Americans have at least some vague notion and will concede, if reluctantly, that although Indian tribes "lost," "surrendered," or "sold" most of America to the United States, railroads, states, and enterprising whites, they rightfully retained through sheer determination or liberal federal Indian policies smaller regions designated as "Indian reservations." In fact, American tourists annually trek to reservations, usually during the summer months, in search of vacations that will expose them to tribal culture and identity.

Interestingly, these same Americans are sometimes taken aback or in some cases become irate when tribal nations and their members move to assert reserved rights—be it a property right such as the right to hunt or gather or fish or a political right such as the power to regulate domestic relations, tax, administer justice, and exercise civil and criminal jurisdiction, among others. Why these Americans concede the greater reserved right—tribal landownership—but refuse to recognize or challenge the lesser rights—rights to tribal property or treaty or civil rights—is an interesting phenomenon and speaks to the ongoing schizophrenia the American public and many lawmakers exhibit toward tribal nations.

From a non-Indian perspective, it comes down to a broader question of whether Indian tribes reserve all those powers and rights they have not surrendered, or whether they may exercise only those rights that have been delegated to them by express act of Congress. This crucial question, unfortunately, has no definitive answer from the United States' perspective, depending, it seems, on the whim of individual justices, congresspersons, or Bureau of Indian Affairs officials.

Two prominent scholars of Indian law and policy, Vine Deloria, Jr., and Charles Wilkinson, adopt a more historically accurate vision of the reserved rights doctrine.[2] They, in fact, compare the reserved rights clause in the U.S. Constitution's Tenth Amendment with that lodged both expressly and implicitly in Indian treaties (and agreements and statutes) that reserved to tribes sovereign powers not expressly surrendered to the federal government.

The Tenth Amendment, ratified in 1791 as part of the Bill of Rights, declares that "the powers not delegated to the United States by the Constitution, nor prohibited by it to the States, *are reserved to the States respectively, or to the people*" (emphasis added). Of all the amendments demanded by the Anti-Federalists in the state conventions that ratified the Constitution, "the one calling for a reserved powers clause was most common."[3]

Although many Federalists, such as Alexander Hamilton, James Madison, and James Wilson, did not believe such an amendment was necessary, the fear of central authority was widely felt, and support for an express guarantee that the states would retain control over their internal affairs proved irresistible. The Tenth Amendment, which embodies the principle of federalism, has been both eroded (by the Civil War and the Great Depression) and embellished (in the years preceding the Civil War and under the Rehnquist Court, which emphasizes dual federalism[4]) over time, but states may generally rest assured that, at any given time, at least some of their inherent sovereign powers are respected and that their existence as distinct polities having been constitutionally established will be protected. They certainly need not fear being "terminated" as political entities.

Indian treaties, similarly, reserve to Indian tribes all those powers specifically stated and those not expressly ceded away. As a federal district court said in *Makah Indian Tribe v. McCauly*,[5] in interpreting a key provision of the 1855 Makah Treaty,[6] "this court is of the opinion that as contended by plaintiffs (Makah) the answer to this question as to the treaty's validity turns upon the sounder theory that the treaty granted nothing to the Indians, but that the treaty in truth and in fact merely *reserved and preserved inviolate to the Indians the fishing rights which from time immemorial they had always had and enjoyed"* (emphasis added). In both cases, the states and the tribes "sought to preserve as much of their original sovereignty, powers and rights as could be done in the face of grasping federal ambitions. As the commerce and welfare clauses became vehicles for federal intrusions on state government, so the trust doctrine became the means of radical federal invasion of Indian political rights. Nevertheless, the treaty performs the same function for Indian nations as does the Tenth Amendment for States."[7]

Of course, state powers have more permanence because they are constitutionally enshrined, whereas Indian treaty rights, according to the Supreme Court, "can be altered without recourse to the constitutional amendment process."[8] It is the fragility, the tenuousness of Indian reserved rights, as interpreted by the courts, that is most problematic, particularly since tribes were not created by the U.S. Constitution and theoretically are not subject to constitutional limitations. That the federal government can justify its abridgments of Indian reserved rights, given the extraconstitutional nature of tribes, the fact that treaties are constitutionally recognized as "the supreme law of the land," and the persistence of the federal trust doctrine, raises important questions of fairness, justice, and intergroup relations. Moreover, if we see tribal sovereignty as a bundle of inherent powers, "then the Indian nation arrives at the treaty-making process with every power possessed by any other nation in the world."[9] Our task is simply to identify what specific attributes of sovereignty tribes have ceded, recognizing that they reserve all other powers, both external and internal, to themselves.

JUDICIAL ORIGINS OF RESERVED RIGHTS

Land and the natural resources appurtenant to land, because of its economic potential, political stability, and cultural impact, have occupied the central role in tribal, federal, and state relations. Issues such as land claims, natural resource allocation and management (e.g., conflicts over water, timber, hunting and fishing, minerals), and environmental regulation (e.g., pollution control, hazardous materials transportation and disposal) have frequently resulted in contentious affairs among the three sovereigns. And it is here that the often conflicting interests of indigenous nations and states are most clearly demarcated because of shared boundaries, shared resources, and shared citizens (with Indians being citizens of their tribe and of the state and nation). When the federal government enters the arena in support of states, in asserting its own position, or is drawn in as a result of its legal obligations to tribes as trustee of tribal property, the situation becomes even more entangled. For instance, when there is a tribal-state conflict, what factors determine whether the federal government will become involved? And if it becomes involved, which of the conflicting parties will it support? States are, of course, an integral part of the constitutionally established federal system; tribes, in contrast, often have explicit treaty-based rights guaranteeing them land and access to and use of natural resources.

Because it is home to many tribal nations, has abundant natural resources, and evidences the early establishment of treaty-based political relations, nowhere are these issues raised as poignantly or with more emotional attachment than in the Pacific Northwest. The intense conflicts between various tribes in that region (Colville, Spokan, Yakama, Lummi, Makah, Quileute, Skokomish, Klamath, Warm Springs, Umatilla, among many others) and the states of Washington and Oregon date back to the 1850s, when the United States entered into several treaties with the tribes.[10] In these bilateral or multilateral agreements, the various tribal nations ceded vast portions of their aboriginal lands, retained all other rights, and established diplomatic relations with the U.S. government.

One of the most important retained rights was the Indians' right to fish at their usual places, both on and off their newly established reservations. The treaty provision stating this, found in each of the so-called Stevens Treaties, reads like the one found in Article 3 of the 1855 Yakama Treaty: "The exclusive right of taking fish in all the streams, where running through or bordering said reservation, is further secured to said confederated tribes and bands of Indians, as also the right of taking fish at all usual and accustomed places, in common with the citizens of the Territory, and of erecting temporary buildings for curing them; together with the privilege of hunting, gathering roots and berries, and pasturing their horses and cattle upon open and unclaimed land."[11]

United States v. Winans[12] was the first Supreme Court case in which the judiciary was called on to interpret the treaty provision reserving to the tribes their right to hunt, fish, and gather, and from this case emerged the reserved rights doctrine. The facts of the case are as follows: In the late 1800s, Lineas and Audubon Winans established a private fishing company at the treaty-recognized fishing grounds of the Yakama Indians on the Columbia River. The Winans brothers claimed an exclusive right to fish there because they had purchased a state license. They also erected fish wheels that were extremely efficient in snaring an abundant amount of fish. The Yakamas complained to federal officials about their depleted fish supply. The United States, "together with certain Indian plaintiffs," filed a suit in federal circuit court for an injunction to stop the Winans brothers from interfering with "fishing rights guaranteed to the Indians of the Yakama Nation, by the terms of the treaty made and concluded between the United States and said Indians."[13]

District Judge Hanford reviewed the appropriate provisions of the 1855 treaty (it had been ratified in 1859) and found that the document acknowledged in the Indians two kinds of rights: exclusive rights, and rights to be enjoyed in common with non-Indians. Hanford supported the federal government and the Yakamas' arguments that the Indians retained exclusive rights to fish within the reservation border and that the Winanses' company could not prevent the Yakamas from fishing at off-reservation sites. "But," said Hanford, "the right of the Indians to erect temporary buildings on any particular spot of ground, according to the terms of the treaty, as I construe it, ceased when the title to that land was transferred from the government, and became vested as private property."[14]

This partial, though significant, tribal victory proved unsatisfactory, and the United States appealed to the Supreme Court on behalf of the Yakama Nation. The solicitor general, in his brief before the justices, noted the importance of the fishery to the Indians. It was, he said, "and always has been a famous one [and is] one of the best, if not the best place, on the Columbia River. The Yakama Indians have resorted to it above all others and depended on it for the supply of fish which was their steady subsistence. *The treaty was negotiated with distinct recognition of this right.*"[15] He went on to say that the Yakamas' "claim is not merely meritorious and equitable; it is an *immemorial right like a ripened prescription.*"[16]

The Winanses' attorneys used two principal arguments, both enunciated in *Ward v. Race Horse.*[17] First, the Court had held that tribal treaty rights were nothing more than temporary and precarious "privileges" and were not firm entitlements. Second, the justices had employed the "equal footing doctrine" to attempt to override the Indians' treaty claims. Justice White in the *Race Horse* case maintained that Wyoming's admitting act had repealed the Indians' treaty rights to hunt, since the admitting act and the treaty provisions were, in his words, "irreconcilable." The equal footing doctrine had been discussed earlier in *Escanaba Co. v. Chicago.*[18] But here the Court held that, on admission, a state "at once became entitled to and possessed of all the rights of dominion and sovereignty which belonged to the original States. She was admitted and could be admitted, only on the same footing as them."[19]

By relying on this doctrine, Winans and company asserted that when Washington became a state, it became sovereign, as had the other states. And as a sovereign, it had the right to regulate fishing, including the right to grant exclusive fishing rights to non-Indians, notwithstanding the Yakamas' treaty provision reserving to tribal members the right to fish.

However, Justice Joseph McKenna in *Winans* wrote a powerful opinion that strongly supported tribal reserved treaty rights.

First, McKenna recited one of the more popular treaty rights doctrines, that treaties should be interpreted the way Indians would read them. A treaty must be construed such "that unlettered people" would have understood, it since it was written in a foreign language and drafted by a military power that was greater than the tribes; that power was nonetheless charged with caring for and protecting Indians. Second, the Court dramatically reaffirmed federal supremacy over certain areas and weakened the "equal footing" argument by declaring that it was within the power of the United States to "secure to the Indians such a remnant of the great rights they possessed," such as fishing at their usual places. This was not viewed as an unreasonable demand on the state. Third, and most importantly, McKenna announced the reserved rights doctrine. An extended quote is appropriate to establish the context for this doctrine:

> The right to resort to the fishing places in controversy was a part of larger rights possessed by the Indians, upon the exercise of which there was not a shadow of impediment, and which were not much less necessary to the existence of the Indians than the atmosphere they breathed. New conditions came into existence, to which those rights had to be accommodated. Only a limitation of them, however, was necessary and intended, not taking away. *In other words, the treaty was not a grant of rights to the Indians, but a grant of rights from them, a reservation of those not granted. And the form of the instrument and its language was adapted to that purpose.* Reservations were not of particular parcels of land, and could not be expressed in deeds, as dealings between private individuals. The reservations were in large areas of territory, and the negotiations were with the tribe. *They reserved rights, however to every individual Indian, as though named therein.*[20]

Interestingly, this emphatic ruling came a mere two years after the repressive *Lone Wolf* decision, which was a clear deprivation of tribal reserved treaty rights. A probable explanation for these two radically disparate judicial views on treaty rights and their interpretation is the role that Congress and the executive branch played, as interpreted by the Court, as well as the Court's own perception of what was in the best interest of the Indians. For instance, in one enlightening passage in *Lone Wolf,* the Court stated that treaty abrogation would be exercised only "when circumstances arise which will not only justify the government in disregarding the stipulation of the treaty, but may demand, in the interest of the country and the Indians themselves, that it should be so."[21] The Court did not attempt to explain how it would be in the Indians' interest to have their treaty rights abrogated, since it was obviously not in their interest. After all, the Kiowa, Comanche, and Apache had filed the lawsuit to protect their treaty rights, not to agree to have them terminated.

A more realistic reading of the case is that the Court was implicitly acknowledging that many whites had already established homesteads on the tribes' former lands. Relocating them, although the proper legal action, would have entailed massive political problems for the state, the squatters, and the president, who had already authorized the settlement. In addition, the Court, in justifying this congressional confiscation of tribal reserved treaty lands, was asserting that as part of the "individualizing" process, Indians simply did not need all the land they had originally reserved to themselves.

Winans, by contrast, was far less threatening and involved no major national political issues. In other words, neither the executive's nor Congress's power was at issue. Moreover, the supremacy of a federally sanctioned treaty was at stake, and the Court understood that fishing represented far more than a simple commercial economic enterprise for the Yakama. It represented, in a physical sense, their life; without the ability to fish, the Indians would surely have faced grave difficulties.

Winans, therefore, was a crucial and timely acknowledgment that a tribe's sovereign rights, recognized and specifically reserved in treaties, warranted respect and were to be enforced. In essence, the United States had not given anything to the tribes, and the only rights lost by the Indians, the Court said, must be specifically granted away; tribes reserved all other rights to themselves. This case represented judicial evidence that despite the twin federal Indian policy goals of individualization and allotment, there was a growing consciousness among federal judges and justices that tribes, as sovereign entities, in certain cases had substantive property rights that were enforceable against states and private citizens.

Three years later, in *Winters v. United States,*[22] the reserved rights doctrine was applied in an implied fashion to water rights on Indian lands. The issue in *Winters* was whether a landowner could construct a dam on his property that prevented water from reaching a downstream Indian reservation, the Fort Belknap Reservation in Montana. Congress had established the reservation several years before the white landowner had bought his property, but the 1888 agreement establishing the reservation did not mention water rights. Because of this absence of language, the landowner argued that the reservation was not entitled to a specific amount of water. However, the Supreme Court ruled otherwise and supported the tribe and, by extension, the federal government as the Indians' water trustee. The Court, again through Justice McKenna, fashioned a creative four-point rationale in ruling for the United States and the Indians: (1) the reservation had been culled from a "much larger tract" that was necessary for a "nomadic and uncivilized people"; (2) the government's policy and the "desire of the Indian" was to transform and elevate tribal culture from a "nomadic" to an "agrarian" lifestyle; (3) this transformation could occur only if the tribal lands were severely reduced in size, making them more amenable to agricultural pursuits; and (4) the capstone argument, since the lands were arid, they would remain "practically valueless" without an adequate supply of water for irrigation.[23] Each of these points represented nearly prescient facts generated by the Court to justify its decision. Although they were not part of the law at the time, they represented the reality of history in the legal field and indicate the Court's ability to sometimes generate plausible arguments to protect tribal reserved rights.

The Court then, in rapid succession, added two more concrete pieces to its already formidable effort to enforce federal supremacy over states with regard to water rights and maintain its "guardianship" of Indian resources. First, Justice McKenna cited the Indian treaty rule of interpretation that ambiguities in the document would be "resolved from the standpoint of the Indians." Second, *Winters'* "equal footing" argument was also disallowed. "The power of the Government," said McKenna, "to reserve the water and exempt them from appropriation under the state laws is not denied, and could not be."[24] In conclusion, the Court noted: "It would be extreme to believe that within a year Congress destroyed the reservation [by admitting Montana to statehood in 1889] and took from the Indians the consideration of their grant, leaving them a barren waste —took from them the means of continuing their old habits, yet did not leave them the power to change to new ones."[25] In short, when the United States entered into diplomatic relations with the tribes, or when it unilaterally created reservations, there was an implicit reserved right to as much water as warranted by the tribes' potential to manage its own needs and for future uses.[26]

On the one hand, *Winters* must be viewed as a landmark case not only supporting a tribe's implied right to water but also reinforcing the doctrine that treaties must be understood as Indians would read them. On the other hand, the case raises an important question regarding who actually owns the reserved water: the tribe or the United States? After all, federal policy and a federally authored agreement were at issue. Further, this is an interesting case because the Court acted in a dual capacity. It functioned first as a legitimator of federal Indian policy, because it supported the federal government's goal of transforming Indians from hunter-gatherers to agriculturists. Second, the Court acted as an initiator of policy, because it succeeded in establishing, for the first time, Indian reserved water rights. The Court apparently felt compelled to articulate federal and Indian reserved water rights because Congress had failed to specifically act on this important matter.

LEGISLATIVE RECOGNITION OF RESERVED RIGHTS

John Collier, Nathan Margold, and Felix Cohen were three of the most important figures in federal Indian policy in the 1930s and 1940s. They deserve equal credit for the following statement on tribal sovereignty issued as part of a crucial solicitor's opinion titled "Powers of Indian Tribes"on 25 October 1934, just four months after the Indian Reorganization Act had become law. It stated in part that "perhaps the most basic principle of all Indian law, supported by a host of decisions hereinafter analyzed, is the principle that *those powers lawfully vested in an Indian tribe are not, in general, delegated powers granted by express acts of Congress, but rather inherent powers of a limited sovereignty which has never been extinguished.* Each Indian tribe begins its relationship with the Federal Government as a sovereign power, recognized as such in treaty and legislation."[27] This declaration of reserved, inherent tribal powers, which included recognition of internal sovereignty, the power to form or change a government, the power to determine tribal citizenship and membership, the power to regulate domestic relations, the power to manage descent and distribution of property, the power to tax, the power to administer justice, and so forth, was later restated as part of Cohen's classic work *Handbook of Federal Indian Law,* first published in 1941, in the chapter titled "The Scope of Tribal Self-Government."

Such a statement on this wider reservoir of tribal reserved powers arose because under section 16 of the Indian Reorganization Act, which authorized tribes that approved the measure to adopt constitutions and bylaws, we find the following important provision: "In addition to all powers vested in any Indian tribe or tribal council by existing law, the constitution adopted by said tribe shall also vest in such tribe or its tribal council the following rights."[28] In fact, only four powers or rights were explicitly granted to tribal governments in the law: (1) to hire legal counsel subject to secretarial approval; (2) to wield veto power over certain land transactions or other tribal assets; (3) to engage in negotiations with federal, state, and local governments; and (4) to expect information from the interior secretary regarding "all appropriation estimates on Federal projects for the benefit of the tribe" before such estimates were submitted to the Budget Bureau or Congress.

But as Elmer Rusco observed, the fact that the Indian Reorganization Act specifies only these few powers "makes sense only if there was the implicit assumption that they [tribal governments] already possessed or legally could assume numerous other areas of authority. What point would there be in establishing governments with such limited authority?"[29] Vine Deloria, Jr., and Clifford M. Lytle also confirm that the combination of the Indian Reorganization Act, the 1934 solicitor's opinion, and de facto and de jure tribal sovereign status all support the view that tribes were possessors of a number of inherent sovereign powers that are not beholden to the U.S. Constitution or federal statutory authority.[30]

In other words, according to the policy triumvirate of Collier, Margold, and Cohen, tribes inherently retained or reserved a panoply of powers and rights based on their preexisting standing as the original sovereigns and proprietors of the United States. These powers, some of which had been diminished over time due to the catastrophic loss of human life and aboriginal territory, specific treaty provisions, and key legislation, endure, and until and unless they are expressly expunged or terminated by tribal or federal action, they remain in force.

RESERVED RIGHTS IN CONTEMPORARY TIMES

The implied reservation of Indian property rights in treaties, agreements, and statutes has been extended to encompass hunting and fishing rights. Such rights are free of state law and survive even congressional termination of the trust relationship. Implied hunting and fishing rights are not ended unless there is a clear indication that Congress intended to sever them.[31] In *Menominee*, the tribe brought suit in the Court of Claims to recover compensation for the loss of hunting and fishing rights that the Wisconsin Supreme Court held had been abrogated by the Menominee Termination Act of 1954. The termination act (the Menominee were the first tribe to lose their status under the termination policy), which had become effective in 1961, provided for the cessation of federal supervision over the property and members of the tribe. State law was also made applicable to the Indians.[32]

Two months after the termination act became law, Congress amended Public Law 280, which granted certain states jurisdiction over offenses committed by or against Indians, to include Wisconsin. However, this law said that "nothing in this section shall authorize the alienation, encumbrance, or taxation of any real or personal property, including water rights, belonging to any Indian tribe, band, or community that is held in trust by the United States . . . or shall deprive any Indian or any Indian tribe, band, or community of any right, privilege, or immunity afforded under Federal treaty, agreement, or statute *with respect to hunting, trapping, or fishing, or the control, licensing, or regulation thereof.*"[33]

Justice Douglas, in a fit of judicial activism, insisted on reading the two acts—the termination act and Public Law 280—together and determined that, notwithstanding the express language of the Menominee Termination Act, the tribe's hunting and fishing rights "survived" the termination. "We decline," said Douglas, "to construe the Termination

Act as a backhanded way of abrogating the hunting and fishing rights of these Indians. While the power to abrogate those rights exists . . . 'the intention to abrogate or modify a treaty is not to be lightly imputed to the Congress' "[34]

The Menominee Nation was not successful, however, in 1998 when it attempted to secure judicial recognition of its *off-reservation* hunting and fishing rights. Those rights had been explicitly recognized in an 1831 treaty. That treaty's provisions regarding hunting and fishing were held to have been extinguished by removal provisions included in later treaties.[35]

THE "TRUSTEE" AND THE "RESERVEE"

The issue of Indian reserved rights and the conditions under which these rights will be respected is intimately connected to the trust doctrine between the federal government and Indian tribes. Further, it often depends on whether there has been some explicit federal recognition of the reserved rights in question. In other words, the courts have generally held that treaty or statutory reserved rights enjoy a higher (though not unassailable) level of legal protection than aboriginal rights—rights arising from Indian use and occupancy of territory since time immemorial, but lacking formal federal recognition.

As the Supreme Court said in the troubling case *Tee-Hit-Ton v. United States*,[36] aboriginal land title of an unrecognized character is, in effect, no title whatsoever. Justice Reed said, "This was true not because an Indian or an Indian tribe has no standing to sue or because the United States has not consented to be sued . . . but because Indian occupation of land without government recognition of ownership creates no rights against taking or extinction by the United States protected by the Fifth Amendment or any other principle of law."[37] In other words, because Congress had never explicitly "recognized" the Tee-Hit-Ton's legal interest in their aboriginal lands, it could take those lands and was not responsible for providing any compensation whatsoever. It was as if the Tee-Hit-Ton had never existed. Otherwise, how could their very presence in Alaska not establish their rights to territory they had inhabited for millennia?

However, in those cases involving "recognized" Indian territory and natural resources, it is the power of the federal government acting either as trustee of Indian lands and resources or as trustee asserting the preexisting rights of the Indians that appears to be the driving force behind these cases. In other words, is the federal government the legal owner of the reserved rights in question, or is the tribal nation? Even on an issue as important as this, the Supreme Court has expressed great ambivalence.

For example, in *Leavenworth Railroad Co. v. United States*,[38] the Court was called on to interpret the meaning of the phrase "reserved to the United States," found in the Osage Treaty of 1825. The Court said, "the treaty reserved them [the lands] as much to one as to the other of the contracting parties. Both were interested therein, and had title thereto. *In one sense, they were reserved to the Indians; but, in another and broader sense, to the United States, for the use of the Indians.*"[39]

In *Winans, Winters,* and *Menominee,* the Supreme Court was asserting federal supremacy (ownership?) over private and states' rights. Of particular importance were the treaty and property clauses of the U.S. Constitution, which, in the Court's consciousness, elevated the federal government above states, corporations, and private parties. The Court acknowledged that since the federal government signed the treaties and established the reservations, it either explicitly or implicitly reserved or, in some cases, created certain rights for tribes to aid in their subsistence and transformation to a civilized status. Any challenges by states or other interests were deemed a direct challenge to federal supremacy, an act that, in these cases, would not be sanctioned by the federal courts.

Of course, the political independence of the Court, vacillations in federal Indian policy (do we forcibly assimilate the Indians or allow them a measured independence?), and conflicts between the federal and state governments over which body has jurisdiction over Indian affairs allow the Court to exercise wide discretionary authority when it comes to Indian issues. In other words, the Court in *Winans, Winters,* and especially *Menominee* could easily have ruled in favor of the non-Indians had it been so inclined, denying the existence of reserved rights. It is this indeterminacy of judicial construction that exasperates Indians:

> One of the frustrating circumstances surrounding Indian law is, not infrequently, the existence of one set of rules that apply specifically to Indian issues and a different set of rules that apply to the law in general. One judge may apply the Indian law precedent and rules of construction, while another judge may ignore these and incorporate the traditional rules of construction, and a third judge may cite the developed rules of construction traditionally used in Indian cases and then announce that the facts of the situation or other circumstances taken together make it necessary to depart from these rules in this particular case. The decisions emanating from the use of different rules may be in marked contrast—one might favor Indian claimants while the other could destroy their chance of prevailing.[40]

For example, in 1999 the Supreme Court handed down two very different rulings involving Indian natural resources and the reserved rights doctrine. In *Minnesota v. Mille Lacs Band of Chippewa Indians*,[41] the Court ruled that the Chippewa, upon ceding millions of acres of land to the United States in 1837, had retained the right to hunt, fish, and gather on those ceded lands, notwithstanding an 1850 presidential executive order that required the tribe to remove. *Mille Lacs* was important for several reasons. First, the Court reaffirmed a long-standing if not always supported doctrine that Indian treaty rights cannot be implicitly terminated; they can be abrogated only by Congress and only when that body has unequivocally expressed its intent to terminate the rights. Second, the so-called canons of treaty construction—the principle that Indian treaties are to be interpreted liberally in favor of the Indians, with any ambiguities in language resolved in the tribes' favor—was also explicitly reaffirmed. Third, states were forcefully reminded that they were without inherent power over Indian rights or resources and that even when territories were admitted to statehood on an "equal footing" with existing states, this did not give the states any constitutional or statutory rights over Indians, and certainly not over Indians exercising treaty-specified rights. The equal footing doctrine, in other words, which had been recently revived in federal court discourse,[42] does not interfere with the federal government's authority to control the nation's Indian affairs under the commerce clause, the property clause, the supremacy clause, and the important treaty-making authority. Finally, the majority implicitly overruled *Ward v. Race Horse*, the 1896 ruling that had upheld states' rights over Indian treaty rights. Justice O'Connor said that "*Race Horse* rested on a false premise. As this court's subsequent cases have made clear, an Indian tribe's treaty right to hunt, fish, and gather on state land are not irreconcilable with a State's sovereignty over the natural resources in the state. Rather, Indian treaty rights can coexist with State management of natural resources. Although States have important interests in regulating wildlife and natural resources within their borders, this authority is shared with the Federal Government when the Federal Government exercises one of its enumerated constitutional powers, such as treaty making."

By contrast, three months later, the Supreme Court in *Amoco Production Co. v. Southern Ute Indian Tribe*,[43] held that the Southern Utes, who had ceded much of their aboriginal territory to the federal government in 1880 but later regained trust title to the ceded lands—including the reserved coal in lands patented under the 1909 and 1910 Coal Lands Acts and still owned by the United States in 1938—did not retain or reserve the methane gas found within the coal formations underlying much of the land. The tribe and the United States argued unsuccessfully that the Coal Acts reserved both coal and the methane gas. But Justice Anthony Kennedy disagreed, saying that this was not Congress's intent because methane gas at the time was considered a dangerous waste product of coal mining, not a valuable energy resource. Thus, in this case, even with the federal government acting as trustee of the tribe, the Court ruled against the Indians' reserved rights and did not even consider the canon of reading ambiguities in treaties or laws in favor of the sovereign—the tribe or the United States.

The reserved rights doctrine is often listed with three other so-called canons of construction as evidence that the federal government supports Indian treaties and the trust doctrine. The other canons are (1) that ambiguities expressed in treaties are to be resolved in the Indians' favor,[44] (2) that treaties are to be interpreted as the Indians themselves would have understood them,[45] and (3) that treaties are to be liberally construed in favor of the tribes.[46]

Of course, as we have seen with the other doctrines, these "canons" —which theoretically stand for a system of fundamental rules and maxims that are recognized as governing the interpretation of written instruments—are not really canons at all, since each has an opposite corollary that may be cited by the courts when it suits the judges' purposes. For instance, although the canon of liberal construction for tribes is supported in cases such as *Worcester v. Georgia* (1832), *Kansas Indians* (1866), and *United States v. Winans* (1905), it has been ignored or shunted aside in cases such as *Cherokee Tobacco* (1871) and *Race Horse* (1896). Other cases have held that the canon of ambiguous phrases does not permit reliance on ambiguities that do not exist, nor does it permit disregarding of the expressed intent of Congress.[47]

More conclusively, the fact that Indian treaties themselves may be expressly abrogated by Congress reveals the tenuous nature of Indian legal rights. In fact, history shows that treaties—including Indian reserved rights—have been "honored more in the breach than the fulfillment," with the treaty process itself being dramatically and problematically transformed in 1871. In that year, Congress informed the president, via an appropriations act rider, that he could no longer recognize Indian nations through treaties, although theoretically, all preexisting treaties were to remain the law of the land.[48] Nevertheless, tribal nations and their treaty- and trust-recognized reserved rights persist, even though their consistent recognition and enforcement lag far behind.

NOTES

1. See many legal definitions of what constitutes Indian country or Indian reservations in Kenneth S. Murchison, comp., *Digest of Decisions Relating to Indian Affairs,* vol. 1 (Washington, D.C.: Government Printing Office, 1901; reprint, Milwood, N.Y.: Kraus Reprint Co., 1973), 5–20.

2. Vine Deloria, Jr., "Reserving to Themselves: Treaties and the Powers of Indian Tribes," *Arizona Law Review*, vol. 38 (fall 1996), 971–72; Charles F. Wilkinson, *American Indians, Time, and the Law: Native Societies in a Modern Constitutional Democracy* (New Haven, Conn.: Yale University Press, 1987), 102–3.

3. Forrest McDonald, "Tenth Amendment," in *The Oxford Companion to the Supreme Court of the United States*, ed. Kermit L. Hall (New York: Oxford University Press, 1992), 861.

4. The concept of dual federalism arose after the Civil War and persisted until the 1930s. It holds that the states and the national government have separate spheres of authority, and each is considered supreme in its own sphere.

5. 39 F.Supp. 75 (1941).

6. 12 Stat. 939 (1855).

7. Deloria, "Reserving to Themselves," 972.

8. Wilkinson, *American Indians*, 102–3.

9. Deloria, "Reserving to Themselves," 972.

10. See, e.g., Treaty of Medicine Creek, 26 December 1854 (10 Stat. 1132); Treaty of Point Elliot, 26 January 1855 (12 Stat. 927); Treaty of Point no Point, 26 January 1855 (12 Stat. 933); Treaty with the Makah, 31 January 1855 (12 Stat. 939); Treaty with the Walla Walla, Cayuse, etc., 9 June 1855 (12 Stat. 945).

11. See the treaty in Charles J. Kappler, comp., *Indian Affairs: Laws and Treaties*, vol. 2 (Washington, D.C.: Government Printing Office, 1903), 524–28.

12. 198 U.S. 371 (1905).

13. 73 Fed. 72 (1896).

14. Ibid., 75.

15. 198 U.S. 371 (1905).

16. Ibid., 374.

17. 163 U.S. 504 (1896).

18. 107 U.S. 678 (1883).

19. Ibid., 512–13.

20. 198 U.S. 381; emphasis added.

21. 183 U.S. 553, 566 (1903).

22. 207 U.S. 564 (1908).

23. Ibid., 576.

24. Ibid., 577.

25. Ibid.

26. Michael C. Nelson, *The Winters Doctrine: Seventy Years of Application of "Reserved" Water Rights to Indian Reservations* (Tucson, Ariz.: Office of Arid Land Studies, 1977), 4.

27. U.S. Department of Interior, *Opinions of the Solicitor: Indian Affairs* (Washington, D.C.: Government Printing Office, 1946), 447.

28. 48 Stat. 985 (1934).

29. Elmer R. Rusco, *A Fateful Time: The Background and Legislative History of the Indian Reorganization Act* (Reno: University of Nevada Press, 2000), 296.

30. Vine Deloria, Jr., and Clifford M. Lytle, *The Nations Within: The Past and Future of American Indian Sovereignty* (Austin: University of Texas Press, 1988), 142.

31. *Menominee Tribe v. United States*, 391 U.S. 404 (1968).

32. See Nicholas C. Peroff, *Menominee Drums: Tribal Termination and Restoration, 1954–1974* (Norman: University of Oklahoma Press, 1982), for a good discussion of this nation's struggles with termination.

33. 67 Stat. 588 (1953).

34. 391 U.S. 404, 412–13.

35. *Menominee Indian Tribe of Wisconsin v. Thompson*, 161 F. 3d 449 (1998).

36. 348 U.S. 273 (1955). See Nell Jessup Newton, "At the Whim of the Sovereign: Aboriginal Title Reconsidered," *Hastings Law Journal*, vol. 31 (July 1980), 1215–85, and David E. Wilkins, *American Indian Sovereignty and the U.S. Supreme Court: The Masking of Justice* (Austin: University of Texas Press, 1997), 166–85 for two accounts that question the legal rationale in the decision.

37. 348 U.S. 285.

38. 92 U.S. 733 (1876).

39. Ibid., 747.

40. Vine Deloria, Jr., and Clifford M. Lytle, *American Indians, American Justice* (Austin: University of Texas Press, 1983), 50.

41. 119 S. Ct. 1187 (1999).

42. *Crow Tribe of Indians and Thomas L. Ten Bear v. Repsis*, 73 F.3d 982 (10th Cir. 1995).

43. 526 U.S. 865 (1999).

44. See, e.g., *McClanahan v. Arizona State Tax Commission*, 411 U.S. 164, 174 (1973).

45. See, e.g., *Choctaw Nation v. Oklahoma*, 397 U.S. 620, 631 (1970).

46. See, e.g., *Tulee v. Washington*, 315 U.S. 681, 684–85 (1942).

47. See, e.g., *Confederated Bands of Ute Indians v. United States*, 330 U.S. 169, 179 (1947); *United States v. Dion*, 476 U.S. 734, 739–40 (1986); and *Menominee Indian Tribe v. Thompson*, 161 F.3d 449, 457 (1998).

48. Deloria, "Reserving to Themselves," 970.

CHAPTER FIVE

Vine Deloria, Jr., and the Development of a Decolonizing Critique of Indigenous Peoples and International Relations

Glenn T. Morris (Shawnee)

Only one thing's sadder than remembering you were once free, and that's forgetting that you were once free. That would be the saddest thing of all. That's one thing we Indians will never do.

Noble Red Man (Mathew King), Oglala Lakota elder[1]

When Vine Deloria, Jr.'s, 1974 book *Behind the Trail of Broken Treaties: An Indian Declaration of Independence*[2] was released, the political landscapes of the United States and the world looked much different than they do today. The Nixon administration was in the throes of Watergate, with Nixon himself teetering on the brink of impeachment and resignation. The wreckage that constituted the war in Vietnam was finally skidding to a grueling repose, accompanied by the domestic social scarring that twenty years of acrimonious conflict had wrought. Legal and political retrenchment around issues of racial justice was in full swing, exhibited particularly by Nixon's opposition to school busing and by Supreme Court appointments calculated to reverse the "liberal" rulings of the Warren Court from the preceding two decades.

The movement for political and economic justice, led by African Americans and Latinos, provided some important ideological and tactical weapons for American Indian activists in the United States. Some of the long-standing bureaucratic Indian organizations, such as the National Congress of the American Indians (NCAI), were being joined on the political scene by more activist, militant organizations such as the National Indian Youth Council (NIYC) and the American Indian Movement (AIM).[3] A significant distinction between the civil rights movement, or the anti–Vietnam War movement, and the struggle of American Indian organizations centered on the foundation for the grievances that were being articulated by American Indians. Additionally, the remedies for Indian grievances were often radically different from those applicable to other contemporaneous movements.

At base, the status of American Indians as the preexisting peoples of the Western Hemisphere was unique to all other groups that were calling for greater inclusiveness and franchisement in the broader U.S. system. When the NAACP Legal Defense Fund began its campaign to dismantle segregated schools and other vestiges of Jim Crow laws, its central complaint involved the lack of application of the Thirteenth, Fourteenth, and Fifteenth Amendments of the U.S. Constitution to African Americans. The remedies that it sought called for the various agencies of government to provide equal protection of the laws to ensure political, social, and economic equity through the elimination of racially discriminatory practices.[4]

For most people of color who had experienced political or social marginalization, their aspiration was the attainment of unimpaired opportunity to participate as coequal members in U.S. society. Remediation in the form of legislation that prohibited race and sex discrimination in education, housing, and employment provided a modicum of relief for historical racism and sexism. For American Indians, however, both the root of the complaints and the remedies for those complaints were significantly different.[5]

The fishing rights struggle of the 1960s in the Pacific Northwest highlighted the differences between strategies constructed upon theories of democratic pluralism and those based on treaties between separate, independent peoples. If it was difficult for the U.S. public to understand and appreciate the nuances and complexities of federal Indian law, it was also difficult for most Indian people. After generations of indigenous children had been socialized in government or missionary boarding schools,[6] and after corrupt government policies had reduced economic and political self-sufficiency for reservation-based Indians to pipe dreams,[7] many American Indians had difficulty continuing to conceptualize—as their ancestors had—a definition of justice that challenged the constraints established by the settler society surrounding them.

Through the operation of its termination and relocation policies of the 1940s, 1950s, and 1960s, the United States had fostered ideological, cultural, and political schisms across Indian country. Entire generations had been severed from their histories, their languages, their families, and their homelands.[8] The consequence of deliberate U.S. policy created a brand of philosophical and political confusion that would not be sufficiently confronted from an indigenous perspective until the late 1960s. Incongruent identities, loyalties, experiences, and aspirations among American Indian people created complex social, political, and economic relations across Indian country that the United States was unable and unwilling to address.

In 1970, terms such as *tribal sovereignty* and *self-determination* were ridiculed, even by elected Indian officials, as the confused jargon of

Indian academics, radicals, or malcontents.[9] Nonetheless, Vine Deloria, Jr., began to demolish the colonizing constructions of U.S. Indian law and policy through his books *Custer Died for Your Sins: An Indian Manifesto* and *We Talk, You Listen.*[10] He began to equip a new generation with a vision for indigenous self-determination, and he began to provide a conscious vocabulary that would allow the expression of a liberatory critique.

Deloria's writings resonated with activists from Alcatraz[11] to the Trail of Broken Treaties to Wounded Knee. American Indian students at colleges and universities across the United States began to read and analyze Deloria's approach. In Washington, D.C., the Institute for the Development of Indian Law was formed,[12] in part, to advance Deloria's critique of U.S. law and policy toward indigenous peoples. Newly graduated Indian lawyers such as Frank Ducheneaux, Kirke Kickingbird,[13] and Tim Coulter[14] worked with Deloria to develop, for its time, a revolutionary approach to federal Indian law that rejected racist assumptions stretching back to the era of Chief Justice John Marshall.[15]

By the time *Behind the Trail of Broken Treaties* was published in 1974, an essential ideological foundation had been laid through Deloria's earlier writings. Additionally, the 1972 election-week confrontation at the Bureau of Indian Affairs (BIA) headquarters in Washington, D.C.,[16] and the seventy-one-day shoot-out between AIM and federal forces at Wounded Knee[17] had propelled issues of indigenous law and politics into a new discursive realm. No longer could indigenous peoples' issues in the United States be deflected solely through the rhetoric of "discovery doctrine," "domestic dependency," "trust responsibility," or "plenary power."[18]

Parallel to the convulsions that were occurring within the United States in the early 1970s, the global stage was in dramatic turmoil. The Cold War between the United States and the Soviet Union was in total engagement, and the bipolar ideological struggles of the day were manifesting in every part of the globe. Although the wars in Indochina were "officially" coming to a conclusion, the underlying political rivalries in the region continued. Similarly, from Angola to Ethiopia, from Nicaragua to the South Moluccas to Lebanon, armed struggles by various national liberation groups were in full swing.

Despite whatever legitimacy the wars of decolonization in places such as Namibia, Eritrea, and East Timor possessed in their own right, it was impossible to ignore the hegemonic interests of both the Americans and the Soviets in attempting to influence the outcomes of anticolonial struggles. The United States was often found installing or supporting extremely repressive regimes in places such as the Philippines, Indonesia, Guatemala, South Africa, and Chile.[19] In several instances, support for colonial regimes placed the United States in diametric opposition to emerging trends in international human rights law. The Soviet Union capitalized on U.S. support of colonizing powers to advance Soviet inter-ests, providing direct military, political, and logistical support to national liberation movements around the world. Similar tugs-of-war occurred in international human rights forums; for every Sakharov or Solzhenitsyn or other Soviet political prisoner championed by the United States, the Soviets held up a Nelson Mandela or Huey Newton of the Black Panther Party or Leonard Peltier of AIM as a counterpoint.

On an ideological level, the differences between the Soviet and U.S. positions regarding people's right of self-determination had been playing out for decades. In the 1920s, Woodrow Wilson and Vladimir Lenin articu-lated dramatically disparate rationales and models justifying nations' and peoples' freedom from colonial domination.[20] Although in the 1970s the cast of characters had changed, the debate regarding self-determination was continuing to be played out in violent struggles around the globe.[21]

This point became particularly important to American Indians and other indigenous peoples, because their cases had been specifically excluded from the development of international legal principles regard-ing the right to self-determination.[22] U.S. courts had constructed legal fic-tions, as Robert A. Williams, Jr., writes, to "assert the West's lawful power to impose its vision of truth on non-Western peoples through a racist, col-onizing rule of law."[23] In the 1970s, the collection of states calling itself the United Nations was also moving toward a construction of international law that excluded the aspirations of indigenous peoples.

One of Deloria's finest contributions to this era can be described in a line from his earlier book, *Custer Died for Your Sins:* "Anyone can get into the headlines by making wild threats and militant statements. It takes a lot of hard work to raise an entire group to a new conception of them-selves."[24] The success of *Broken Treaties* was rooted in its coherent histor-ical and analytical framework and in its accessibility to everyone from the street to the ivory tower.

Broken Treaties is divided into four distinct but related areas of dis-cussion. The first (chapters 1, 9, and 10) gives some historical insight into why many indigenous people in the United States and Canada were so disaffected by U.S. law and policy, leading to an intense period of indige-nous activism by the 1970s. The second area describes the legal doctrines of discovery, domestic dependency, and plenary power (all discussed in detail later) and how these doctrines led to territorial, political, economic, and cultural destruction of indigenous nations. The third is a specific dis-cussion of the Indian Reorganization Act and the Indian Claims Com-mission, and the fourth treats the international character of indigenous nations.

It is in this fourth area that Deloria proceeded "to raise an entire group to a new conception of themselves." Deloria challenged members of an entire generation to imagine themselves liberated from the confines of an existence that had been defined by the settler-state society that wished them exterminated. He had the foresight and the temerity to compare indigenous nations in a coequal light with other existing nations and states around the globe; he welcomed the application of international law (especially the Convention against the Crime of Genocide), as well as a reinstallation of the treaty-making process between indigenous peoples and the U.S. government. By taking this tack, Deloria gave permission to a new generation of indigenous activists, academics, and technicians not only to challenge colonial convention but also to reconceptualize the entire nature of indigenous peoples' reality in the contemporary era. Deloria recognized and respected that the contemporary flexing of indigenous rights activism was seated in a long and honorable tradition that simply needed to be revealed. He noted that the movement "has its roots in the tireless resistance of generations of unknown Indians who have refused to melt into the homogeneity of American life and accept American citizenship."[25]

Fortunately, *Broken Treaties* raised the clarion call for indigenous activists, scholars, and lawyers to reconceptualize the semiotics of colonial legal discourse and to situate analyses of the circumstances of indigenous peoples beyond the boundaries established by settler-society institutions. The impact of Deloria's framework on the construction of an analysis that has held the extension of destructive legal fabrications at bay cannot be exaggerated. Questions remain about the degree to which Deloria's lessons from 1974 are being pursued in the unipolar new world order of the twenty-first century. To what extent are the hallmarks established by Deloria being recalled in the new political landscape in which the U.S. views itself as the indispensable power in the world? Perhaps most important, to what degree are Deloria's successors extending and expanding his vision for indigenous peoples' liberation, and to what degree is a new generation rising to the challenge of resisting the contemporary expressions of Nebrija, Columbus, Marshall, Jackson, and Custer?

Robert Allen Warrior crystallizes an essential point of Deloria's writings: that the struggle for indigenous identity and self-determination is a dynamic and ongoing process, demanding constant self-assessment and evaluation. As will be discussed later, the militancy of the early 1970s prompted significant movement—action and reaction—from settler institutions, including the United Nations. Deloria was concerned that the Indian movement would "get stalled in its own rhetoric," "losing its sense of historical perspective and becoming a victim of its own success."[26]

Deloria was calling for a continuing revolution. He was "warning against making the rhetoric of sovereignty and tradition a final rather than a beginning step" for those who engage in the vindication of indigenous peoples' rights.[27] Deloria provided the intellectual base from which important political action sprang, but he contended that political action alone would be insufficient to liberate indigenous peoples. He was not saying "that direct action or even violence are intrinsically wrong, but that any political activism must bring with it critical reflection and constructive strategy."[28] *Broken Treaties* sowed the seeds that would germinate challenges to the racist underpinnings of federal Indian law utilizing international forums. The following sections discuss the degree to which those seeds have been nurtured and cultivated, or the degree to which they have been allowed to languish and wither.

SEMANTICS AS A COLONIZING WEAPON

David Wilkins reminds us of Deloria's insistence that fully understanding or appreciating the operation of settler-state law and policy affecting indigenous peoples is impossible "without total immersion in a historical context."[29] With that admonition in mind, the participation of indigenous peoples in the international arena cannot be viewed as a new phenomenon that commenced at the League of Nations in the 1920s or the United Nations (UN) in the 1970s. Indigenous peoples have been engaged in international relations throughout the Americas from time immemorial,[30] and with European and other foreign powers from first contact.[31] Evidence of indigenous diplomacy, either pre- or post-invasion, is often difficult to access "because the cultural archives maintained by the conquering society frequently neglect to record or adequately document the many different and distinct visions of law that have contributed to the traditions of resistance forged by colonized peoples."[32]

In more contemporary times, indigenous peoples asserted their right to self-determination in an international relations context even before the creation of the League of Nations or the United Nations.[33] The publication of *Behind the Trail of Broken Treaties,* however, was an important catalyst for the most recent movement to take the grievances of indigenous peoples into the international arena.[34]

Although considerable time and space could be expended discussing the emergence of an indigenous people's presence at the UN and in other international forums,[35] those issues have been discussed extensively elsewhere.[36] The focus of this chapter is to outline the elements of *Broken Treaties* that served as a foundation for at least a generation of activists, lawyers, and others to enter the international arena. It also provides an appraisal of the degree to which the first principles of *Broken Treaties* have been subsequently advanced or betrayed.

One of the most important contributions of Deloria's writings was the deconstruction of the colonizing semantics of federal Indian law. In particular, three concepts without which the colonizing project of the United States would have been impossible—the doctrine of discovery, domestic dependent nation status, and the plenary power doctrine— came under scathing critique by Deloria. Through this discussion, Deloria was able to begin the process of "decolonizing the minds" of generations of American Indian people who had internalized the essential components of the colonizer's constructed reality. The oppressive semantics of colonialism proved to be much more pervasive and extensive than perhaps even Deloria could have imagined in 1974. It is, however, from the seeds planted in his earliest writings that Deloria inspired new inquiries and analyses to expose and root out the racist origins of settler-state law imposed on indigenous peoples.[37] The discussion that follows is an attempt to elaborate and deepen the historical underpinnings of U.S. law and policy affecting indigenous peoples that Deloria addressed in *Broken Treaties*.

LANGUAGE AS THE LEGAL AND POLITICAL INSTRUMENT OF EMPIRE

In August 1492, Elio Antonio de Nebrija, the bishop of Avila, set into motion the "most massive act of genocide in the history of the world."[38] Yet Nebrija commanded no armies. He was neither a politician nor a military strategist. He was neither financier nor mercenary. He was a linguist and a scholar at the University of Salamanca, in what later would become Spain. Nebrija's actions on that hot summer day, just fifteen days after Columbus set sail from Palos on his way to find a new route to Asia, were quite deliberate and would change the world forever. For indigenous peoples around the globe, Nebrija began a nightmare, the final extent of which has yet to be realized.[39]

When Nebrija entered the royal court on 18 August, he held in his hands the freshly printed first edition of his *Gramatica Castellana*, the first grammar[40] and semantic road map for Christian Europeans[41] intent on colonization. In the introduction to his *Gramatica*, Nebrija informed Queen Isabella of the importance of his new invention: "Language has always been the consort of empire, and forever shall remain its mate. Together they come into being, together they grow and flower."[42]

When the noted scholar presented the queen with the book, she is reported to have asked quite pointedly, "What is this good for?" Nebrija, with the foresight of an expansionistic clairvoyant, is reported to have replied, "Your Majesty, language is the perfect instrument of empire."[43] Nebrija's vision was not limited solely to formalizing language and education for the masses in the emerging Spain. His much more expansive plan was designed to turn

> the mate of empire into its slave. Here the first modern language expert advises the Crown on the way to make, out of a people's speech and lives, tools that benefit the state and its pursuits, Nebrija's grammar is conceived as a pillar of the nation-state. The new state takes from people the words on which they subsist, and transforms them into the standardized language which hence-forth they are compelled to use. . . . Henceforth, people will have to rely on the language they receive from above, rather than to develop a tongue in common with one another. . . . Both the citizen of the modern state and his state provided language come into being for the first time—both are without precedent anywhere in history.[44]

Nebrija's clear intent was to create a vehicle that would totalize the official position of the Spanish state in its new colonizing project. Artificial linguistic constructions would be imposed on the social, spiritual, legal, and political conditions of indigenous peoples first in the Americas and then across the globe. "The modern European state cannot function in the world of the vernacular [read indigenous-subsistent]. The new national state needs an *artificio*. . . . This kind of polity requires a standard language understood by all those subject to its laws and for whom the tales written at the monarch's behest (that is propaganda) are destined."[45]

Confident in his project, Nebrija then outlined to Isabella the precise intended impact of semantic imperialism on the indigenous peoples that the Spanish seem destined to encounter: "Now, Your Majesty, let me come to the last advantage that you shall gain from my grammar. . . . Soon Your Majesty will place her yoke upon many barbarians who speak outlandish tongues. By this, your victory, these people shall stand in a new need; *the need for the laws the victor owes to the vanquished,* and the need for the language we shall bring with us."[46] As will be discussed later, the legacy of Nebrija continues to reside in the official positions and high court (especially U.S. Supreme Court) decisions of settler and neocolonial states around the world. The creation, manipulation, and subversion of language in the pursuit of conquest and colonization of indigenous peoples continue to the present. The United States has declared itself to be "the only superpower . . . and the indispensable power"[47] in the world today, and in its effort to "democratize" the world and integrate all peoples into the new world order, the United States has accepted the role of successor to Isabella and Nebrija.[48]

The rest of this chapter provides a few brief and sporadic examples of the continuation of Nebrija's design through the colonial period. It then relates the colonial period to the development and expansion of federal Indian law in the United States and the manner in which the U.S. courts have continued to use language as the perfect instrument of colonial expansion and indigenous dispossession. Discussion of the linguistic manipulations by U.S. courts is followed by a historical overview of indigenous peoples' emergence into the contemporary international legal and political arenas. Finally, a specific discussion of the role that the U.S. government has assumed in the global indigenous peoples' rights discourse, especially regarding the UN Draft Declaration on the Rights of Indigenous Peoples, segues into some possible strategies for a more powerful indigenous peoples' rights position into the future.

NEBRIJA'S PROGENY: COLONIAL EXAMPLES

In his own time, the bishop of Avila was required to wait only two months before Christopher Columbus began implementing Nebrija's vision throughout the Caribbean.[49] Columbus immediately began the Christian, European project of negating the existence, the voice, and the location of indigenous identity in the Americas. Columbus's christening of places and peoples in the Caribbean "entail[ed] the cancellation of the native name—the erasure of the alien, perhaps demonic identity—and hence a kind of making new.[50] The imposition of Christian, European ideological constructs on the physical and human geography of indigenous America "in effect converts them from their former status to a new, European one: the external body of the land remains the same, but its essence is redefined by a new name."[51] Todorov explains that "Columbus knows perfectly well that these islands already have names . . . however, he seeks to replace names . . . to give them the *right* names."[52]

The process of devaluing, dispossessing, dehumanizing, and redefining indigenous peoples by the colonial-settler powers has been, and continues to be, relentless and pervasive—in religion,[53] history,[54] law,[55] politics,[56] economics,[57] science,[58] and popular culture.[59] Despite some European opponents[60] of the process of denying and replacing the identity of indigenous peoples through the use of language and, if necessary, force of arms, the effect of semantic displacement for indigenous peoples was profound. In describing the analogous process through which virtually all women have been historically marginalized, silenced, or otherwise erased from the collective voice of the United States, feminist legal scholar Catherine MacKinnon could have been describing ongoing practices employed against indigenous peoples:

> Imagine that for hundreds of years your most formative traumas, your daily suffering and pain, the abuse you live through, the terror

you live with are unspeakable—not the basis of literature. . . . You cannot tell anyone. When you try to speak of these things, you are told that it did not happen, you imagined it, you wanted it, you enjoyed it. Books say this. No books say what happened to you. Law says this. No law imagines what happened to you, the way it happened. You live your life surrounded by this cultural echo of nothing where your screams and your words should be. . . . Consider what [this experience] does to one's relation to expression: to language, speech, the world of thought and communication. You learn that language does not belong to you, that you cannot use it to say what you know, that knowledge is not what you learn from your life, that information is not made out of your experience.[61]

When you are powerless, you don't speak differently. A lot, you don't speak at all. Your speech is not just differently articulated, it is silenced. Eliminated, gone. You aren't just deprived of a language with which to articulate your distinctiveness, although you are; you are deprived of a life out of which articulation might come.[62]

The imposition of manipulated semiotics (especially semantics) that was begun immediately by Columbus, through the process of imposing European names on locations inhabited for millennia by indigenous peoples, was followed by legalistic measures intended to wrap colonialism in the cloak of legitimacy. The linguistic construction of reality appears obvious in the Royal Ordinances on "Pacification" (1573), which stated, "discoveries are not to be called conquests."[63] Such a legal admonition seems ludicrous, given the complete physical and cultural decimation of the indigenous peoples by the European invaders of the region by that time.[64]

The 1573 Ordinances also ordered any Spaniard "discoverers" to impose names "on all the land, each province for itself, the principle mountains and rivers which are there, and towns and cities that they find in the land."[65] European representations did not end with the physical landscape of indigenous America. In fact, the concept of "America" was "a European invention. Certainly the mass of land existed, Amerindians and their own conceptual territorial and cosmological representation existed, but they were not Americans, because American, as a way of conceiving the four parts of the world, did not exist."[66] Beyond that most important realization, Europeans began the process of redefining the peoples of the Americas and their relationship to their homeland.

One illustration of the movement of indigenous peoples to the periphery of their own existence through semiotic sleights of hand by the colonizing invaders is provided by Kirkpatrick Sale with regard to cannibalism and the Carib Indians. After reviewing the original accounts purporting to establish human flesh eating as a regular practice by the Caribs, Sale concludes that the charges amount to no more than a myth. Sale goes on to quote W. Arens in his book *The Man-Eating Myth:* "there is little reason to assume that the very aborigines whose name now means man-eaters [Carib] actually were so."[67]

Despite the mythology surrounding the Caribs and countless other indigenous peoples, defamatory representations are pervasive and are often believed, even by indigenous peoples themselves. Logically, one might ask, if the Caribs were not cannibals, why would the Europeans characterize them as such? Sale provides two explanations. First, accounts of human flesh eaters filled the fantastic prejudices of Europeans about the "Other" across the ocean.[68] By projecting aberrant practices onto the indigenous peoples of the Americas, Europeans could attain a sanctimonious, "civilized" power position in their dealings with the Indians. A much more important, and I believe much more accurate, reason was that, in order to present a legal justification for the subjugation and dispossession of indigenous nations, Europeans had to find violations of European projections of "natural law." Today, a general ignorance exists among jurists, lawyers, and the general public regarding the development of European legal doctrines and the rights of non-Christian peoples prior to 1492.

Williams provided a useful history of those developments, particularly regarding the decisions of the Council of Constance in 1414.[69] The Constance proceedings involved the question of whether "infidels" possessed rights (or, more accurately, *dominium,* control and jurisdiction over their territory) that Christians were required to respect. The Roman Catholic Church, in the person of Pope Innocent IV, decided that infidels were possessed of *dominium* and that Christian rulers could wage "just wars" against infidels only with the approval of the pope, and only to "punish violations of natural law or to facilitate the spread of the gospel."[70]

Despite an expanded view of the humanity and the rights of "infidels," the Constance Council ruling provided an opening for colonizing Christian powers to attack indigenous peoples "according to a rule of law that recognized the right of non-Christian people either to act according to Europe's totalizing normative vision of the world or to risk conquest and subjugation for violations of this Eurocentrically understood natural law."[71] The projection of these principles onto the European invasion of the Caribbean and Central and South America meant that there were now legal, political, and economic motives to find violations of European constructions of "natural law." It is not difficult to imagine the process by which mercenaries and treasure seekers could fabricate such violations where none existed.[72]

Consequently, the humanity of Indian peoples was appropriated and converted by calculating entrepreneurs and political bureaucrats for the purpose of expanding the empire. In place of Indian humanness was injected the grotesque fabrication of indigenous peoples as subhumans and barbarians. By 1698, signifiers of indigenous barbarity were becoming firmly ensconced in European law. The Italian law professor Alberico Gentili memorialized racist characterizations of indigenous peoples through his endorsement "of the opinion of those who say that the cause of the Spaniards is just when they make war upon the Indians, who practiced abominable lewdness even with beasts, and who ate human flesh. . . . And against such men . . . war is made as against brutes."[73] The dehumanization of indigenous peoples made the construction of legal fictions to dispossess, subjugate, enslave, or murder native nations much more palatable. The contortions developed to provide a veneer of semantic legality to otherwise indefensible genocidal practices were extraordinary.[74]

Immediately after Columbus returned to Spain from his first voyage, the Spanish monarchy wasted no time in requesting, and receiving, the sanction of the Roman Catholic Church for Spain's venture into indigenous America. The rulings of the Constance Council notwithstanding, Pope Alexander VI issued two papal bulls purporting to grant the islands and the mainland of the Americas to Spain, simultaneously granting authority to "subjugate" and "subdue" the "barbarous nations" found there.[75] Despite the questionable legal force of the bulls to transfer territory, the practical effects in the Americas were disastrous for indigenous peoples.[76]

Williams masterfully demonstrates that repeatedly throughout the invasion of the Americas by various European powers, a juridically derived necessity to diminish the humanity of indigenous peoples was present. After the creation of the United States, the legal fabrications continued under John Marshall when, in the case of *Johnson v. M'Intosh* (discussed later), Marshall caricaturized indigenous peoples as barbarians, writing that "the tribes of Indians inhabiting this country were fierce savages, whose occupation was war. . . . To leave them in possession of their country, was to leave the country a wilderness."[77] The purpose of Marshall's fabrications was to reinforce a socialized belief in the natural inferiority of indigenous peoples in order to establish that "Indians are inferior [to Christian Europeans] as a matter of law."[78]

The noted federal Indian law scholar Felix Cohen acknowledged that Indians were widely oppressed under Spanish rule, but he concluded that "the oppression was in defiance of, rather than pursuant to, the laws of Spain."[79] Cohen's point, along with that of Lewis Hanke,[80] that the Spanish were meticulous in the formalistic application of their "rule of law" to justify the expansion of their empire, must have been little consolation to the indigenous peoples it was purporting to protect but ultimately dispossessed. Williams contends that although the Constance Council had pronounced the right of infidels to be free from unprovoked attacks by invading Christian Europeans, actual practice in the Americas "revealed a frightening gap between law on the books in the Old World and law in action in the New World."[81]

Not to be outdone by the Spanish, the English perfected their own instruments of empire, eventually without the cumbersome constraints of the papacy. Commencing with the Cabot Charter of 1493, Henry VII authorized Englishmen, under the pretense of law, to "subdue, occupy and possess"[82] the territories and nations of all indigenous peoples with whom all Christians were decreed to be in a "perpetual state of war."[83] By 1608, after fabricating elaborate legal justifications for the invasion and enslavement of the Irish, the English courts decided *Calvin's Case*, in which all infidels or indigenous peoples "are in law perpetual enemies" of Christians, and once they are subdued, "the laws of the infidels are abrogated." Utilizing these doctrines, coupled with the semantic constructions and the legal manipulations that emanate from them, the English exported the lessons of their Irish colonial war to the Americas and began systematically to compose their semiotic tools to seize physical, philosophical, and cultural control of the northern sections of indigenous America.[84]

From its hierarchical base, the colonizing project of the English was passed to their kindred colonial successors in the newly formed United States. Eventually, the seed of *Calvin's Case* was constructed into the edifice of U.S. federal Indian law, replete with its own pretentious doctrines and self-serving jurisprudence. Using *Broken Treaties* as his sledgehammer, Deloria sets upon the processes of demolishing the ideological and juridical structure that has imprisoned indigenous peoples the world over, beginning his task with the United States.

DISMANTLING THE MASTER'S HOUSE

Deloria's design for "dismantling the master's house"[85] focuses on the three pillars of U.S. Indian law on which all other legal justifications have been constructed: the discovery doctrine, domestic dependent nation status, and the plenary power doctrine. Each of the doctrines has been described and discussed in significant detail, but Deloria's perspective provided one of the first unapologetic critiques of those ideas that constitute the foundation of the "master's house." This chapter does not discuss these doctrines in detail but mentions them to highlight their continuing application in the international relations policy of the United States regarding the rights of indigenous peoples.

One of the most powerful dimensions of *Broken Treaties* is Deloria's courage in exposing the pretentiousness of federal Indian law. He was able to remove the blinders that had allowed U.S. courts and politicians to pretend that somehow the occupation of America had been a justifiable enterprise. He laid bare the a priori assumptions of the foundational cases of Indian law and liberated a generation of activists and lawyers to imagine a different strategic approach to vindicating the inherent rights of indigenous peoples.

The question at the commencement of the twenty-first century concerns the degree to which current activists and advocates will embrace the intellectual freedom Deloria has provided. One point is unquestionable: the precepts that Deloria confronts in *Broken Treaties* are still the foundation of U.S. indigenous law and policy today.[86] Unfortunately, since the publication of *Broken Treaties,* two generations of attorneys, both Indian and non-Indian, have been trained—most of them indoctrinated to accept the very assumptions that Deloria so vigorously challenged, and most of them internalizing those assumptions.[87] It is almost as though, as Wilkins would say, the law has been "masked,"[88] so that lawyers (Indian and non-Indian alike) are able to read and discuss only those ideas and issues that reinforce the dominating ideology of colonialism.

Doctrine of Discovery

The first aspect of Indian law that Deloria attacks is the doctrine of discovery and the fabrication of "aboriginal title" as a rationalization for the European occupation of indigenous peoples' territory. In the case of *Johnson v. M'Intosh,* Chief Justice John Marshall is transparent in his admission that the U.S. Supreme Court is engaging in a self-serving justification of empire building. Deloria provides one of the most salient passages from *Johnson*: "However extravagant the pretension of converting the discovery of an inhabited country into conquest may appear, if the principle has been asserted in the first instance, . . . it becomes the law of the land, and cannot be questioned."[89]

Despite Deloria's exposé of Marshall's charade of relying on a set of objective notions of law, especially some pretense of respect for a European notion of natural rights, very few lawyers or activists advanced Deloria's critique on the point of "aboriginal title"[90] or his conclusion that the constructions of the U.S. Supreme Court could not legitimately "be considered as taking away from the tribes their national recognition or their residual rights as nations."[91] The opinions of the U.S. Supreme Court, through the person of John Marshall, were often contradictory and "ambiguous."[92] Nonetheless, most lawyers, scholars, and activists tend to ignore the contradictions and ambiguities of the opinions and seem to reject Deloria's invitation to begin the process of deconstruction. Instead, most lawyers in the field pursue the path of least resistance, internalizing and reinforcing the foundation of the structure that maintains indigenous peoples in bondage.[93] Consequently, the U.S. government has been emboldened to prescribe its federal Indian law and policy as a model for the world.[94]

Twenty-four years after *Broken Treaties* was published, Deloria's critique of *Johnson v. M'Intosh* was honed to a fine point. David Wilkins wrote that Marshall's admission (quoted above) "is an amazing confession. The Chief Justice was candidly admitting that the doctrine of discovery and of conquest were nothing more than extravagant pretenses without any basis in fact. Nevertheless, the Supreme Court had decided for purely political and economic reasons to transform these legal fictions into legal concepts."[95]

Wilkins also provides important illumination on the role of the creation of legal "doctrines" in federal Indian law. Although three of the most fundamental are discussed here, several others that have impaired and eroded indigenous peoples' independence have also been fabricated. Wilkins acknowledges that these doctrines "have developed without any constitutional basis" and "have been presented by the justices as if they were essential or eternal verities."[96]

More recent research indicates that "there was no real 'case or controversy' [in *Johnson v. M'Intosh*], like another leading early Supreme Court land case, *Fletcher v. Peck*, [*Johnson*] appears to have been a sham."[97] Apparently, the tracts of land involved in *Johnson* did not overlap, and there was no actual dispute. Eric Kades argues that Marshall and the Supreme Court fabricated the opinion in *Johnson* in order to establish a consistent and orderly regime of expropriating the territories of indigenous peoples in the most economically efficient manner. *Johnson* "was an essential part of the regime of efficient expropriation because it ensured that Europeans did not bid against each other to acquire Indian lands, thus keeping prices low."[98] Marshall fabricated one of the foundational pillars of federal Indian law because "he thought the stakes were important enough to warrant a universal rule barring private purchases from the Indians."[99] By manipulating the Court and customary law to his own design, Marshall "solved a collective action problem and left the Indians facing a single buyer [monopsony] assured of no competition."[100] With one bogus decision, Marshall began the process of exterminating the Indian race with, as described by Tocqueville, "singular felicity, tranquilly, legally, philanthropically, without shedding blood, and without violating a single great principle of morality in the eyes of the world.[101] It is impossible to destroy men with more respect for the laws of humanity."[102]

The doctrine of discovery comprises the foundation of the master's house that Deloria has called to be dismantled. Not only does every federal Indian law casebook continue to reprint *Johnson v. M'Intosh*, but the case is often taught with an assumption of inevitability, with the most uncritical analysis. Most property law casebooks in law schools across the United States begin with *Johnson*, for without *Johnson*, there could be no body of property law in the country that would justify the current configuration of the United States, nor could there be the current configuration of federal Indian law. More important, without *Johnson*, there could be no joinder of the two.

The total acreage of the continental United States is approximately 1.9 billion acres.[103] Today, the BIA claims that it holds slightly over 56 million acres of land in trust for Indian nations and individuals. The process by which the indigenous nations lost control of 1.85 billion acres of land remains a mystery not only to non-Indian people but also to most Indians. *Johnson*, a fabricated case and a controversy in its whole, provides a smoke screen of fictionalization in the legal rationalizations that obscure the methods through which the United States created its unique brand of colonialism and implemented it against a variety of indigenous peoples. More important, according to Deloria's admonitions, indigenous lawyers, as well as their nonindigenous colleagues, have internalized the holding and Marshall's perverse logic, to the point where *Johnson*, despite its illegitimate roots and unjust reasoning, is almost universally perceived as "good law," defining the decision as settled and beyond challenge. Despite all the problems related to *Johnson's* legitimacy, the U.S. government continues to use the case religiously as a justification for ongoing U.S. policy. In response to inquiries from the UN Committee on the Elimination of All Forms of Racial Discrimination, the United States justified its taking of indigenous peoples' territories by citing *Johnson* and the attendant legal proposition that "as a result of European discovery . . . discovery gave exclusive title to those who made it, [and] indigenous peoples' ability to sell or convey the property was subject to the approval of the [invading, colonizing] sovereign."[104]

Domestic Dependent Nations

In 1831 the U.S. Supreme Court was fighting for its life. Political tensions between Chief Justice John Marshall and President Andrew Jackson, as well as states' rights members of Congress, led to a series of constitutional crises. The future of the Supreme Court as a coequal partner in the federal governmental structure was far from secure, and Marshall understood that the "Indian problem" could spawn reactions that might lead to a permanent marginalization of the Court in the federal government.[105] The central question of whether Marshall was going to allow his understanding of international law to protect indigenous nations' territories and political independence at the expense of the survival of his Supreme Court is answered by Jill Norgren: "Certainly in *Cherokee Nation* Marshall calculated the issues of politics and the issues of law and ruled in a manner far more protective of the interests of the Court than those of the Cherokee Nation. The final two paragraphs of the opinion in particular offer clear evidence of Marshall's mental exhaustion and abandonment of the Indian cause."[106]

In *Johnson v. M'Intosh*, "Marshall invented the category of occupancy of title and needed a legal rationalization to his confection. He found it in the concept Western jurists call the doctrine of discovery. . . . If, however, John Marshall doubted the international or moral legitimacy of discovery doctrine, he did not say so in *Fletcher*[107] [or *Johnson*]. Instead Marshall used the doctrine as a starting point for the development of an American law of continental real estate [and colonialism]."[108] Similarly, in *Cherokee Nation*, Marshall consciously manufactured juridical doctrines to suit his political ends and the political and economic needs of U.S. expansionism.[109] Evidence of Marshall's willingness to costume political expedience as law is reflected in the assurances of Jeremiah Evarts, a pro-Indian lobbyist from the American Board of Commissioners for Foreign Missions who told the Cherokees that on the question of independent Cherokee nationhood, "all of the great lawyers in the country are on your side."[110] William Wirt, former attorney general of the United States who was now the Cherokee Nation's primary attorney, confirmed that the greatest legal minds of the time—John Sergeant, Ambrose Spencer, Daniel Webster, James Kent, and Horace Binney—all sided with the legal position that the Cherokee Nation was a foreign, independent state.[111] Despite the jurisprudential correctness of the Cherokee's position (even from a Euro-American perspective), Marshall decided that the more important interest was "that the Court and the [U.S.] Constitution, as the justices interpreted it, always came first,"[112] even if the Cherokees were to be sacrificed in the bargain.

In the process of crafting a jurisprudential strategy designed to save the Court, Marshall deliberately tried to walk a razor's edge in describing the status of the Cherokee Nation (and, by implication, other indigenous peoples) in a diminished political light. Marshall never actually wrote that the Cherokees were a "domestic dependent nation," as is so widely accepted. Instead, he used a passage that is so qualified as to be almost meaningless, unless one is pursuing a specific political agenda. Marshall wrote that although the Cherokees could not be described as "foreign nations," because their territories were contiguous with the United States, "They may, more correctly, perhaps be denominated domestic dependent nations. . . . Their relation to the United States resembles that of a ward to his guardian."[113]

Nowhere does Marshall conclude that the Cherokees constituted, *in fact,* a domestic dependent nation. He writes that *perhaps* their current condition could be *denominated* that way. Nonetheless, lawyers (Indian and non-Indian alike) read, teach, and argue that *Cherokee Nation* created and affirmed the status of indigenous peoples as being in a domestic dependent relationship to the United States. Even if the passage above is given the most liberal interpretation in favor of domestic dependency, the judgment about the Cherokees in 1831 could not possibly be extrapolated to the Seminoles at the same time, who remained engaged in full-fledged war with the United States, not to mention other indigenous nations such as the Lakotas or Comanches,[114] who remained in a condition of unquestioned and unassailable political independence from the United States. One of the most valuable lessons of Deloria's writing in *Broken Treaties* is the plea to all Indian people to engage in the critical process of parsing language, and not merely to accept blindly the legal constructions of the leadership of the settler state that has flourished in our homeland.

Parallel to his treatment of the discovery doctrine in *Broken Treaties,* Deloria viewed the United States' fabrication of the notion of indigenous peoples as domestic dependent nations as a self-serving imposition that many Indians have been socialized to accept and internalize. Deloria supported the assertion of those who occupied Wounded Knee in 1973 that indigenous peoples are citizens of their own nations, which "remain in a very real sense foreign nations with respect to the United States."[115] During the consolidated federal cases after Wounded Knee held in Lincoln, Nebraska, Deloria testified about the historical view of the Lakota and Dakota (Sioux) vis-à-vis their political independence from the United States: "The Sioux people not only considered themselves a nation but they were prepared, some were even eager, to fight to the death against the United States. They definitely considered themselves a distinct and separate sovereignty which had to receive the respect of other nations, particularly the United States."[116]

The imposition of "domestic dependency" by John Marshall fits completely within Wilkins's explanation of Supreme Court sleight of hand in Indian law.[117] The rationale of the doctrine is provided by one of Deloria's early student-colleagues, Tim Coulter, now the director of the Indian Law Resource Center (ILRC):

One reason Marshall calls Indian nations "dependent" is that the United States claims title to the Cherokee land. But, as we saw in *Johnson* . . . , this U.S. claim to aboriginal Indian land is not a legal claim at all, only a political position taken by the United States which the Supreme Court refused to question. Marshall himself had admitted that there was no basis for the assertion in established legal principles. [Marshall's holding] is not a position based on independent legal principles. Marshall's remarks do not state what the law is but what the political position of the United States is.[118]

The political, legal, and economic motivations of the U.S. decision makers were strengthened and emboldened subsequent to *Cherokee Nation* and its jurisprudential twin, *Worcester v. Georgia*.[119] Eventually, U.S. invasion into additional territories of indigenous peoples necessitated the invention of the third major doctrine criticized by Deloria: the plenary power doctrine.[120]

Plenary Power Doctrine

Wilkins succinctly describes plenary power as that coercive authority of the state that is "complete in all aspects or essentials."[121] He proceeds to elaborate that in federal Indian law, three brands of plenary power are exercised: exclusive, preemptive, and unlimited or absolute.[122] In its essence, though, the plenary power doctrine was developed and articulated by the Supreme Court in earnest between 1886[123] and 1903.[124] In practice, the doctrine means that "U.S. courts, rather than assessing the constitutionality of governmental action, defer to the 'political' branches of government, Congress and the Executive."[125] Congress and the president possess essentially unbridled freedom to make any decision in relation to indigenous peoples, and the Court will defer to the legislative and executive authority. In practice, this has meant that Congress has unlimited power to legislate to the detriment of Indian nations, that the president has unlimited power to sign executive orders to the same detriment, and that the United States can legislate indigenous nations out of political, cultural, or economic existence, abrogate treaties, and misuse or lose billions of dollars in trust funds for Indian people, apparently without consequence.[126]

The doctrine has allowed the Court to invent, manufacture, and enforce myth as history, and ethnocentric dogma as law. The consequence of this judicial hooliganism, represented by the "absolute power which the Court arrogated to itself and Congress . . . [has] set a destructive precedent for tribal nations that continues to affect their daily operations and intergovernmental relations . . . [with] no obvious limitation on Congress' presumed plenary power regarding tribal sovereignty."[127]

In discussing the contrivance of the plenary power doctrine in *Lone Wolf*, one U.S. senator compared the Supreme Court's action there to the infamous slave case of *Dred Scott v. Sandford* (described as "undoubtedly the greatest disaster in the history of the Court"[128]). Senator Quey of Pennsylvania said that *Lone Wolf* "was *Dred Scott* decision #2, except that in this case the victim is red instead of black. [It suggests] that the red man has no rights which the white man is bound to respect, and, that no treaty or contract made with him is binding."[129]

As Deloria suggested in *Broken Treaties,* the plenary power doctrine is an inexcusable maneuver by the Court to replace the independent political status of indigenous nations and the international treaty relationship between indigenous peoples and the United States. Perhaps more than any other single indigenous author, David Wilkins has taken up the challenge posed by Deloria in stripping back the veneer of legitimacy from the plenary power doctrine. Although Norgren posits the relatively safe and diluted conclusion that *"Kagama, Lone Wolf,* and the early twentieth century cases that followed appear . . . to have made a mockery of Marshall and *Worcester,"*[130] it is Wilkins who puts the fine point on the cases: "Reified in the Court's consciousness, the justices employed masks like 'wardship,' 'dependency,' 'savagery,' 'primitivism,' 'plenary power,' 'political question,' in various ways to achieve whatever ends they deem viable. And it was the Court, not the [indigenous nation], the individual, the states or even Congress, which retained plenary discretion to decide the scope of Congress's powers and the degree, if any, to which treaty rights were to be protected."[131]

The discussion above provokes the question, what is to be done? More succinctly, what was Deloria's prescription in *Broken Treaties?* Norgren reminds us that *Lone Wolf* was decided in the same era as *Plessy v. Ferguson,* the infamous "separate but equal" case that legitimized "American apartheid" for fifty-eight years. *Lone Wolf* was also compared to *Dred Scott* as a judicial vehicle that effectively stripped indigenous peoples of any vestiges of self-determination. In that regard, Norgren seems to propose a legal attack on the foundations of federal Indian law: "While *Plessy* has been denounced and principles underlying it have been rejected as reflecting unabashed racism and intolerance, *Lone Wolf* continues to be cited as precedent, its underlying principles still unquestioned by the courts."[132] To this day, there has been no indigenous equivalent to *Brown v. Board of Education,* the case that overturned *Plessy* and "American apartheid" for African Americans. Doctrines of discovery, domestic dependency, and plenary power remain apparently safe in the halls of U.S. jurisprudence, without any apparent design on the horizon to cut them out, root and branch, as *Brown* was intended to do with *Plessy.*

DEVELOPMENTS IN THE POLITICAL ATMOSPHERE SURROUNDING *BROKEN TREATIES*

Commencing in the late 1960s, members of AIM were emboldened by the counsel of traditional elders of various indigenous nations to advance principles of self-determination, as their ancestors had, on the grounds of the inherent authority of indigenous nations as acknowledged by the United States in hundreds of treaties.[133] It was AIM and some strategic allies from other activist indigenous organizations that brought national prominence to the issues discussed here during the actual Trail of Broken Treaties (from which Deloria's book title is derived), a cross-country caravan during the presidential election week of November 1972.[134]

AIM joined with traditional indigenous political forces and a few legal interests to utilize the U.S. federal courts to advance indigenous peoples' claims. Soon, the obstacles to challenging the entrenched ideological roots of U.S. law and policy affecting indigenous peoples became insurmountable. In 1974, guided in part by Deloria's arguments in *Broken Treaties*, AIM formed the International Indian Treaty Council (IITC) to advance positions of treaty rights and indigenous self-determination at the United Nations and other international forums.[135]

By 1977, AIM, along with traditional representatives of the Six Nations Iroquois Confederacy and the ILRC, had helped organize the first major UN gathering to address indigenous peoples' concerns. The International Nongovernmental Organization (NGO) Conference on Discrimination against Indigenous Peoples of the Western Hemisphere[136] represented the first time since 1923 that indigenous peoples had asserted an international personality on the world stage. In the 1920s the Cayuga leader Deskaheh had unsuccessfully approached the League of Nations in the hope of gaining recognition for the international standing of the Six Nations (Haudenosaunee) Confederacy.[137] In 1977, and at subsequent conferences in 1981 and beyond, indigenous peoples were not going to be denied as Deskaheh had been.[138]

In the late 1970s the entry of American Indians and other indigenous peoples onto the global stage was perplexing to officials and citizens of settler states, as well as to less politicized indigenous people. After all, settler-state law had ordained that indigenous peoples were "domestic" matters, completely within the jurisdiction of the colonizing state.

Tim Coulter, director of the ILRC, which by then was also an NGO with consultative status at the UN, decided to explain why international avenues were appearing more attractive to indigenous peoples.[139] In his analysis, Coulter utilized Deloria's outline in *Broken Treaties* to explain in painful detail why the operation of the discovery doctrine, conquest doctrine, domestic dependency (trust) doctrine, and plenary power–political question doctrines provided persistent, insurmountable obstacles to indigenous peoples seeking justice in the courts of the United States. Coulter concluded, "The U.S. legal system does not . . . offer legal procedures for the most fundamental Indian claims and controversies."[140] Regarding legal questions of indigenous governance, territoriality, validity and interpretation of treaties, and equal relations between the United States and indigenous peoples, "it can be stated with certainty that no remedy is available and no legal relief is possible under U.S. law."[141]

In 1981 a second conference was held at the UN in Geneva. The NGO Conference on Indigenous Peoples and the Land was fundamentally important for two reasons. First, the conference included not only indigenous peoples from the 1977 NGO conference but also representatives from UN-acknowledged national liberation organizations, notably the Palestine Liberation Organization (PLO), FRETELIN from East Timor, the Polisario Front from Western Sahara, and the South West Africa People's Organization (SWAPO) from Namibia. The significance of this development was that it situated the conference and the movement for indigenous peoples' rights solidly in the midst of the Cold War between the United States and the USSR. The question of whether decolonization principles under international law should be extended to indigenous peoples was now squarely on the UN's table. The willingness of national liberation organizations such as the PLO and SWAPO to weigh in on the question of indigenous peoples' rights clearly situated the discourse in a place that made the United States and other settler states with significant surviving indigenous nations uncomfortable.

The second important development from the 1981 NGO conference was the direct evolution of the UN Working Group on Indigenous Populations. What was yet to be determined was the scope, the context, and the orientation of the working group's mandate. The history of the UN Working Group on Indigenous Populations, as well as its recent history and the Draft Declaration on the Rights of Indigenous Peoples, has been discussed elsewhere.[142] This discussion is limited to a few particular issues around the Draft Declaration[143] and the similarities in semantic manipulation that occurred in U.S. federal Indian law and that developed with respect to the Draft Declaration.

SEMANTICS, COLONIALISM, AND LAW: CREATING A COLONIZATION OF THE MIND

> We say no to the lie. The colonial inheritance obliges [us] to accept as our own the memory of the victors who conquered it and to take the lies of others and use them as its own reality. They reward our obedience, punish our intelligence, and discourage our creative energy. We are opinionated, yet we cannot offer our opinions. We have a right to the echo, not to the voice, and those who rule praise our talent to repeat parrot fashion. We say no: we refuse to accept this mediocrity as our destiny.
>
> We say no to fear. No to the fear of speaking, of doing, of being. Visible colonialism forbids us to speak, to do, to be. Invisible colonialism, more efficient, convinces

us that one cannot speak, cannot do, cannot be. Fear disguises itself as realism: to prevent realism from becoming unreal . . . morals must be immoral. . . . By saying no to the devastating empire of greed, whose center lies in North America, we are saying yes to another possible America, which will be born of the most ancient of American traditions, [that] Indians have defended, desperately, defeat after defeat, during the last five centuries.[144]

In November 1996, during a particularly acrimonious meeting of the UN Intersessional Working Group to Consider the Draft Declaration on the Rights of Indigenous Peoples, an informal conversation was held between members of the U.S. Mission to the United Nations and several indigenous delegates from the territory now claimed by the United States. During the conversation, which revolved mostly around the question of self-determination and the United States' unwillingness to use the term *indigenous peoples*,[145] one of the indigenous participants asked the U.S. delegation if the United States considered the Draft Declaration to be an important international legal-political instrument.

The response from a member of the delegation, whose name was never clear and whom the indigenous delegates assumed to be a CIA political attaché to the U.S. Mission, replied, "To the extent that words have meaning, and to the extent that meanings configure reality, the Draft Declaration has importance."[146] Although the profound candor and depth of the statement was not immediately clear to the indigenous delegates, over time, the United States' advancement of particular semantic markers with regard to indigenous peoples became clearer.

What the U.S. representative's statement reflected was an understanding of two schools of linguistic theory and analysis: sociology of knowledge[147] and sociology of language.[148] These two intellectual strains reflect the understanding that power is not achieved solely through political or economic decisions enforced through the use or the threat of coercive physical force. Rather, power is also exercised by influential societal actors who can construct or reconfigure perceptions of reality through the deliberate and methodical imposition of semantic rules and practices. The actions of the U.S. representatives to the UN not only advance the semantics of control but simultaneously serve to muffle the voice of indigenous peoples. Bourdieu describes this process as the creation of "censorship by limiting the universe of political discourse, and thereby the universe of what is politically thinkable."[149] It is obvious to the United States and all other settler states that their very existence is dependent on a rational (and legally consistent) justification that subordinates the right of indigenous peoples to self-determination to the claim of territorial integrity by the settler state. The operation of settler-state governments requires the construction of a normalized or "correct" language, the use of which establishes the standard for acceptable discourse. The "correct" language becomes a kind of code within the settler society that is reinforced in law, policy, and the educational system. The legitimation of the normalized semantics of the dispossession of indigenous peoples takes on the veneer of objectivity in the courts and the schools, but in fact, what is created is a state ideology designed to establish a totalizing rationalization and excuse for state expansion over indigenous peoples.

Bourdieu reminds us that "ideologies serve particular interests which they tend to present as universal interests . . . [and contribute] to the fictitious integration of society as a whole, and thus to the apathy (false consciousness) of the dominated classes; and it contributes to the legitimation of the established order by establishing distinctions (hierarchies) and legitimating these distinctions."[150] U.S. law and policy toward indigenous peoples have consistently highlighted the deficiencies in indigenous civilization, development, and culture in order to justify the imposition of "higher" standards on indigenous peoples by settler states.[151]

The debates over the Draft Declaration provide the most recent example of U.S. attempts to legitimate its processes of domination of indigenous peoples through language. The importance of semiotic, especially semantic, manipulation in this regard is very important, because "it is as structured and structuring instruments of communication and knowledge that 'symbolic systems' fulfill their political function, as instruments which help to ensure that one class dominates another . . . by bringing their own distinctive power to bear on the relations of power which underlie them and thus by contributing, in Weber's terms, to the 'domestication of the dominated.' "[152]

The United States has consistently refused to use a category of specific terms (peoples, self-determination, collective rights) that might acknowledge the international character and aspirations of indigenous peoples. The attempted U.S. control of international indigenous peoples' rights discourse is hauntingly analogous to the U.S. Supreme Court's semantic constructions in *Johnson, Cherokee Nation,* and the other cases that fabricated colonizing legal doctrines destructive to indigenous nations.

As discussed earlier, the Supreme Court created the terms *discovery doctrine* and *domestic dependent nation* to reconfigure reality both for indigenous peoples and for the colonizing society. Despite the decades over which the right to self-determination had evolved into customary international legal force,[153] the United States assumed the authority to contort and redefine the terminology of decolonization to suit its own purposes.[154]

In an unclassified, internal State Department memorandum of July 1993, the United States acknowledged that for the first dozen years of debate over the Draft Declaration on the Rights of Indigenous Peoples, the United States had "invested little effort" in the Working Group on Indigenous Populations, where the draft was crafted. Now, the memo continued, the United States would take a more active role and "try to shape the text [of the draft] to reflect U.S. interests," prior to the declaration going for ratification to the UN Commission on Human Rights.[155] That stated aspiration is precisely what has occurred.

The United States insists that any declaration on the rights of indigenous peoples must conform to the doctrines of U.S. domestic law that have been so laboriously crafted over the past two centuries. The United States also forced discussion of the declaration into a completely new working group mandated solely to reconsider the Draft Declaration, which had already been under debate for a dozen years. The transparent purpose of the U.S. maneuver was to enable the United States and its allies to stall consideration of the draft by the full UN General Assembly and to dilute the language of self-determination. The United States and like-minded states have now prevented the advancement of a declaration, which is merely an aspirational document with no particular force in international law, for nearly a decade. Within the so-called Intersessional Working Group to consider the Draft Declaration, the United States has concertedly attacked the application of the international right of self-determination to indigenous peoples. Like John Marshall before them, U.S. State Department officials are constructing new semantic meanings to suit state interests at the expense of indigenous peoples.

In another unclassified memo, this time originating in the U.S. National Security Council (NSC), the United States decided to inject its distorted definition of self-determination into the Draft Declaration, writing that "the USDEL [United States delegation to the UN or to the Organization of American States (OAS)] should support the use of the term 'internal self-determination' in both the UN and OAS declarations. . . . In exercising their right of internal self-determination [indigenous peoples] have the right to autonomy or self-government in matters relating to their local affairs."[156] Any brand of the U.S. version of indigenous self-determination "must be exercised within the existing state."[157] The United States acknowledged that "under international law, self-determination means the full enjoyment of civil and political rights . . . [and] the right of all 'peoples' to choose their political status, including the right to choose independence . . . and to exercise permanent sovereignty over natural resources."[158] Despite U.S. recognition of what self-determination has been interpreted to mean for all other colonized peoples[159] of the earth, in the case of indigenous peoples, the United States only concedes "the right of internal self-determination [that] does not include rights of independence or permanent sovereignty over natural resources."[160]

The consequence of the embodiment of "internal self-determina-tion" as the international legal standard for indigenous peoples is that domestic "autonomy" within the confines of the state system will consti-tute the external limit of freedom for the world's most consistently oppressed peoples. Some indigenous peoples might be satisfied with a subordinate relationship to the state, and for them, "internal self-deter-mination" may satisfy all their political, economic, and social aspirations. However, for those indigenous nations that have been marginalized and oppressed since colonialism first visited their homelands and that aspire to reassert their freedom, not only will international law prevent them from expressing their self-determination, but states will be justified in using any level of force desired to frustrate self-determination move-ments, resulting in protracted and perhaps even genocidal wars against indigenous peoples.[161]

The next tactic in the NSC memo was to impose a narrow interpre-tation of "peoples" to indigenous nations, consistent with the U.S. con-struction of limiting language in International Labor Organization (ILO) Convention No. 169, Article 1(3), which specifically states: "The use of the term 'peoples' in this convention shall not be construed as having any implications as regards the rights which attach to the term under inter-national law."[162] Although some commentators dispute that this lan-guage, per se, denies the right of self-determination to indigenous peoples,[163] the United States interprets the ILO language explicitly to limit the right of indigenous peoples to assert any version of self-deter-mination that would impair or disrupt the current state system. In its 2001 NSC memo, the United States clearly states that it will accede to the use of the term *peoples* only if the qualifying language from ILO Conven-tion No. 169 is included in the Draft Declaration.[164]

The refusal of the United States and other settler states to even con-sider application of the customary definitions of terms such as *self-deter-mination* and *peoples* to indigenous peoples constitutes a politically powerful control of the markers of international human rights discourse. The attempt to control the meaning of the most important terms in indige-nous peoples' rights development through the fabrication of multiple def-initions is what Robin Tolmach-Lakoff and Deborah Tannen might label "pragmatic homonyms," that is, "word forms that look the same but have two or more distinct interpretations depending on context."[165]

In this instance, the pragmatic homonyms mask the United States' intention to create a double standard in international human rights law. Through redefining the meaning of *peoples* to exclude indigenous peo-ples, the United States is implicitly returning to previous eras in which indigenous peoples were marginalized as "the other," less human, less civilized, less worthy of inclusion in the community of nations. This process is a complex construction of a coded lexicon from a system that, as Edward Said has observed, is "supported and perhaps even impelled by impressive ideological formations that include notions that certain territories and people require and *beseech* domination, as well as forms of knowledge affiliated with domination."[166] In practice, this process is described by Susan Opotow as "moral exclusion"; that is, "when a distinction is made between those entitled to the fullest privileges of membership in the community and those whose privileges are restricted or non-existent."[167] Similarly, it is the process through which "individuals or groups are perceived *as outside the boundary in which moral values, rules and considerations of fairness apply.*"[168]

The juncture of pragmatic homonyms with moral exclusion in the field of indigenous peoples' rights discourse is no more graphic than in use of the term *self-determination*. In practice, as mentioned above, the United States perverts self-determination to mean, variously, self-administration, autonomy, or self-government. In each instance, the opportunistic, pragmatic homonym devised by the United States is a frustration both of the international character of indigenous peoples and nations and of the potential for indigenous peoples to realize a future free of external domination.

Deloria himself seemed to recognize that U.S. manipulations of terms such as *self-determination* and *self-government* were mere extensions of Marshall's fabrication of domestic dependency and discovery doctrine. Indigenous elected officials and bureaucrats regularly fall into the linguistic traps set by the settler state, internalizing the language of colonization. By incorporating terms such as *government-to-government relationship*,[169] uncritically engaging in "consultations"[170] with U.S. officials, and accepting self-government or internal self-determination as a substitute for the *international right* to self-determination, indigenous officials confirm Max Weber's definition of the "domestication of the dominated." On the self-determination–self-government dichotomy, Deloria is clear:

> When we distinguish between *nationhood [self-determination] and self-government,* we speak of two entirely different positions in the world. *Nationhood* implies a process of decision-making that is free and uninhibited within the community, a community in fact that is almost completely insulated from external factors, as it considers its possible options. *Self-government,* on the other hand, implies a recognition by the superior power [the United States] that some measure of local decision-making is necessary, but that this process must be monitored very carefully so that its products are compatible with the goals and the policies of the larger political power. . . . *Self-government is not an Indian idea.* It originates in the minds of non-Indians who

have reduced the traditional ways to dust, or believe they have, and now wish to give as a gift, a limited measure of local control and responsibility.[171]

Despite the enormous physical costs that have been paid by indigenous peoples in terms of lives, territory, and natural resources, the ultimate catastrophe for indigenous nations may rest in the destruction of the raw materials of consciousness development through the operation of what Linda Tuhiwai Smith labels colonial "hierarchies of knowledge," which create a systematic "imposition of Western authority over all aspects of indigenous knowledges, languages and cultures"[172] through colonial educational systems, laws, and compelled socialization. In this process, the colonized must, as Frantz Fanon suggests, either choose to accept and assimilate his immobility and "stay in his place" or decide "to put an end to the history of colonization and to bring into existence the history of decolonization." Fanon unambiguously describes this process as "the meeting of two forces, opposed to each other by their very nature . . . [through which] there is therefore the need for a complete calling in question of the colonial situation."[173]

Some skeptics might question the appropriateness of describing the relationship of indigenous peoples to the settler or neocolonial states that surround them as colonialism. The three emerging phenomena of the colonial process, in both its historic and its current form, have been artfully described by V. Y. Mudimbe and are useful to the discussion here. Mudimbe concludes that colonialism is constituted of (1) the domination of the physical space of another by the colonizer, (2) the reformation of the minds of the indigenous peoples of the dominated space, and (3) the integration of the local indigenous economic histories into the Western perspective.[174] One would be hard-pressed to find a single indigenous people in the world for whom these conditions could not be satisfied.[175]

The consequence of colonialism for indigenous peoples has been the exertion of pressure on indigenous territories, cultures, and histories by a global capitalist system in three major ways: parts of the system of global capitalism always develop at the expense of other parts; the creation of a Western-dominated globalized capitalist structure requires greater and greater integration of non-Western territories and peoples; and despite significant economic resources within the territories of indigenous peoples, the structural capacity of colonized peoples for political, economic, and cultural autonomy is largely defined and decided by other key actors in a globalized new world order.[176]

Deloria refines the point concerning the comprehensive control that external forces exert over the economic, political, and ideological condition of American Indians. In describing the seemingly inevitable, dire consequences of state domination of indigenous peoples, Deloria writes that "many Indians speak of this condition as colonialism, but it is considerably more devastating than simple colonialism. It is the final and systematic and perhaps even ruthlessly efficient destruction of Indian society."[177] Although the economic implications of colonization are critical, the discussion here is concerned primarily with the methods and mechanisms that have been, and continue to be, utilized by the colonizing powers in convincing others that the colonizer's signs, markers, and constructions of language are legitimate. This process of conversion is critical in the process of systems acceptance by members of the colonizing society. Perhaps of greater importance is the way the colonized internalize the colonizer's language, soon accepting and adopting not only the superficial forms of the words but also the overt and implied meanings attached to them—in other words, the colonization of the mind.

For indigenous peoples, the "colonization of the mind" is described by Taiaiake Alfred as "the intellectual dimension in the group of emotional and psychological pathologies associated with internalized oppression . . . recognizable in the gradual assumption of the values, goals, and perspectives that make up the status quo." The consequence of this process is a "mental state that blocks recognition of the existence or viability of traditional [indigenous] perspectives [preventing] people from seeing beyond the conditions created by white society to serve its own interests."[178]

Mental and psychological colonization of indigenous peoples has always been an integral part of the algebra of power relations in indigenous peoples' territories. The control or the deliberate destruction of indigenous peoples' languages, and the imposition of foreign signifiers, has been an indispensable component of settler-state indigenous policy. At root, the debate taking place in Geneva over the Draft Declaration is an ideological battle pitting the legitimacy of hundreds of ancient nations of indigenous peoples against the asserted legitimacy of Westphalian states'[179] attempt to force on them "the West's view of itself as the center of legitimate knowledge, the arbiter of what counts as knowledge, and the source of 'civilized' knowledge."[180]

Tolmach-Lakoff explains that this process

> presupposes and re-creates a narrative in its very utterance: the story of who has power over whom, and how that power is maintained, and what will happen to anyone who challenges that power. As long as narrative continues uninterrupted and unquestioned, language can be used (at whatever level of consciousness) by those with language-making power against those without it: to remind them that they are them but we are us; and to let them know by words that we can do actions that harm, by that utterance doing word-harm. So

word and action merge in narrative meaning-making. The status quo is maintained. Control of the story is control of history.[181]

Illuminating the enormous, invisible power of words and the meanings with which they are associated, Alfred Korzybski, founder of a general theory of semantics, explained that "a language, any language, has at its bottom certain metaphysics, which ascribe . . . some sort of structure to the world. . . . We do not realize what tremendous power the structures of a habitual language has. It is not an exaggeration to say that it enslaves us through the mechanisms of semantic reactions and that the structure which language exhibits and impresses on us unconsciously, is automatically projected upon the world around us."[182] Korzybski went on to remind us that language is a symbol, not a reality; the map, not the territory. Yet words "become powerful because they can be used as tools . . . [with] tremendous potency, often more than the reality they stand for."[183] The deliberate manufacture and use of specific language for specific ends create the juncture of politics and meaning. The practical implications of the intersection of semantics and power are made clear as "politics brings the brute physical reality of power into the sphere of human mind and heart, [and] language is the means of that transformation. Language drives politics and determines the success of political machinations. Language is the initiator and interpreter of power relations."[184]

The practice of Euro-American subjugation of indigenous America, and the role of deliberate semiotic projection in the enterprise, serves as a poignant example of the accuracy of Korzybski's appraisal. The juridical, political, economic, and cultural underpinnings of European actions have created a treacherous ideological imbroglio through which indigenous peoples, both collectively and individually, are forced constantly to maneuver.

Through the repetitious and unchallenged creation and use of certain signifiers throughout indigenous America, "evolution, conquest and difference become signs of a theological, biological and anthropological destiny, and assign to things and beings both their natural slots and social mission."[185] The consistent use and abuse of terms such as *savage, primitive, barbarous, ignorant, pagan, infidel,* and *heathen,* among many others both in common usage and with particular legal and political connotations, have had the profound effect, at one time or another, of legitimizing the marginalization of indigenous peoples in every aspect of their existence.[186]

The profound importance of the subjugation of indigenous languages and systems of meaning by European ones cannot be minimized. What has occurred in this brutal process is not merely the replacement of one vocabulary set with another. In this struggle, the entire worldviews of indigenous peoples and nations, which were created and evolved over tens of millennia, were eradicated, sometimes within one generation.

The enormity of the project to colonize indigenous peoples around the globe does not cease with the body count from the physical genocide, nor with the chronicling of the millions upon millions of square miles of territory that was stripped from indigenous peoples' homelands. Perhaps the deepest, most enduring, and least discussed is the process through which indigenous peoples have been forced to reconceptualize the universe and their place in it. This reconceptualization is virtually undetectable from the perspective of the colonizer, but it can be viscerally destructive to the colonized.

The ongoing process of situating indigenous peoples within the ideological and semantic confines of Western legal and political discourse continues to the present in the UN, the OAS, and the ILO. In his admonitions and prescription in *Broken Treaties* and beyond, Deloria seemed to be able to predict the current evolution. While praising the vision of Lakota and Haudenosaunee traditionals in advancing issues in the international arena, he also recognized the need to produce a huge moral shift within both the United States and the UN. In a 1989 law review article, Deloria appeared pessimistic at the prospect that such fundamental change could occur within the U.S. legal system, or that a paradigmatic shift could be produced by lawyers who had been immersed for so long in accepted doctrines of federal Indian law:

> The overwhelming proportion of lawyers practicing federal Indian law will no doubt continue to use the various versions of the Handbook of Federal Indian Law as their bible, and we will no doubt continue to see casebooks and law review articles [interpret this material]. The mythical, doctrinally determined history which is now entrenched in federal Indian law will be replaced with more accurate history only with exceptional difficulty and hardship. Not only are we dealing with a fictional history promulgated by the winners, we are dealing with a belief long fostered by the legal profession that federal Indian law is comparable to other fields of law which are informed by a few basic principles and doctrines. This attitude must fall before anything significant can be accomplished.[187]

A similarly cautious view could be advanced in the international arena. Many of the original indigenous leaders who opened the international arena have either passed on[188] or abandoned hope[189] that the UN can provide an effective vehicle for the vindication of indigenous peoples' rights. On other fronts, indigenous peoples have developed a highly effective communication network via the Internet. The effectiveness of one particular indigenous resistance movement in the Mexican state of Chiapas provoked the U.S. Army to commission a study on the ability of the

Ejercito Zapatista Liberacion Nacional (Zapatistas) to utilize Internet communication effectively.[190]

Despite some important developments in the international arena, such as the creation of the UN Working Group on Indigenous Peoples, and a number of influential reports by rapporteurs and panels of experts,[191] questions remain about the coherence of a long-term resistance by indigenous peoples to settler-state colonialism and to the negative impacts of a globalized political economy. After more than two decades of being a presence in the international arena, some of the original stalwarts of indigenous rights discourse appear fatigued.[192] This is not to detract from the continuing good works of essential indigenous organizations. The ILRC recently won two exceptional cases at the Inter-American Commission on Human Rights (IACHR) that would have been unimaginable just a few years ago.

In one opinion, the IACHR held that U.S. treatment of Mary and Carrie Dann of the Western Shoshone Nation violated the norms and principles of international law as embodied in the American Declaration of the Rights and Duties of Man. It also held that the processes of the Indian Claims Commission (roundly criticized by Deloria in chapter 10 of *Broken Treaties*) "were not sufficient to comply with contemporary international human rights norms, principles and standards that govern the determination of indigenous property interests."[193]

In the second opinion, the ILRC assisted the Sumo Indians of Nicaragua in defense of their historical territory against the collusion of the Nicaraguan state and transnational corporate timber interests. The opinion states that Nicaragua violated international human rights standards by allowing the taking of timber in the Sumo territory, over the objections of the indigenous nation. The 2001 case represented a major victory for indigenous peoples.[194]

Other developments, such as indigenous participation in the debates over the Convention on Biological Diversity,[195] World Bank Operational Directive 4.20, and adoption of the Convention on Elimination of All Forms of Racial Discrimination, mark some positive movement on the international stage. Yet questions remain about the vitality of the kind of new, innovative thinking by indigenous scholars that Deloria suggested was necessary in the mid-1970s.

KEEPING INDIGENOUS REVOLUTIONARY CONSCIOUSNESS ALIVE: THE NEXT WAVE

We have to think about the terminology that we use. We must think about thoughts that go with that terminology. . . . Because if we do not think about this struggle we

are engaged in, if we do not use our minds to think about the coming generations,
then [the invaders] will win their psychological genocide against us.

John Trudell, Dakota poet and musician
and former national director of AIM

How are indigenous thinkers heeding Deloria's "warning against making the rhetoric of sovereignty and tradition a final rather than a beginning step"?[196] The generation immediately following the publication of *Broken Treaties* produced a pool of fine scholars and thinkers who continued and extended Deloria's critique of U.S. colonial law toward indigenous peoples. Authors that have been cited repeatedly here[197] have made important contributions in ensuring the vitality and the continuation of a decolonizing discourse for indigenous peoples. Yet simultaneously, theorists and technicians for the statist position were even more prolific in their defense of the status quo.

The logical questions are: Who is on the horizon to elaborate Deloria's critique? What will be the contribution of the next wave of revolutionary thinking? I believe that Deloria would agree with the late critical pedagogist Paolo Freire, who once told his students, "You don't have to follow me. You have to reinvent me." Deloria is interested not in adulation but rather in a succeeding generation taking the fruit of his work and expanding and extending it.

Three particular authors are reflecting the acceptance of Deloria's challenge to lift and extend the critical examination of every aspect of the colonial settler state and to provide important alternatives from an indigenous perspective. Jeanette Armstrong,[198] Robert Porter,[199] and Taiaiake Alfred[200] all give reason for optimism that various segments of indigenous society will be pushed beyond its social and intellectual comfort zones, just as Deloria fulfilled that role in the 1970s and 1980s.

A common thread connecting all three of these authors is their belief in the resilience of indigenous peoples to transcend the individual and collective damage of colonialism. They also construct their work from a foundational knowledge that, prior to the invasion of the Americas by Europeans, vibrant indigenous political traditions flourished within indigenous nations and confederacies, as well as in collective relationship to one another. Armstrong, Porter, and Alfred face a difficult task in educating settler-state political and educational actors that preinvasion indigenous political traditions were more complex than settler-state mythology suggests and were constituted of more than a "big chief" dictating pronouncements from on high. The authors face an even greater challenge in reversing the pervasive collective amnesia that is often present among indigenous peoples about their own history. Porter refers to this phenomenon as "colonization amnesia"; it is a phenomenon resulting in "little understanding amongst Indigenous peoples today of how colonialism has generated the radical transformation of Indigenous life over the past 200 years,"[201] born of a process "that strips the colonized people of their ability to generate their own history."[202]

Porter describes the antidote to colonization amnesia as the "Path of Indigenization," a seven-point strategy that is premised on the conclusion that all indigenous peoples have been adversely "socially engineered" by the colonial process.[203] All indigenous peoples in colonial contexts who are interested in a modicum of genuine self-determination must therefore recapture and refocus their indigenous consciousness "so that they can dedicate their life energies towards the survival of their indigenous societies."[204] Although his specific prescriptive solutions could benefit from elaboration, particularly as he envisions the application of his design from individual to collective consciousness-raising and translation into praxis,[205] his challenge to the colonizing process is valuable. Alfred engages in a similar discussion under the heading of "self-conscious traditionalism" which is somewhat more comprehensive than Porter's, in that it speaks in terms of a "process of decolonization [that] is personal as well as public" and is outlined in eight points that speak to a reconnection to community through, among other things, greater communication, respect, consensus building, and improved self-image through cultural and ceremonial renewal.[206]

Central to Porter's approach, and found equally in Armstrong and Alfred, is the orientation of a liberatory strategy springing from an indigenous understanding of place, and the ability to describe reality through indigenous language. Armstrong explains that "the Okanagan word for 'our place on the land' and 'our language' are the same."[207] Alfred discusses justice from an indigenous perspective as "the imperative of respectful, balanced coexistence among all human, animal, and spirit beings, together with the earth. Justice is seen as that crucial balance and demonstrating true respect for the power and dignity of each part of the circle of interdependency."[208]

Lest those who have yet to read these three powerful voices of indigenous liberation would assume that they gravitate toward lightweight, multicultural pap, make no mistake that their discussion of human harmony and balance with the environment is coupled with the most relentless and unapologetic attack on the forces of colonialism from the settler state. In particular, Alfred provides extremely timely and important extensions of Deloria's earlier writing and is courageous enough to challenge one of the most sacrosanct terms that has been internalized from the colonial political tradition: *sovereignty.*

As mentioned earlier,[209] use of the term *sovereignty* was an important political device in the 1970s to raise the consciousness of indigenous communities and to free indigenous leadership from the throes of "domestic dependent" colonial psychology. In its time, the term *sovereignty* was a critical tool that enabled indigenous activists to imagine a liberated existence beyond the Indian Reorganization Act or the BIA. At the time, no one much considered the philosophical or political origins of the notion of sovereignty, nor the inconsistency between definitions of European sovereignty and our own indigenous political traditions. On the contrary, AIM, Deloria, and other scholars attempted to contort the status of indigenous nations to conform with international legal criteria of statehood.[210] Alfred has exposed the futile nature of this exercise by revealing that "the common criteria of statehood—coercive force, control of territory, population numbers, international recognition—come to dominate discussion of indigenous peoples' political goals as well."[211]

Fortunately, in recent years, a critique of the entire notion of the state has emerged, including in the context of the rights of indigenous peoples. In forums such as the Working Group on Indigenous Peoples, indigenous delegates openly question whether the ultimate expression of self-determination for indigenous peoples should be to emulate states.[212] In the context of American Indian nations, the uncritical embrace of the term *sovereignty* provokes immediate and virulent reaction from indigenous people who have come to equate sovereignty with freedom and self-determination for indigenous nations.

Consistent with Deloria's statement that self-government is not an Indian concept, neither is sovereignty. As Alfred correctly points out, "sovereignty is an exclusionary concept rooted in an adversarial and coercive western notion of power."[213] Sovereignty is a political construct that was first articulated by Jean Bodin,[214] building on the parameters outlined earlier by Nicolo Machiavelli.[215] Thomas Hobbes[216] elaborated on the nature of sovereignty, based on a perception that humans are natural enemies to one another, leading brutish lives defined by selfishness and competition. Central to Bodin's conception of the state, which has its origins in the Peace of Westphalia in 1548, is that the state must be absolute and unitary by its very nature, possessing the ultimate power to command obedience through its monopoly on the "legitimate" use of violence. Similarly, the sovereign must have all the power that can be legitimately possessed, and there must be a single individual in whom the entire power of the state is concentrated. Bodin assumed that stability in the state system required a coercive, hierarchical organization. Similarly, "the power of the law lies in him who has the sovereignty."[217]

Bodin carried a negative view of human nature, as did his successor, Hobbes. Hobbes's most famous work, *Leviathan* (1651), outlined his belief that the exercise of sovereign authority by the state is pragmatically necessary. The force of law, as expressed by John Marshall in *Johnson* and *Cherokee Nation*, has its roots in Bodin and Hobbes. Hobbes wrote that the purpose of the state is to control the inherently bad nature of people in order to prevent a war of all against all. Consequently, the state consists of a system of organized coercive power. One commentator has written that "Bodin constructed sovereignty as the power to make law, but Hobbes treated it as the power to coerce, by law and in accordance with law, or without law and in disregard of it."[218] Machiavelli laid the foundation for the works of Bodin and Hobbes, clearly rationalizing the idea of calculated political behavior by political elites toward the end of coercing the obedience of citizens. So the obvious questions are: If the worldview of Machiavelli, Bodin, and Hobbes is the foundation of sovereignty, why should indigenous peoples strive so tenaciously to accept an authoritarian system developed in sixteenth- and seventeenth-century Renaissance Europe? Of what benefit could this political philosophy be to indigenous peoples today?

Alfred's short answer is: none. He writes, "The concept of sovereignty is incompatible with traditional indigenous notions of power. . . . Traditional indigenous nationhood stands in sharp contrast to the dominant understanding of 'the state': [in indigenous political traditions] there is no absolute authority, no coercive enforcement of decisions, no hierarchy, and no separate ruling entity. . . . 'Sovereignty' implies a set of values and objectives in direct opposition to those found in traditional indigenous philosophies."[219]

Alfred consciously and effectively questions the continuing practice of indigenous peoples emulating and becoming identified with the very models of Western political thought that assaulted indigenous nations in the first place. He quotes Boldt and Long, who conclude that by indigenous peoples defaulting to an acceptance of Western political values, indigenous leadership provides an "endorsement of hierarchical authority and a ruling entity [that] constitutes a complete rupture with traditional indigenous principles."[220] Without question, Alfred's, Armstrong's, and Porter's critique of the state system is not targeted exclusively at individual states but rather at the various systems that emanate from statist ideology, including the UN processes. Armstrong describes the "people without hearts"[221] embodied in "large nation-states continuously reconfiguring economic boundaries into a world economic disorder to cater to big business."[222]

All three of these indigenous thinkers appreciate the pervasive entrenchment of statist ideology in international relations and the unwillingness of statist actors to acknowledge the legitimacy of indigenous alternatives to a hierarchical global ideology. Alfred acknowledges that states "will not easily release [their] grip on control-power and accept the alternative of [indigenous] knowledge-power."223 The battle over one single letter (the *s* on *peoples* versus the singular *people* in the Draft Declaration) is emblematic of the ongoing "intellectual violence done to indigenous peoples through the continued denial of their reality in the dominant mythology."224 Some of the battles occurring in international forums, such as the ILO, the UN, and the OAS, between indigenous peoples and states indicate that those states that continue to dictate the terms of debate in the international arena, such as the United States and its allies, are "determined to eliminate the intellectual threat posed by the idea of a politics beyond state sovereignty, and to that end [are] prepared to use terror—including not only physical force but the intellectual violence inherent in state policies."225

Alfred's alternative political strategy is for indigenous peoples to develop a forward-looking vision while recalling their own traditions of honoring "the autonomy of individual conscience, non-coercive authority, and the deep interconnection between human beings and other elements of the creation."226 Neither Alfred, Porter, nor Armstrong should be confused with some stripe of millenarian who hearkens back to a mythical and romantic past and longs for a return to life in a wigwam or chasing down buffalo on the windswept plain. What they do promote, as stated by Alfred, is a new political model "that challenges the destructive and homogenizing force of Western liberalism and free-market capitalism . . . to de-think the concept of sovereignty and replace it with a notion of power that is based on more appropriate premises . . . such as the *Kaienerekowa*"227 (the Rotinohshonni Great Law of Peace) as an indigenous model of a postcolonial alternative to state sovereignty. Although it is certainly not the primary point of any of their analyses, the inevitable consequence of a transformative indigenous strategy is the opportunity for even the successors of the original invaders to embrace a future of justice, humanity, and balance with their environment.228

The importance of the critique and suggestions provided by Alfred, Armstrong, and Porter does not rest in agreeing with every point of their analysis or with their recommendations. Rather, it resides in their willingness to take the necessary risks to challenge colonialism against indigenous peoples and nations, even in the face of opposition and resistance to their critique by other indigenous people. They have taken seriously Deloria's "warning against making the rhetoric of sovereignty and tradition a final rather than a beginning step."229 Alfred reinforces Deloria's call for a new generation of indigenous philosophical and strategic innovation on the road to self-determination by recognizing Deloria's warning "against the sort of simplistic thinking that puts tradition on a pedestal and refuses to recognize the changes that have taken place in response to colonization . . . that simple reimmersion in tradition is useless without conscious reflection on how traditional teachings can be applied to the contemporary crisis."[230]

Alfred's interpretation of Deloria's balanced model of applying core traditional indigenous values that do not rely on a Western system of compartmentalization is insightful. He recalls Deloria's point that in traditional indigenous societies, law and politics and spirituality and culture were not separate, specialized spheres of knowledge, understanding, and praxis but were intimately interconnected and described as a way of life, or "our way of doing things."[231] Alfred applies those lessons in outlining four essential objectives in commencing the process of decolonizing the indigenous national experience in the twenty-first century: structural reform, reintegration of native languages, economic self-sufficiency, and nation-to-nation relations with the state.[232] He then couples this design with four essential principles of action to guide and inspire liberatory action: (1) undermine the intellectual premises of colonialism, (2) act on the moral imperative for change, (3) do not cooperate with colonialism, and (4) resist further injustice.[233] In this crystallization of his manifesto, Alfred provides two critical elements to those who seek a path to freedom from colonial oppression: first, license to think, critique, and act in a principled, revolutionary way; and second, a succinct foundation from which to develop the methods and tactics that best suit the conditions in their own indigenous contexts.

As with Deloria, Alfred's outline is a starting point, not a final destination. It is, however, along with the prescriptions of Armstrong and Porter, reason for optimism that the seeds of intellectual decolonization that Deloria planted in the 1970s have continued to sprout and grow. The future challenge will be to continue to encourage more innovation, more critical inquiry, more principled praxis, and more courageous risk taking in the atmosphere of the also growing ideological, political, and economic environment of "people without hearts," known also as predatory globalization.[234]

NOTES

1. Harvey Arden, *Noble Red Man: Lakota Wisdomkeeper Mathew King* (Hillsboro, Ore.: Beyond Words Publishing, 1994), 82.

2. Vine Deloria, Jr., *Behind the Trail of Broken Treaties: An Indian Declaration of Independence* (1974; reissued, Austin: University of Texas Press, 1985); hereafter, *Broken Treaties*.

3. For a discussion of the growth of American Indian activism in the 1960s and 1970s, see Paul Chaat Smith and Robert Allen Warrior, *Like a Hurricane: The Indian Movement from Alcatraz to Wounded Knee* (New York: New Press, 1996).

4. Richard Kluger, *Simple Justice* (New York: Vintage Books, 1977); Clay-

borne Carson, David G. Garrow, Gerald Gill, Vincent Harding, and Darlene Clark Hine, *The Eyes on the Prize Civil Rights Reader: Documents, Speeches and Firsthand Accounts from the Black Freedom Struggle, 1954–1990* (New York: Penguin Books, 1991).

5. Deloria expressed concern that American Indian activists would emulate some of the tactical mistakes of civil rights organizations, where "activism has been substituted for power itself." He was similarly concerned about the potential acceptance of piecemeal, reformist change that could co-opt the larger, structural confrontation required in the indigenous peoples' rights context. Deloria referred to this process of co-optation as "a quicksand of assimilationist theories which destroy the power of the group to influence its own future." Robert Allen Warrior, *Tribal Secrets: Recovering American Indian Intellectual Traditions* (Minneapolis: University of Minnesota Press, 1995), 90–91, citing Vine Deloria, Jr., *We Talk, You Listen: New Tribes, New Turf* (New York: Macmillan, 1971), 114, 118.

6. David Wallace Adams, *Education for Extinction: American Indians and the Boarding School Experience, 1875–1928* (Lawrence: University Press of Kansas, 1995).

7. On the creation of a relationship of economic dependency between the United States and indigenous peoples, see Angie Debo, *And Still the Waters Run: The Betrayal of the Five Civilized Tribes* (Princeton, N.J.: Princeton University Press, 1940); Donald Fixico, *The Invasion of Indian Country in the 20th Century: American Capitalism and Tribal Natural Resources* (Boulder: University of Colorado Press, 1998); H. Craig Miner, *The Corporation and the Indian: Tribal Sovereignty and Industrial Civilization in Indian Territory, 1865–1907* (Columbia: University of Missouri Press, 1976); Roxanne Dunbar Ortiz, *Economic Development in American Indian Reservations* (Albuquerque: Native American Studies, University of New Mexico, 1979).

8. On the insidious design of the U.S. government's relocation and termination policies, see Richard Drinnon, *Keeper of the Concentration Camps: Dillon S. Meyer and American Racism* (Berkeley: University of California Press, 1987), 163–269; see also Donald Fixico, *Termination and Relocation: Federal Indian Policy, 1945–1960* (Albuquerque: University of New Mexico Press, 1986).

9. Russell Means, one of the original leaders of the American Indian Movement (AIM), recounts a 1970 meeting of the National Congress of American Indians (NCAI), the largest organization of tribal government officials recognized by the United States. One of the NCAI officials derided AIM and the notion of sovereignty that was printed on an "AIM for Sovereignty" bumper sticker. "'Here's what we think of AIM and their sove-rain-itty,' and he cut up the bumper sticker with scissors. He got a wild ovation from hundreds of tribal officials." Russell Means, *Where White Men Fear to Tread: The Autobiography of Russell Means* (New York: St. Martin's Press, 1995), 165.

10. Vine Deloria, Jr., *Custer Died for Your Sins: An Indian Manifesto* (New York: Avon Books, 1969); Deloria, *We Talk, You Listen.*

11. Smith and Warrior, *Like a Hurricane*, 81–82; Wilma Mankiller, *Mankiller: A Chief and Her People* (New York: St. Martin's Press, 1993), 191; Adam Fortunate Eagle and Tim Findley, *Heart of the Rock: The Indian Invasion of Alcatraz* (Norman: University of Oklahoma Press, 2002); Troy Johnson, *We Hold the Rock: The Indian Occupation of Alcatraz, 1969–1971* (San Francisco: Golden Gate National Parks Association, 1997). Mankiller (191) wrote, "Vine Deloria, Jr., the Sioux who wrote the book which became our manifesto, *Custer Died for Your Sins*, was a visitor [to Alcatraz]."

12. The initial funding for the institute came from royalties for *Custer Died for Your Sins*. "A Letter from the Publisher," *American Indian Journal*, vol. 7, no. 1 (January 1981), 2.

13. Kickingbird coauthored (with Karen Ducheneaux) an important analysis of indigenous territorial dispossession entitled *One Hundred Million Acres* (New York: Macmillan Press, 1973). In what some have viewed as a contradiction, he went on to serve as a member of the U.S. government delegation to the International Labor Organization revision of Convention 107 and has served on other U.S. government delegations in international forums discussing indigenous peoples' rights. He is now a professor at Oklahoma City University School of Law.

14. Coulter left the institute and founded the Indian Law Resource Center (ILRC) in 1978 in Washington, D.C. ILRC has consultative status as a nongovernmental organization at the United Nations and has been involved for many years in the development of the Draft Declaration on the Rights of Indigenous Peoples. Coulter, who continues as ILRC's president, was instrumental in organizing the 1977 United Nations Conference on Discrimination against the Indigenous Peoples of the Americas. Coulter also published (among several other important works) a seminal article describing one rationale for indigenous peoples seeking redress in international forums: "The Denial of Legal Remedies to Indian Nations under U.S. Law," *American Indian Journal*, vol. 3, no. 9 (September 1977), 5.

15. Scores of other indigenous and nonindigenous scholars and activists have acknowledged the writings and speeches of Vine Deloria, Jr., as an integral component in their intellectual, political, and cultural development, including Taiaiake Alfred, S. James Anaya, Duane Champagne, Ward Churchill, Winona Laduke, Wilma Mankiller, Russell Means, Robert Porter, Tink Tinker, Sharon Venne, Robert Allen Warrior, Robert Williams, Jr., David Wilkins, and virtually every student or teacher of American Indian policy and law in the United States and Canada today.

16. The occupation of the BIA has been discussed extensively. Deloria, *Broken Treaties*, 43–62; Smith and Warrior, *Like a Hurricane*, 149–68; Means, *Where White Men Fear*, 222–35; Robert Burnette and John Koster, *The Road to Wounded Knee* (New York: Bantam Books, 1974), 195–219; Rex Weyler, *Blood of the Land: The Government and Corporate War against the American Indian Movement* (New York: Everest House, 1982), 35–57.

17. Similarly, Wounded Knee II (Wounded Knee I being the original massacre of Lakotas by the U.S. 7th Cavalry in 1890) has been described as the most catalytic event in contemporary U.S.-Indian relations. See Deloria, *Broken Treaties*, 63–83; Smith and Warrior, *Like a Hurricane*, 194–268; Means, *Where White Men Fear*, 258–310. The essential demands from the Trail of Broken Treaties and the siege at Wounded Knee can be found in *Chronicles of American Indian Protest* (New York: Council on Interracial Books for Children, 1979), 322–39.

18. These "doctrines" are purported to emanate from the so-called Marshall Trilogy (*Johnson v. M'Intosh, Cherokee Nation v. Georgia,* and *Worcester v. Georgia*) and their progeny. For critical assessments of the fabrication of these doctrines, see David Wilkins, *American Indian Sovereignty and the U.S. Supreme Court: The Masking of Justice* (Austin: University of Texas Press, 1997); Jill Norgren, *The Cherokee Cases: The Confrontation of Law and Politics* (New York: McGraw-Hill, 1996); Sidney Harring, *Crow Dog's Case: American Indian Sovereignty, Tribal Law, and United States Law in the Nineteenth Century* (New York: Cambridge University Press, 1994); Robert A. Williams, Jr., *The American Indian in Western Legal Thought: The Discourses of Conquest* (New York: Oxford University Press, 1990), 308–23. The

construction of legal semantic sleights of hand for the purpose of colonizing indigenous peoples is discussed in detail later.

19. John Prados, *The President's Secret Wars: CIA and Pentagon Covert Operations from World War II through the Persian Gulf* (Chicago: I. R. Dee, 1996); Jonathan Kitney, *Endless Enemies: The Making of an Unfriendly World* (New York: Congdon and Weed, 1984); Noam Chomsky, *Year 501: The Conquest Continues* (Boston: South End Press, 1993); William Blum, *Rogue State: A Guide to the World's Only Superpower* (Monroe, Me.: Common Courage Press, 2000), 125–67.

20. Antonio Cassese, *Self-Determination of Peoples: A Legal Reappraisal* (Cambridge: Cambridge University Press, 1995), 13–23; Umozurike O. Umozurike, *Self-Determination in International Law* (Hamden, Conn.: Archon Books, 1972), 11–26, 161–68; Walker Connor, *The National Question in Marxist-Leninist Theory and Strategy* (Princeton, N.J.: Princeton University Press, 1984), 28–42.

21. Patrick Brogan, *The Fighting Never Stopped: A Comprehensive Guide to World Conflict since 1945* (New York: Vintage, 1990).

22. Catherine J. Iorns, "Indigenous Peoples and Self-Determination: Challenging State Sovereignty," *Case Western Reserve Journal of International Law*, vol. 24 (1992), 165, 251.

23. Williams, *American Indian in Western Legal Thought*, 325.

24. Deloria, *Custer Died for Your Sins*, 270.

25. Deloria, *Broken Treaties*, 20.

26. Warrior, *Tribal Secrets*, 95.

27. Ibid., 97.

28. Ibid.

29. Wilkins, *American Indian Sovereignty and the Supreme Court*, 1.

30. Robert A. Williams, Jr., "Pre-Encounter Indigenous Diplomacy," in *Linking Arms Together: American Indian Treaty Visions of Law and Peace, 1600–1800* (New York: Routledge, 1999), 32–34.

31. Howard Berman, "Perspectives on American Indian Sovereignty and International Law, 1600–1776," in *Exiled in the Land of the Free: Democracy, Indian Nations and the U.S. Constitution* (Santa Fe, N.M.: Clear Light Publishers, 1992), 126–88.

32. Williams, *Linking Arms Together*, 12.

33. Douglas Sanders, "The Re-emergence of Indigenous Questions in International Law," *Canadian Human Rights Yearbook*, no. 3 (1983), 13. Maori and Rotinoshonni (Iroquois) delegations were rebuffed in their petitions for recognition at the League of Nations in the 1920s, but their assertion of their rights as indigenous peoples served as inspiration for later generations. This was especially the case for Deskaheh, a Cayuga speaker for the Council of the Iroquois Confederacy, who spent two years advancing the case for self-determination for the Rotinoshonni. Akwesasne Notes, *A Basic Call to Consciousness* (Summertown, Tenn.: Book Publishing Co., 1978), 19–35.

34. A critical mass of events converged in the years 1970–1974 that infused energy into the international indigenous peoples movement. Already mentioned was the series of confrontations in the United States beginning with Alcatraz and culminating with the siege at Wounded Knee in 1973. In addition to the publication of *Broken Treaties* in 1974, the First International Indian Treaty Conference was held on the Standing Rock Indian Reservation in North Dakota. The conference issued a document entitled the "Declaration of Continuing Independence," which asserted the international personality of American Indian nations and mandated the establishment of an indigenous presence at the United Nations.

AIM leader Russell Means established the offices of the International Indian Treaty Council, which received consultative status as a nongovernmental organization at the UN in 1977. Since that time, twelve other indigenous organizations have received NGO status, but scores of other indigenous organizations participate at UN meetings on a regular basis.

35. For example, considerable efforts have been expended by indigenous peoples at the International Labor Organization (ILO) and at the Inter-American Commission for Human Rights, a subunit of the Organization of American States (OAS).

36. See S. James Anaya, *Indigenous Peoples in International Law* (New York: Oxford University Press, 1996), 39–71; Maivan Clech-Lam, *At the Edge of the State: Indigenous Peoples and Self-Determination* (Ardsley, N.Y.: Transnational Publishers, 2000); Sharon Helen Venne, *Our Elders Understand Our Rights: Evolving International Law Regarding Indigenous Rights* (Penticon, B.C.: Theytus Books, 1998); Franke Wilmer, *The Indigenous Voice in World Politics: Since Time Immemorial* (Newbury Park, Calif.: Sage Publications, 1993), 162–210; Roxanne Dunbar Ortiz, *Indians of the Americas: Human Rights and Self-Determination* (London: Zed Books, 1984), 29–72; Siegfried Wiessner, "Rights and Status of Indigenous Peoples: A Global Comparative and International Legal Analysis," *Harvard Human Rights Journal,* vol. 12 (spring 1999), 56–128; Iorns, "Indigenous Peoples and Self-Determination"; Robert A. Williams, Jr., "Encounters on the Frontiers of International Human Rights Law: Redefining the Terms of Indigenous Peoples' Survival in the World," *Duke Law Journal* (September 1990), 660.

37. Two of the most important indigenous scholars in continuing and extending Deloria's fundamental challenge to colonizer semantics in law and politics, in my opinion, are Robert A. Williams, Jr., and David Wilkins. Concerning the refinement and elaboration of Deloria's discussion of the application of the UN Genocide Convention to the Americas, Ward Churchill's contributions are unrivaled. See Ward Churchill, *A Little Matter of Genocide: Holocaust and Denial in the Americas, 1492 to the Present* (San Francisco: City Lights Books, 1998).

38. David Stannard, *American Holocaust: Columbus and the Conquest of the New World* (New York: Oxford University Press, 1992), x. Of course, Nebrija's actions were not the sole impetus for or cause of genocide against indigenous peoples, but as Illich points out, Nebrija's *Gramatica* intentionally issued "the declaration of war against subsistence [read, in part, indigenous peoples] which the new state was organizing to fight." Ivan Illich, *Shadow Work* (Boston and London: Marion Boyars, 1981), 51. Stannard's book deals exclusively with the genocide against indigenous peoples in the Americas, but the genocide by Europeans against other indigenous peoples was equally widespread and devastating. Kanaka Maoli (Native Hawaiians) suffered at least a 90 percent demographic destruction (Stannard, *American Holocaust,* 244). In Australia, the Aborigine population experienced a 97 percent population collapse, with the Tasmanian population virtually exterminated. Mark Crocker, *Rivers of Blood, Rivers of Gold: Europe's Conflict with Tribal Peoples* (London: Jonathan Cape, 1998), 115–84. A similar fate befell the Maori of Aotearoa (New Zealand) and other indigenous nations of the Pacific (Crocker, 178–81). In Africa, it is estimated that in the Congo alone, 10 million indigenous people were destroyed at the hands of Belgian colonizers in a scant forty years. Adam Hochschild, *King Leopold's Ghost: A Story of Greed, Terror and Heroism in Colonial Africa* (New York: Houghton Mifflin, 1998), 223.

39. The continuing, horrific experiences of indigenous peoples at the hands of settler states and neocolonial powers are recounted on an annual basis at the

United Nations Working Group on Indigenous Populations in Geneva, Switzerland. See, e.g., *Report of the Working Group on Indigenous Populations on Its Seventeenth Session*, E/CN.4/Sub.2/1999/19, 12 August 1999.

40. "Grammars were not new. The most perfect of them, unknown to Nebrija, was already two thousand years old—Panini's grammar of Sanskrit." Illich, *Shadow Work*, 35. According to Hanke, however, this was the first grammatica of a modern European language. Lewis Hanke, *Aristotle and the American Indians: A Study in Race Prejudice in the Modern World* (Bloomington: Indiana University Press, 1959), 8.

41. The term *Christian Europeans* is used deliberately throughout this discussion to expose the secular revisionism that has taken place in colonizer law, especially in the United States. The legal and political justifications for the dispossession of indigenous peoples in the Americas were explicitly ordained through Christian doctrine, as mentioned by Chief Justice John Marshall in *Johnson v. M'Intosh*, discussed later. For a detailed discussion of the Christian underpinnings of federal Indian law, see Steve Newcomb, "The Evidence of Christian Nationalism in Federal Indian Law: The Doctrine of Discovery, *Johnson v. M'Intosh*, and Plenary Power." *Review of Law and Social Change*, vol. 20 (1993), 303.

42. Illich, *Shadow Work*, 34.

43. Hanke, *Aristotle and the American Indians*, 8; Williams, *American Indian in Western Legal Thought*, 74, citing J. Trend, *The Civilization of Spain* (1944), 88.

44. Illich, *Shadow Work*, 43–44.

45. Ibid., 47. The long-term impact of Nebrija's work is described by Illich: "his important innovation was to lay the foundation for a linguistic ideal without precedent: the creation of a society in which the universal ruler's bureaucrats, soldiers, merchants and peasants all pretend to speak one language, a language the poor [and the colonized] are presumed to understand and obey. . . . Isabella's claim to historical fame depends on forging a language of propaganda . . . capable of penetrating every village and farm, to reduce subjects into modern citizens."

46. Ibid., 49; emphasis added.

47. The more complete quote by the U.S. secretary of state was: "The United States is the only superpower. We have responsibilities as such. . . . We are the United States, and we are the indispensable power." Interview of Secretary of State Madeleine Albright on ABC-TV *Nightline* with Ted Koppel, 18 February 1998; the transcript can be found at www.usembassy-israel.org.il/publish/armscontrol/archive/1998/february/aco0220d.html.

48. Official U.S. Indian policy in the nineteenth and twentieth centuries sought to destroy indigenous languages and replace them with English. The sentiment found in the 1887 annual report of the U.S. Commissioner of Indian Affairs could have been taken directly from Nebrija: "The impracticability, if not impossibility, of civilizing the Indians of this country in any other tongue other than our own would seem to be obvious. . . . Teaching an Indian youth in his own barbarous dialect is a positive detriment to him. The first step to be taken toward civilization . . . is to teach them the English language." *Annual Report of the Commissioner of Indian Affairs*, 21 September 1887, reprinted in Francis Paul Prucha, ed., *Document of United States Indian Policy* (Lincoln: University of Nebraska Press, 1990), 176.

Two years later, U.S. Indian Commissioner Thomas J. Morgan made the intent of the destruction of indigenous languages clear: "The Indian must conform to the 'white man's ways,' peaceably if they will, forcibly if they must. . . . They cannot escape it, and must either conform or be crushed by it. . . . Education is the Indian's only salvation. . . . Especial attention should be directed toward giving them a ready command of the English language. To this end, only English should be allowed to be spoken, and only English-speaking teachers should be employed in schools supported wholly or in part by the Government." Prucha, *Document*, 177–79.

49. Despite Columbus's erroneous conclusions regarding his location and the nature of the peoples he encountered, he followed preordained legalistic procedures in documenting and attempting to seize new territories and resources. See Williams, *American Indian in Western Legal Thought*, 81–83; Robert A. Williams, Jr., "Columbus' Legacy: Law as an Instrument of Racial Discrimination against Indigenous Peoples' Rights of Self-Determination," *Arizona Journal of International and Comparative Law*, vol. 8, no. 2 (1991), 51, 63–67.

50. Steven Greenblatt, *Marvelous Possessions: The Wonder of the New World* (Chicago: University of Chicago Press, 1991), 58.

51. Patricia Seed, "Taking Possession and Reading Texts: Establishing the Authority of Overseas Empires," *William and Mary Quarterly*, vol. 49, no. 2 (1992), 199.

52. Tzvetan Todorov, *The Conquest of America: The Question of the Other* (New York: HarperPerennial, 1984), 27. See notes 145–172 and the accompanying text for contemporary examples of this practice.

53. Bartolomé de Las Casas, *The Devastation of the Indies: A Brief Account*, trans. Herman Briffault (Baltimore: Johns Hopkins University Press, 1992); George E. Tinker, *Missionary Conquest: The Gospel and Native American Cultural Genocide* (Minneapolis: Fortress Press, 1993); Gerard Colby with Charlotte Dennett, *Thy Will Be Done, the Conquest of the Amazon: Nelson Rockefeller and Evangelism in the Age of Oil* (New York: HarperCollins, 1995).

54. "Theories of American historiography . . . exclude Amerindians from participation, except as foils for Europeans, and thus assume that American civilization was formed by Europeans in a struggle against savagery or barbarism of the nonwhite races." Francis Jennings, *The Invasion of America: Indians, Colonialism, and the Cant of Conquest* (New York: W. W. Norton, 1975), 327–28; Michel-Rolph Rouillot, *Silencing the Past: Power and the Production of History* (Boston: Beacon Press, 1995); James W. Loewen, *Lies My Teacher Told Me: Everything Your American History Textbook Got Wrong* (New York: New Press, 1995), 90–129.

55. Williams, *American Indian in Western Legal Thought*; Wilkins, *American Indian Sovereignty and the Supreme Court*; Harring, *Crow Dog's Case*.

56. Reginald Horsman, *Race and Manifest Destiny: The Origins of American Racial Anglo-Saxonism* (Cambridge: Harvard University Press, 1981); Richard Drinnon, *Facing West: The Metaphysics of Indian-Hating and Empire-Building* (Minneapolis: University of Minnesota Press, 1980); Vine Deloria, Jr., ed., *American Indian Policy in the Twentieth Century* (Norman: University of Oklahoma Press, 1985); Debo, *And Still the Waters Run*.

57. Winona Laduke, *All Our Relations: Native Struggles for Land and Life* (Boston: South End Press, 1999); Jerry Mander, *In the Absence of the Sacred: The Failure of Technology and the Survival of the Indian Nations* (San Francisco: Sierra Club Books, 1990); H. Craig Miner, *The Corporation and the American Indian: Tribal Sovereignty and Industrial Civilization in Indian Territory, 1865–1907* (Norman: University of Oklahoma Press, 1989).

58. Vine Deloria, Jr., *Red Earth, White Lies: Native Americans and the Myth of Scientific Fact* (New York: Scribner, 1995).

59. Shari M. Huhndorf, *Going Native: Indians in the American Cultural Imagination* (Ithaca, N.Y.: Cornell University Press, 2001); Duane Champagne, *Contem-*

porary Native American Cultural Issues (Walnut Creek, Calif.: AltaMira Press, 1999); Susan Scheckel, *The Insistence of the Indian: Race and Nationalism in Nineteenth-Century American Culture* (Princeton, N.J.: Princeton University Press, 1998); Ward Churchill, *Indians Are Us? Culture and Genocide in Native North America* (Monroe, Me.: Common Courage Press, 1994).

60. Among them Bartolomé de Las Casas, Antonio de Montesinos, and Franciscus de Victoria. See Glenn T. Morris, "In Support of the Right of Self-Determination for Indigenous Peoples under International Law," *German Yearbook of International Law,* vol. 29 (1986), 277, 280–88, and accompanying notes.

61. Catharine A. MacKinnon, *Only Words* (Cambridge: Harvard University Press, 1993), 1, 6.

62. Catharine A. MacKinnon, *Feminism Unmodified: Discourses on Life and Law* (Cambridge: Harvard University Press, 1987), 9.

63. Cited in Lewis Hanke, ed., *History of Latin American Civilization: Sources and Interpretations,* vol. 1 (Boston: Little, Brown, 1967), 149.

64. Stannard reports credible population estimates for the island of Hispaniola (Haiti, Dominican Republic) of 3 million to 8 million in 1492 . The official census of the island in 1514 listed 22,000 adult Indians. In 1542 Bartolomé de Las Casas reported a Taino population of only 200, based on his eyewitness examination. Stannard, *American Holocaust,* 266–67. "The two leading researchers here, Sherburne Cook and Woodrow Borah of the University of California at Berkeley, have calculated a population decline [on the island of Hispaniola] after 1496 . . . with an estimate of the original island population of just under 8 million. [The population declined] from 8 million to 28,000 in just over twenty years. That is a carnage of more than 99 percent." Kirkpatrick Sale, *The Conquest of Paradise: Christopher Columbus and the Columbia Legacy* (New York: Plume, 1990), 160–61.

65. Francisco de Solano, *Documentos Sobre Politica Linguistica en Hispanoamerica (1492–1800)* (Madrid: Consejo Superior de Investigaciones Cientificas, 1991), 72, cited in Zhenja La Rosa, "Language and Empire: The Vision of Nebrija," *Student Historical Journal,* Loyola University, 1995–1996.

66. Walter Mignolo, "On the Colonization of Amerindian Languages and Memories: Renaissance Theories of Writing and the Discontinuity of the Classical Tradition," *Comparative Studies in Sociology and History,* vol. 34, no. 2 (1992), 48.

67. Sale, *Conquest of Paradise,* 133.

68. For a discussion of the marginalization of the "other" in U.S. law, see Natsu Taylor Saito, "Asserting Plenary Power over the 'Other': Indians, Immigrants, Colonial Subjects and Why U.S. Jurisprudence Needs to Incorporate International Law," *Yale Law and Policy Review,* vol. 20, no. 2 (2002), 427.

69. Williams, *American Indian in Western Legal Thought,* 62–67.

70. Ibid., 65.

71. Ibid., 67.

72. One perspective that suggests extensive fabrication is Peter Hassler, "The Lies of the Conquistadors: Cutting through the Myth of Human Sacrifice," *World Press Review* (December 1992), 28–29, and Peter Hassler, *Human Sacrifice among the Aztecs? A Critical Study* (Bern: Peter Lang, 1992).

73. Williams, *American Indian in Western Legal Thought,* 196. Perhaps the three most egregious violations of natural law were cannibalism, human sacrifice, and bestiality. Not surprisingly, all were used regularly as grounds to wage "just wars" throughout the Americas.

74. The transparent motives for these practices were exposed by journalist T. D. Allman: "[Indians] were not human beings; they were only obstacles to the

inexorable triumph of American [i.e., Anglo-Saxon] virtue, who must be swept away to make room for a new reality of American freedom. Our own solemnly proclaimed rights to life, liberty and the pursuit of happiness totally superseded the rights of the peoples whose life, liberty and happiness we were expunging from the face of the earth." Quoted in Noam Chomsky, *The Chomsky Reader*, ed. James Peck (New York: Pantheon, 1987), 123. The methods by which the initial racist assumptions about indigenous peoples have been reinforced over time, to become enshrined in the fabric of contemporary legal and political doctrines, are described by Deloria in his discussion of indigenous peoples' origins in the Americas. Deloria exposes a mind-set in which "scholars and scientists are wedded to an outmoded framework of interpretation and spend their time arranging facts and evidence to fit these old ideas." These scholars seem unable "to see more than one explanation for data or phenomena, and they apparently hold in great disdain all traditions except the one in which they have grown up and received awards." Deloria, *Red Earth, White Lies*, 251.

75. An excellent discussion of the bulls and their subsequent legacy in the U.S. law affecting indigenous peoples is provided in Newcomb, "Evidence of Christian Nationalism." There is ongoing debate about the legal effect of the papal donations. See Franciscus de Victoria, "On the Indians Lately Discovered," in *Classics of International Law*, ed. James Brown Scott (New York: Ocean Publications, 1964). As early as 1542, Victoria (widely viewed as the father of modern international law) concluded that the emperor was not entitled "to seize the provinces of the Indian aborigines," and "the Pope has no temporal authority over the Indian aborigines" (129). Bartolomé de Las Casas, *In Defense of the Indians*, trans. Stafford Poole (DeKalb: Northern Illinois University Press, 1974), 353–62. Williams, *American Indian in Western Legal Thought*, 74–81.

76. Las Casas, *Devastation of the Indies*.

77. *Johnson v. M'Intosh*, 21 U.S. (8 Wheat.) 543 (1823).

78. Steve Russell, "Indigenous Peoples: The Jurisprudence of Colonialism," *Legal Studies Forum*, vol. 25 (2001), 605. We know that Marshall's description is an opportunistic fabrication because he knew from personal experience that indigenous peoples were not "fierce savages." Marshall was raised on the "frontier," primarily in sparsely populated Fauquier County, Virginia. Marshall's father served as a surveyor and advance man for frontier land speculators like George Washington. Marshall's perspective on Indians, unlike his characterizations in *Johnson*, was quite sympathetic, and "his sensitivity to the Indians' cause was heartfelt." Jean Edward Smith, *John Marshall: Definer of a Nation* (New York: Henry Holt, 1996), 104, 162–63. Marshall's accurate understanding of indigenous societies, as well as his sympathies, makes his betrayal of Indian peoples that much more troubling. Tim Alan Garrison, *The Legal Ideology of Removal: The Southern Judiciary and the Sovereignty of Native American Nations* (Athens: University of Georgia Press, 2002), 97–102.

79. Felix Cohen, "The Spanish Origins of Indian Rights in the Law of the United States," in *The Legal Conscience: Selected Papers of Felix Cohen*, ed. Lucy Kramer Cohen (New Haven, Conn.: Yale University Press, 1960), 243.

80. "Sixteenth-century Spaniards were thoroughly saturated also with the spirit of legal formalism, and the New World offered many opportunities for the exercise of juridical formalities." Lewis Hanke, *The Spanish Struggle for Justice in the Conquest of America* (Philadelphia: University of Pennsylvania Press, 1949), 6.

81. Williams, *American Indian in Western Legal Thought*, 92. Williams continues: "Law, which Europeans have long revered as their instrument of civilization,

became the West's perfect instrument of empire in the heart of darkness that was America" (93).

82. Newcomb, "Evidence of Christian Nationalism," 311 and accompanying notes.

83. Williams, *American Indian in Western Legal Thought*, 200.

84. For a detailed examination of these processes, see ibid., 121–225; Jennings, *Invasion of America*; James Muldoon, "The Indian as Irishman," *Essex Institute Historical Collections*, vol. 11 (1975); Nicholas Canny, "The Ideology of English Colonization: From Ireland to America," *William and Mary Quarterly*, vol. 30 (1973), 575–98.

85. With acknowledgment to Audre Lorde. "The master's tools will never dismantle the master's house. They may allow us temporarily to beat him at his own game, but they will never enable us to bring about genuine change." Audre Lorde, *Sister Outsider: Essays and Speeches by Audre Lorde* (Freedom, Calif.: Crossing Press, 1984), 112.

86. See David Getches, "Beyond Indian Law: The Rehnquist Court's Pursuit of State's Rights, Color-Blind Justice and Mainstream Values," *Minnesota Law Review*, vol. 86 (December 2001), 267. Getches exposes the astounding statistic that, in the past ten terms of the Rehnquist Supreme Court, indigenous interests have lost 82 percent of their cases. Getches concludes that this record of defeat is the worst of any litigant group appearing before the Supreme Court, even worse than that of incarcerated criminals seeking reversal of their convictions (280–81).

87. The process by which critical discourse is stifled in law schools, especially regarding the case of *Johnson v. M'Intosh*, is brilliantly exposed in Matthew L. M. Fletcher, "Listen," *Michigan Journal of Race and Law*, vol. 3 (spring 1998), 523: "The story of *Johnson v. M'Intosh*, the story of conquest, murder, starvation, disease, betrayal, has been laid down before all of us to hear. No reason to go over it again. The lesson has been learned already. It's a real downer. Why dwell on it at eight o'clock in the morning on a freezing January day when there is so much ahead to learn—an almost unimaginable amount of information to master about property in only four months. I can hear students now, agreeing silently with the professor: we already know this story, we have heard it before, let us not waste time. Let's move on. . . . The story was told. It was over. The wheels had been greased over time to make the story move so effortlessly, it made no ripple. No one will argue with it. No discussion. No dissent."

88. Wilkins, *American Indian Sovereignty and the Supreme Court*, 6–10, 297–310.

89. *Johnson v. M'Intosh*, 21 U.S. (8 Wheat.) 543, 591, cited in Deloria, *Broken Treaties*, 102.

90. A couple of noteworthy exceptions to this point are Indian Law Resource Center, "United States Denial of Indian Property Rights: A Study in Lawless Power and Racial Discrimination," in *Rethinking Indian Law* (New York: National Lawyers Guild, 1982), 15–25; Newcomb, "Evidence of Christian Nationalism," and accompanying notes; Williams, *American Indian in Western Legal Thought*, "Principles of federal Indian law set down by Marshall in *Johnson v. M'Intosh* . . . ensured that future acts of genocide would proceed on a rationalized, legal basis" (Williams, 317).

91. Deloria, *Broken Treaties*, 110.

92. Anaya, *Indigenous Peoples in International Law*, 16–17.

93. It is worth noting that the seminal cases of federal Indian law that Deloria criticizes have been exported to other countries, promoting other conflicts

between states and indigenous peoples. Australia: *Cooper v. Stuart*, 14 App. Case 286 (1889); *Milirrpum v. Nabalco*, 17 FLR 141 (1971); *Mabo v. Queensland (No. 2)*, 175 CLR1 (1992). Aotearoa (New Zealand): *Queen v. Symonds*, NZPCC 387 (1847); *Wi Parata v. Bishop of Wellington*, 3 NZ Jurist 72 (1877). Canada: *Calder v. Atty. Gen. for British Columbia*, SCR 313 (1973); *Sparrow v. The Queen*, 1 SCR 1075 (1990); *Guerin v. The Queen*, 2 SCR 335 (1984). Africa: *In re Southern Rhodesia*, [1919] AC 211 (Privy Council).

94. "The United States can offer a working model of how [indigenous peoples'] rights can be recognized and implemented." Observer Delegation of the Government of the United States of America, "Statement to the Working Group on Indigenous Populations," United Nations, Geneva, Switzerland, 26 July 1994.

95. Wilkins, *American Indian Sovereignty and the Supreme Court*, 34.

96. Ibid., 299.

97. Eric Kades, "The Dark Side of Efficiency: *Johnson v. M'Intosh* and the Expropriation of American Indian Lands," *University of Pennsylvania Law Review*, vol. 148 (April 2000), 1065, 1092; Eric Kades, "History and Interpretation of the Great Case of *Johnson v. M'Intosh*," *Law and History Review*, vol. 19, no. 1 (2001), 67.

98. Kades, "Dark Side," 1071.

99. Ibid., 1095.

100. Ibid., 1105.

101. Justice Story, who originally joined Marshall's unanimous decision in *Johnson*, later concluded that the case violated both "natural law and moral right." R. Kent Newmyer, *Supreme Court Justice Joseph Story: Statesman of the Old Republic* (Chapel Hill: University of North Carolina Press, 1985), 213.

102. Alexis de Tocqueville, *Democracy in America* (New York: Alfred A. Knopf, 1945), 355.

103. "Comparison of Federally Owned Land with Total Acreage of State, Fiscal Year 1998," U.S. General Services Administration, Washington, D.C. Total acreage, including Alaska and Hawaii, is 2.27 billion acres.

104. *Reply of the United States to Questions from the UN Committee on the Elimination of Racial Discrimination*, at http://www.state.gov/g/drl/rls/rm/2001/4486.htm.

105. For a general discussion of these issues, see Helen W. Winston, "An Anomaly Unknown: Supreme Court Application of International Law Norms on Indigenous Rights in the Cherokee Cases (1831–32)," *Tulsa Journal of Comparative and International Law*, vol. 1 (1994), 339; Philip P. Frickey, "Marshalling Past and Present: Colonialism, Constitutionalism and Interpretation in Federal Indian Law," *Harvard Law Review*, vol. 107 (1993), 381; G. Edward White, *The Marshall Court and Culture Change* (New York: Oxford University Press, 1991); Joseph C. Burke, "The Cherokee Cases: A Study in Law, Politics and Morality," *Stanford Law Review*, vol. 21 (February 1969), 500–31.

106. Norgren, *The Cherokee Cases*, 105.

107. *Fletcher v. Peck*, 10 U.S. (6 Cranch) 87 (1810). Regarding a discussion of the fraud perpetrated by the Georgia state legislature to extinguish Indian title, later upheld by John Marshall in *Fletcher*, see C. Peer Magrath, *Yazoo: Law and Politics in the New Republic* (Providence, R.I.: Brown University Press, 1966).

108. Norgren, *The Cherokee Cases*, 89.

109. "The Court drew selectively on existing Western legal traditions to create a federal Indian law that was consonant with many of the political and economic goals of the United States. Where it served the Court's purposes, its members built a case on familiar rules. But where this approach worked against

the interests of the United States, the judges rejected or manipulated older legal traditions, arguing that the United States was a new nation and that such rules were foreign to it" (ibid., 8). "Using complex, obfuscating and sometimes incorrect interpretations of history and treaties as well as English and international law, the Court attempted to forge a compromise that would permit the United States to view itself as a nation under rule of law while continuing its quest to control the continent. . . . According to law, it appeared that the United States had little basis for its claims" (ibid., 6).

110. Cited in Burke, "The Cherokee Cases," 511.

111. Ibid.

112. Ibid., 530.

113. *Cherokee Nation v. Georgia,* 30 U.S. (5 Pet.) 1, 17 (1832).

114. Deloria specifically discusses the independent political status of the Comanches and Wichitas into the mid-nineteenth century: "There was no acknowledgement by the Comanches that they recognized the United States as their sovereign. . . . Far from being subservient to either the United States or Mexico, the Comanches and Wichitas held control over a vast area into which neither Americans nor Mexicans strayed without permission" (*Broken Treaties,* 133).

115. Ibid., 138.

116. Roxanne Dunbar Ortiz, *The Great Sioux Nation: Sitting in Judgment on America. An Oral History of the Sioux Nation and Its Struggle for Sovereignty* (San Francisco: Moon Books, 1977), 141.

117. See note 88 and accompanying text.

118. Robert T. Coulter, "A History of Indian Jurisdiction," in *Rethinking Indian Law* (New York: Committee on Native American Struggles of the National Lawyers' Guild, 1982), 8.

119. 31 U.S. (6 Pet.) 515 (1832). Time and space do not permit an adequate discussion of the important issues of *Worcester* here, other than to observe, as have others, that *Worcester* seems to be a kind of apologia by Marshall for his other "Indian" opinions in *Fletcher, Johnson,* and *Cherokee Nation.* Although consumed by what he repeatedly called "the actual state of things" (i.e., nineteenth century realpolitik), Marshall acknowledged that "Indian nations had always been considered as distinct, independent political communities, retaining their original natural rights. . . . The words 'treaty' and 'nation' are words of our own language. . . . We have applied them to the Indians, as we have applied them to the other nations of the earth" (ibid., 559). With this language, written in ill health during the last year of his life, Marshall seemed to be opening the door for lawyers for indigenous nations to challenge the assumptions of cases such as *Johnson* and *Cherokee Nation.* Until *Broken Treaties,* no one seemed interested in accepting Marshall's tacit invitation to walk through the door to confront the racism of cases like *Johnson.* After *Broken Treaties,* a disappointing number of lawyers, scholars, and activists have walked through the door held open by Deloria's manifesto.

120. For a more comprehensive discussion of this doctrine, see Wilkins, *American Indian Sovereignty and the Supreme Court,* 64–117; Nell Jessup Newton, "Federal Power over Indians: Its Sources, Scope, and Limitations," *University of Pennsylvania Law Review,* vol. 132 (1984), 195–288; Natsu Taylor Saito, "Asserting Plenary Power over the 'Other': Indians, Immigrants, Colonial Subjects and Why U.S. Jurisprudence Needs to Incorporate International Law," *Yale Law and Policy Review,* vol. 20, no. 2 (2002), 427–80.

121. Wilkins, *American Indian Sovereignty and the Supreme Court,* 372.

122. Ibid.

123. *U.S. v. Kagama*, 118 U.S. 375 (1886). *Kagama* upheld the Major Crimes Act (1885) and recognized the authority of Congress unilaterally to diminish the inherent criminal jurisdiction of indigenous nations.

124. *Lone Wolf v. Hitchcock*, 187 U.S. 553 (1903), recognized the authority of Congress unilaterally to abrogate treaties with indigenous nations, in a conflation of the plenary power and political question doctrines. In *Lone Wolf*, the Court held that Congress "had not only unlimited but unreviewable authority over Indian tribes, their treaties and their properties." Wilkins, *American Indian Sovereignty and the Supreme Court*, 115.

125. Taylor Saito, "Asserting Plenary Power," 429.

126. These issues are discussed in detail in other sources, such as Wilkins, but regarding trust funds, litigation is currently under way to force an accounting by the Department of Interior for between $10 billion and $100 billion in trust funds that have been "lost" or misappropriated since 1887. See Michael J. Kennedy, "Truth and Consequences on the Reservation," *Los Angeles Times*, 16 July 2002.

127. Wilkins, *American Indian Sovereignty and the Supreme Court*, 81.

128. Daniel Farber, William N. Eskridge, Jr., and Philip P. Frickey, *Constitutional Law: Themes for the Constitution's Third Century*, 2nd ed. (St. Paul, Minn.: West Law Group, 1998), 13.

129. *Congressional Record* (1903), 2028, cited in Wilkins, *American Indian Sovereignty and the Supreme Court*, 116.

130. Norgren, *The Cherokee Cases*, 147.

131. Wilkins, *American Indian Sovereignty and the Supreme Court*, 117.

132. Norgren, *The Cherokee Cases*, 152–53.

133. AIM leader Russell Means explained that the seventy-one-day confrontation between AIM and U.S. authorities at Wounded Knee in 1973 "happened because traditional chiefs and holy men of the Oglala people directed and supported our attempt to assert the treaty rights of the Lakota people based on the 1868 Sioux treaty. We did not break any laws, but in fact went into Wounded Knee . . . to force the U.S.A to live up to its own laws." Quoted in *Chronicles of American Indian Protest*, 377.

134. The Trail of Broken Treaties is discussed in chapter 2 of *Broken Treaties* and more extensively in Akwesasne Notes, ed., *B.I.A. I'm Not Your Indian Anymore* (Rooseveltown, N.Y.: Akwesasne Notes, 1973); Smith and Warrior, *Like a Hurricane*.

135. The founding document of the IITC, "The Declaration of Continuing Independence," asserted the sovereignty of indigenous nations and charged the United States with gross violations of international law in the form of treaty violations and human rights abuses. The text can be found in *Chronicles of American Indian Protest*, 339–42. For a chronology of the creation of the IITC and other indigenous NGOs, as well as the general entry of indigenous peoples into the contemporary international arena, see, Weyler, *Blood of the Land*, 212–50; Means, *Where White Men Fear to Tread*, 325–26; Ortiz, *Indians of the Americas*, 32–38; Douglas Sanders, "The UN Working Group on Indigenous Populations," *Human Rights Quarterly*, vol. 11 (1989), 406, 414–19; Sanders, "Re-emergence of Indigenous Questions in International Law," 3.

136. Akwesasne Notes, *Basic Call to Consciousness*, 36–64; Ortiz, *Indians of the Americas*, 29–32.

137. Akwesasne Notes, *Basic Call to Consciousness*, 18–33.

138. One result of the conference was the emergence of the "Declaration of Principles for the Defense of the Indigenous Nations and Peoples of the Western Hemisphere," which stated unambiguously that "Indigenous people shall be accorded recognition as nations and proper subjects of international law." Although similar pronouncements may have become commonplace in the twenty-first century, for its time, the statement represented a revolutionary declaration. The entire document may be found in *Chronicles of American Indian Protest*, 367–71.

139. Robert T. Coulter, "The Denial of Legal Remedies to Indian Nations under U.S. Law," *American Indian Journal*, vol. 3 (September 1977), 5–11; later updated as "United States Denial of Indian Property Rights: A Study in Lawless Power and Racial Discrimination," in *Rethinking Indian Law*, 15–25.

140. Ibid. Reprinted in *Chronicles of American Indian Protest*, 345–46.

141. Ibid.

142. See Robert B. Porter, "Pursuing the Path of Indigenization in the Era of Emergent International Law Governing the Rights of Indigenous Peoples," *Yale Human Rights and Development Law Journal*, vol. 5 (2002), 123; Patrick Cleveland, "Apposition of Recent U.S. Supreme Court Decisions Regarding Tribal Sovereignty and International Indigenous Rights Declarations," *Pace International Law Review*, vol. 12 (fall 2000), 397; Clech-Lam, *At the Edge of the State*; Anaya, *Indigenous Peoples in International Law*, 39–71; Venne, *Our Elders Understand Our Rights*; Wilmer, *The Indigenous Voice in World Politics*, 162–210; Ortiz, *Indians of the Americas*, 29–72; Wiessner, "Rights and Status of Indigenous Peoples"; Irons, "Indigenous Peoples and Self-Determination"; Williams, "Encounters on the Frontiers of International Human Rights Law."

143. The Draft United Nations Declaration on the Rights of Indigenous Peoples is reproduced in the appendix of this book, but it can also be located on the Internet at http://www.indianlaw.org/un_draft_decl.htm.

144. Eduardo Galeano, *We Say No: Chronicles 1963–1991* (New York: W. W. Norton, 1992), 241–44.

145. The importance of the terms *peoples* and *self-determination* is discussed below, but the international right of all peoples to self-determination is found in the United Nations Charter and the UN Human Rights Covenants. The substance of the right to self-determination was elaborated in *General Assembly Resolution 2625*, also known as the *Declaration on Friendly Relations and Cooperation among States*, which reads: "By virtue of the principle of equal rights and self-determination of peoples enshrined in the [UN] Charter, all peoples have the right freely to determine, without external interference, their political status and to pursue their economic, social and cultural development." Resolution 2625(XXV) UN Doc. A/8028(1971). A major debate within the United Nations has involved the degree to which the international meanings of self-determination apply to indigenous nations and peoples.

146. Author's personal notes from the 24 October 1996 meeting, United Nations, Geneva, Switzerland.

147. This school of thought examines the socially constructed sources of knowledge, as well as the consequences of socially constructed knowledge in various power relations. Advanced initially by Karl Mannheim, this body of analysis has been advanced through the writings of such notables as Emile Durkheim, Max Weber, and Michel Foucault, who analyze the ways in which social position can determine the strength or force of an articulated idea. In the context of the discussion with U.S. officials, sociology of knowledge can be important in assessing

the ways in which terminology is being coded and decoded to achieve a desired meaning. Coding in this instance is conducted by those who are considered the "experts" in the State Department in defining legalese and government jargon and transmitting its "meaning" to the general public. Specifically, the "experts" in this case are charged with redefining the terms *peoples, self-determination,* and *collective rights,* ignoring the historical application of the terms and applying new definitions to comport with U.S. interests. For a general understanding of sociology of knowledge, see Karl Mannheim, *Ideology and Utopia: An Introduction into the Sociology of Knowledge,* trans. Louis Wirth and Edward Shils (New York: Harvest Books, 1936, 1985); Volker Meja and Nico Stehr, eds., *The Sociology of Knowledge,* International Library of Critical Writings in Sociology, no. 12 (Cheltenham, UK: Edward Elgar Reference Collection, 2000); Michel Foucault, *Power/Knowledge: Selected Interviews and Other Writings 1972–1977* (New York: Pantheon, 1980).

148. See, generally, *International Journal of the Sociology of Language;* Basil B. Bernstein, *Class, Codes and Control: Theoretical Studies toward a Sociology of Language* (London: Routledge and Kegan Paul, 1971).

149. Pierre Bourdieu, *Language and Symbolic Power* (Cambridge: Harvard University Press, 1991), 172.

150. Ibid., 167.

151. Federal Indian law "confirmed the superior rights of a European-derived nation to the lands occupied by 'infidels, heathens and savages,' encouraged further efforts by white society to acquire the Indians' 'waste' lands . . . according to national interest, security and sometimes even honor." Williams, *American Indian in Western Legal Thought,* 317. See Williams generally on these points.

152. Ibid.

153. Cassese, *Self-Determination of Peoples,* 11–100.

154. One of the first attempts at semantic obfuscation involves the term *self-determination* itself. Despite decades of debate and evolution of the term in international legal and political debate, Congress and the president passed the so-called Self-Determination and Education Assistance Act of 1975 (P.L. 93-638, 25 U.S.C. 450, 88 Stat. 2203-14). Under the law, not a single mention is made of the international right of peoples to control their political, economic, and social decisions without external interference. Instead, the United States decided to devolve the administration of contracts for specific federally funded programs to Indian tribes. More accurately, the law provided for *self-administration* under the continuing colonial processes of U.S. Indian policy. The manipulation of the international lexicon of self-determination was no accident but was designed to preempt an extension of the international formulation of self-determination to the U.S. context. Jack D. Forbes, *Native Americans and Nixon: Presidential Politics and Minority Self-Determination* (Los Angeles: American Indian Studies Center, UCLA, 1981).

155. Unclassified internal U.S. State Department position paper, "Draft Universal Declaration on Indigenous Peoples," written by John Crook, counselor for legal affairs, U.S. Mission to the United Nations, Geneva, Switzerland, 9 July 1993, 1.

156. National Security Council (NSC), "Indigenous Peoples," unclassified internal memorandum, 18 January 2001 (on file with author).

157. Ibid., 2.

158. Ibid.

159. Precise definitions of a "people" have been elusive in international law. One UN rapporteur stated that the UN Charter, Articles 1 and 55, used the term

nations "in the sense of all political entities, states and non-states, whereas 'peoples' refers to groups of human beings who may or may not comprise states or nations." He continued by defining the responsibility of states "to apply the principle [of self-determination] in relations both with other states and with peoples which have not yet constituted themselves independent states." Aureliu Cristescu, *The Right to Self-Determination: Historical and Current Developments on the Basis of United Nations Instruments,* UN Doc. E/CN.4/Sub.2/404/Rev.1(1981), para. 262, 266. Cristescu continued by suggesting that the right to self-determination is not to be narrowly construed, but that it is based on a universal commitment to "fight against the unequal relations and domination deriving from colonialism and related forms of domination" (690). In this regard, indigenous peoples around the globe can easily match the criteria as "peoples," and their conditions, if not complying with the classic definitions of colonialism, certainly constitute "related forms of domination" by settler states.

160. The United States is certainly not alone in embracing this perspective. Very few states acknowledge the unbridled right of indigenous peoples to self-determination. Because this chapter focuses on U.S. policy on indigenous peoples, and because the U.S. deportment is critical in the evolution of standards in this area, the focus is primarily on U.S. statements.

161. The vast majority of armed conflicts in the world today are between indigenous peoples or nations and the settler states that desire the natural resources under indigenous peoples' territories or that seek to frustrate the self-determination aspirations of indigenous peoples. See Bernard Neitschmann, "The Fourth World: Nations versus States," in *Reordering the World: Geopolitical Perspectives on the 21st Century,* ed. George J. Demko and William B. Wood (Boulder, Colo.: Westview Press, 1994); Kathy Seton, "Fourth World Nations in the Era of Globalization: An Introduction to Contemporary Theories Posed by Indigenous Nations," *Fourth World Journal,* vol. 4, no. 1 (1999), http://www.cwis.org/fwj/41/fworld.html.

162. Convention No. 169 Concerning Indigenous and Tribal Peoples of Independent Countries (1989). The text can be found at: http://www.unhchr.ch/html/menu3/b/62.htm.

163. Clech-Lam, *At the Edge of the State,* 45; Lee Sweptson, "A New Step in the International Law on Indigenous and Tribal Peoples: ILO Convention 169 of 1989," *Oklahoma City University Law Review,* vol. 15 (1990), 677; but compare Sharon H. Venne, *The New Language of Assimilation: A Brief Analysis of ILO Convention 169* (Washington, D.C.: *Without Prejudice,* 1990), 53.

164. NSC memo, 3.

165. Robin Tolmach-Lakoff and Deborah Tannen, "Communicative Strategies and Metastrategies in Pragmatic Theory," *Semiotics,* vol. 17, nos. 3–4 (1984), 324–46.

166. Edward W. Said, *Culture and Imperialism* (New York: Alfred A. Knopf, 1994), 9.

167. Cited in Wilmer, *The Indigenous Voice in World Politics,* 67.

168. Susan V. Opotow, "Moral Exclusion and Injustice: An Introduction," *Journal of Social Issues,* vol. 46 (1990), 1–20, cited in ibid.

169. *Government-to-government relationship* has evolved into a near-mantra in Indian country in the United States. Although the precise genesis of the term is elusive (Deloria places it in the 1972 State and Local Fiscal Assistance Act, only reinforcing the point below that the U.S. government views indigenous nations as little more than federal municipalities), the phrase was used extensively during

the Clinton administration (1993–2001) as a classic case of a pragmatic homonym. Among indigenous peoples, the term implied recognition of the *nation-to-nation* relationship between the United States and Indian nations, suggesting an independent, perhaps even international character to the relationship. The United States, however, has been consistently clear in the parameters of the term, which of course, it developed. In its April 2001 statement before the Organization of American States, the U.S. delegation reiterated that the United States deals "on a government-to-government basis with federally recognized indigenous *groups* within U.S. territory. The nature of this *domestic right* to self-determination is an *internal* one, existing *within the framework of the U.S.*" (italics added; underline in original). "Opening Statement of U.S. Delegation," Working Group on the Proposed American Indigenous Rights Declaration, Organization of American States, Washington, D.C., 3 April 2001, 1. For indigenous political leaders to delude themselves that the United States uses the term *government-to-government* in relation to indigenous nations any differently than it uses the term to describe its dealings with municipalities or other subordinate "sovereignties" within the U.S. federal system simply ignores the United States' own repeated statements on the issue.

170. Although numerous federal statutes require the U.S. government to engage in consultations with indigenous nations when a federal project affects indigenous peoples' interests, it was only in 1995 that the United States began consultations with indigenous peoples regarding the Draft Declaration. Once again, the interpretation of critical terms is vital. For indigenous delegates to the "consultation," an expectation exists of genuine collaboration and discussion. Haskew describes what John Marshall might have called "the actual state of things": "Consultations, therefore, may confuse the real consent of Indian communities to federal actions with the procedural illusion of participation, in which Indian consent is never *really* asked for, and advice is never *really* heeded." Derek C. Haskew, "Federal Consultation with Indian Tribes: The Foundation of Enlightened Policy Decisions, or Another Badge of Shame?" *American Indian Law Review*, vol. 24 (2000), 21, 24. See also Executive Order 13084 of 14 May 1998, Consultation and Coordination with Indian Tribal Governments, and revisions of 6 November 2000. In its 1996 statement to the Intersessional Working Group on the Draft Declaration, the U.S. delegation made great fanfare of "a series of consultations with U.S.-based indigenous people," noting that the July consultation was attended by "more than 100 tribal representatives." The purpose of the statement was to invest legitimacy in the U.S. position by suggesting that indigenous peoples had given their consent, or at least their acquiescence, to a position that continued to deny international personality to indigenous peoples, their treaties, or their territorial and natural resource rights. See "Opening Statement of the U.S. Delegation," Working Group on the Draft United Nations Declaration on the Rights of Indigenous Peoples, Geneva, Switzerland, 24 October 1996.

171. Vine Deloria, Jr., and Clifford Lytle, *The Nations Within: The Past and Future of American Indian Sovereignty* (New York: Pantheon Books, 1984), 13–15; emphasis added.

172. Linda Tuhiwai Smth, *Decolonizing Methodologies: Research and Indigenous Peoples* (London: Zed Books, 1999), 64.

173. Frantz Fanon, *The Wretched of the Earth* (New York: Grove Press, 1965).

174. V. Y. Mudimbe, *The Invention of Africa: Gnosis, Philosophy and the Order of Knowledge* (Bloomington: Indiana University Press, 1988), 2.

175. Julian Burger, *Report from the Frontier: The State of the World's Indigenous Peoples* (London: Zed Books, 1987). Wilmer, *The Indigenous Voice in World Politics.*

176. Mudimbe, *The Invention of Africa,* 3; Jerry Mander and Edward Goldsmith, *The Case against the Global Economy: And for a Turn toward the Local* (San Francisco: Sierra Club Books, 1996), 33–179.
177. Deloria and Lytle, *The Nations Within,* 258.
178. Taiaiake Alfred, *Peace, Power, Righteousness: An Indigenous Manifesto* (Don Mills, Ontario: Oxford University Press, 1999), 70.
179. For a critical discussion of the evolution of the contemporary state from the time of the Peace of Westphalia in 1648 to the present, see Richard Falk, *Predatory Globalization: A Critique* (Cambridge: Polity Press, 1999), 20–47.
180. Smith, *Decolonizing Methodologies,* 63.
181. Robin Tolmach-Lakoff, *The Language War* (Berkeley: University of California Press, 2000), 116–17.
182. Cited in S. I. Hayakawa, ed., *The Use and Misuse of Language* (Greenwich, Conn.: Fawcett, 1964), ix.
183. Robin Tolmach-Lakoff, *Talking Power: The Politics of Language* (New York: Basic Books, 1990), 15.
184. Ibid., 12–13.
185. Mudimbe, *The Invention of Africa,* 17.
186. Newcomb, "Evidence of Christian Nationalism," 314 and accompanying footnotes.
187. Vine Deloria, Jr., "Laws Founded on Justice and Humanity: Reflections on the Content and Character of Federal Indian Law," *Arizona Law Review,* vol. 31 (1989), 203, 223.
188. Among those who have passed over are Phillip Deere, David Monongye, Larry Red Shirt, Dan Bomberry, Tadadaho Leon Shenandoah, Bill Wahpepah, and Thomas Banyaca.
189. Notable among this group is Russell Means of AIM, who led a walkout of all the indigenous delegates at the UN Intersessional Working Group on the Draft Declaration, saying that the process had been entirely captured by state interests and that many indigenous representatives had forgotten the original principles indigenous peoples had used to open the UN process in the first place. See Ward Churchill, "Subterfuge and Self-Determination: Suppression of Indigenous Self-Determination in 20th Century United States," http://www.horizons.k12.mi.us/~aim/papers/subterfugeandself.html.
190. David E. Ronfeldt, John Arquilla, Graham E. Fuller, and Melissa Fuller, *The Zapatista Social Netwar in Mexico* (Los Angeles: RAND Corporation, 1999).
191. For a comprehensive listing of international reports affecting indigenous peoples, visit the United Nations High Commission for Human Rights web site at http://www.unhchr.ch/indigenous/forum.htm#doc.
192. Even the Indian Law Resource Center (ILRC), one of the original indigenous NGOs at the UN and a stalwart in the fight to maintain the integrity of the Draft Declaration, has succumbed to "pragmatism" on occasion. In an intervention at the UN in 2000, the ILRC statement concluded, "There is a limit to what we can win [in the debate with states over the Draft Declaration] especially in light of the political realities and the nature of the political arena that we now find ourselves within . . . we know that the attempts to weaken the draft are a probability not merely a possibility." Statement of the Indian Law Resource Center and the National Congress of American Indians, 8 August 2001, 19th Session of the United Nations Working Group on Indigenous Populations, Geneva, Switzerland.
193. *Mary and Carrie Dann v. United States of America,* Inter-American Com-

mission on Human Rights, Report No. 113/01, Case No. 11.104, decided 15 October 2001 (released publicly 26 July 2002), 36.

194. *The Case of the Mayagna (Sumo) Awas Tingni Community v. Nicaragua,* Inter-American Commission on Human Rights, 3 August 2001.

195. For discussion of the role of indigenous peoples in challenging the corporatization of the natural world, see the web site for the Indigenous Peoples Council on Biolcolonialism, http://www.ipcb.org/pub/index.htm. The text of the convention can be found at http://www.ipcb.org/pub/index.htm, with additional discussion of the impact of the loss of biological diversity at http://www.biodiv.org/doc/meetings/wg8j/wg8j-01/information/wg8j-01-inf-04-en.pdf.

196. See note 27 and accompanying text.

197. In particular, indigenous scholars such as David Wilkins, Robert Williams, Jr., Ward Churchill, Winona LaDuke, and Jim Anaya have pushed convention and normative interpretations in challenging federal Indian law.

198. Armstrong comes from the Okanagon indigenous people and is a member of the traditional council of the Penticton Band. She is a prolific artist and author of poetry, short stories, and a very popular novel, *Slash*. For purposes of this discussion, the concepts from her essay "Sharing One Skin: Okanagon Community" serve as the focal point. She was the first director of the En'owkin International School of Writing in Penticton. For a more complete bibliography, see http://quarles.unbc.edu/kbeeler_html/research/arm2.html.

199. Porter, from the Heron Clan of the Seneca Nation, currently serves as an associate professor of law at the University of Kansas School of Law, where he also directs the Tribal Law and Governance Center. He has an impressive list of publications in law and policy journals, including, "Pursuing the Path of Indigenization in the Era of Emergent International Law Governing the Rights of Indigenous Peoples," *Yale Human Rights and Development Law Journal*, vol. 5 (2002), 123, and "A Proposal to the Hanodaganyas to Decolonize Federal Indian Control Law," *University of Michigan Journal of Law Reform*, vol. 31 (summer 1998), 899.

200. Alfred comes from the community of Kahnawake in the Mohawk Nation in the Rotinoshonni (Six Nations Iroquois) Confederacy. He currently holds the Indigenous Peoples Research Chair at the University of Victoria in British Columbia and is the author of numerous articles and books, including *Peace, Power, Righteousness: An Indigenous Manifesto* (New York: Oxford University Press, 1999). His personal web site may be found at http://www.taiaiake.com/.

201. Porter, "Pursuing the Path of Indigenization," 135.

202. Ibid., 170.

203. Ibid., 171–72.

204. Ibid., 171.

205. Praxis is the process by which theory and practice merge through a cycle of action and reflection that converts to further action in the development of critical consciousness, resulting in the implementation of liberatory strategy. Paolo Freire, *Pedagogy of the Oppressed* (New York: Seabury Press, 1974), 75.

206. Alfred, *Peace, Power, Righteousness,* 80–82.

207. Armstrong, "Sharing One Skin," 464.

208. Alfred, *Peace, Power, Righteousness,* 42.

209. See notes 9 and 10 and accompanying text.

210. I include myself in this category. In my article "In Support of the Right of Self-Determination for Indigenous Peoples under International Law," *German*

Yearbook of International Law, vol. 29 (1986), 277, I went to great lengths to prove that indigenous nations were the equal of existing states and could satisfy the criteria of statehood under the 1933 Montevideo Convention on the Rights and Duties of States, which establishes that states must have a permanent population, a defined territory, effective self-government, and the capacity to enter into relations with other states. Although many indigenous nations obviously satisfy these criteria, the question is whether indigenous nations should measure the legitimacy of their existence against the very states that have actively pursued the extermination of indigenous peoples. See also *Broken Treaties*, chap. 8; John Howard Clinebell and Jim Thomson, "Sovereignty and Self-Determination: The Rights of Native Americans under International Law," *Buffalo Law Review*, vol. 27 (1978), 669–714; Joe Ryan, "Like Other Nations," *American Indian Journal*, vol. 3, no. 8 (August 1977).

211. Alfred, *Peace, Power, Righteousness*, 56–57.

212. In response to this point, indigenous peoples have issued a series of documents that reflect the power of indigenous peoples and nations to formulate positions and relations in international arenas that are independent of states. See "Kari-Oca (Brazil) Declaration," World Conference of Indigenous Peoples on Territory, Environment and Development, 25–31 May 1992 (in direct opposition to the UN Conference on Environment and Development held simultaneously in Rio de Janeiro); "The Mataatua Declaration on Cultural and Intellectual Property Rights of Indigenous Peoples," First International Conference on the Cultural and Intellectual Property Rights of Indigenous Peoples, Whakatane, Aotearoa (New Zealand), 12–18 June 1993; "Ukupseni Declaration on the Human Genome Diversity Project," Ukupseni, Kuna Yala (Panama), 12–13 November 1997, as only three examples of an emerging practice. Also, see Anaya, *Indigenous Peoples in International Law*, chap. 3, discussing a variety of interpretations of the right to self-determination other than aspiring to statehood.

213. Alfred, *Peace, Power, Righteousness*, 56–57.

214. Jean Bodin, *On Sovereignty: Four Chapters from the Six Books of Commonwealth*, trans. Julian Franklin (1576; Cambrige: Cambridge University Press, 1992).

215. Nicolo Machiavelli, *The Prince* [1513] *and the Discourses* [1517] (New York: Modern Library Collection, 1950).

216. Thomas Hobbes, *Leviathan*, ed. Richard Tuck (1651; Cambridge: Cambridge University Press, 1991).

217. Bodin, *On Sovereignty*, 55.

218. Scott Gordon, *Controlling the State: Constitutionalism from Ancient Athens to Today* (Cambridge: Harvard University Press, 1999), 28.

219. Alfred, *Peace, Power, Righteousness*, 55–57.

220. Menno Boldt and J. A. Long, "Tribal Traditions and European Political Ideologies: The Dilemma for Canada's Native Indians," *Canadian Journal of Political Science*, vol. 17 (1984), 548; cited in ibid., 56.

221. "People without hearts" translates from the Okanagan language, which describes the "discord that we see around us . . . at a level that is not endurable without consequences and therefore to everything that the human influences. A suicidal coldness is seeping into and permeating all levels of interaction; there is a dispassion of energy that has become a way of life in illness and other forms of human pain. People without hearts means people who have lost the capacity to experience the deep generational bond to other human beings and their surroundings. It refers to collective disharmony and alienation from the land." Armstrong, "Sharing one Skin," 466–67.

222. Ibid.

223. Alfred, *Peace, Power, Righteousness,* 64

224. Ibid.

225. Ibid. Evidence of this state tendency can be found in numerous examples, ranging from Mexican state repression against indigenous self-determination in Chiapas to Canadian military force against Mohawks at Oka in 1990. Further evidence is found in recent threats by the U.S. government that if popular indigenous leader Evo Morales were to succeed in his Bolivian presidential bid, the United States would work to undermine his administration. Otto Reich, U.S. undersecretary of state for Western Hemisphere affairs, threatened the majority indigenous population of Bolivia by stating that "the Bolivian electorate must consider the consequences of choosing leaders" like Morales; "we do not believe that we could have normal relations with someone who espouses [his] kind of policies." Duncan Campbell, "Bolivia's Leftwing Upstart Alarms U.S.," *Guardian of London,* 15 July 2002. On 4 August 2002, Morales's indigenous party came in second for the presidency of Bolivia, but he remains the leader of the opposition in the Bolivian legislature, and his party controls more than a quarter of the legislative seats. Craig Mauro, "Bolivia's Downtrodden Indian Majority Gains Political Voice," *Washington Post,* 15 August 2002.

226. Alfred, *Peace, Power, Righteousness,* 60.

227. Ibid., 63.

228. Some members of the settler-state society have begun to develop an analysis that actively questions or betrays the privilege of their legacy and encourages others to do likewise. See Wes Jackson, *Becoming Native to This Place* (Washington, D.C.: Counterpoint Books, 1996); Mander and Goldsmith, *The Case against the Global Economy;* Chellis Glendinning, *Off the Map: An Expedition Deep into Imperialism, The Global Economy and Other Earthly Whereabouts* (Boston: Shambhala Books, 1999).

229. See note 27.

230. Alfred, *Peace, Power, Righteousness,* 135.

231. Ibid., 67.

232. Ibid., 136–37. Space does not permit an adequate elaboration of Alfred's finer points of these objectives, and no suggestion is made that he intends these points to represent a definitive strategy for reversing the devastating impact of colonialism on indigenous peoples and nations.

233. Ibid., 145.

234. Richard Falk, *Predatory Globalization: A Critique* (Cambridge: Polity Press, 1999). One of the progressive international legal scholars of our time, Falk "explores both the detrimental impact of globalization and the creative initiatives that are emerging as a response" (8).

CHAPTER SIX

International Law and U.S. Trust Responsibility toward Native Americans

S. James Anaya (Purepecha/Apache)

A central feature of U.S. law and policy concerning Native Americans is the doctrine of a federal "trust responsibility" toward them. This doctrine is multidimensional, functioning variously as an extraconstitutional source of broad power by the federal government, as a limitation on government abuse, as an engine of paternalism, and as a source of affirmative obligation beneficial to Native peoples. This chapter does not detail or unravel the intricacies of the trust doctrine but rather describes in broad terms its evolution in relation to international legal developments. One of Vine Deloria, Jr.'s, important contributions to the study of Indian affairs has been to inspire, through example and otherwise, attention to the wider international context within which domestic Indian law and policy are located. An examination of the trust doctrine in an international context leads to an understanding of the discrete patterns of thought that have shaped the doctrine over time and that give the doctrine its highly textured character.

A common thread in the development of both international law and U.S. federal law is the doctrine embracing a special duty of care toward indigenous or aboriginal peoples. In its broadest sense, the doctrine includes a general duty on the international community at large and more particularized state obligations to ensure the well-being of indigenous peoples and the full enjoyment of their rights. This doctrine has been associated with the terms *trusteeship, wardship,* or *fiduciary obligation,* although its development in the law only roughly approximates the legal regimes ordinarily attached to those terms. The special-duty doctrine is sui generis, arising from a nucleus of jurisprudential and practical considerations unique to the conditions of indigenous peoples.

A special duty to ensure the just treatment of indigenous peoples has been a constant doctrine in legal thought since at least the nineteenth century, prominent today in international law's burgeoning human rights program as well as in aspects of U.S. federal Indian law. The normative elements of the doctrine and their implications, however, have changed as dominant thinking about the substantive content of indigenous peoples' rights and well-being has shifted over time. Diverse strains of

155

thought shaped the historical evolution of the special-duty doctrine and continue to manifest themselves, often in tension with one another, in U.S. law and policy. The more recent international developments concerning indigenous peoples favor precepts of indigenous self-determination and cultural integrity. Although they have to compete with some of the legacies of older dominant thinking, such modern precepts can also been found in the contemporary United States' exercise of its acknowledged trust responsibility toward Native Americans.

HISTORICAL STRAINS OF THOUGHT IN
THE DEVELOPMENT OF TRUSTEESHIP DOCTRINE

Prior to the middle part of the twentieth century, three discrete strains of thinking fed into the notion that independent states owe special duties or trusteeship obligations to the indigenous populations falling under their authority or control. For the sake of simplicity, I call these the *consent/protectorate* strain, the *white man's burden* strain, and the *liberal assimilation* strain. These jurisprudential and philosophical strains can be seen in developments both in the international realm and in the domestic law of the United States.

Consent/Protectorate Strain

Under the consent/protectorate strain, a state owes a duty of protection to an indigenous people on the basis of mutual consent. Both the existence and the terms of the duty, or trusteeship, are based on the agreement between otherwise independent sovereigns. This strain of trusteeship doctrine arose in association with the theory of international relations espoused by Emerich de Vattel, the eighteenth-century Swiss publicist generally regarded as one of the most influential early theorists on international law. In his major work *The Law of Nations or the Principles of Natural Law* (1758),[1] Vattel envisioned an international system comprised of presumptively independent, mutually exclusive nations or states (terms he used interchangeably). Within this state-centered model, he discussed the practice whereby weaker nations or states voluntarily placed themselves under the protection of stronger ones. Vattel held that such states retained their sovereign status and powers of self-government over matters not voluntarily given up to the stronger power.[2]

The concept of a consensual protectorate relationship between sovereign nations surfaced in the U.S. Supreme Court's early decisions considering the status of the Indian tribes living within the exterior boundaries of the country. In the now famous case of *Cherokee Nation v.*

Georgia,[3] Chief Justice John Marshall, writing for the Court, characterized the tribes as having "acknowledge[d] themselves in their treaties to be under the protection of the United States."[4] Marshall described the tribes as "domestic dependent nations. . . . Their relation to the United States resembles that of a ward to his guardian."[5] In a later Supreme Court decision also involving the Cherokee, *Worcestor v. Georgia*,[6] Marshall again wrote for the Court and clarified his characterization of the tribes. Citing Vattel, Marshall stressed the common usage of the term *nations* to refer to the tribes, and he analogized them to the "'tributary and feudatory states'" of Europe,[7] which Vattel ranked among sovereign states subject to the law of nations despite their having assented to the protection of a stronger power.[8]

The consent/protectorate strain of trusteeship doctrine reflected in the Marshall decisions waned as nineteenth-century states, including the United States, discontinued treaty making with non-European aboriginal peoples and instead unilaterally asserted more and more power over them.[9] It resurfaced in a limited way, however, in a line of jurisdictional statutes and court decisions allowing tribes in the United States, on their own initiative, to sue in federal court to enforce trust responsibilities deemed incumbent on executive officials.[10] The concept of a consensual protectorate can also be seen today to influence federal-tribal relations, increasingly defined by federal regulatory and assistance programs to which tribes expressly or tacitly have consented while maintaining sovereign powers.

White Man's Burden Strain

A second and more influential strain of thought in the early evolution of the special-duty or trust doctrine is in the philosophy associated with the British colonial phrase *the white man's burden*. Under this strain of thought, which has intellectual underpinnings in the now infamous school identified as "scientific racism,"[11] trusteeship exists over indigenous peoples irrespective of their consent and instead arises due to their "backward" and "uncivilized" character. Because of their inferior status, indigenous peoples are deemed incapable of adequately managing their own affairs, so "civilized" humanity must place them under its tutelage and bring them the "blessings of civilization." Trusteeship is thus a source of unilateral state power over indigenous peoples, and indigenous peoples' rights are reduced to those consistent with the "civilizing" mission.

An early version of this thinking is reflected in the work of Francisi de Victoria, the sixteenth-century Spanish theologian and jurist who, like Vattel, is considered one of the fathers of international law. In his lecture *On the Indians Lately Discovered* (1532),[12] Victoria analyzed a series of arguments advanced to justify Spanish authority over already occupied lands of the Western Hemisphere. Victoria concluded his analysis as follows:

> There is another title which can indeed not be asserted, but brought up for discussion, and some think it a lawful one. I dare not affirm it at all, nor do I entirely condemn it. It is this: Although the aborigines in question are (as has been said above) not wholly unintelligent, yet they are little short of that condition, and so are unfit to found or administer a lawful State up to the standard required by human and civil claims. Accordingly they have no proper laws or magistrates, and are not even capable of controlling their family affairs; they are without any literature or arts, not only the liberal arts, but the mechanical arts also; they have no careful agriculture and no artisans; and they lack many other conveniences, yea necessaries, of human life. It might, therefore, be maintained that in their own interests the sovereigns of Spain might undertake the administration of their country, providing them with prefects and governors for their towns, and might even give them new lords, so long as this was clearly for their benefit. I say there would be some force in this contention; for if they were all wanting in intelligence, there is no doubt that this would not only be a permissible, but also a highly proper, course to take; nay, our sovereigns would be bound to take it, just as if the natives were infants. The same principle seems to apply here to them as to people of defective intelligence.[13]

The argument floated by Victoria gained backing in Western intellectual circles as European colonizing states consolidated power over non-European lands. Among the colonial powers of the nineteenth century, Great Britain was a leader in devising special administrative regimes over Native peoples with the objective of reengineering their cultural and social patterns in line with European conceptions of civilized behavior. In 1837 a special committee of the British House of Commons concluded that such a policy was required by the "obligations of conscience to impart the blessings we enjoy,"[14] as well as by practical considerations: "We have abundant proof that it is greatly for our advantage to have dealings with civilized men rather than with barbarians. Savages are dangerous neighbors and unprofitable customers, and if they remain as degraded denizens of our colonies they become a burden upon the State."[15]

The British policy, and its premise of indigenous inferiority, is reflected in the following excerpt of a letter by Prime Minister Lord John Russell written on 23 August 1840 to Sir George Gipps, the governor of New South Wales, Australia:

Between the native, who is weakened by intoxicating liquors, and the European, who has all the strength of superior civilization and is free from its restraints, the unequal contest is generally of no long duration; the natives decline, diminish, and finally disappear. . . .

The best chance of preserving the unfortunate race . . . lies in the means employed for training their children. The education given to such children should consist in a very small part of reading and writing. Oral instruction in the fundamental truths of the Christian religion will be given by the missionaries themselves. The children should be taught early; the boys to dig and plough, and the trades of shoemakers, tailors, carpenters, and masons; the girls to sew and cook and wash linen, and keep clean the rooms and furniture.[16]

The views advanced by Great Britain and adopted by other colonizing powers were internationalized through a series of conferences and related efforts aimed at regulating continued European penetration into Africa. Most notable in this respect was the first Berlin Conference on Africa, which concluded in 1885 with the signing of a general act intended to set the basic parameters for what has been dubbed the "scramble for Africa."[17] Under Article VI of this Berlin General Act, the signatory powers agreed to "bind themselves to watch over the preservation of the native tribes, and to care for the improvement of the conditions of their moral and material well-being," with the ultimate purpose of "instructing the natives and bringing home to them the blessings of civilization."[18] In his 1926 work *The Acquisition and Government of Backward Territory in International Law*, British jurist M. F. Lindley argued that the trusteeship doctrine as advanced by the Berlin General Act had become widely accepted and should be understood as part of general international law.[19]

The United States firmly embraced the white man's burden strain of trusteeship doctrine in its domestic law and policy. In the late nineteenth century, a vast government bureaucracy emerged under the U.S. commissioner of Indian affairs to consolidate and manage the system of reservations, pueblos, rancherias, and settlements that were home to the surviving Indian people within the country's external boundaries. In 1868 the Indian commissioner wrote of his task: "What, then, is our duty as the guardian of all the Indians under our jurisdiction? To outlaw, to pursue, to hunt down like wolves, and slay? Must we drive and exterminate them as if void of reason, and without souls? Surely, no. It is beyond question our most solemn duty to protect and care for, to elevate and civilize them."[20]

Pursuant to its "civilizing" mission, the Indian Office assumed virtual despotic powers over Indian people through the early part of the twentieth century, even though judicial doctrine supported the view that the tribes continued to possess inherent sovereign powers. With most Indian people rendered dependent on government programs for their subsistence, government officials effectively supplanted or eliminated autonomous structures of tribal governance. On the reservation, the government "Indian agent was the new taskmaster bringing a multitude of new programs foreign to Indian ideas of the proper role of man in his society."[21] Government programs designed to break Indian culture ran in collusion with those of Christian missionary institutions.

In this same period, the Supreme Court invoked the white man's burden to buttress the exercise of broad congressional power over Indians. In *United States v. Kagama*,[22] the Court upheld federal legislation regulating certain criminal behavior implicating Indians on Indian lands. The Court reasoned: "After an experience of a hundred years of the treaty-making system of government [vis-à-vis the Indians], Congress has determined upon a new departure—to govern them by Acts of Congress. . . . The power of the General Government over these remnants of a race once powerful, now weak and diminished in numbers, is necessary to their protection, as well as to the safety of those among whom they dwell."[23]

In *Lone Wolf v. Hitchcock*,[24] the Supreme Court confirmed the trusteeship doctrine as a source of congressional power and held that it could even be exercised unilaterally to contravene prior treaty commitments. That case involved a challenge to a land distribution statute on the grounds that the statute violated treaty rights. The Court rejected the challenge, stating: "To uphold the claim would be to adjudge that the indirect operation of the treaty was to materially limit and qualify the controlling authority of Congress in respect to the care and protection of the Indians, and to deprive Congress, in a possible emergency, when the necessity might be urgent for a partition and disposal of the tribal lands, of all power to act, if the assent of the Indians could not be obtained."[25]

Kagama and *Lone Wolf* were precedents for the now controversial doctrine of plenary congressional power over Indian affairs.[26] Under current judicial doctrine, Congress continues to be regarded as having broad powers over Indians pursuant to its trusteeship obligation, reviewable only by a minimal rationality standard.[27]

Liberal Assimilation Strain

In the early part of the twentieth century, the white man's burden strain of thinking diminished with the rise of what may be called the liberal assimilation strain. Under this more modern strain of thought, trusteeship doctrine continues as a source of official power, but only a transient one. The object of trusteeship under this view is *not* to watch over the affairs of indigenous peoples *indefinitely*. Rather, its goal is to go beyond infusing members of indigenous groups with Western skills and values and, ultimately, to assimilate them into nontribal societies constructed on the basis of individualistic precepts of equality. Purged of pseudoscientific notions of racial hierarchy, trusteeship over tribal aborigines is to lead to, and be replaced by, their full and equal citizenship in a modern liberal state.

During the turmoil surrounding World War I, President Woodrow Wilson promoted the liberal model of political organization as a basis for world order. In a major foreign policy address, Wilson said: "No peace can last, or ought to last, which does not recognize and accept the principle that governments derive all their just powers from the consent of the governed. . . . I speak of this, not because of any desire to exalt an abstract political principle which has always been held very dear by those who have sought to build up liberty in America, but for the same reason that I have spoken of the other conditions of peace which seem to me clearly indispensable."[28] Wilson's comments were concerned primarily with the conflicts over competing territorial claims in Europe; however, they had clear implications for the forms of governance imposed and maintained through colonial patterns in other parts of the world, especially as theories of white racial superiority became discredited.

A certain merger of Wilsonian liberalism and notions of trusteeship was incorporated into the Covenant of the League of Nations in its system of mandates, which applied to territories taken from the European powers defeated in World War I. The covenant declared the "well-being and development" of the people of the subject territories to be a "sacred trust of civilization."[29] Although manifesting elements of trusteeship doctrine common to the white man's burden strain of thought,[30] the provisions of the covenant establishing the mandate system reflect a policy of moving indigenous populations away from conditions of classic dependency.[31]

The merger of liberalism into trusteeship notions was strengthened, and its impact enhanced, with the United Nations (UN) Charter and the human rights frame of global organization it spawned at the close of World War II. The human rights frame of the charter included a heightened international concern over the segments of humanity that continued to experience colonization or its legacies. In particular, Chapter XI of the charter established special duties for UN members "which have or assume responsibilities for the administration of territories whose peoples have not yet attained a full measure of self-government."[32] Under Article 73 of Chapter XI, such members commit themselves to "accept as a sacred trust the obligation to promote to the utmost . . . the well-being of the inhabitants of these territories."[33]

Following adoption of the charter, the international community simultaneously promoted, on the one hand, independent statehood for overseas colonial territories with their colonial boundaries intact[34] and, on the other hand, assimilation and rights of full citizenship for members of aboriginal groups living within the boundaries of independent states.[35] In both cases, little or no value was placed on indigenous patterns of association and political ordering originating prior to European colonization. Instead, within the operative normative frame, the model pursued was that of the culturally homogeneous, non–racially discriminatory, fully self-governing state. Nation building entailed a corresponding policy of breaking down competing ethnic or cultural bonds, a policy even (or perhaps especially) engaged in by newly independent states.[36] Through assimilation and rights of full citizenship, members of indigenous or tribal enclaves would be brought to equality and self-government.

The major embodiment in international law of the liberal assimilation strain of thinking in the specific context of enclave indigenous groups is International Labor Organization (ILO) Convention No. 107 of 1957.[37] While requiring states to take extraordinary measures to benefit members of indigenous groups, the convention's operative premise is assimilation, and hence it treats such measures as transitory. The thrust of Convention No. 107 is to promote improved social and economic conditions for indigenous populations generally, but within a perceptual scheme that does not seem to envisage a place in the long term for robust, politically significant cultural and associational patterns of indigenous groups. Convention No. 107 is framed in terms of *members* of indigenous populations and their rights as equals within the larger society.[38] Indigenous *peoples* or *groups* as such are only secondarily, if at all, made beneficiaries of rights or protections. The convention does recognize indigenous customary laws and the right of collective landownership. Such recognition, however, is overshadowed by a persistent call for national programs of integration and noncoercive assimilation that ultimately render themselves unnecessary. The following provisions illustrate the tenor and thrust of the convention:

Article 2

1. Governments shall have the primary responsibility for developing co-ordinated and systemic action for the protection of the populations concerned and their progressive integration into the life of their respective countries. . . .

3. The primary objective of such action shall be the fostering of individual dignity, and the advancement of individual usefulness and initiative. . . .

Article 3

1. So long as the social, economic and cultural conditions of the populations concerned prevent them from enjoying the benefits of the general laws of the country to which they belong, special mea-

sures shall be adopted for the protection of the institutions, persons, property and labour of these populations.

2. Care shall be taken to ensure that such special measures of protection—

(a) are not used as a means of creating or prolonging a state of seg-regation, and

(b) will be continued only so long as there is need for special protection and only to the extent that such protection is necessary.

The liberal assimilation strain of thought promoted internationally and reflected in Convention No. 107 guided a series of legislative measures enacted by Congress in exercising its judicially sanctioned power of trusteeship over Native Americans. The Dawes General Allotment Act of 1887[39] was an early manifestation of the philosophy of breaking up Indian tribes and assimilating their members into the American immigrant society. The act established a policy framework to be implemented at the discretion of the executive. The basic design of the framework was to allot communal tribal lands into separate parcels and distribute them to individual tribal members who, after a period of transition from tribal life, were to hold their allotted parcels by fully alienable title. "Excess" Indian lands could then be open to non-Indian settlement or other disposition negotiated by the secretary of interior. Under the allotment scheme, allottees could become U.S. citizens once they abandoned their tribes and demonstrated their "competency."[40]

In 1924, after President Wilson had established the United States as the vanguard of liberalism, Congress passed a statute conferring citizenship on all Indians born in the United States.[41] By that time, the allotment policy had come under increasing attack. It had largely failed to produce a new generation of acculturated Indians sustaining themselves on allotted lands or otherwise assimilated into the dominant social and economic fabric. Instead, the Dawes Act had primarily facilitated the passing of Indian lands to non-Indians,[42] heightened levels of poverty, and worsened conditions of health and education among Indians. At the same time, Indian cultural bonds had proved resilient, and the federal Indian Office continued its pervasive grip on the governance of Indian people in a manner increasingly at odds with twentieth-century conceptions of democracy.[43]

Along with the conferral of rights of full citizenship for Indian people, the Indian Reorganization (Wheeler Howard) Act of 1934[44] was supposed to be the answer to the failures of the allotment policy. The 1934 act included measures to secure the Indian land base from further erosion and established a framework for Indians to adopt constitutions for reservation governance under the authority of the secretary of interior. The chief architect of the act was then U.S. Indian Commissioner John Collier, who is still revered today by many Indian sympathizers for his reformist efforts. Whatever Collier's intentions, however, it is evident that Congress intended the act as an alternative way of supplanting traditional tribal political institutions and cultural patterns and of educating Indians in American-style democracy and entrepreneurship.[45] In a prepared statement before a committee of the House of Representatives during the deliberations leading to the 1934 act, Collier himself provided the following assurance: "Does it contemplate for the Indian a permanent tribal status, isolation from the white man, collective as distinguished from individual enterprise, and nonassimilation into American civilization? The answer is a clear-cut one: No."[46] Collier also told the House committee that the legislation would provide the Indians "experience" in "civic and business responsibility and the opportunity to manage property and money," which would prepare them for "real assimilation."[47]

The Indian Reorganization Act no doubt was devised as a major reform effort aimed at bringing Indians the possibility of greater economic security and freedom from the federal bureaucracy's authoritarian control experienced under previous policy regimes; nonetheless, it was an effort within a larger design of Indian assimilation. Accordingly, under the act, Indian governments were, with little variation, organized pursuant to a model constitution developed by federal bureaucrats in Washington, which was not unlike the charter of the average American municipality.[48] Further, the basic unit for organizing under the 1934 act was the reservation, as opposed to the historical tribal grouping. Many reservations with more than one tribal grouping were constituted under a single authority without regard to, and often in defiance of, preexisting traditional institutions.[49]

In the 1950s the U.S. government attempted to complete its program of assimilation by adopting and pursuing a policy of "termination." The express object of this policy was "as rapidly as possible, to make the Indians within the territorial limits of the United States subject to the same laws and entitled to the same privileges and responsibilities as are applicable to other citizens of the United States, [and] to end their status as wards of the United States."[50] The termination policy was eventually abandoned as dominant thinking about the objective of trusteeship over indigenous peoples evolved beyond the liberal assimilation strain and began to take on its contemporary form.

CONTEMPORARY INTERNATIONAL LAW AND U.S. TRUSTEESHIP

The United States continues to acknowledge a special duty or trusteeship obligation toward Native Americans, and the doctrinal contours of this

obligation continue to be shaped by precepts that are operative internationally. In their current formulation, relevant international norms are
grounded in an unprecedented measure of respect for the dignity of
indigenous peoples and their cultures. This section discusses contemporary developments giving rise to a reformed body of international law
concerning indigenous peoples and demonstrates how new international
norms parallel certain trends in the contemporary exercise of the United
States' acknowledged trusteeship.

Indigenous Rights Movement

International law's contemporary treatment of indigenous peoples has
taken form over the last few decades as a result of activity that has
involved, and has substantially been driven by, indigenous peoples
themselves. Indigenous peoples have ceased to be mere objects of the discussion of their rights and have become real participants in an extensive
multilateral dialogue facilitated and sanctioned by the United Nations
and other international institutions.[51]

   During the 1960s, armed with a new generation of men and women
educated in the ways of the societies that had encroached on them, indigenous peoples began drawing increased attention to their demands for continued survival as distinct communities with unique cultures, political
institutions, and entitlements to land.[52] Indigenous peoples articulated a
vision of themselves different from that previously advanced and acted on
by dominant sectors.[53] In the 1970s indigenous peoples extended their
efforts through a series of international conferences and direct appeals to
international intergovernmental institutions.[54] These efforts coalesced into
a veritable campaign, aided by concerned international nongovernmental
organizations (NGOs) and an increase in supportive scholarly and popular
writings from moral and sociological, as well as juridical, perspectives.[55]

   The heightened international concern over indigenous peoples generated through years of work was signaled by the UN General Assembly's designation of 1993 as "The International Year of the World's
Indigenous People."[56] With this heightened concern has come a reformulated understanding of the contours of general human rights principles
and their implications for indigenous peoples. And grounded on this
reformulated understanding is a new—though still developing—body of
international law governing state behavior toward indigenous peoples.

ILO Convention No. 169

The ILO Convention on Indigenous and Tribal Peoples (Convention No.
169) of 1989[57] is contemporary international law's most concrete statement

of states' specific obligations toward indigenous peoples. Convention No. 169 is a revision of the ILO's Convention No. 107 of 1957, and it represents the marked departure in world community policy from the philosophy of integration or assimilation underlying the earlier convention.[58]

The basic thrust of Convention No. 169 is indicated by its preamble, which reiterates "that in many parts of the world [indigenous] peoples are unable to enjoy their fundamental human rights to the same degree as the rest of the population of the States within which they live, and that their laws, values, customs and perspectives have often been eroded."[59] The preamble additionally recognizes "the aspirations of [indigenous] peoples to exercise control over their own institutions, ways of life and economic development and to maintain and develop their identities, languages and religions, within the framework of the States in which they live."[60] Based on these premises, the convention places affirmative duties on states to advance indigenous cultural integrity,[61] uphold land and resource rights,[62] and secure nondiscrimination in social welfare spheres[63]; the convention generally enjoins states to respect indigenous peoples' aspirations in all decisions affecting them.[64]

The convention avoids use of the terms *trust* and *trusteeship,* just as indigenous peoples themselves have in pressing their demands in the international arena. These terms apparently have become disfavored due to their historical linkage with philosophies no longer acceptable. The concept of a special or extraordinary duty to secure the rights and well-being of indigenous peoples, however, is implied by the convention's very existence and, further, by its requirements of affirmative programmatic action. Within the normative frame reflected by the convention, this special duty arises not because of some presumed inferiority of indigenous groups but because of their especially disadvantaged condition resulting from a long history of colonization and its legacies.[65]

The convention has been subject to criticism because several of its provisions contain caveats or appear in the form of recommendations.[66] Additionally, the convention includes language that qualifies the term *peoples* used to refer to the subject groups. The qualifying language, together with an explanatory note, disassociates the term *peoples* from its linkage in other international instruments with the term *self-determination.*[67] The International Covenant on Civil and Political Rights and other international instruments affirm that "all *peoples* have the right of Self-determination."[68] The International Labour Office has taken the position that the qualifying language regarding the term "peoples . . . did not limit the meaning of the term, in any way whatsoever," but was simply a means of leaving a decision on the term's implications to procedures within the United Nations.[69] Nonetheless, the qualifying language in the convention reflects an aversion on the part of states to expressly acknowledge a right to self-determination for indigenous groups, out of the fear that it may effectively imply a right of secession.

At the same time, however, even the qualified use of the term *peoples* implies a certain affirmation of indigenous group identity and corresponding attributes of community. Whatever the convention's limitations, its aggregate effect is to affirm the value of indigenous communities and cultures and to establish in states a special duty to secure basic rights and pursue policy objectives in that regard. As an ILO official closely associated with the development of Convention No. 169 observed, the convention "contains few absolute rules but fixes goals, priorities, and minimum rights" that are to be realized through affirmative programmatic action by states.[70]

New and Emergent Customary International Law

ILO Convention No. 169 is significant to the extent it creates treaty obligations among ratifying states in line with current trends concerning indigenous peoples. The convention is further meaningful as part of developments that can be understood as giving rise to new customary international law with the same normative thrust. Largely as a result of indigenous peoples' efforts over the last several years, concern for indigenous peoples has assumed a prominent place on the international human rights agenda.[71] Since the 1970s, the demands of indigenous peoples have been addressed continuously in one way or another within the United Nations, the Organization of American States, and other international venues of authoritative normative discourse.[72] The extended multilateral discussion promoted through the international system has involved states, NGOs, independent experts, and indigenous peoples themselves.

It is now evident that states and other relevant actors have reached a certain new common ground about minimum standards that should govern behavior toward indigenous peoples, and it is further evident that those standards are already guiding behavior. Under modern theory, such a controlling consensus following from widely shared values of human dignity constitutes customary international law. As a general matter, norms of customary international law arise when a preponderance of states and other authoritative actors converge on a common understanding of the norms' content and generally expect future behavior in conformity with the norms. The traditional points of reference for determining the existence and contours of customary norms are the relevant patterns of actual conduct on the part of state agencies. Today, however, actual state conduct is not the only or necessarily the determinative indicia of customary norms. With the advent of modern international intergovernmental institutions and enhanced communications media,

states and other relevant actors increasingly engage in prescriptive dialogue. Especially in multilateral settings, explicit communication may
itself bring about a convergence of understanding and expectation about
rules, establishing in those rules a pull toward compliance, even in
advance of a widespread corresponding pattern of physical conduct. It is
thus increasingly understood that explicit communication, of the sort that
has been ongoing in the United Nations and other international forums
with regard to indigenous peoples' rights, is itself a form of practice that
builds customary rules. [73]

The new and emergent consensus of normative precepts concerning
indigenous peoples is reflected at least partly in Convention No. 169.[74]
Since the convention was adopted in 1989, government comments
directed at developing a universal indigenous rights declaration for
adoption by the UN General Assembly have affirmed the basic precepts
set forth in the convention; in fact, the comments indicate an emerging
consensus that even more closely accords with indigenous peoples'
demands.[75]

The 1993 Draft Declaration on the Rights of Indigenous Peoples,[76]
produced by the five independent experts who make up the UN Working
Group on Indigenous Populations, stands as an authoritative statement
of norms concerning indigenous peoples based on generally applicable
human rights principles, and it also manifests a corresponding consensus
on the subject among relevant actors. The 1993 Draft Declaration goes
beyond Convention No. 169, especially in its bold statements concerning
indigenous self-determination,[77] land and resource rights,[78] and rights of
political autonomy.[79] Although the Draft Declaration is phrased mostly in
terms of rights, it incorporates the concept of a special duty on the part of
states to engage in programmatic action to implement those rights and
safeguard their enjoyment. This is evident in Article 37: "States shall take
effective and appropriate measures, in consultation with the indigenous
peoples concerned, to give full effect to the provision of this Declaration.
The rights recognized herein shall be adopted and included in national
legislation in such a manner that indigenous peoples can avail themselves of such rights in practice."

Not everyone is satisfied with *all* aspects of the Draft Declaration
developed by the working group for consideration by its parent bodies.
Some indigenous peoples' representatives have criticized the draft for not
going far enough, while governments typically have held that it goes too
far. Nevertheless, a new generation of common ground of opinion is discernible among experts, indigenous peoples, and governments about
indigenous peoples' rights and attendant standards of government
behavior, and that widening common ground is in some measure
reflected in the working group's draft.

Further manifesting, as well as contributing to, a new generation of international consensus on indigenous peoples' rights are the revised policy directive of the World Bank concerning Bank-funded projects that affect indigenous peoples[80]; Chapter 26 of Agenda 21 of the UN Conference on Environment and Development, which reiterates precepts of indigenous peoples' rights and seeks to incorporate them within the larger program of global environmentalism and sustainable development; and the 1994 resolution of the European Parliament on "Action Required Internationally to Provide Effective Protection for Indigenous Peoples."[81]

The existence and content of customary norms are especially evident in government statements about relevant domestic policies and initiatives made before international bodies concerned with promoting indigenous peoples' rights. The government practice of reporting on domestic policies and initiatives has been a regular feature of numerous UN-sponsored and other international forums at which the subject of indigenous peoples has been addressed.[82]

Governments' written and oral statements reporting domestic initiatives to international bodies are doubly indicative of customary norms. First, the accounts of government conduct provide evidence of behavioral trends by which the contours of underlying standards can be discerned or confirmed, notwithstanding the difficulties in agreeing on normative language to include in written texts. Second, because the reports are made to international audiences concerned with promoting indigenous peoples' rights, they strongly indicate subjectivities of obligation and expectation attendant on the discernible standards. Illustrative are the following statements to the 1993 World Conference on Human Rights in Vienna under the agenda item "Commemoration of the International Year of the World's Indigenous People":

Statement of Colombia on behalf of the
Latin American and Caribbean Group:
> In Latin America there exists a process of recognizing the role played by indigenous cultures in the definition of our identity, a process which takes the form of State measures, through constitutional and legislative means, to accord respect to indigenous cultures, the return of indigenous lands, indigenous administration of justice and participation in the definition of government affairs, especially as concerns their communities.
>
> Within the framework of the State unity, this process is characterized by the consecration in some constitutions of the multiethnic character of our societies.[83]

Statement on behalf of the Delegations by Finland, Sweden and Norway:
In the Nordic countries, the Sami people and their culture have made most valuable contributions to our societies. Strengthening the Sami culture and identity is a common goal for the Nordic governments. Towards this end, elected bodies in the form of Sami Assemblies, have been established to secure Sami participation in the decision making process in questions affecting them. Cross border cooperation both between Sami organizations and between local governments in the region has also provided a fruitful basis for increasing awareness and development of Sami culture.[84]

Statement by the Delegation of the Russian Federation:
We have drawn up a stage-by-stage plan of work. . . .
At the first stage we elaborated the draft law entitled "Fundamentals of the Russian legislation on the legal status of small indigenous peoples" which was adopted by the Parliament on June 11, 1993.
This Law reflects . . .
—collective rights of small peoples in bodies of state power and administration, in local representative bodies and local administration;
—legitimized ownership rights for land and natural resources in regions where such peoples traditionally live;
—guarantees for the preservation of language and culture.
The next stage consists in elaborating the specific mechanism for the implementation of this law. Work is underway on draft laws on family communities and nature use.[85]

The foregoing statements, made without reference to any specific treaty obligation, manifest the existence of customary norms. Evident in each of these statements is the implied acceptance of, and tendency toward compliance with, certain normative precepts grounded in general human rights principles. This is so notwithstanding continuing shortcomings in state behavior that are not reflected in the government accounts.

The specific contours of a new generation of international customary norms concerning indigenous peoples are still evolving and remain somewhat ambiguous. Yet the norms' core elements increasingly are confirmed and reflected in the extensive multilateral dialogue and decision processes focused on indigenous peoples and their rights.[86] These core elements can be summarized as follows.

Self-determination. Although several states have resisted express use of the term *self-determination* in association with indigenous peoples, it is possible to look beyond the rhetorical sensitivities to a widely shared consensus of opinion. That consensus is the view that indigenous peoples are entitled to continue as distinct groups and, as such, to be in control of their own destinies under conditions of equality. This principle has implications for any decision that may affect the interests of an indigenous group, and it bears generally on the contours of related norms.

Cultural integrity. There is little controversy that indigenous peoples are entitled to maintain and freely develop their distinct cultural identities, within the framework of generally accepted, otherwise applicable human rights principles. Culture is generally understood to include kinship patterns, language, religion, ritual, art, and philosophy; additionally, it increasingly is held to encompass land use patterns and other institutions that may extend into political and economic spheres. Further, governments increasingly are held, and hold themselves, to affirmative duties in this regard.

Lands and resources. In general, indigenous peoples are acknowledged to be entitled to ownership of, or substantial control over and access to, the lands and natural resources that traditionally have supported their respective economies and cultural practices. Where indigenous peoples have been dispossessed of their ancestral lands or lost access to natural resources through coercion or fraud, the norm is for governments to have procedures that permit the indigenous groups concerned to recover lands or access to resources needed for their subsistence and cultural practices and, in appropriate circumstances, to receive compensation.

Social welfare and development. In light of historical phenomena that have left indigenous peoples among the poorest of the poor, it is generally accepted that special attention is due indigenous peoples in regard to their health, housing, education, and employment. At a minimum, governments are to take measures to eliminate discriminatory treatment or other impediments that deprive members of indigenous groups of social welfare services enjoyed by the dominant sectors of the population.

Self-government. Self-government is the political dimension of ongoing self-determination. The essential elements of a sui generis self-government norm developing in the context of indigenous peoples are grounded in the juncture of widely accepted precepts of cultural integrity and democracy, including precepts of local governance. The norm upholds local governmental or administrative autonomy for indigenous communities in accordance with their historical or continuing political and cultural patterns, while at the same time upholding their effective participation in all decisions affecting them left to the larger institutions of government.

Special duty of care. Full implementation of the foregoing norms and the safeguarding of indigenous peoples' enjoyment of all generally accepted human rights and fundamental freedoms are the objectives of a continuing special duty of care toward indigenous peoples. With heightened intensity over the last several years, the international community has maintained indigenous peoples as special subjects of concern and sought cooperatively to secure their rights and well-being. Additionally, it is evident that authoritative international actors expect states to act domestically, through affirmative measures, to safeguard the rights and interests of the indigenous groups within their borders. Any state that fails to uphold a duty of care toward indigenous peoples and allows the flagrant or systematic breach of the standards summarized above, whether admitting to their character as customary law or not, risks international condemnation.

As noted previously, the terms *trust* or *trusteeship* are not commonly used in contemporary international discourse concerning indigenous peoples. Today, the principle of a special duty of care is largely devoid of the paternalism and negative regard for non-European cultures previously linked to trusteeship rhetoric. Instead, the principle rests on widespread acknowledgment, in light of contemporary values, of indigenous peoples' relatively disadvantaged condition resulting from centuries of oppression. Further, in keeping with the principle of self-determination, the duty of care toward indigenous peoples is to be exercised in accordance with their own collectively formulated aspirations. In this respect, there is a certain reemergence of the consent/protectorate strain of trusteeship doctrine discussed earlier, without the state-centered conception of humanity that requires envisioning indigenous peoples as "nations" or "states" for them to count as self-determining units.

JUNCTURE OF CONTEMPORARY INTERNATIONAL LAW AND EXERCISE OF U.S. TRUST RESPONSIBILITY

As in earlier periods, U.S. law and policy regarding Native peoples have much in common with international trends, although earlier doctrinal formulations and policy perspectives have not entirely yielded to those trends. The U.S. government continues to describe its relationship with Native peoples in terms of a trusteeship, and, as in the past, the federal government's role as a trustee refers in part to its substantial power over Indian affairs. An extensive bureaucracy, the Bureau of Indian Affairs (BIA), continues to exercise substantial influence over tribal affairs. Besides managing tribal resources, the BIA has programs for education, housing, building and maintaining roads, providing emergency relief, and administering grant programs. The United States also holds legal title to tribal lands and other major tribal assets.

Although courts still invoke the trusteeship doctrine to uphold federal discretion in regulating Indian affairs as the government carries out its duty to protect Indians,[87] the trust relationship also imposes some limitations on executive authority. Particularly in cases involving claims of federal mismanagement of Indian natural resources, courts have held the federal government liable for breach of fiduciary duty to Indians.[88] The trusteeship responsibility thus imposes a limited judicially enforceable duty on the federal government in its specific role as a legal trustee over assets it holds for the benefit of Indians.

The trusteeship doctrine also supports a broader, non–judicially enforceable obligation accepted by the legislature and the executive in treating Native peoples. Although courts have not directly enforced a broad trust responsibility on the federal government, they have relied on the trust doctrine in resolving issues brought on other grounds, particularly in construing federal statutes conferring benefits on Indians.[89] And although courts have viewed the trusteeship duties of Congress largely in terms of justifying its plenary power over Indians, Congress itself has come to view its duties as tied to the federal policy of promoting Indian self-determination. In addition, the BIA increasingly views its trusteeship responsibility from the perspective of a federal policy of Indian self-determination, moving away from its tradition of paternalism toward Native peoples.

A new U.S. policy to promote Indian self-determination, in line with contemporary developments leading to reformulated international norms concerning indigenous peoples, began to take shape around 1970. At that time, President Richard Nixon declared the assimilation policy a failure and urged Congress to "begin to act on the basis of what the Indians themselves have long been telling us . . . to create the conditions for a new era in which the Indian future is determined by Indian acts and Indian decisions."[90] Nixon called for legislative measures to ensure Indian self-determination by preserving the integrity of Native tribes and allowing them to manage their own affairs.

The reform of U.S. Indian policy urged by President Nixon was set into motion by the Indian Self-Determination and Education Assistance Act of 1975.[91] The act was designed to place control of the planning and administration of federal programs for the benefit of Native Americans primarily in the hands of the tribes themselves. The secretaries of the interior and health and human services are authorized under the act to enter "self-determination contracts" with tribes to negotiate arrangements for them to plan, conduct, and administer federal programs for their benefit.[92] The Indian Financing Act of 1974 established a $50 million revolving fund to establish loan and grant programs for the development of Indian resources.[93] An additional effort to improve the economic self-determination of tribes is evident in the Indian Tribal Government Tax Status Act, which conferred on tribes many of the tax benefits enjoyed by states.[94]

The 1988 amendments to the Indian Self-Determination Act created a self-governance demonstration project to allow a limited number of tribes to enter into self-governance "compacts" with the federal government.[95] Under these "compacts," tribes that have successfully managed other contracts under the act can extend their self-governance to all other functions and activities performed by the BIA or the Indian Health Service.[96] Federal assistance under the amended act is allocated to qualifying tribes in the form of a block grant, allowing tribes to determine what their needs are and how to meet them. Under 1991 amendments, the demonstration project was extended from five to eight years, the number of eligible tribes was expanded, and funding was increased.

The development of programs incorporating Native American cultural perspectives involved the enactment of legislation such as the Indian Child Welfare Act of 1978 (ICWA).[97] That act sought to remedy the widespread practice of placing Indian children in adoptive and foster homes, as well as placing Indian children in boarding schools, often as a result of misconceptions about Indian family structures by social workers.[98] The ICWA, designed to maximize tribal jurisdiction over child placement decisions and limit state intervention in such decisions, recognized that deciding whether Indian children should be separated from their families is of vital importance to tribes.[99] Congress stated the purpose of the act as "to protect the best interests of Indian children and to promote the stability and security of Indian tribes and families by the establishment of minimum Federal standards for the removal of Indian children from their families and the placement of such children in foster or adoptive homes which will reflect the unique values of Indian culture, and by providing for assistance to Indian tribes in the operation of child and family service programs."[100] The act, making express reference to the United States' trusteeship duties toward Indian tribes, further recognized "that there is no resource that is more vital to the *continued existence and integrity of Indian tribes* than their children and that the United States has a direct interest, as *trustee,* in protecting Indian children who are members of or are eligible for membership in an Indian tribe."[101] By linking the trusteeship responsibility directly to the continued integrity of Indian tribes, Congress envisioned anew the trusteeship role in accordance with modern international expectations about the treatment of indigenous peoples by states.

Similarly, Congress invoked the federal government's "historical and unique legal relationship with, and resulting responsibility to, the American Indian people" as part of its findings in enacting the Indian Health Care Improvement Act.[102] That act, designed to improve federal health services for Native Americans in light of evidence of low Indian health status compared with the general population, pledged to "encourage the maximum participation of Indians in the planning and management of those services." Again, Congress stressed both the historical trusteeship duties of the United States and the importance of Indian participation in providing services for their benefit.

The Indian Religious Freedom Act of 1978 underlined the federal policy to "protect and preserve for American Indians their inherent right of freedom to believe, express, and exercise the traditional religions."[103] The act requires the president to direct federal agencies to consult with Indian religious leaders to determine appropriate changes in policy or procedures needed to protect and preserve cultural rights and practices.[104] Although the act has been declared non–judicially enforceable,[105] it stands as an important policy statement to guide administrative decisions within the federal bureaucracy.

In 1983 President Ronald Reagan reaffirmed the goal of reducing tribal dependence on the federal government and increasing tribal self-governance in accordance with President Nixon's self-determination policy.[106] Reagan criticized the patterns of "excessive regulation and self-perpetuating bureaucracy" that "have stifled local decisionmaking, thwarted Indian control of Indian resources, and promoted dependency rather than self-sufficiency."[107] He called for a reversal of this trend, announcing a policy "to reaffirm dealing with Indian tribes on a government-to-government basis," while at the same time continuing to "fulfill the Federal trust responsibility for the physical and financial resources we hold. . . . The fulfillment of this unique responsibility will be accomplished in accordance with the highest standards."[108]

In the Native American Graves Protection and Repatriation Act, the "special relationship" between the federal government and Indian tribes was again invoked in the context of a framework for the repatriation of Indian human remains and funerary objects held by museums or federal agencies.[109]

Continuing this trend in legislative and executive policy, President Bill Clinton met at the White House on 29 April 1994 with representatives of hundreds of American Indian tribes, becoming the first president to summon the leaders of all 547 federally recognized tribes to a meeting with the executive.[110] Clinton issued two executive orders, the first of which called on his administration to treat tribes with the same deference given to state governments, requiring federal agencies to deal directly with Indian nations, rather than referring their concerns to the Interior Department.[111] A second order modified the Endangered Species Act to facilitate the collection of eagle feathers for use in Indian religious ceremonies.

Following the meeting with Clinton, more than 200 Native American leaders met in Albuquerque with Attorney General Janet Reno and Interior Secretary Bruce Babbitt for an unprecedented two-day National American Indian Listening Conference.[112] The conference was organized as a forum for negotiating ways to strengthen tribes' sovereign status and to resolve conflicts with the federal government over the management of tribal natural resources and the power of tribal courts.[113]

These and similar developments are in line with the concurrently emerging international norms relating to indigenous peoples. Central to these developments is the long-standing doctrine of a special duty of care, or trusteeship, toward Native peoples. But unlike in earlier periods, the objective of the trusteeship is to advance the integrity of indigenous cultures and communities and to promote indigenous self-determination. In a 1993 concurrent resolution, the U.S. Senate appeared to acknowledge the *international* character of the country's obligations toward Native Americans. In response to the UN resolution declaring 1993 the International Year of the World's Indigenous Peoples, the Senate urged the United Nations to proclaim an International Decade of the World's Indigenous Peoples. The Senate resolution expressed the "sense of Congress" that the United States should support the United Nations in its efforts to raise public awareness and to establish international standards on the rights of indigenous peoples, and further, that the United States should "address the rights and improve the social and economic conditions of its own indigenous peoples."[114]

In both its domestic and international manifestations, the doctrine of a special duty of care toward indigenous peoples rests on notions of what is required to achieve just treatment of this segment of humanity, in light of the particular genre of historical and ongoing circumstances they have faced. As the foregoing demonstrates, however, notions of what is required to achieve just treatment of indigenous peoples have changed over time, and these changes are reflected in the development of law and policy at both the international and domestic levels. As international law and policy in this field are now settling on normative assumptions that favor the cultural survival and self-determination of indigenous peoples, the development of domestic law and policy exhibits the same tendency. Still, strains of trusteeship doctrine that are rooted in the past and at odds with contemporary international norms persist in the political and legal discourse of the United States. For those who want to see the modern normative assumptions take hold in the United States, the challenge is to purge from the country's legal and political discourse the legacies of older thinking that has no place in today's world. Invoking contemporary international law can be a tool in this effort.

NOTES

1. Emerich de Vattel, *The Law of Nations or the Principles of Natural Law*, trans. Charles G. Fenwick, Classics of International Law, vol. 3 (Washington, D.C.: Carnegie Institution of Washington, 1916).

2. Ibid., 3.

3. 30 U.S. (5 Pet.) 1 (1831).

4. Ibid., 17.

5. Ibid.

6. 31 U.S. (6 Pet.) 515 (1832).

7. Ibid., 560–61 (quoting Vattel).

8. A few years after the Cherokee cases, Supreme Court reporter Henry Wheaton published a treatise on international law in which he explained the character of the consensual protectorate concept invoked by Marshall, stressing that the protectorate relationship between nations or states exists on the basis of "express compact." Henry Wheaton, *Elements of International Law*, 8th ed. (Boston: Little, Brown, 1866), 52.

9. See notes 20–27 and the accompanying text.

10. See, e.g., *Menominee Tribe v. United States*, 101 Ct. Cl. 10 (1944) (special jurisdictional act allowing the tribe to sue for mismanagement of resources under the same standards applicable to a private trustee); *Seminole Nation v. United States*, 316 U.S. 286 (1942) (action against the government for failure to meet fiduciary standards in disbursing treaty annuity payments); *United States v. Mitchell*, 463 U.S. 206 (1983) (action for money damages for breach of fiduciary obligations arising from a statutory scheme). See, generally, Reid Chambers, "Judicial Enforcement of the Federal Trust Responsibility to Indians," *Stanford Law Review*, vol. 27, no. 5 (May 1975), 1213–48.

11. See, generally, Philip D. Curtin, ed., *Imperialism* (New York: Harper and Row, 1971), 1–40 (excerpts from original nineteenth-century texts explaining the inherent inferiority of nonwhite cultures and races through pseudoscientific reasoning).

12. Francisi de Victoria, *De Indis et de Iure Belli Relectiones*, ed. Ernest Nys, trans. John Pawley Bate, Classics of International Law (Washington, D.C.: Carnegie Institution of Washington, 1917).

13. Ibid., 160–61.

14. House of Commons, Select Committee on Aboriginal Tribes, Report (1837) quoted in Russel Barsh and James Youngblood Henderson, *The Road: Indian Tribes and Political Liberty* (Berkeley: University of California Press, 1980), 86.

15. Ibid.

16. Lord John Russell, letter to Sir George Gipps, 23 August 1840, quoted in Alpheus Henry Snow, *The Question of Aborigines in the Law and Practice of Nations*, 1972 ed. (Northbrook, Ill.: Metro Books, 1918), 29–30.

17. See R. J. Gavin and J. A. Bentley, eds., *The Scramble for Africa: Documents on the Berlin West African Conference and Related Subjects 1884–1885* (Ibadan, Nigeria: Ibadan University Press, 1973), 291.

18. General Act of the Conference of Berlin, art. VI, quoted in Gavin and Bentley, *Scramble for Africa*, 291. See also M. F. Lindley, *The Acquisition and Government of Backward Territory in International Law* (London and New York: Longmans, Green, 1926), 333–34 (citing similar provisions in the concluding acts of subsequent conferences).

19. Lindley, *Acquisition and Government*, 324–36. But see *South West Africa*

Case: Phase 2, 1966 I.C.J. 34–5 (declining to recognize the juridical character of such trusteeship precepts operative on peoples in the late nineteenth to early twentieth centuries).

20. Indian Commissioner Taylor on Indian Civilization, from the Annual Report of the Commissioner of Indian Affairs, 23 November 1868, quoted in David Getches et al., *Federal Indian Law*, 3rd ed. (St. Paul, Minn.: West, 1993), 174–75.

21. S. Lyman Tyler, *A History of Indian Policy* (Washington, D.C.: Government Printing Office, 1974), 86.

22. 118 U.S. 375 (1886).

23. Ibid., 382–85.

24. 187 U.S. 553 (1903).

25. Ibid., 564.

26. See, generally, Irene K. Harvey, Note: "Constitutional Law: Congressional Plenary over Indian Affairs—A Doctrine Rooted in Prejudice," *American Indian Law Review*, vol. 10, no. 1 (1982).

27. The contemporary rational basis test for review of congressional exercise of its trusteeship powers is reflected in *Morton v. Mancari*, 417 U.S. 535 (1974) (upholding, against an equal protection challenge, a statutory provision granting Indian employment preference on the ground that the provision was "rationally tied to Congress' unique obligation toward the Indians"); and *Delaware Business Comm. v. Weeks*, 430 U.S. 73 (1977) (upholding an Indian claims settlement statute on the same ground). Compare *United States v. Sioux Nation of Indians*, 448 U.S. 371 (1980) (finding that Congress, in taking Indian lands in the nineteenth century, had not effected a good-faith transaction as trustee, and thus compensation was due pursuant to constitutional standards).

28. R. S. Baker and W. E. Dodd, eds., *War and Peace: Presidential Messages, Addresses, and Public Papers (1917–1924)* (New York: University Press of the Pacific, 1927), 411.

29. Covenant of the League of Nations, art. 22, para. 1.

30. For example, ibid., art. 22, para. 2 ("the tutelage of such peoples should be entrusted to advanced nations").

31. Depending on the circumstances of each one, the territories placed under League mandate were to be (1) assisted toward independent statehood, (2) loosely administered by the designated Mandatory power to provide basic guarantees of public order and security, or (3) included under the general administrative and legal regime of the Mandatory power as an integral part of its territory. Ibid., art. 22, paras. 3–6. In addition to establishing the system of mandates, the covenant committed *all* League of Nations members to "undertake to secure the just treatment of the native inhabitants of territories under their control." Ibid., art. 23(a).

32. UN Charter, art. 73; see also ibid., arts. 75–85 (establishing parallel international trusteeship system).

33. Ibid.

34. General Assembly Resolution 1514 of 1960 confirmed the practice establishing the norm of independent statehood for colonial territories with their colonial boundaries intact, regardless of the arbitrary character of most such boundaries. See Declaration on the Granting of Independence to Colonial Countries and Peoples, G.A. Res. 1514, UN GAOR, 15th Sess., Supp. No. 16, at 67, UN Doc. A/4684 (1960) ("Immediate steps shall be taken, in . . . Non-Self-Governing Territories . . . to transfer all powers to the peoples of those territories"); Malcolm

Shaw, *Title to Territory in Africa* (Oxford: Clarendon Press, 1986), 93 (discussing the arbitrary character of colonial boundaries in Africa in terms of the ethnic composition of the indigenous populations, boundaries left intact through decolonization). Under the companion Resolution 1541 and related international practice, self-government was also deemed implemented through the association or integration of a colonial territory with an independent state, as long as the resulting arrangement entailed a condition of equality for the people of the territory concerned and was upheld by their freely expressed wishes. See G. A. Res. 1541, UN GAOR, 15th Sess., Annex, Agenda Item 38, at 10, UN Doc. A/4651 (1960). Ofuatey-Kodjoe concludes that Resolution 1541 generally reflects international practice in the application of the principle of self-determination to the colonial territories. W. Ofuatey-Kodjoe, *The Principle of Self-Determination in International Law* (New York: Nellen, 1977), 115–28.

35. See notes 37–40 and the accompanying text.

36. See Rodolfo Stavenhagen, *The Ethnic Question: Conflicts, Development, and Human Rights* (Tokyo: United Nations University Press, 1990), 5–6.

37. International Labor Organization Convention (No. 107) Concerning the Protection and Integration of Indigenous and Other Tribal and Semi-Tribal Populations in Independent Countries, 26 June 1957 (entered into force 2 June 1959).

38. The first article of the convention states: "This Convention applies to . . . *members* of tribal or semi-tribal populations." Ibid., art. 1, para. 1; emphasis added.

39. Ch. 119, 24 Stat. 388, codified as amended at 25 U.S.C. sec. 331 et seq. (1887).

40. See generally Robert Clinton et al., *American Indian Law: Cases and Materials* (Charlottesville, Va.: Michie Company, 1991), 147–52 (describing in greater detail the provisions and implementation of the Dawes Allotment Act).

41. 8 U.S.C. sec. 1401(b) (1924).

42. "The primary effect of the Allotment Act was a precipitous decline in the total amount of Indian-held land, from 138 million acres in 1887 to 48 million in 1934." William C. Canby, Jr., *American Indian Law,* 3rd ed. (St. Paul, Minn.: West Group, 1998), 22.

43. The failures of the allotment policy from the standpoint of liberal assimilationist ideals were brought to light in the famous Merriam report. Lewis Merriam et al., *The Problem of Indian Administration* (Baltimore: Johns Hopkins Press, 1928).

44. Ch. 576, 48 Stat. 984, codified at 25 U.S.C. secs. 461–79 (1934).

45. This is evident in the summary of the congressional debate leading to passage of the Indian Reorganization Act in Barsh and Henderson, *The Road,* 96–111.

46. House Committee on Indian Affairs, 73rd Cong., 2nd sess., *Hearings: Readjustment of Indian Affairs* (Washington, D.C.: Government Printing Office, 1934), 20.

47. Ibid., 21.

48. In theory, Indians had a choice as to the form of constitution to adopt, or whether to adopt any constitution under the provisions of the act. In practice, however, the choice was most often manipulated by the federal bureaucracy, which continued to exercise substantial power over reservations. Russell Barsh, "Another Look at Reorganization: When Will Tribes Have a Choice," *Indian Truth,* no. 247 (October 1982), 4–5, 10–12.

49. For further explanation of the Indian Reorganization Act and a stinging critique of its assimilationist design, see ibid.

50. H.R. Con. Res. 108, 83rd Cong., 1st Sess., 67 Stat. B132 (1952).

51. See, generally, Franke Wilmer, *The Indigenous Voice in World Politics: Since Time Immemorial* (Newburg Park, Calif.: Sage, 1993).

52. In the United States, for example, several young Indians, among them college graduates, appeared uninvited at the 1961 conference on Indian policy organized with the help of the University of Chicago Anthropology Department. They issued a statement declaring "the inherent right of self-government" of Indian people and that they "mean to hold the scraps and parcels [of their lands] as earnestly as any small nation or ethnic group was ever determined to hold on to identity and survival." The young activists also used the conference as a springboard for the creation of the National Indian Youth Council and, with it, a new form of Indian advocacy connected with the larger civil rights movement. Later developments included the formation of other Indian activist organizations, including the American Indian Movement and its international arm, the International Indian Treaty Council.

53. Important elements of this process included widely read works by indigenous authors, e.g., Vine Deloria, Jr., *Custer Died for Your Sins* (New York: Macmillan, 1969) (Deloria is Standing Rock Sioux); Ramiro Reinaga, *Ideología y Raza en América Latina* (La Paz, Bolivia: Ediciones Futuro, 1972) (Reinaga is Quechua).

54. Indigenous peoples' representatives have appeared before UN human rights bodies in increasing numbers and with increasing frequency, grounding their demands in generally applicable human rights principles. See, generally, National Lawyer's Guild, *Rethinking Indian Law* (New York: National Lawyers Guild, 1982), 139–76 (discussing indigenous peoples' efforts of the late 1970s to early 1980s within the UN Human Rights Commission and its Subcommission on Prevention against Discrimination and Protection of Minorities); see also note 72 (discussing indigenous peoples' participation in the UN Working Group on Indigenous Populations, which was created in 1982).

Indigenous peoples have enhanced their access to these bodies as several organizations representing indigenous groups have achieved official consultative status with the UN Economic and Social Council, the parent body of the UN human rights machinery. These organizations include the Consejo Indio de Sud-America (CISA), Four Directions Council, Grand Council of the Crees (of Quebec), Indian Law Resource Center, Indigenous World Association, International Indian Treaty Council, International Organization of Indigenous Resources Development, Inuit Circumpolar Conference, National Aboriginal and Islander Legal Services Secretariat, National Indian Youth Council, and World Council of Indigenous Peoples. Additionally, indigenous peoples have invoked procedures within the Organization of American States, particularly its Inter-American Human Rights Commission. See Getches et al., *Federal Indian Law*, 1032–33 (discussing cases brought by representatives of indigenous peoples before the Inter-American Human Rights Commission). The use of international human rights procedures by indigenous peoples was encouraged by the publication in 1984 of *Human Rights—Indian Rights: Handbook for Indians on International Human Rights Complaint Procedures*, a small book written with the nonlawyer in mind. This publication by the Indian Law Resource Center (which now has offices in Helena, Montana, and Washington, D.C.) was subsequently published in Spanish and widely distributed throughout the Americas.

55. See, generally, Burnadette Kelly Roy and Gudmundur Alfredsson, "Indigenous Rights: The Literature Explosion," *Transnational Perspectives*, vol. 13, no. 1 (1987), 19.

56. G. A. Res. 45/164 (12 March 1991). See, generally, S. James Anaya, ed., "Inauguration of the 'International Year of the World's Indigenous People,'" *Transnational Law and Contemporary Problems*, vol. 3, no. 1 (spring 1993) (a compilation of related statements before the UN General Assembly by the UN secretary-general, indigenous peoples' representatives, and others).

57. International Labor Organization Convention (No. 169) Concerning Indigenous and Tribal Peoples in Independent Countries, 27 June 1989 (entered into force 5 September 1990).

58. With indigenous peoples increasingly taking charge of the international human rights agenda, Convention No. 107 of 1957 came to be regarded as anachronistic. In 1986 the ILO convened a "meeting of experts" that recommended that the convention be revised. Report of the Meeting of the Experts, quoted in International Labor Organization, *Partial Revision of Indigenous and Tribal Populations Convention, 1957* (No. 107), Report VI(1), International Labour Conference, 75th session, Geneva, 1988, 100–18. The meeting unanimously concluded that the "integrationist language" of Convention No. 107 is "outdated" and "destructive in the modern world" (ibid., para. 46, 107). The discussion on the revision continued at the 1988 and 1989 sessions of the International Labour Conference, the highest decision-making body of the ILO. At the close of the 1989 session, the conference adopted new Convention No. 169 and its shift from the prior philosophical stand. For detailed descriptions of Convention No. 169 and the process leading to it, see Lee Swepston, "A New Step in the International Law on Indigenous and Tribal Peoples: ILO Convention No. 169 of 1989," *Oklahoma City University Law Review*, vol. 15, no. 3 (fall 1990); Russel Barsh, "An Advocate's Guide to the Convention on Indigenous and Tribal Peoples," 15 *Oklahoma City University Law Review*, vol. 15, no. 1 (spring 1990). The convention came into force in 1991 with its ratification by Norway and Mexico. It was subsequently ratified by Argentina, Bolivia, Colombia, Costa Rica, Ecuador, Fiji, Guatemala, Honduras, Netherlands, Paraguay, and Peru.

59. ILO Convention No. 169, preamble, sixth para.

60. Ibid., fifth para.

61. For example, ibid., art. 5 ("the social, cultural, religious and spiritual values and practices of these peoples shall be recognized and protected").

62. Ibid., part II (Land).

63. Ibid., part III (Recruitment and Conditions of Employment), part IV (Vocational Training, Handicrafts and Rural Industries), part V (Social Security and Health), part VI (Education and Means of Communication).

64. For example, ibid., art. 7(1): "The peoples concerned shall have the right to decide their own priorities for the process of development as it affects their lives, beliefs, institutions and spiritual well-being and the lands they occupy or otherwise use, and exercise control, to the extent possible, over their own economic, social and cultural development. In addition, they shall participate in the formulation, implementation and evaluation of plans and programmes for national and regional development which may affect them directly."

65. This is recognized in the convention's preamble, quoted in the text at note 59. The need for special state and international programs directed at indigenous peoples has been established and widely accepted through years of expert study and official inquiry coordinated by international organizations. See note 72.

66. For example, Convention No. 169, art. 8.1 ("In the application of national laws and regulations to the peoples concerned, *due regard* shall be had to their customs or customary laws"); art. 9.1 ("*To the extent compatible with the national legal*

system and with internationally recognized human rights, the methods customarily practiced by the peoples concerned for dealing with offenses committed by their members shall be respected"); art. 10.1 ("In imposing penalties laid down by general law on members of these peoples *account shall be taken* of their economic, social and cultural characteristics"); emphasis added.

67. The convention includes the following: "The use of the term 'peoples' in this convention shall not be construed as having any implications as regards to the rights which may attach to the term under international law." Convention No. 169, art. 1 (3). Further, it was agreed that the following appear in the record of the proceedings: "It is understood by the Committee that the use of the term 'peoples' in this Convention has no implications as regard to the right to self-determination as understood in international law." *Report of the Committee on Convention No. 107,* Provisional Record 25, International Labour Conference, 76th session, Geneva, 1989, 27'/7, para. 31.

68. International Covenant on Civil and Political Rights, 16 December 1966, art. 1, para. 1, (entered into force 26 March 1976).

69. Statement of Lee Swepston of the International Labour Office to the UN Working Group on Indigenous Populations, 31 July 1989 (on file with the author).

70. Swepston, "A New Step," 689. Representatives of indigenous peoples' organizations expressed dissatisfaction with the new Convention No. 169 at the 1989 International Labour Conference. See statement of Ms. Venne, representative of the International Work Group for Indigenous Affairs (speaking on behalf of indigenous peoples from North and South America, the Nordic countries, Japan, Australia, and Greenland), Provisional Record 31, at 31/6, International Labour Conference, 76th session, Geneva, 1989. Since the convention was adopted in 1989, however, indigenous peoples' organizations and their representatives have increasingly expressed support for the convention's ratification. Indigenous peoples' organizations from Central and South America have been especially active in pressing for ratification. Other organizations that have expressed support for the convention include the Nordic Sami Council, the Inuit Circumpolar Conference, the World Council of Indigenous Peoples, and the National Indian Youth Council.

71. See notes 52–56 and the accompanying text.

72. A watershed in relevant United Nations activity was the 1971 resolution of the Economic and Social Council authorizing the UN Subcommission on Prevention of Discrimination and Protection of Minorities to conduct a study on the "Problem of Discrimination against Indigenous Populations." E.S.C. Res. 1589(l), UN ESCOR (21 May 1971). The study, which was issued originally as a series of partial reports from 1981 to 1983, is in UN Subcommission on Prevention of Discrimination and Protection of Minorities, "Study on the Problem of Discrimination against Indigenous Populations," UN Doc. E/Cn.4/Sub.2/1986/7 and Adds. 1–4 (1986) (Jose Martinez Cobo, special rapporteur); hereafter Martinez Cobo study. The original documents comprising the study are, in order of publication, UN Docs. E/CN.4/Sub.2/476/Adds. 1–6 (1981); E/CN.4/Sub.2/1982/2/Adds. 1–7 (1982); and E/CN.4/Sub.2/1983/21/Adds. 1–7 (1983). The Martinez Cobo study initiated further information gathering and evaluation of the subject by experts working under the sponsorship of international organizations, such as seminars organized by the UN Technical Advisory Services on racism and indigenous-state relations (Geneva, 1989), indigenous self-government (Greenland, 1991), and the role of indigenous peoples in sustainable development (Chile, 1992).

On the recommendation of the Martinez Cobo study and representatives of indigenous groups, the UN Human Rights Commission and the Economic and

Social Council approved in 1982 the establishment of the UN Working Group on Indigenous Populations. UN Human Rights Commission Resolution 1982/19 (1982); E.S.C. Res. 1982/34, UN ESCOR (1982). Through its policy of open participation in its annual one- or two-week sessions, the working group has become an important international forum for the sustained dissemination of information and exchange of views focused on indigenous peoples' demands. The subject of indigenous peoples has also been taken up regularly by the working group's parent bodies, particularly the Subcommission on Promotion and Protection of Human Rights; the subject has also appeared on the agendas of the recent major UN-sponsored global conferences, including the UN Conference on the Environment and Development (Rio de Janeiro, 1992) and the World Conference on Human Rights (Vienna, 1993).

Within the Organization of American States (OAS), the Inter-American American Indian Institute and the Inter-American Commission on Human Rights have maintained an ongoing interest in indigenous peoples. In November 1989 the OAS General Assembly resolved to "request the Inter-American Commission on Human Rights to prepare a juridical instrument relative to the rights of indigenous peoples." AG/Res. 1022 (XIX-0/89). The Inter-American Commission on Human Rights has drafted a Proposed American Declaration on the Rights of Indigenous Peoples, which currently is under consideration by OAS member states.

73. See, generally, Statute of the International Court of Justice, art. 38(1)(a) (describing "international custom, as evidence of a general practice accepted as law"); Louis B. Sohn, "Unratified Treaties as a Source of Customary International Law," in *Realism in Law-making: Essays on International Law in Honour of Willem Riphagan*, ed. Adriaan Bos and Hugo Siblesz (Boston: Martinus Nijhoff, 1986) (discussing how multilateral dialogue in the context of treaty negotiations may give rise to customary law in advance of ratification of a treaty). The theoretical grounding for identifying new customary international law concerning indigenous peoples is described more fully in S. James Anaya, *Indigenous Peoples in International Law* (Oxford and New York: Oxford University Press, 1996), 48–59 and notes.

74. Convention No. 169 was approved by consensus by the conference committee that drafted it (see 1989 ILO Provisional Record 25, 25/24–25), and the convention was adopted by the full conference by an overwhelming majority of the voting delegates. The vote was 328 in favor, 1 against, with 49 abstentions. Provisional Record 32, International Labour Conference, 76th session, Geneva, 1989, 32/17–19. None of the government delegates voted against adoption of the text, although a number abstained. Government delegates who abstained, however, expressed concern primarily about the wording of certain provisions or about perceived ambiguities in the text; in many instances, they indicated support for the core precepts of the new convention.

75. A sampling of such comments appears verbatim or is summarized in *Analytical Compilation of Observations and Comments Received Pursuant to Subcommission Resolution 1988/18*, UN Doc. E/CN.4/Sub.2/1989/33/Adds. 1–3; *Analytical Commentary on the Draft Principles Contained in the First Revised Text of the Draft Declaration on the Rights of Indigenous Peoples*, UN Doc. E/CN.4/Sub.2/AC.4/1990/1 and Adds. 1–3; *Revised Working Paper Submitted by the Chairperson/Rapporteur*, UN Doc. E/CN.4/Sub.2/1991/36.

76. *Draft Declaration on the Rights of Indigenous Peoples as Agreed upon by the Members of the Working Group at Its Eleventh Session*, UN Doc. E/CN.4/Sub.2/1993/29, Annex I (1993).

77. See ibid., 3: "Indigenous peoples have the right of self-determination. By

virtue of that right they freely determine their political status and freely pursue their economic, social and cultural development."

78. See, e.g., ibid., art. 26: "Indigenous peoples have the right to own, develop, control, and use the lands and territories, including the total environment of the lands, air, waters, coastal seas, sea-ice, flora and fauna and other resources which they have traditionally owned or otherwise occupied or used. This includes the right to the full recognition of their laws, traditions and customs, land-tenure systems and institutions for the development and management of resources, and the right to effective measures by States to prevent any interference with, alienation of or encroachment upon these rights."

79. See, e.g., ibid., art. 31: "Indigenous peoples, as a specific form of exercising their right to self-determination, have the right to autonomy or self-government in matters relating to their internal and local affairs, including culture, religion, education, information, media, health, housing, employment, social welfare, economic activities, land and resources management, environment and entry by non-members, as well as ways and means for financing these autonomous functions."

80. World Bank Operational Directive 4.20 (1991).

81. European Parliament Resolution Action Required Internationally to Provide Effective Protection for Indigenous Peoples, Eur. Parl. Doc. PV 58(II) (9 February 1994).

82. Such reporting has occurred on a regular and sustained basis in the annual meetings of the UN Working Group on Indigenous Populations pursuant to the group's mandate "to review developments pertaining to the promotion and protection of indigenous populations." Subcommission Resolution 1985/22 (29 August). See discussion of "Review of Developments Pertaining to the Promotion and Protection of Human Rights and Fundamental Freedoms of Indigenous Populations," which appears in three annual reports of the UN Working Group. Written government submissions on domestic developments appear in UN Doc. E/CN.4/Sub.2/AC.4/1989/2 and Add. 1 (information received from Australia, Brazil, Canada, and Venezuela); UN Doc. E/CN.4/Sub.2/AC.4/1990/4 (information received from Bangladesh); UN Doc. E/CN.4/Sub.2/AC.4/1991/4 (information received from Colombia).

83. Declaración de Colombia en Nombre del Grupo Latinoamericano y del Caribe en la Conmemoración del Año Internacional de las Poblaciones Indígenas (Tema 8), Conferencia Mundial de Derechos Humanos (18 June 1993) (translation from Spanish is the writer's).

84. H. E. Ambassador Haakon B. Hjelde, head of the Norwegian delegation, statement on behalf of the delegations of Finland, Sweden, and Norway to the World Conference on Human Rights in Vienna (18 June 1993).

85. Z. A. Kornilova, statement by member of the delegation of the Russian Federation at the World Conference on Human Rights on Agenda Item 8 "International Year of the World's Indigenous People" (18 June 1993).

86. A discussion of the content and general contours of new and emergent international norms concerning indigenous peoples is in Anaya, *Indigenous Peoples in International Law*, 97–125.

87. See, e.g., cases cited in note 10. See also *Lincoln v. Vigil*, 508 U.S. 182 (1993) (holding that the trust relationship did not limit the discretion of the Indian Health Service to eliminate its Indian Children's Program in the southwestern United States in favor of a nationwide program).

88. See, e.g., *United States v. Mitchell*, 463 U.S. 206 (1983) (finding a breach of

fiduciary duty by the United States for mismanagement of timber resources; the Court found that this duty arises not from express statutory language, but "necessarily arises" when the government exercises substantial control over Indian property).

89. See, e.g., *McNabb v. Bowen*, 829 F.2d 787 (9th Cir. 1987) (holding that the Indian Health Service's refusal to pay for medical care of an Indian child because the state had primary responsibility was "inconsistent with the trust doctrine" and that Congress's intent under the Indian Health Care Improvement Act was "brought into sharper focus by the trust doctrine").

90. Message from the President of the United States Transmitting Recommendations for Indian Policy, H.R. Doc. No. 363, 91st Cong., 2nd sess. (1970).

91. 25 U.S.C.A. 450a–450n (1975).

92. 25 U.S.C.A. 450f (as amended).

93. 25 U.S.C. 1451 et seq. (1974).

94. 96 Stat. 2607 (1982).

95. Getches et al., *Federal Indian Law*, 257–58.

96. Ibid.

97. 25 U.S.C.A. 1901–1963 (1978). For a summary of the act, see Getches et al., *Federal Indian Law*, 605–24. Under the act, the Indian tribe has jurisdiction in most Indian child custody proceedings, and the act requires that a preference be given to other members of the child's tribe for adoptive placement.

98. From 1969 through 1974, these practices resulted in approximately 25 to 35 percent of Indian children being separated from their families. Manuel P. Guerrero, "Indian Child Welfare Act of 1978," *American Indian Law Review*, vol. 7, no. 1 (1979), excerpts reprinted in Getches et al., *Federal Indian Law*, 606, 607.

99. Getches et al., *Federal Indian Law*, 607.

100. 25 U.S.C. 1902 (1978).

101. 25 U.S.C. 1901(3) (1978); emphasis added.

102. 25 U.S.C. 1601(a) (1976).

103. 42 U.S.C. 1996 (1978).

104. 42 U.S.C. sec. 2 (1996).

105. See *Lyng v. Northwest Indian Cemetery Protective Association*, 485 U.S. 439, 455 (1988).

106. President Ronald Reagan, Statement on Indian Policy, *Weekly Compilation of Presidential Documents*, vol. 19 (24 January 1983), 98. See Canby, *American Indian Law*, 31.

107. Ibid.

108. Ibid.

109. 25 U.S.C. 3001 et seq. (1990). Section 3010 states, "This chapter reflects the unique relationship between the Federal Government and Indian tribes and Native Hawaiian organizations and should not be construed to establish a precedent with respect to any other individual, organization, or foreign government."

110. See William J. Clinton, "Remarks to American Indian and Alaska Native Tribal Leaders," 29 April 1994, *Weekly Compilation of Presidential Documents*, vol. 30, no. 18 (9 May 1994), 941, 942.

111. Ibid.

112. "Tribal Leaders Meet, Voice Sovereignty Concerns," *Los Angeles Times*, 6 May 1994, sec. A, p. 12.

113. Ibid.

114. Senate Concurrent Resolution 44, 103rd Cong. 1st sess. (1993).

PART III: NATIVE AMERICAN RELIGIOUS TRADITIONS AND RESISTANCE

When God Became Red
Cecil Corbett (Nez Percé)

In the 1960s the mainline denominations in the United States were beginning to look at "Indian work" in a different light. Although Indian mission outreach had deteriorated since World War II, general interest in civil rights and racial unrest brought Indian peoples back into focus. In 1963 several denominations affiliated with the National Council of Churches arranged an orientation workshop on the old campus of Cook Christian Training School in Phoenix to train "new" workers how to work among Indians. And they brought in their best white experts to inform and train these neophytes in the subtleties of Indian culture, social structures, politics, and so forth. The expert staff included scholars such as Eugene Nida and Ruth Underhill. Part of the resurgence of Indian work by the churches was an attempt to recruit and train Indian persons for positions of service to Indian people, positions that in the past had fallen to white persons by default. Both Vine Deloria, Jr., and I were among those workers selected for this training event. I had been working among the Santee Sioux and had just accepted a ministry at Sacaton, Arizona. Deloria, also a seminary graduate, was working with a program of the United Scholarship Service to secure scholarships to send Indian students to eastern colleges and universities.

The idea of the conference had merit, in that it was a first attempt to compensate for curricular deficiencies in seminaries with respect to cross-cultural knowledge. Churches provided several months of preparation, orientation, and language study for missionaries who were going to serve overseas, but little was being done to prepare non-Indians to work with American Indian people, in spite of the fact that Indians also had unique cultures, languages, and heritages. The churches had not given much thought to the concept of Indian nationhood. After Manifest Destiny was introduced in the west, all Western institutions generally had a superior-inferior form of relationship with Indians. The orientation program was an attempt to complement theological courses with anthropological and Indian cultural cognition. Seminary course work did not recognize the unique cultural gifts of Indian students from many Indian nations.

After two or three lectures from the knowledgeable scholars, the Indian people recognized who had taught them. The scholars needed to learn first from the aboriginal people themselves, so Deloria suggested that the Native people at the conference establish a panel and critique the lectures from the perspective of the personal experiences of Indian people. After lengthy discussion by the conference planners, consent was given to create the panel. In the evaluation at the conclusion of the conference, people found the panel of young Indian people to be the highlight of the conference. The planners went home quite satisfied that the young Indians had learned their lessons well in such a short time. I knew then that Indian missions had reached a new day. It was time to consider what our elders had taught us about life and how we must conduct ourselves with respect, dignity, and intellect. Change was in order.

In his first book, *Custer Died for Your Sins,* Deloria introduces himself at the end by reciting his pedigree:

> My great grandfather was a medicine man named Saswe, of the Yankton Tribe of the Sioux Nation. My grandfather was a Yankton chief who was converted to Christianity in the 1860's. He spent the rest of his life as an Episcopal missionary on the Standing Rock Sioux reservation. So earnest was his work that he was called the Phillip Brooks of the Indians and his statue was placed in the national Cathedral in Washington, D.C. My father was an Episcopal missionary for thirty seven years in South Dakota. . . . He worked among our people all his life and ended his career as an Archdeacon of the Missionary District of South Dakota.[1]

With such spiritual genes, it was natural that Deloria would speak and write about the morality of a country and society such as the United States and its dealings with Indian peoples. Deloria expected much from the church in terms of righting the wrongs that had been perpetrated on American Indians in the course of the European conquest of North America. History shows that there has always been an inextricable link between the federal government and the church in their common conquest of Native peoples on this continent. The government was interested in "civilizing," while the church was interested in "Christianizing." And it has always been clear that these were two sides of the same coin.

About that time, 1964, the Program Board of the Division of Christian Life and Mission of the National Council of Churches established the National Indian Goals Study. Once again, Deloria and I found ourselves working together, two of eleven Indians on a panel of twenty-two. It was the first time in 350 years of denominational history in North America that Indian people had been invited to participate in planning and evaluating mission work among Indian people. Formerly the studies had been done to and for Indians, not with and by Indians. In another first, Robert Bennett had been employed as the first Indian commissioner of

Indian affairs since Ely Parker, a Ulysses S. Grant appointee. Bennett invited the committee members to attend eighteen field hearings that were to be held in Indian country, which gave even more credence to the committee. Yet after only a single meeting, Deloria decided precipitously to withdraw from the committee and from church work.

Unlike Don Quixote, Deloria decided that he could best work for Indian peoples in the legal and political arena. He used his sharp intellect to challenge legal and scientific thinking, as well as challenging the theological thinking of the churches. In a sense, he was hardest on those from whom he expected the most. As he said in *Custer*, "this book has been hardest on those people in whom I place the greatest amount of hope for the future—Congress, the anthropologists, and the Churches. They have been spinning their wheels either emotionally or programmatically."[2] Thus Deloria's voice became the most prominent Indian voice of the 1960s, challenging the morality of both church and state as civil rights issues were being raised by the black community. Morality became a theme and a battle cry.

> Until America begins to build a moral record in her dealings with the Indian people she should not try to fool the rest of the world about her intentions on other continents. America has always been a militantly imperialistic world power eagerly grasping for economic control over weaker nations. . . . When one considers American history in its imperialistic light, it becomes apparent that if morality is to be achieved in this country's relations with other nations a return to basic principles is in order. Definite commitments to fulfill extant treaty obligations to Indian tribes would be the first step toward introducing morality into American foreign policy.[3]

During the Indian Goals Study, Deloria had delivered a document called "Missionaries and the Religious Vacuum," which became chapter 5 in *Custer*. I saw it as a challenge to the Indian committee to maintain its integrity and not be co-opted by the church. Later I came to understand his suspicion about the goals committee.

It was in a men's room at 475 Riverside Drive, the nineteen-story headquarters of the National Council of Churches and several different denominations, where I was queried about the progress of the committee. Finally the question came, "How many Indian churches have you closed?" I was dumbfounded and returned the question, "What do you mean, close Indian churches?" He replied, "Well, you don't think white church executives are going to close the Indian churches, do you?" Suddenly, Deloria's intuition was strongly reaffirmed. I remained to fight the fight and was gratified that instead of closing churches, the Indian Goals

Study came out strongly in favor of self-determination for Indians in both church and society. Ultimately, the Indian Goals Study proposed something that had never been considered, that every denomination employ an Indian executive and establish national Indian boards within each.

Deloria continued to call and tease me every now and then. When the "God is dead" theology briefly became prominent in theological and church circles, Deloria wryly commented, "Now that God is dead, I guess all the church executives at '475' have moved up a floor."

It was a busy time in Indian affairs. The National Conference on American Indian Poverty was held in Washington, D.C., in 1964, and the War on Poverty was launched. For the first time, Indian tribes could go to other departments of government, many of which established Indian desks to work with the tribal nations. Deloria came to feel that he could best use his talents working with tribal governments, and shortly thereafter he was elected to serve as the executive director of the National Congress of American Indians (NCAI). Not many people know about Deloria's personal sacrifice to keep the offices open during the early days of his administration. Often, because of lack of funds, he could not pay himself and would sleep on the couch in the NCAI office to save money.

Some years later, Deloria and I attempted to bring some of his disparate worlds together in a series of symposia on theology and law, beginning with an initial meeting at Princeton; a follow-up conference at Cook School with Dr. Robert Bellah, author of *Habits of the Heart*; and a third at Harvard, bringing together traditional Indian medicine men, lawyers, and theologians. Deloria argued that the seminars sought ways to deal realistically with the patterns of behavior that the modern world was bringing to Indian communities. He wanted to know to what degree we rely on law and legal practitioners to establish the boundaries and procedures for proper social behavior, and to what degree we expect the shaman/medicine man/priest/therapist to draw the boundaries that law must respect.

The meeting at Harvard was particularly timely. Museums across the country were debating and considering whether to return funerary implements and skeletal remains of Indian people who had been removed from their graves and placed in basements of museums, ostensibly to foster "science." The prestigious Peabody Museum staff participated in the symposium, and later its administration announced that the museum would place two Indian people on the board. Today, "our ancient ones" are respected with dignified burials across Indian country as skeletal remains are returned to the various tribes.

Even as we count these occasional victories, the debate around "Kennewick Man" raises anew the question of Indian origin—as anthropologists attempt to argue that this 10,000-year-old skeleton unearthed in

Washington State is that of a "Caucasian" man. This appears to be a gross example of political academics, an attempt to negate any Indian claim to original occupancy of the continent and to aboriginal title to the land. Fortunately for Indians, Vine Deloria was deeply involved in creating the Native American Graves Protection and Repatriation Act, and he continues to put his energies into exposing the political underbelly of "objective" scholarship, whether it be legal, historical, social, or scientific.

NOTES

1. Vine Deloria, Jr., *Custer Died for Your Sins: An Indian Manifesto* (New York: Macmillan, 1969(, 269. See Deloria's more extended family history in his *Singing for a Spirit: A Portrait of the Dakota Sioux* (Santa Fe, N.M.: Clear Light Publishers, 1999).

2. Deloria, *Custer Died for Your Sins*, 275.

3. Ibid., 51.

CHAPTER SEVEN

Earth Mother and Prayerful Children: Sacred Sites and Religious Freedom

Henrietta Mann (Cheyenne)

Nistaomeno (In the past of long ago), the Great Mysterious Life-Giver planted the first people in the ground-womb of the Great Mother Earth and gave them spiritual-rooted lifeways that are anchored in the dirt and soil of this land comprising the Western Hemisphere. The Cheyenne word *Xamaa-vo'estaneo'o* linguistically illustrates this special relationship between humans and the land. The word translates into English as the indigenous, aboriginal, ordinary people, or the natural, simple people of this land. Thus, the natural people of this land, the culturally and spiritually diverse first nations, have long-standing and continuous caretaking responsibilities for maintaining the sanctity of earth. This is affirmed by their beliefs that they come from the earth, that they must live in mutual relationship with the earth, that they must constantly and responsibly observe ceremonies that revitalize and renew the earth, and that in the end they return to the earth. As earthborn people, they have a sense of place that has been deepened throughout the thousands of years they have lived on and with this land. Their spiritual earth roots have resulted in a kinship like that of a mother to her children. It is a sacred relationship that is characterized by prayerful love and deep religious reverence for holy ground.

There are numerous holy places on this island-continent. As Vine Deloria, Jr., states: "Holy places are well known in what have been classified as primitive religions. The vast majority of Indian tribal religions have a center at a particular place, be it river, mountain, plateau, valley, or other natural feature. . . . In part the affirmation of the existence of holy places confirms tribal people's rootedness."[1] This indigenous spiritual rootedness to place has been in jeopardy since the Anglo-European invasion. Those that left their homelands to immigrate to this country held differing attitudes toward earth, based on their belief in Manifest Destiny. "The White Man excused his presence here by saying that he had been guided by the will of his God; and in so saying absolved himself of all responsibility for his appearance in a land occupied by other men."[2] His God had commanded him to multiply, subdue the earth, and to have dominion over everything on it. Following the "fall of man," however, God exacted punishment, which included cursing the ground. Ground that is cursed cannot be sacred; consequently, land is nothing more than a commodity to be subdued, which is justifiable under the doctrine of Manifest Destiny.

It is against this background of conflicting attitudes toward the land and all life that historical and contemporary indigenous religious rights issues had their genesis. Many of the earliest Anglo-American immigrants to this hemisphere fled their homelands to escape religious persecution. Ironically, some forgot their religious fears and ethnocentrically presumed that their religions were superior to indigenous sacred ways, an attitude that found its way into federal Indian policy.

Despite its doctrine of separation of church and state, the newly established federal government worked with Christian denominations in carrying out its so-called American Indian civilization and assimilation policy. Because of heavy church involvement, Christianization also became a goal of federal Indian policy. In his 1869 Indian "peace policy," President Ulysses S. Grant, in an unprecedented delegation of authority, entrusted the nomination of federal agents in charge of reservations to the several religious bodies interested in Indian missionary work. Such Indian agents also were responsible for administering Indian education activities, which incorporated religious instruction along with a rudimentary English education and vocational instruction. Essentially, the federal education system consisted of federally subsidized church group schools.

Assessing the impact of Grant's policy on reservations, Alvin Josephy, Jr., notes that the peace policy was damaging to Indian peoples: "Many reservations had come under the authority of what had amounted to stern missionary dictatorships whose fanatic zealousness had crushed Indian culture and institutions, suppressed religious and other liberties, and punished Indians for the least show of independence."[3] The peace policy was a failure, and it was abandoned in the 1880s.

Although policy supposedly changed, the suppression of Indian religions continued. The government had banned the sweat lodge in 1873. "Thus the Sun Dance, the Snake Dance, the Ghost Dance, the Potlatch Ceremony, and the use of peyote for religious purposes were outlawed or administratively discouraged. 'Superstition,' or 'cruelty,' 'licentiousness,' 'idleness,' 'indifference to family welfare,' and the like were frequently cited as reasons for suppressing Indian religious ceremonies."[4] Such prohibitions were effected through regulations governing courts of Indian offenses or policy directives sent to the superintendents of Indian agencies. In one instance, however, the federal government utilized military force to extinguish a religious movement called the Ghost Dance. This event is known as the Wounded Knee Massacre of 1890. At Wounded Knee over 300 Lakota people, mostly women and children, were killed.

The repressive policy governing American Indian ceremonies and religious expression was reversed by John Collier when he became the commissioner of Indian affairs in 1934. He issued Circular No. 2970, "Indian Religious Freedom and Indian Culture," which says in part, "No interference with Indian religious life or ceremonial expression will hereafter be tolerated. The cultural liberty of Indians is in all respects to be considered equal to that of any non-Indian group. . . . In no cases shall punishments for statutory violations or for improprieties be so administered as to constitute an interference with, or to imply a censorship over, the religious or cultural life, Indian or other."[5] Despite the First Amendment's free-exercise clause, Commissioner Collier's policy directive was necessary to provide a degree of religious freedom to this country's first nations.

Based on the cherished freedoms enshrined in the U.S. Constitution, no individual or cultural group should ever have to worry about freedom of worship. Nonetheless, this harsh reality of the indigenous experience was, unfortunately, not curtailed by the Collier policy directive. Ongoing religious rights violations necessitated the passage in 1978 of the American Indian Religious Freedom Act (AIRFA). A joint resolution of Congress enacted as Public Law 95-341, AIRFA commits the United States "to protect and preserve for American Indians their inherent right of freedom to believe, express, and exercise the traditional religions of the American Indian, Eskimo, Aleut, and Native Hawaiians, including but not limited to access to sites, use and possession of sacred objects, and the freedom to worship through ceremonials and traditional rites."[6] It is difficult to imagine that a democratic nation such as the United States would need special legislation to ensure First Amendment protection to its indigenous population. Further, it lends validity to the analogy of a "miner's canary," which has been used to describe the role that tribal people play in the country's political arena.

The second section of AIRFA mandated the president to "direct the various Federal departments, agencies, and other instrumentalities responsible for administering relevant laws to evaluate their policies and procedures in consultation with native traditional religious leaders in order to determine appropriate changes necessary to protect and preserve Native American religious cultural rights and practices."[7] The president was given twelve months to compile a report for Congress, which was to include recommendations for administrative changes and legislative action.

The Federal Agencies Task Force submitted its AIRFA Report in August 1979. The document included nearly forty pages of recommendations for administrative and legislative changes regarding land, cemeteries, sacred objects, and ceremonies.[8] The report also contained over 500 incidents of documented government infringements on American Indian religious freedom.[9]

Generally, the recommendations of the AIRFA Report have resulted in minimal action. One positive outcome from the AIRFA Report, however, was passage of the 1990 Native American Graves Protection and Repatriation Act (NAGPRA), which addresses the return of human skeletal remains and sacred objects to their cultural homelands. NAGPRA is a means of reversing the insensible collection policies of museums and their warehousing of hundreds of thousands of ancestral human remains, which are sacred. The blatant disrespect exhibited in such collection practices is as much a violation of a people's religious rights as is the lack of First Amendment protection for Indian sacred sites, the religious rights of Indian prisoners, and the religious use of eagle feathers and other animal parts. Such violations continue to exist within the boundaries and politics of the greatest democracy in the world.

In attempting to understand the wrongs committed against indigenous people and their sacred beliefs, there appear to be considerable differences in the understanding of what is sacred and how one shows respect for the sacred. "When we try to do things we want to do and have done in the past," complained Cheyenne spokesperson Bill Tallbull at a 1991 sacred sites caucus, "we always run up against a person who came to us that held nothing sacred. This person began to probe the earth, probe the sky, treads on everything, touches everything. He has no taboos. . . . We have tried to educate this person in many different ways. We are trying to do our best to convey the cultural values of our people."[10]

Indigenous people have great reverence and love for the earth and all that lives on, in, above, below, and all around it. That the earth is mother and sacred are two beliefs passed on through the generations. As I wrote some years ago, "My great-grandmother taught her son and grandson, and through them she passed on to me her profound respect for the earth. . . . Because of her, I know the earth as a wise, loving, generous, and powerful woman, who will continue to sustain us as a people so long as we continue to revere her and maintain a balance in life. A stable, solid earth, fresh air, continuing heat from the sun, and clear water are important to us because they were important to our beloved ancestors."[11]

Because our ancestors lived in respectful interdependence with these life-giving spiritual elements, so must we. It is both painful and horrifying for indigenous people to see excessive pollution of the air and water and to see the desecration of places that are sacred. Sacred site development is antithetical to the indigenous interdependent view of life, which requires one to live in a balanced, prayerful way and to protect and renew all earth through ceremonies. How horrifying it must have been for the Cherokee to witness the culturally destructive flooding of their sacred birthplace and historic capital of Chota, their ancestral burial grounds, and their ceremonial medicine-gathering area caused by the Tellico Dam.

Some members of the Cherokee Nation attempted to stop the Tennessee Valley Authority from constructing the dam by filing a lawsuit, *Sequoyah v. Tennessee Valley Authority*. They sought relief under AIRFA but lost, proving that AIRFA is indeed a "toothless tiger" that provides no legal protection.[12]

Cherokees remember a devoted and courageous Cherokee man who refused to abandon the grave of his wife, who weighted himself down so he would drown alongside her burial site when the floodgates of the Tellico Dam were opened.[13] Thus, this Cherokee man rests alongside his beloved wife in their ancestral homeland, covered over by water, a human monument to how much indigenous people love their dead. *Sequoyah v. Tennessee Valley Authority* was the first Indian sacred site case lost after the passage of AIRFA, which diminished the hope of many in Indian country that their sacred landscape would be protected. Fortunately, the inner spiritual terrain of the indigenous mindscape preserves those sacred places.

For some first nations, like the Cherokee, AIRFA has not provided the necessary First Amendment protection. For others, AIRFA came too late. Bear Butte is located on the periphery of the Black Hills in northwestern South Dakota. This mountain is sacred to the Cheyenne, Lakota, Arapaho, and Kiowa since the Grandfather Great One sent each of them a powerful sacred object from that mountain to guide and protect them as they walk their respective roads of life.[14] These holy gifts that the Creator sent as blessings spiritually bind them and embed them in the sacred landscape, just as a tree, flower, or blade of sweetgrass is embedded in the soil.

For the Cheyenne, Bear Butte is the sacred center of their universe and is the place from which their power as a people flows. It is *Noahavose*, the "giving hill," which gave them their way of life. All the powers of the world assembled deep within the mountain and taught their great prophet all that makes them unique as a people. As a former Keeper of the Sacred Buffalo Hat of the Cheyenne stated: "All of our spiritual history surrounds Bear Butte. Our point of origin as a people. And also it is a reference point for our existence as a people in this land. It's a symbol and physical thing that substantiates our existence as a people."[15] It is the spiritual Cheyenne home.

Today, Cheyenne, Lakota, and other tribal people make pilgrimages to Bear Butte to fast, make prayer offerings, gather ceremonial items, or formalize ceremonial vows. They do this even though the mountain and the surrounding ground is a South Dakota State Park and the natural landscape has been desecrated by geographic modifications. The state has developed the area for tourism, complete with a visitor center and parking lots. The hiking trails and overlook platforms are incongruent with the awe-inspiring features of the land, which are heightened by a sense of sacredness. The incongruity is especially noticeable among some of the trees to which sacred offering cloths, which represent prayers, have been tied. Park officials have attempted to be sensitive to those fasting in designated fasting areas and have posted signs, "Indians praying—do not pass beyond this point," which some "find alienating and dehumanizing."[16] Some hikers unintentionally or perhaps intentionally intrude on fasters and often make loud noises; this is highly disruptive to spiritual thinking, which requires silence.

Places designated for tourism can hardly remain quiet or unnoticed. Another site located northwest of Bear Butte is Devil's Tower. To the Lakota it is *Mato-tipila,* Bear's Lodge.[17] It is an ancient Lakota Sun Dance site and is also sacred to many other tribes, among them the Kiowa, who came to this place on their pilgrimage to the south. N. Scott Momaday writes:

> Two centuries ago, because they could not do otherwise, the Kiowas made a legend at the base of the rock. My grandmother said: *Eight children were there at play, seven sisters and their brother. Suddenly the boy was struck dumb; he trembled and began to run upon his hands and feet. His fingers became claws, and his body was covered with fur. Directly there was a bear where the boy had been. The sisters were terrified; they ran, and the bear after them. They came to the stump of a great tree, and the tree spoke to them. It bade them climb upon it, and as they did so it began to rise into the air. The bear came to kill them, but they were just beyond its reach. It reared against the tree and scored the bark all around with its claws. The seven sisters were borne into the sky, and they became the stars of the Big Dipper.* From that moment, and so long as the legend lives, the Kiowas have kinsmen in the night sky.[18]

This event in Kiowa history affirms indigenous interrelated views of land, sky, and life. It also explains the origin of an unusual land formation that protected their children, just as the land protects them as a people. The Kiowa revere this place they call *Tosai,* which means Rock Tree.

For the more than twenty Plains Indian tribes that consider Devil's Tower the equivalent of a cathedral or temple, rock climbing is a sacrilege, to say nothing of the visual and geologic impact created by pitons, some of which are driven permanently into the rock face. The National Park Service attempted to mitigate the multiple-use situation and developed a management plan that discouraged rock climbing during the month of June, since many tribes hold their ceremonies and Sun Dance around the summer solstice. Rock climbers opposed the plan and filed a lawsuit. In April 1998, the presiding judge ruled in favor of the National Park Service and supported its authority to provide for private worship without external distractions.

This ruling was long overdue, and although tribal people can observe the Sun Dance and other ceremonies at this place of worship, the site is still available for climbing the remaining eleven months of the year. This is equivalent to individuals being allowed to climb places of sanctity such as the Vatican, St. John's Cathedral, or any synagogue, temple, or church, whether services are being conducted or not. The act of climbing a sacred structure for sport or its defacement or disturbance simply would not be tolerated. Indigenous people feel this way about their sacred sites as well.

Devil's Tower, Bear Butte, and Chota are but a sampling of what has happened, is happening, and can happen at other Indian sacred sites throughout the United States. Indigenous people have caretaking and protective responsibilities for the land, and their spirituality is rooted in the land.

> American Indian religious practices are land-based theologies whose effectiveness is dependent upon access to specific sacred sites. Consequently, dispute over land has become, undoubtedly, the most significant and pressing dilemma facing Native North Americans today. Sacred geography is the essential feature of that struggle. Tourism and accelerated mineral exploration by the U.S. government over the past three decades have heightened the ongoing battle by Native Americans for land rights. The essence of Native American religious freedom is the land. . . . Native peoples, however—alone among American citizens—are effectively denied access to their sacred sites.[19]

Policy makers, primarily federal officials and corporate executives, have no understanding of or respect for sacred geography. The Constitution and AIRFA do not afford any protection for Indian sacred sites, and neither do the courts.

In 1988, the U.S. Supreme Court in *Lyng v. Northwest Indian Cemetery Protective Association* clearly articulated its position concerning sacred sites located on federal property by ruling in favor of then Secretary of Agriculture Richard E. Lyng. The lawsuit involved the U.S. Forest Service's proposed construction of a six-mile paved logging road through the Chimney Rock area, where three Northern California tribes hold their world renewal ceremonies in which they pray for the earth and all life. The Supreme Court reversed lower court rulings that had found that construction of this road (commonly referred to as the GO Road, short for Gasquet and Orleans) would violate the Free Exercise Clause of the First Amendment. Yurok spokesperson Chris Peters concludes, "This precedent-setting case established that Native Americans do not have First

Amendment protection under the United States Constitution. The public majority outweighs Native Rights. Federal agencies intend to extermi- nate a belief system. . . . *Lyng* deems that the total destruction of three Native American religions (that of the Yurok, Karok, and Tolowa Indians in northern California) is not a violation of the First Amendment Free Exercise Clause."[20] The precedent also affirmed that federal land man- agement agencies can do whatever they want with public land, even if it results in the death of a people's religion. This has ominous implications for American democratic traditions and "should deeply concern all citi- zens who cherish religious freedom principles, because, under *Lyng,* United States law guarantees less religious freedom than most other democracies and some non-democratic nations."[21]

A scant two years later, in April 1990, American Indians were still reeling from the judicial insult to their religions when the Supreme Court handed down an equally devastating decision in *Employment Division, Department of Human Resources of Oregon v. Smith et al.,* involving the Native American Church and its traditional use of peyote.

> Al Smith was a Klamath Indian who had been fired from a private alcohol and drug abuse treatment program because he admitted par- ticipating in a Native American Church ceremony. His employers had designated peyote as a drug. They claimed that when Smith used peyote in a Native American Church meeting, he violated the rules of their organization. Al Smith filed for unemployment benefits and was upheld by the Appeals Court in the State of Oregon. He was upheld all the way to the State Supreme Court in Oregon, but Ore- gon's attorney general took the case to the United States Supreme Court. The Supreme Court's decision was shocking, not only because it jeopardizes Native Americans, but because of its detri- mental effect on the whole religious life of the American people.[22]

Indian rights leaders and the 250,000 members of the Native American Church who use peyote as their supreme sacrament were shocked by the decision, as were mainstream churches. Most disturbing about *Smith* was that the Supreme Court did not apply the compelling state interest appli- cable to free-exercise cases. It then directed all concerned to go to Con- gress for relief, which Indians and mainstream churches did.

Indigenous people created a broad-based coalition of organizations spearheaded by the National Congress of American Indians, the Associa- tion on American Indian Affairs, the Native American Rights Fund, and the Native American Religious Freedom Project. Their basic strategy was to lobby Congress for legislative amendments to AIRFA. Coalition lead- ership took into account the findings of the 1969 AIRFA Report, critical traditional religious rights violations, and other pressing situations in light of *Lyng*. The four broad, priority categories of proposed amendments to AIRFA were: (1) Protection of Indian sacred sites. (2) Protection of traditional use of peyote by Indians. (3) Protection of religious rights of Native prisoners to the same extent as prisoners of other religious faiths. (4) Protection of religious use of eagles and other animals and plants. AIRFA coalition members exerted considerable lobbying efforts with key congressional representatives, and on 25 May 1993 the proposed amendments were introduced in the Senate as the Native American Free Exercise of Religion Act of 1993. The bill was referred to the Committee on Indian Affairs, but it was never enacted.

Early the following year, Representative Bill Richardson introduced H.R. 4230 in the House, which targeted only the peyote section of the AIRFA amendments. It was referred to the Committee on Natural Resources on 14 April 1994, and on 6 October 1994 President Bill Clinton signed it as Public Law 103-344, the American Indian Religious Freedom Act Amendments of 1994. This ended the threat of religious persecution against Indians who are practitioners of the peyote religion. "The bill provides that the use, possession or transportation of peyote by Indians for religious purposes is lawful and shall not be prohibited by any state or the Federal government, and no Indian shall be penalized or discriminated against for peyote possession."[23] This legislation was a significant triumph for the protection of Indian rights. Peyotists, their attorneys, coalition members, and the family of the late Reuben Snake, peyote Road Man and former director of the Native American Religious Freedom Project, celebrated their victory. The national Indian celebration was held on the campus of Haskell Indian Nations University in Lawrence, Kansas. It began with a forum, which was followed that night by traditional prayer services held in four tepees that had been erected around Haskell's sacred medicine wheel earthwork. Finally free to worship as they believed, the participants echoed the words of a Navajo man, a Road Man, who had walked the peyote road for forty years and who had been incarcerated for his religious beliefs: "Peyotism has endured."[24]

The peyote way is enduring. Historians have traced the use of peyote back 10,000 years. Indigenous people developed their land-based theologies over the thousands of years they lived here, which has resulted in sacred geography. Over that time they also maintained a respectful relationship with all other life-forms and incorporated them into their ceremonies, which is why they must have continued access to eagle feathers, animal parts, and plants. Because of their humane and just ways, there were no prisons in this country in pre-Columbian times. Regardless of circumstances, a person's most treasured possession is his or her spirituality. Although the traditional religious use of peyote is now protected, the three remaining categories of proposed amendments have yet to be brought under the protective umbrella of the Bill of Rights.

The mainstream churches formed the Coalition for the Free Exercise of Religion, which pursued a separate federal legislative remedy after *Smith*. It became a powerful political influence group, and its congressional lobbying efforts resulted in enactment of Public Law 103-141 on 16 November 1993. Reversing the Supreme Court's ruling in *Smith,* the Religious Freedom Restoration Act of 1993 (RFRA) was intended to protect the free exercise of religion, "restore the compelling interest test . . . and to guarantee its application in all cases where free exercise of religion is substantially burdened; and . . . to provide a claim or defense to persons whose religious exercise is substantially burdened by government."[25] Although RFRA restored religious freedom to all Americans, it did not address the unique, unwritten, and often misunderstood needs of American Indians in the free exercise of their religious practices. At a time when majority America was again free to enjoy religious liberty, indigenous people were left to confront their disheartening struggle for religious freedom.

Earlier, the 1990 enactment of NAGPRA had provided some religious and human rights protection for indigenous people. NAGPRA protected grave sites, provided for the repatriation and reburial of remains, and mandated the return of sacred objects, in consultation with traditional spiritual leaders. Contemporary Indian tribal leaders had worked diligently for the enactment of this legislation for cultural, legal, and moral reasons. They recognized the power contained in sacred objects, which can be dangerous when they are not handled properly or are in the wrong hands. Further, indigenous people have a deep respect for human remains, which should not be disturbed. "It has been estimated that museums, federal agencies, other institutions, and private collectors retain between 300,000 and 2.5 million dead bodies taken from Indian graves, battlefields, and POW camps by soldiers, museum collectors, scientists, and pothunters."[26] This has created a crisis, which underscores arrogant cultural insensitivity and disrespect.

Nonetheless, repatriation is occurring, but at a slow rate. Museums initially were given five years to inventory their holdings identified in NAGPRA and to consult with traditional leadership on their return. No one anticipated the emotional cost of repatriation, not to mention the exorbitant expense to low-budget tribal governments and communities. In addition, the return of human remains has thrust some first nations into a cultural dilemma in terms of the absence of ceremonies for reburial. Return of sacred objects also requires serious consideration of possible health risks associated with handling such items, which may have been contaminated with hazardous substances, such as arsenic, formerly used in standard preservation techniques. Indigenous people continue to be challenged by the entire repatriation issue. In general, however, they are grateful for the return of the beloved human remains of their ancestors and for the sacred objects that have come back home to their motherland.

After several years of sustained efforts to convince Congress of the need for legislation to protect the unprotected, AIRFA coalition members decided to explore relief through the executive branch of government. After all, both the judicial and the legislative branches had proved to be either hostile or unresponsive to the lack of Bill of Rights protections for the first people of this country.

Subsequently, on 24 May 1996, President Clinton issued an executive order on "Indian Sacred Sites." It ordered federal land management agencies to be "as responsive as possible to the concerns of American Indian tribes regarding sacred sites."[27]

> EO 13007 requires five actions of Federal agencies: 1. Accommodate access to and ceremonial use of Indian sacred sites by Indian religious practitioners, as long as such accommodation is not inconsistent with the law or with essential agency functions. 2. Avoid adverse effect on physical integrity of such sacred sites, subject to the same caveats. 3. Maintain information on such sites in confidence where appropriate. 4. Implement procedures to carry out the provisions of the order, including providing notice to Indian tribes of actions potentially affecting sacred sites or access to them, in a manner that respects the sovereignty of Indian tribal governments. 5. Report to the President about any changes needed in law, regulation, or procedure to accommodate access to and ceremonial use of Indian sacred sites, to avoid adverse affect on such sites, and to facilitate consultation with tribes, and religious leaders, including provision for the resolution of disputes.[28]

Indigenous people appreciated the administration's action, but to them it essentially was an echo of AIRFA, in that the executive order lacks enforcement provisions. They were hoping to have some guarantee of religious freedom, particularly in protecting the natural integrity of their most holy places.

Accepting the fact that holy places are not restricted to lands across the ocean would help in maintaining the sacred landscape in this country. Majority society, lawmakers, policy makers, and federal land managers must remember and respect that indigenous people have a sacred, umbilical-like attachment to the land, which is rooted in the past of long ago. The same people in power would do well to remember that indigenous people evolved their own distinct cultures and land-based theologies thousands of years prior to 1492. Their spiritual traditions differ from

Judeo-Christian ones in many respects. American Indians believe in natural spiritual laws, but they are also required to adhere to the laws that govern this country.

On 25 June 1997 the Supreme Court once again considered a ruling on religious freedom in the case of *City of Boerne v. P. F. Flores, Archbishop of San Antonio, and United States*. The Court struck down the four-year-old RFRA as unconstitutional. The Court said that the Congress had overstepped its Fourteenth Amendment power and had unconstitutionally usurped the power of federal courts and the states by enacting RFRA. What is significant is that indigenous people were not accorded First Amendment protection in RFRA, and their First Amendment rights were violated in *Lyng* and *Smith* while others enjoyed religious liberty. Their treatment as this country's "miner's canary" should have acted as a democratic barometer of what can happen to others if civil rights are violated.

America is looked on as the greatest democratic nation in the world, and other world powers would find it virtually impossible to believe that indigenous religious rights violations have been allowed to occur here at all. The reality is that such violations are occurring presently, and this country's culturally distinct Native people are engaged in a struggle for their very existence. Their sacred sites are especially vulnerable, and the ones that have been identified number in the hundreds. Some, like Bear Butte, have been developed; others are slated for development, including recreation, tourism, mining, logging, New Age vandalism, oil and gas exploration, and geothermal development, to name but a few.

These blessed and holy places are located throughout this great island and across the ocean in Hawaii. Indigenous people have their equivalents of Mount Sinai, Mount Moriah, and the Mount of Olives in such places as Mount Shasta, Mount Graham, San Francisco Peaks, and the Sweetgrass Hills. The major difference is that biblical sites are revered, and it would be sacrilege to even think of their development. Regrettably, the majority of land developers in this country have no such respect for sites that are paradise to American Indian people.

One of them, Mount Graham, is sacred to the Apache, and Ola Cassadore-Davis, a San Carlos Apache, was charged with protecting this place, which to them is "Big Seated Mountain." It is home to their Spirit Crown Dancers, the sacred gateway for their prayers, and the original Apache homeland to which they are tied. Mount Graham International Observatory, the world's largest seven-telescope observatory, has been under construction at the mountaintop. The Vatican constructed the first telescope, the Max Planck Institute of Germany completed the second, and the University of Arizona is to build the third. "On the U of A's own campus, Roger Lynds of the National Optical Astronomy Observatory co-authored a 1984 report that ranked Mount Graham 38th out of 56 peaks as a possible large telescope location."[29] It is puzzling why thirty-seven better sites were ignored and Mount Graham was selected.

One also has to wonder about the motives underlying the Vatican's involvement. "The astronomer who runs the already-functioning Vatican telescope on Mount Graham once explained that he's doing it partly to scan the skies for aliens to convert to Catholicism."[30] Apparently, the discussion of conversion of possible life-forms in space has taken place in church circles. "Father Chris Corbally, an English Jesuit who is the observatory's deputy director, said: 'If civilisation were to be found on other planets and if it were feasible to communicate, then we would want to send missionaries to save them, just as we did in the past when new lands were discovered.'"[31] Statements of this nature make perfect sense to indigenous peoples, based on the 500-year history of proselytizing and their experience with Manifest Destiny. The Vatican is still on track in terms of subduing the earth and having dominion over every living thing on it, but it has now extended this concept to space—thus, the telescope.

The objection is not to telescopes, just to where they are situated. The Vatican is the center of the Catholic world, and Catholics, too, would feel disrespected and violated if the steeple of St. Peter's Church became an observatory. The collective cultural and spiritual memory of indigenous people rests solely in this sanctified land. The land-based cultures and theologies of the first nations are rooted in the landscape of earth as mother. The earth is their altar where they carry out their divinely ordered mandates to protect the earth and all life. It is from their various altar sites that they send their prayers to the four sacred directions of this earth, to the powers of the four directions, who guide their hearts and spirits. They are spiritual people, the prayerful children of this earth.

Despite the contemporary mandates of Manifest Destiny, which have resulted in incredible desecration, and despite indigenous people's cultural loss, they are still rich in spiritual wealth. Perhaps government and corporate America will stop to think and come to understand this sacred, interdependent relationship with the land and afford those who were here first their divine right to worship at their sacred places, in their own ceremonies that keep this earth alive for everyone. It is a simple but critical matter of respecting sacred sites and the freedom of religion so that indigenous people can pray in culturally appropriate ways for all their relations on earth. It has been that way from the past of long ago, *Nistaomeno*.

NOTES

1. Vine Deloria, Jr., *God Is Red* (New York: Grosset and Dunlap, 1973), 81.

2. Luther Standing Bear, *Land of the Spotted Eagle* (Boston and New York: Houghton Mifflin, 1933), 249.

3. Alvin M. Josephy, Jr., *The Indian Heritage of America* (New York: Alfred A. Knopf, Bantam Books, 1968), 340.

4. Sandra L. Cadwalader and Vine Deloria, Jr., eds., *The Aggressions of Civilization: Federal Indian Policy since the 1880s* (Philadelphia: Temple University Press, 1984), 52.

5. Arlene Hirschfelder and Paulette Molin, *The Encyclopedia of Native American Religions* (New York: MJF Books, 1992), 48.

6. Christopher Vecsey, ed., *Handbook of American Indian Religious Freedom* (New York: Crossroad Publishing Company, 1991), 138.

7. Ibid.

8. Sharon O'Brien, "A Legal Analysis of the American Indian Religious Freedom Act," in *Handbook of American Indian Religious Freedom,* ed. Christopher Vecsey (New York: Crossroad Publishing Company, 1991), 30.

9. U.S. Department of the Interior, Federal Agencies Task Force, *American Indian Religious Freedom Act Report, P.L. 95-341,* Washington, D.C., August 1979.

10. Bill Tallbull, "On the Tongue River Valley," in *Proceedings of the National Sacred Sites Caucus* (New York: Association on American Indian Affairs, August 1991), 8.

11. Henrietta Mann, "The Beautiful Earth Woman: American Myth and Reality," in *The Way of the Earth: Encounters with Nature in Ancient and Contemporary Thought,* ed. T. C. McLuhan (New York: Simon and Schuster, 1994), 417.

12. O'Brien, "Legal Analysis," 35.

13. Dr. Lee Piper, Overhill Cherokee, panel discussant, "Religious Freedom and Sacred Sites," international gathering sponsored by Anne Wilson Schaef, Ph.D., Boulder Hot Springs, Montana, July 1998.

14. Telephone interview, Vernon Sooktis, Northern Cheyenne Sun Dance Priest, fifth-generation Chief Dull Knife descendant, Lame Deer, Montana, July 1999.

15. Joe Little Coyote, quoted in *A Song from Sacred Mountain,* ed. Anita Parlow (Pine Ridge, S.D.: Oglala Lakota Legal Rights Fund, 1983), 76; McLuhan, *The Way of the Earth,* 379.

16. *Proceedings of the National Sacred Sites Caucus* (New York: Association on American Indian Affairs, August 1991), 2.

17. It seems axiomatic to add that nearly all places in North America that have the name "devil" in English are sites of special sacredness to the Native peoples and were named to discourage Native ceremonial attention to the sites.

18. N. Scott Momaday, *The Way to Rainy Mountain* (1969; paperback ed., Albuquerque: University of New Mexico Press, 1993), 8.

19. McLuhan, *The Way of the Earth,* 378.

20. Chris Peters, "On Chimney Rock," in *Proceedings of the National Sacred Sites Caucus,* 4.

21. Walter R. Echo-Hawk, "Native American Religious Liberty: Five Hundred Years after Columbus," *American Indian Culture and Research Journal,* vol. 17, no. 3 (1993), 43.

22. Jay C. Fikes, *Reuben Snake Your Humble Serpent: Indian Visionary and Activist* (Santa Fe, N.M.: Clear Light Publishers, 1996), 183.

23. "President Clinton Signs Law Protecting Ceremonial Use of Peyote by Native American Church Practitioners: A Victory for the Religious Freedom

Coalition," *Indian Affairs* (newsletter of the Association on American Indian Affairs), vol. 132 (spring 1995), 5.

24. Peggy V. Beck, Anna Lee Walters, and Nia Francisco, *The Sacred: Ways of Knowledge, Sources of Life* (1977; Tsaile, Ariz.: Navajo Community College Press, 1992), 243.

25. Religious Freedom Restoration Act of 1993.

26. Walter R. Echo-Hawk and Roger C. Echo-Hawk, "Repatriation, Reburial, and Religious Rights," in Vecsey, *Handbook of American Indian Religious Freedom*, 67.

27. Fact Sheet, "Implementation Procedures for Executive Order 13007: Indian Sacred Sites," 24 May 1996, 1.

28. Ibid.

29. John Dougherty, "The Long, Bitter Battle over Mount Graham," *High Country News*, 24 July 1995, 15.

30. Lisa Jones (opinion by), "The University Aimed for the Stars and Hit Mount Graham," *High Country News*, 24 July 1995, 16.

31. "Pope Builds Telescope to Find God," *London Sunday Times*, 14 December 1997.

CHAPTER EIGHT

Religious Studies on the Margins: Decolonizing Our Minds

Michelene E. Pesantubbee (Choctaw)

As members of the first generation of indigenous scholars of American Indian religious traditions near the end of their academic careers and the second generation begins its journey through the halls of academia, it seems appropriate to reflect on the state of religious studies as it pertains to Native traditions. Such an examination begins by looking at the careers of those first American Indian scholars who paved the way for others not only to enter the field of religious studies but also to specialize in American Indian religious traditions. This entry is not simply one of American Indian integration into a traditionally white enterprise, of becoming part of the Western hegemonic study of American Indian religious traditions; it is one of challenging the classic way of studying and theorizing about American Indian religious traditions. The first generation of American Indian scholars began a process of depriviliging a Western approach to the study of American Indian religious traditions; this enabled those of us who followed to engage in an emic study of indigenous traditions in a way that intersects meaningfully with comparative studies of religion. The road between emic and etic ways of studying indigenous traditions, however, is not a simple one to negotiate from either an indigenous or a Western academic perspective.

Many of us entered the field of religious studies with change in mind. We had read the histories of religion and anthropological studies of American Indian culture. We knew that what we were reading in the scholarly texts minimized and in many ways vilified our people's cultures and histories. Many, like myself, wanted to change the way academia portrayed American Indians, and we wanted to learn about our traditions in ways that did not relegate us to specimens of evolutionary development. The best way to do that was through the platform of religious studies, because the interdisciplinary nature of the field provided us with the multiple tools needed to study American Indian religions not as a separate aspect of society but as an integral part of culture and history.

We are fortunate to have entered the field of religious studies at a time when three American Indian scholars, in particular, had already provided exemplars of how the study of American Indian religious traditions should proceed. This chapter looks at how these three scholars, Vine Deloria, Jr. (Standing Rock Sioux), Inés Talamantez (Mescalero Apache), and George Tinker (Osage/Cherokee) have pushed the boundaries of the study of American Indian religious traditions in ways that opened up new paths of study for the next generation. By addressing the contributions of these scholars, as well as contemporary issues in the study of American Indian religious traditions, I hope to offer ideas about the future of the field that will contribute to further discourse about religious studies.

Each of the above-named scholars has forged new paths in the study of American Indian religious traditions that have challenged the status quo. Often, however, their work has been dismissed by others as irrelevant or lacking a purely scientific or analytic approach, or for failure to engage in disinterested studies. In his statement on the future study of Native American religions, Ake Hultkrantz urged that "great efforts should be concentrated on elevating the research on native religions to a scientific level equal with that of the studies of Old World religions." He also felt it necessary to "link the studies of native religions to the study of the religious traditions of the Old World" (132).

Vine Deloria, Jr., professor emeritus of history at the University of Colorado–Boulder, has probably done more than any other American Indian scholar to challenge the notion of a purely objective scientific study of American Indian religious traditions, and in the process, he has drawn the ire of academia. He urges scholars to recognize the limitations of the classic way of studying American Indians. Removing ourselves from Western-centric idealizations of scholarship, however, is not easy. Like Deloria, we have all grown up "on the edges of two very distinct cultures, western European and American Indian." Even Deloria, as he admits in the introduction to his book *Red Earth, White Lies,* at one time believed in the myth of the objective scientist, until he reasoned otherwise and later became a passive dissenter (if Deloria can ever be considered passive) of harmless scientific doctrine, until he saw how science was used to "smear American Indians" (9–10).

Deloria has often voiced his concern that young American Indian scholars are too passive in their scholarship and in their relationship to the academic study of religion. He has been the voice challenging Indian and non-Indian scholars to look at Indian culture and history from perspectives different from the generally accepted ones. Deloria's motivation comes not from the intellectual exercise of rehashing history in order to introduce new interpretations of the old; rather, he seeks to redress the hegemonic interpretations of the histories and needs of indigenous people. In the preface of the 1988 reprint of *Custer Died for Your Sins,* Deloria wrote, "Indians are alive, have certain dreams of their own, and are being overrun by the ignorance and the mistaken, misdirected efforts of those who would help them" (xiii). He implicitly and explicitly argues for the legitimacy of Indian-centered responses to the intellectual study of Indian cultures and histories. Through his books and lectures, American Indian scholars have recognized the reasons for their own discomfort with Western academia and have begun to seek culturally centered interpretations of American Indian religious traditions.

Deloria has exemplified the notion of scholar as activist through his groundbreaking interpretations and analyses of law, particularly as it pertains to American Indian religious freedom. He has pointed out the problems inherent in court decisions based on "analyzing tribal religions within the same conceptual framework as Western organized religions" (*For This Land,* 205). For example, about the 1988 Supreme Court decision in *Lyng v. Northwest Indian Cemetery Protective Association,* in which the Court ruled that the Free Exercise Clause did not prevent the government from using its property in any way it saw fit, Deloria argues that the Court based its decision partly on the erroneous assumption that belief and behavior can be separated (205). Conversely, problems also arise when decision makers do not treat American Indians in the same way as white Americans. In his article "A Simple Question of Humanity: The Moral Dimensions of the Reburial Issue," Deloria attacks the exploitation of American Indian burial remains by science and other institutions. In the process, he raises questions about how Indians are studied. He points out the practice of treating Indian remains as natural resources and argues for the religious freedom of Indians to determine the fate of those remains. In essence, he states that it is not possible for a scholar, no matter how well educated, to know more about the religious beliefs, feelings, and practices of a religion than a practitioner. Thus, in order to make determinations about burial remains, scholars must include and accept the testimony of Indians (200).

The inclusion of American Indians in the study of their religious traditions, however, poses a problem for many scholars. As Hultkrantz writes, too often in the past, fieldwork was undertaken as "extra trips of historians of religion who have been specialists in other subjects." He urges increased attention to fieldwork by specialists in the field (94). In response to this need for specialists, Inés Talamantez, professor of religious studies at the University of California–Santa Barbara, has taken on the task of training American Indian scholars in the study of American Indian religious traditions. As a strong advocate of fieldwork, Talamantez has directed numerous graduate students in new ways of thinking about the interaction between scholar and practitioner. Traditionally, scholars have been viewed as the experts and practitioners as the objects of their gaze. American Indian communities were little more than valuable laboratories "where different theories may be tested and different interrelationships investigated" (Hultkrantz, 105). Indian practitioners were not viewed as legitimate interpreters of their own beliefs and actions. Only an outside observer could provide the objectivity needed to analyze the religious ideas of American Indians.

Talamantez refused to accept the objective scientific approach as the only legitimate study of religion and engaged in a culturally centered approach to fieldwork. She mandated that graduate students go to Indian communities not with the idea of applying an existing theory to their observations but with the goal of constructing theories based on indigenous knowledge and experience. And as she often tells her students, theorizing from the culture means learning the language and listening to the people. Talamantez has spent many years studying her own culture, with the goal of developing theories drawn from Mescalero culture. She has taken many graduate students to Mescalero Apache and Navajo Nation reservations to give them valuable field experience, but also to impress on them the importance of generating theory from the culture itself (Insider's, 20). Through Talamantez's guiding fieldwork, many American Indian scholars have begun working with their own nations or other Indian nations to develop theories that come out of the culture rather than forcing theories onto the culture.

Talamantez's fieldwork has influenced her own study of Mescalero Apache religious traditions. In her work on the girls' puberty ceremony, she has demonstrated how Apache conceptions of time and space differ from Western conceptions. For example, in "Images of the Feminine in Apache Religious Traditions," she describes the life cycle of Apache women as "movement on a path or trail, 'intine, protected by a complex of ceremonies" (133). Rather than undergoing a violent detachment from one stage in the social structure before entering another (liminality) in a rite of passage (Van Gennep, 74–75; Turner, 94), the Mescalero girl experiences something more like a massaging along the path of life, a ceremony that creates more a sense of fluidity than of separation. In reading the above-mentioned article in conjunction with "The Mescalero Apache Girls' Puberty Ceremony: The Role of Music in Structuring Ritual Time" (Shapiro and Talamantez), one gains a sense of that fluidity or massaging through music and dance.

One of the most difficult arenas in which to challenge the status quo in academia is in seminaries or schools of theology. The separation of Christianity from its Western European heritage has not been easy. Most studies of the history of Christian mission work among Indian people are typically apologetic works of Christian theology. Yet George Tinker, professor of cross-cultural ministries at Iliff School of Theology, refuses to romanticize Christian mission history and has taken up the challenge through his work in liberation theology. He has written numerous works on mission history that demonstrate that even good intentions and sincerity have had devastating effects on American Indians. American Indians interested in the ministry have not easily broken into the halls of seminaries. For those who have, Tinker encourages them to go beyond the typical good-works notion of mission history to examine the more insidious effects on Indian culture. Tinker has impacted the thinking of many seminary and religious studies students and has changed the way many now study and think about Christian mission history.

In his book *Missionary Conquest,* Tinker responds to the challenge of writing an Indian point of view by reexamining the lives of four highly acclaimed missionaries to indigenous peoples. Countless works have been written about the sacrifices and good intentions of John Eliot, Junipero Serra, Pierre-Jean De Smet, and Henry Benjamin Whipple as they struggled to convert indigenous peoples to Christianity. Rather than accept the success stories of these missionaries as the full story, Tinker redefines conversion stories as a genre that does violence to non-Western religious traditions. Embedded in this genre is the accepted inevitability of recognition of the superiority of Western Christian civilization. Thus, the dominant discourse is about missionaries who used positive religious means to aid the natural course of history by facilitating the rejection of indigenous cultural traditions for the more civilized and true Christian religion. Tinker challenges this interpretation of missionary efforts by raising questions about the entire missionary agenda. He emphasizes missionary participation in the cultural genocide of Indian people, which included not only military conquest or police action but any political, economic, social, or religious action that consciously or unconsciously served to destroy, "in whole or in part, a national, ethnic, racial or religious group, as such" (5). Through Tinker's book, readers learn that missionary action was experienced and interpreted by Indian people as acts of violence, of systematic persecution, rather than as the more commonly assumed "good intentions."

Although these three scholars have advocated studying and interpreting Indian religious traditions in culturally centered ways, the academy and, perhaps more importantly, scholars in the field have not always been receptive to their ideas or concerns. Resistance to concerns about the academic study of American Indian religious traditions has been complicated by different conceptions of learning or ways of knowing. American Indian scholars have experienced the tension of existing on the edges of two cultures, two ways of knowing. Poised on the edges of Western and indigenous cultures, they operate within a constrictive Western paradigm while experiencing the realities of non-Western cultures. On the one hand, success in the academy necessitates applying theories and methodologies developed out of Western scholarship to studies of cultures. On the other hand, cultural experience and community responsibility demand legitimization of cultural concerns and categories. The two do not always make amenable bedfellows. Despite the difficulties inherent in working for two masters, these three scholars have negotiated this often unforgiving terrain between Western and Indian ways of knowing.

Primary to their work is concern with how American Indians are studied. In his plenary address at the 1996 meeting of the American Academy of Religion, Deloria asked, "To what degree do we do violence to non-Western religious traditions when we try and force them into pre-existing categories? When are we going to free ourselves up and just look at these things?" His question was not directed particularly at American Indian scholars, but it did strike at the heart of the problem for those of us engaged in studying our own cultures. How do we engage in emic studies without consciously or unconsciously doing injustice to our own cultures by applying Western paradigms to the study of indigenous religious traditions? How do we resist the pull toward academic homogeneity?

As many of us engage in the intellectual pursuit of culturally centered theories, our efforts are often met with a less than enthusiastic reception by those who would maintain the status quo. As scholars of religion, we must find ways of engaging the approaches of the imagined or real two sides in the field of religious studies. Our task is one of resisting the hegemonic discourse of the academy while simultaneously encouraging multiple dialogues at the margins of the Western and non-Western. Before real dialogue can begin, however, some degree of equanimity between the Western and non-Western approach must be achieved. Equanimity in this case means developing culturally centered studies to the degree necessary to enable effective dialogue among various cultures represented in the study of religion.

The first step toward effective dialogue arguably begins with, "unabashedly and without apology," American Indian points of view. Tinker acknowledges that his approach may seem unduly biased, but he argues that it is necessary to counter a history of one-sided conversations. He tells American Indians that they must own their history, a task made difficult by the "self-serving illusion of white superiority," an illusion that Indian people have internalized just as deeply as white Americans have (Tinker, 2). In *Missionary Conquest*, we see the dilemmas facing American Indian scholars. We must, as Deloria says of his own experience, deal with our conscious and unconscious acceptance of Western scholarship. It is not easy to recognize within our own scholarship the internalization of much of the bias of Western scholarship, and we must continually second-guess our assumptions.

As scholars of religion, we are trained in Western academic institutions and often find ourselves drawn into the homogenizing study of religion. Not only must we question our own assumptions, which are informed in part by Western scholarship; we must also deconstruct other Indians' construction of events, which are influenced by the internalization of "white superiority." This dilemma is exemplified by Tinker's assumption or acceptance of missionaries' "good intentions" in spite of his own arguments to the contrary. He writes, "I have presumed a certain naivete with respect to the complicity of the missionaries in acts of cultural genocide. They surely did not intend any harm to Indian people" (15). We can see in his book the struggle to resist the hegemonic interpretation of missionary work with his own internalized, unquestioned acceptance of missionaries' "good intentions." *Missionary Conquest*'s significance lies not so much in its resistance of the hegemonic interpretation but in alerting us all to the insidious ways hegemonic discourse influences our thinking.

In an effort to articulate an indigenous perspective, we often struggle with various Western ideologies in order to find a discourse that allows us to express the subtleties of indigenous thought. Such is the case in Talamantez's article "Images of the Feminine in Apache Religious Traditions." There, she seeks to counter male-biased interpretations of the Mescalero girls' puberty ceremony by demonstrating how the ceremony embodies and expresses the female aspects of the Mescalero world. Through her knowledge of Mescalero Apache language and years spent listening to her people talk about the ceremony, Talamantez is aware of subtle differences in various references to the ceremony that have informed her study of Mescalero culture. For example, whether the ceremony is referred to as a "feast" or a "dance" shifts the attention from one meaning or emphasis to another. The feast references the concluding meal of the four-day ceremony and embodies ideas of communal cooperation and social gathering. Dance, in contrast, focuses on the rite of passage of the young girl and her importance to the well-being of the community. The distinctions are complicated by the tendency of men to use "feast" and women to use "dance." Is this a factor of Mescalero culture or of Western ideologies?

The difficulties that American Indian scholars face when framing non-Western ideas within a Western paradigm can be demonstrated by examining Talamantez's use of the term *power* in "Images of the Feminine in Apache Religious Tradition." She distinguishes Mescalero Apache traditions from those that may be deemed patriarchal, citing other cultures in which authority and leadership roles are specifically considered male.

She states that in the case of the Mescalero Apache, women "have worked toward a balanced sense of power." The term *power*, in this instance, takes on multivalent meanings. On the one hand, power, as it is used in the context of patriarchy, suggests authority and leadership over another. On the other hand, in the case of the Mescalero Apache, power implies movement toward balance (not necessarily between men and women) and harmony. Power can also refer to *diye*, ultimate spiritual strength (131). Thus, Talamantez is comparing one culture to another by utilizing a referent—power—that could suggest that the girls' puberty ceremony is intended to give girls control or authority equal to that of men rather than developing their ultimate spiritual strength and molding girls into ideal Apache adults who, by fulfilling their role, will help society maintain balance and harmony. Yet, as a result of Western colonization, we must also consider how power as an expression of control and authority may be informing contemporary Mescalero Apache ideas about the purpose of the ceremony. Such subtleties of language are paramount in articulating an Indian perspective. We must deconstruct and reconstruct language to get at the particular or cultural meanings embedded in words. We must understand meaning in a cultural context in order to dialogue at the margins. We cannot assume that words have the same meanings across cultures, and we have to consider the blurring or blending of meanings between cultures as a process of interaction.

Constructing cultural meanings from historical accounts is not an easy task, because the Native side of the story is often translated into English, which necessarily leads to distortion. The story is not recorded in the Native language or, worse, the Native voice is never recorded. Thus, as we see in the case of Tinker's study, reconstruction of a viable version of events may depend on a combination of reports of events as recorded by non-Indians and on common sense, patterns, oral history, and even speculation. Whereas some scholars might argue a biased and intuitive approach, as though history could be unbiased or noninterpretive, *Missionary Conquest* presents a significant challenge to the validity of how American religious history has been taught, particularly in relation to Christian missionary efforts on what Western scholars commonly refer to as "the frontier." Tinker's approach reflects the problems faced by those scholars who work to counter the legacy of hegemonic discourse in the academic study of American Indian religious traditions. Often, what non-Indians chose to record about Indians is so steeped in Western conceptions and biases that only common sense and patterns based on contemporary knowledge can offer interpretations from the margins. Such interpretations are legitimate ways of reconstructing theory about indigenous history and culture when other sources of information have been lost through suppression or disinterest. To argue that only certain sources of information or methods of reconstruction of history constitute legitimate scholarship limits opportunities to understand the experiences of the world in alternative ways.

Although Deloria, Talamantez, and Tinker have pushed the boundaries of religious studies, American Indian scholars have a long way to go to reach equanimity in the field. Our efforts to facilitate dialogue at the margins, "where real people interact respectfully in order to learn what constitutes coherence and meaning for the other" (Irwin, 888), have become part of a larger process of growing pains of the academic study of religion as scholars debate the direction and maturity of the field (see *Journal of the American Academy of Religion*, vol. 62, no. 4 [1994]; vol. 65, no. 1 [1997]; vol. 66, no. 4 [1998]). Questions have been raised about the Western tradition of academia in relation to scholars who study specific religious traditions rather than developing normative theories and methodologies. This emphasis on the normative by a Western-dominated academy risks limiting real discourse at the margins. Peter Hitchcock, a Bahktinian specialist, argues that the act of "defining is a form of monological contraction, a limitation, that is, of the 'terms of the debate'—but only in the voice of the speaker" (2). His logic can be extended to the debate within the field of religious studies whereby an emphasis on normative theory at the cost of specific cultural theories is a monological contraction, a limitation of the development of the field. It is possible to embrace a dialogue that is simultaneously normative and particular, while being cognizant of the pressures to homogenize the experiences of the particular or cultural into some perceived normative construct.

However, as stated earlier, some degree of equanimity is necessary to resist the tendency toward homogenizing academic discourse. Scholars like Deloria, Talamantez, and Tinker have helped move the discourse away from the center toward the margins. In fact, the 1970s and 1980s witnessed a flourishing of the study of particular cultures, and that approach still has many adherents. However, I sense a growing impatience or tiredness with the attention to the particular at some perceived cost of developing the field of religious studies. The perception that the study of specific religious traditions represents immature scholarship (Gill, Academic Study, 966) has the potential to draw the study of religion back toward the center. The implication is that a mature field is one that develops normative theories, theories that distinguish the field of religious studies from other academic fields. Although normative theories and language are desirable and can facilitate dialogue, they also present the danger of hegemonic discourse.

Perhaps the maturity of the field lies in resisting the traditional Western tendency to develop normative theories. A history of setting limiting conditions within academic studies (Gill, 967) is not sufficient reason to continue setting boundaries. The mature study of religion may be envisioned as one that develops the ability to move beyond the normative to dialogue at the margins. As Lee Irwin (Cherokee) argues, "The strength of religious studies, as a profession, lies in its diversity and rich, multi-ethnic roots in all world cultures. The realization of that strength lies not in some 'super-science' of an inherited 'western' tradition but as a place 'at the boundaries' where many diverse peoples can meet, share perspectives, and learn from each other in the mutual formulation of critical theories that seek to illuminate the many cross-currents in religious studies" (889–90). The cost of realizing that strength may be a sense of unconventionality and even vagueness, but as dialogue at the margins improves, that amorphousness may come to embody a more mature study of religion.

The move away from particular studies may be triggered in part by debates over who should study those cultures. Deloria, Talamantez, and Tinker have challenged the hegemonic study of American Indian cultures. They have argued that scholars of religion who study Indian cultures should learn the languages of the people they study, should involve the people being studied in more of the theorizing about their cultures, and should be activists in changing the way Indian cultures are studied and interpreted. The unfortunate consequence appears to be one of polarization between those who would continue hegemonic discourse and those who want to develop the field at the margins. Rather than focusing the study of religion on the interactive possibilities of the particular and normative, the tendency is to see the particular and normative as oppositional. As scholars of religion, we must work not only to bring the particular and the normative together in our own research but also to engage in dialogue on the necessity and viability of such an approach in the academic study of American Indian religious traditions.

In addition to the polarization between advocates of the particular and the normative, I sense a climate of impatience with the revisualization and reshaping of the field that is necessary to move the discourse toward the margins. While the age of deconstruction and postmodernism has witnessed attention to the issues of the particular, the pendulum now seems to be swinging back toward normative studies of religion. The argument that the development of the field necessitates an emphasis on normative studies of religion is reminiscent of the impatience shown toward various Indian policies and programs. From John Collier's New Deal of the 1930s to the Indian Job Corps of the 1970s, the expectation is immediate results. Rather than allowing the necessary time for a program to overcome centuries of colonization, politicians and the public have often declared programs a failure within a few years and demanded a new approach. The call for a mature academic study of religion has the same tone of impatience.

The academic study of religion has its roots in Enlightenment philosophy, and in America, it has 500 years of colonial history informing its development. The field itself has existed for approximately 40 years, and American Indian religious traditions as an area of specialty has been around for less than 30 years. Yet the move toward developing normative theories of religion suggests that 30 years should be sufficient time to counter the 500 years of Western influence on the study of American Indian religious traditions. Rather than continuing the process of developing the field by encouraging culturally centered theories and drawing indigenous thought into the academic study of religion, some want to focus attention on the development of an imagined normative approach. Such an approach may swing the study of religion toward hegemonic discourse and thus inhibit discourse at the margins. In fact, I suggest that the normative approach to the study of religion is itself a hegemonic impulse. We must be cognizant of the human tendency to represent the interests of the dominant academic study of religion as the interests of all scholars of religion (Hitchcock, 5). Thus, as scholars of religion, we are invested in ensuring that the normative approach does not replace the study of the particular and that the two approaches are engaged simultaneously in ways that encourage discourse at the margins.

Another issue is the question of who should study Native cultures, or the insider-outsider debate. One concern is whether American Indian scholars can adequately problematize their own positions while studying their own cultures. Gill argues that "this questioning of oneself is most effectively motivated, as anthropology has demonstrated, if one is studying a subject other than one's own tradition and culture" (Rejoinder, 179). A related issue is the argument that American Indian scholars of religion are trained in Western thought and thus are influenced by the same ideas and impulses as non-Indian scholars. The idea that an outsider is the most effectively motivated scholar to question his or her own views and sense of the world in order to study a culture serves the hegemonic practice in the study of religion. All scholars bring their own histories, cultures, and philosophies into the study of religion, whether it is their own tradition or someone else's. The question, then, seems to be one of degree of motivation to question one's own position. I argue that motivation, like many other emotions such as love or sorrow, cannot be objectively measured because it is an individual experience. The manifestations of motivation can be documented, but the internal experience of motivation cannot be. The argument that an outsider is more motivated is a product of hegemonic positioning based on Western interpretations and assumptions about outward manifestations of motivation. If the field is to move toward equitable discourse, then assumptions about the motivations of insiders must be recognized for what they are—assumptions.

The argument that American Indian scholars are Western trained and thus are part of the hegemonic discourse on American Indian religious traditions is a particular concern for all of us. We recognize the tremendous impact of Western scholarship on the study of American Indian religions. We also realize that to facilitate dialogue at the margins, the broader academic study of religion and the specific study of religious traditions must take place on a level playing field; otherwise, the violence to non-Western religious traditions will continue. For scholars like Deloria, Talamantez, and Tinker, the leveling of the field begins by offering an American Indian point of view. This means that we have to first deconstruct our own Western thinking, to separate Western interpretations from indigenous ones, which in actuality may no longer be fully separable, and reconstruct an indigenous-centered approach. It also means that we have to employ the discourses available until more appropriate ones are developed. This is not an easy task. As we work to free ourselves from preexisting categories, we must strive to find our own epistemologies, discourses, and constructive histories (Irwin, 888).

As we struggle with our own internalization of Western scholarship, we also have to contend with the illusion that the academic study of religion is necessarily Western (Gill, Academic Study, 967). There is no question that the field grew out of Western intellectual history, that the field continues to be shaped by its Western history, and that the academic study of religion is by and large a predominantly Western scholar–controlled field. Yet to say that the academic study of religion is Western and must be Western denies the contributions of the other (in terms of gender, ethnicity, or religion) in shaping the field, no matter how suppressed or unrealized they may be. The position that the field is necessarily Western fails to acknowledge the "dialogical relationship between 'religion,' as invented by scholars (center), and religion, as engaged in by practitioners and/or believers (margins)" (Churchill, 12). One does not exist without the other. The other has shaped the academic study of religion in recognizable and, more often, unrecognizable or unacknowledged ways.

It is an illusion that American Indian scholars, by virtue of having been trained in a Western academic arena, are entirely Western in thought as well. To make this claim denies that we bring distinct ideas, experiences, and interpretations to our Western experience. We may sit in the same classrooms, read the same materials, succeed by the same criteria, but the reality is that we approach and understand the material and experience it in individual ways that are influenced by our histories, families, communities, religions, and cultures, Western and non-Western. The construction of the academic study of religion is a complex one that involves multiple reciprocal interactions in which the interpretation of the Western is often assumed to represent the culture or the field as a whole. In reality, there is no normative understanding of the academic study of religion, nor can there ever be. To argue such is to deny the complex dialogical interaction that informs the field.

As scholars of American Indian religious traditions, we necessarily work from the edges of two cultures. Thus, it is incumbent on us to constantly be cognizant of how our use of Western discourse limits dialogue on the margins. We have to avoid the homogenizing discourse in which we are trained. This is not to say that we must avoid Western discourse or Western theories, but that we must employ them in a conscientious way that avoids the dismissive and demeaning way American Indian religious traditions have been studied in the past. We need to work with other scholars in the academy to facilitate dialogue at the margins. This means working toward greater equanimity by presenting an American Indian point of view, with dialogue at the margins in mind. Instead of applying Western theories to American Indian religious traditions, we should develop theories that "will draw on substantive, critical studies of alternative epistemologies (and cultures) whose articulation constitutes a necessary theoretical pluralism in the teaching of religions" (Irwin, 891). Only then can the academic study of religion mature into a field that embraces multiple systems of epistemologies and theories.

American Indian scholars like Vine Deloria, Jr., Inés Talamantez, and George Tinker have led the way toward decolonizing our minds and opening up the field to ideas and perspectives that serve "as a corrective to an over-reliance on a strictly rationalized application of abstract ideas and theories often highly alien and antagonistic to the self-definitions of the communities to which they are applied" (Irwin, 889). To enhance dialogue at the margins, to facilitate theoretical pluralism, American Indian scholars, as well as all scholars who study the particular, must continue to question their assumptions about Western scholarship, resist the tendency toward homogenization of theory and scholarship, and develop alternative theories based on the epistemologies of Native cultures. The future of the study of religion lies in developing multiple, culturally determined theories. Such an approach should not be determined by concerns about whether one is an insider or an outsider but rather should be based on problematizing one's stance. The reality is that, as American Indian scholars, we are both insider and outsider, and the distinctions between the two are not always obvious. Our place on the edges of two cultures puts us in the particularly challenging situation of questioning our presuppositions from both a Western and an indigenous perspective. Yet it also puts us in a distinctly other place from which to theorize about religion. As American Indian scholars of American Indian religious traditions, we are in a position to bridge the chasm between the center and the margin and, in the process, contribute to "theoretical pluralism in the teaching [and studying] of religions" (Irwin, 891).

REFERENCES

I want to thank Mary C. Churchill, Christopher Jocks, and Lee Irwin for their essays on the study of American Indian religious traditions. Their interpretations and analyses contributed significantly to the development of my ideas on the future of the field.

Churchill, Mary. "'The White Path': Finding Our Way in the Study of Indigenous Women and Religion." In *Creative/Critical Representations by Native American Women*, ed. Ines Hernandez-Avila. Manuscript.

Deloria, Vine, Jr. *Custer Died for Your Sins: An Indian Manifesto*. New York: Macmillan, 1969. Reprint, Norman: University of Oklahoma Press, 1988.

———. *For This Land: Writings on Religion in America*. New York: Routledge, 1999.

———. "Origins: Physical Reality and Religious Belief." Audiotape recording of plenary address at the annual meeting of the American Academy of Religion, New Orleans, La., 23 November 1996.

———. *Red Earth, White Lies: Native Americans and the Myth of Scientific Fact*. New York: Scribner, 1995.

Gill, Sam. "The Academic Study of Religion." *Journal of the American Academy of Religion*, vol. 62, no. 4 (1994), 965–75.

———. "Rejoinder to Christopher Jocks." *Journal of the American Academy of Religion*, vol. 65, no. 1 (1997), 177–82.

Hitchcock, Peter. *Dialogics of the Oppressed*. Minneapolis: University of Minnesota Press, 1993.

Hultkrantz, Ake. *The Study of American Indian Religions*. New York: Crossroad Publishing Company and Scholars Press, 1983.

Irwin, Lee. "American Indian Religious Traditions and the Academic Study of Religion." *Journal of the American Academy of Religion*, vol. 66, no. 4 (1998), 887–92.

Jocks, Christopher. "American Indian Religious Traditions and the Academic Study of Religion: A Response to Sam Gill." *Journal of the American Academy of Religion*, vol. 65, no. 1 (1997), 169–76.

Shapiro, Anne Dhu, and Inés Talamantez. "The Mescalero Apache Girls' Puberty Ceremony: The Role of Music in Structuring Ritual Time." In *Yearbook for Traditional Music*. New York: International Council for Traditional Music, 1986.

Talamantez, Inés. "Images of the Feminine in Apache Religious Traditions." In *After Patriarchy: Feminist Transformations of the World Religions*, ed. Paula M. Cooey, William R. Eakin, and Jay B. McDaniel. Faith Meets Faith Series. Maryknoll, N.Y.: Orbis Books, 1991.

———. "An Insider's Point of View." In *Center for the Study of Women in Society Review: Annual Magazine for the Study of Women in Society*. Eugene, Ore.: Center for the Study of Women in Society, University of Oregon, 1990.

Tinker, George. *Missionary Conquest*. Minneapolis, Minn.: Fortress Press, 1993.

Turner, Victor. *The Ritual Process*. Ithaca, N.Y.: Cornell University Press, 1969.

Van Gennep, Arnold. *The Rites of Passage*. Chicago: University of Chicago Press, 1960.

CHAPTER NINE

American Indian Religious Traditions, Colonialism, Resistance, and Liberation

George E. Tinker (Osage/Cherokee)

That the People May Live!

Self-mutilation. Self-torture. These were the judgments expressed by appalled missionaries and U.S. government officials. And the ceremony is indeed demanding and even brutal in ways: months of preparation and days of hard physical labor culminating in four days of dry fasting (no food; no liquids); dancing from dawn to dusk under a 100-degree sun in a confined sacred center; and finally offering the flesh of one's chest to be skewered and tied to a tree until dancing tears the skin. Few people in their right mind would willingly choose to engage in such a religious act of self-abuse.

And yet, as the dancers leave the center at the end of the fourth day, tears of sadness roll down one dancer's cheeks and drip onto the wounds of the day before. The impending separation from the center, from the tree that has given its life even as the dancers sacrificed themselves, generates this bittersweet melancholy, and the dancer finds himself mumbling a prayer of commitment, promising to return the following summer.

They come to dance for a great variety of reasons. Actually each Indian person has his (or increasingly, her) own discrete reasons that may or may not be shared with others. Yet in actuality, there is only one reason to dance this ceremony: That the people may live! Anyone who does not understand this simple fact should stay home or at least stay out of the center, perhaps remaining under the arbor where learning can take place and where one can support those in the center. There is too much at stake. The well-being of the whole community depends on the hard spiritual work of a few who have made the commitment on behalf of the whole.

Beginning in the 1880s, in the interests of the doctrine of Manifest Destiny, it became U.S. government policy to outlaw specific American Indian ceremonies that were deemed dangerous impediments to the twin projects of civilizing Indian peoples and systematically relieving them of their landholdings. U.S. churches contributed significantly to this cause of colonial expansion by providing on-site policing services (missionaries) to ferret out secret performances of ceremonies, disrupt them, and destroy religious artifacts that were seized in the process. Although these

223

missionaries had no official sanction to perform such civil police services, they were never restrained by civil authorities; rather, their vigilante activities appear to have been greatly appreciated.

These outlawed ceremonies quite often continued in one fashion or another in spite of attempts to end their observance. They were performed in hidden locations, often in abbreviated form, and often transformed in other ways to make concealment and continuation possible. One particular category of Lakota ceremony became a nighttime ceremony that even now is typically conducted in complete darkness, a remnant of the earlier necessity for concealment. The perseverance of these ceremonial forms and of Indian cultures in general in the face of such intense repression and oppression is itself a testament to the tenacity of Indian peoples and their ongoing commitment to resistance and struggle. Needless to say, the combined efforts of church and state to rid North America of pagan Indian ceremonial life never quite succeeded.

With the intensification of the modern indigenous movement of resistance, beginning in the 1960s and reaching an apex in the emergence of the American Indian Movement after 1968,[1] a renewed pride in Indian identity began to erupt, and along with it, a renewed interest in the ancient ceremonial life of the peoples. What had been hidden or practiced by only a few in remote locations suddenly began to claim a place in the public consciousness of Indian communities in one nation after another, with Lakota ceremonial practice taking center stage among both urban Indians and New Age whites. What had been revived as a tourist attraction at Pine Ridge in the 1960s was brought back into the open as legitimate ceremonies with stricter and more traditional observance on the Pine Ridge and Rosebud reservations during the 1970s with Sun Dances at Porcupine and Kyle, Ironwood Hilltop, and Crow Dog's Paradise. With this spiritual renaissance, Indian identity was rekindled with a new pride, all of which became more intimately connected with the Indian political resistance of the day. This renaissance of Indian traditional ceremonial life continues unabated even today and shows little sign of ebbing soon. It speaks to the persistent and enduring attachment of Indian people to their traditional cultures and structuring of society.

Yet there is also a cost to pay related to the complex and lingering effects of European and Amer-European colonialization on the well-being of Indian communities. The emergence of Indian ceremonial traditions into the larger public consciousness has generated a sexy appeal of the exotic among the spiritually exhausted colonizer community of North America and Europe, resulting in a new invasion of Indian peoples. This time the invasion is not a colonial attempt to appropriate Indian lands. Rather, it is an invasion of the intimate and private religious space of Indian communities trying to heal themselves from 500 years of colonial abuse. In this moment of late colonial capitalism, the invaders see their intentions as benign, yet the effect is a globalization of private community acts as a new commodity fetish.

This chapter looks at the non-Indian appropriation of Indian ceremonial life as a means of unraveling some of the complexity.

COMMITMENT AND VICARIOUS SUFFERING

All Indian ceremonies contain some aspect of commitment—both to the ceremony itself, that is, to the spiritual presence that empowers a particular ceremony, and to the community in the context of which the ceremony is performed.[2] Many ceremonies also contain some aspect of vicarious suffering. Although the purpose of the suffering is usually expressed in terms of some benefit for the community as a whole, its intensity can be of considerable magnitude for the individual. The strong sense of "doing" is part of what makes these ceremonies so appealing to American Indians as oppressed peoples living in the late stages of colonization and conquest.[3] In the midst of political and social hopelessness marked by extreme poverty and continued pressures from the systemic power structure of church and state, which still urges Indian peoples toward compliance with the terms of colonization, these ceremonies provide hope. It is in the commitment and the performance of these ceremonies that many Indian people achieve a sense of doing something concrete about their community's ongoing sense of injustice, degradation, and alienation and all the dysfunctionality that emerges from successive generations of colonial imposition. In the suffering we experience in these ceremonies, there is hope for the people. Our pain is short in comparison to the pain of the community. The suffering in these ceremonies (called "self-mutilation" or "self-torture" in the "professional" literature) is always an act engaged in by personal choice, and the personal commitment is always made for the sake of the people.

Vicarious suffering of any Indian person on behalf of the community is also part of the ritual drama typical of the Purification Ceremony, or sweat lodge, as it is colloquially known. In this ceremony, the heat can be so intense for so long that the participants must encourage one another to "remember" why they are there, to concentrate on their prayers, and not to focus on their own pain. Some Amer-Europeans have asked over the years whether this ceremony is not similar to a sauna. Although I have never *prayed* in a sauna, and therefore find the question somewhat bewildering, I can attest that the Purification Ceremony is typically a couple of hours longer than the ten-minute sauna stay recommended by physicians, and certainly much hotter. The lodge itself is a symbolic microcosm of the earth. Our suffering is the substance of our prayer and is willingly endured for the sake of the earth and all our relatives who live on it. Our prayer is especially for the community in which we thrive.

Likewise, the Rite of Vigil requires a commitment to a period of rigorous fasting—abstaining from both food and water—while bivouacked on a hillside far from the center of the community, confined in a small, ceremonially marked area perhaps a body length and a half long and wide. The duration of the ceremony varies from a single day and night, perhaps for an adolescent completing his first Rite of Vigil, to a more typical four-day period in the modern context. In ancient times there were stories of people completing six-day ceremonies with regularity and even up to ten or eleven days, far in excess of what modern medical science would allow as possible without the replenishing of body fluids. Although I have made a conscious choice *not* to provide an "instruction manual" for Indian ceremonial life and therefore do not discuss the technical aspects of the spiritual experiences associated with these ceremonies, it should be apparent that the spiritual commitment needed to complete such a regimen far exceeds the physical requirements. There is always a personal benefit from completing this ceremony, and even personal accretions of spiritual power, but these benefits are always experienced as intended to help that person in her or his commitment to the well-being of the whole. Quite typically in the Lakota context, for instance, the community greets the individual upon completion of the ceremony not with an exclamation of "congratulations" but rather with a simple handshake and the words "thank you"—thank you, because the community has benefited from the person's successful completion of the commitment.

Although variations of both the Purification Ceremony and the Rite of Vigil are common to many Indian nations in North America, the Sun Dance is a more regional ceremony native to the Great Plains and Great Basin, north and west into Canada, and south into the prairies west of the Mississippi River. Again, one commits to this ceremony on behalf of the community as a whole, even when each participant has personal reasons for initiating the commitment. The ceremony involves a pledge to personal deprivation (no food and no water) and the physical effort of sustained dancing over a three- or four-day period, depending on the particular national tradition,[4] through the heat of midsummer days and sometimes even extending through the nighttime. In the Lakota tradition, the vicarious nature of the ceremony is captured in a common acclamation: "That the people might live!" The ceremony is sometimes referred to as an annual world renewal ceremony and can be described as a ceremony for maintaining the balance and harmony of life. Thus, whatever the personal reasons for an individual's commitment to complete the ceremony, the greater good of community well-being is always most prominently at stake.

COLONIALISM, NEOCOLONIALISM, AND RESISTANCE

These three ceremonies are the most common ones practiced today by a variety of Indian peoples, but they are by no means the only ones. They have also become common in urban multitribal Indian communities. They have become symbolic of our continuing cultural resistance to the colonizer at religious, social, and political levels. Although the ceremonies have important aspects of spiritual power associated with them, they also have a distinct political and social power related to the cohesion of the community and its focus on resistance and liberation.

Countless Indians on virtually every U.S. reservation have been withdrawing from the Christian churches into which they were missionized and are returning to these sorts of traditional ceremonies. The incongruity of maintaining Indian self-pride and self-conscious identity as "Indian" communities while participating in a religion imposed on us by our colonizer finally began to break down the inroads made by several generations of missionary imposition on our Indian communities.

Many young Indian clergy and some of their congregations have moved to reshape the Christianity they have embraced through a reinterpretation of the European and Amer-European theological and faith categories in language and material forms that better reflect our Indian identity. Yet for the majority, this shift is inadequate and still leaves the colonized with a religious tradition that belongs to and derives from the colonizer. In the unhealthy and dysfunctional colonized world that we Indian people inhabit in North America today, it seems that the healthiest persons are those who have engaged in full-voiced resistance to continuing colonization and have returned to traditional ceremonial life as a significant part of this resistance. Thus, the boldest of the young Indian clergy have hearkened to the call of these traditionalists and can be found participating in the traditional ceremonies, praying in ways that an earlier generation of missionaries would have criticized as devil worship.

INDIAN RELIGIOUS TRADITIONS AS COMMODITY IN A MASS-CONSUMPTION SOCIETY

The young man had wandered in early to the site of an urban Indian community religious ceremony. The ceremonial leader met the man cordially. Because of the colonial phenomenon of "mixed blood," it is often not possible to ascertain by sight whether a person is Indian, so the leader asked the man whether he was Indian and what tribe he might be. The young man's honest reply was, "No, I am just a white man who is a pipe carrier." Just as easily and genuinely, the leader responded by

asking, "Oh! Who do you carry a pipe for?" Possessing an Indian community reli-
gious symbol, but living a polar reality existence in a non-Indian world, the young
white man had no answer to the question but, rather, had to ask the meaning of the
question. In reality, he knew who he carried this pipe for; he carried it for himself and
for his own spiritual empowerment. Someone had sold this young man a pipe and a
bill of goods to go with it.

Colonization and the processes of assimilation are not yet finished with
Indian peoples. Even as we seek new ways to embrace ourselves as Indian
communities, the colonizer has found new ways to impede Indian healing
and to steal what is left of Indian identity, cultural values, and traditional
lifeways. The newest threat to Indian well-being actually builds on the
impoverishment that has been established by five centuries of invasion
and conquest, yet it involves a seeming affirmation of Indian cultures. Per-
versely, however, it includes inoculation with a robust strain of the mass-
consumption virus. The appeal of easy cash accumulation for individuals
who are accustomed to poverty is sometimes too great to refuse.

Over the past three decades, Amer-European entrepreneurs have
discovered that Indian culture has a dramatic appeal to those New Age
aficionados whose sense of spiritual poverty has whetted their appetites
for the exotic and reduced their economic wealth proportionately. First
Carlos Castaneda and then Lynn Andrews found that even wholly fabricated but exotically romanticized tales of Indian mysteries could gain
them both academic credibility and wealth.[5] These parodies of Indian
spiritual traditions have spawned countless copycats, some of whom
have gained credibility by spending a short time in actual Indian ceremonies indulging their fantasies. More recently there was a report from
the Florida American Indian Movement that a white woman calling herself "Bear" (a catchy, Indian-sounding name), having danced in a Lakota
Sun Dance ceremony, had established herself in the "how-to" workshop
business and drew 250 people at $1,500 per person to a recent event. The
susceptible are quickly separated from their wallets in return for some
illusion of spiritual well-being, but Indian people are left the poorer as
misperceptions and falsified interpretations of our world are sold for
profit. Thus, Indian cultural traditions, particularly those that are identified as spiritual or religious traditions, have emerged as commodities of
trade in the Great American Supermarket of Spirituality.

With this discovery of Indian spirituality as a growth industry, many
Indian people with a little knowledge—that is, significantly more knowledge than Castaneda or Andrews—began to move into the marketplace
as well. Andrews and Castaneda made up fantasies that sounded Indian
but were actually fabrications, and the Indian purveyors of spirituality
are also engaged in selling a lie. In their case, the lie is decorated with

enough genuine Indian forms and structures that the purchasers are led to believe that they are buying the genuine item. Yet there remains a significant and substantial set of differences between Amer-European New Age belief structures and those of Indian peoples. In the next section, I describe a single but definitive distinction between the two.

NEW AGE INDIVIDUALISM AND INDIAN COMMUNITY: A COLONIAL CLASH OF VALUES

Beginning with Aristotle (in the fourth century B.C.E.), but accelerated by the next generation of Hellenistic philosophers (Stoics, Epicureans, Skeptics) from 300 B.C.E. on, Mediterranean thinking and, hence, European thinking took a decided turn toward the emergence of the individual. With the conquest of Alexander the Great, Aristotle's pupil, Europe began to experience the steady decline of the importance of community. The city-state was supplanted by empire followed by empire, and Greek philosophy shifted subtly away from Aristotle's search for the "good" toward the Hellenistic search for the wise individual. Both religion (the "mystery religions") and philosophy in the three centuries leading up to the emergence of Christianity became increasingly concerned with the salvation or the behavior of the individual, a trajectory that led directly to the emergence of the Cartesian "self" more than a millennium and a half later (and the ludic postmodern American selfish self at the end of the second millennium C.E.).

It should not be surprising, then, to discover in New Age aficionados a spiritual focus on the self and the engagement of spiritual experience for the sake of personal, that is, individual, self-enhancement or the accrual of personal spiritual power. Whether this is good or ill is beyond the purview of this chapter. I only intend to emphasize that this modus operandi is diametrically opposed to ceremonial intentionality in any traditional American Indian cultural context.

When New Age aficionados invade Indian ceremonies, they represent another sort of colonizing virus that threatens the health of the communities into which they have invited themselves or finagled invitations from Indian people unaccustomed to saying no and too weak from generations of colonization to change that cultural habit of hospitality, even when their own survival depends on it. Many of these spiritual seekers are genuinely well intentioned and are seriously searching for something more substantial than the spiritual experiences of the churches into which they were born and raised. Typically, they see themselves as sharing a worldview with Indian people, including a concern for environmental issues, an openness to the universe as an expression of pervasive divinity, a sense of the interrelationship of all things and especially all people, and a sense of the immanence and accessibility of spiritual power. All these may be thought of as laudable, but they are not yet Indian, and indeed, these New Age seekers may find that they are the distinct opposite of what Indian religious traditions represent. Namely, the New Ager is a prime example of the Western, European, Amer-European cultural value of individualism in its starkest naiveté.[6]

The viral aspect of this situation is that the individualist belief introduced by the New Age adherent can quickly infect an indigenous community, especially the younger generation. This is a common experience in urban Indian communities, where there may not be immediate access to traditional teaching elders. Thus, we have a generation of young people who are learning—or mislearning—how to be Indian from non-Indian individualists. New Agers, to this extent, are much more effective in destroying Indian cultural values than were several generations of missionaries and government functionaries, especially in this late period of neocolonialism.

CHRISTIANIZING THE LANGUAGE
OF CEREMONIAL TRADITIONS

As the Amer-European virus of individualism infects Indian traditional communities, the final conquest of the colonizer is most apparent in the way Indian people themselves talk about their ceremonies. This shift to individualism, marked by participation in a ceremony so that the individual might gain personal power, is what I refer to as the Christianizing of Indian religious traditions. It represents a serious colonization of the American Indian mind, one that may or may not be immediately recognizable by the person whose mind is so affected. The gospel of this Christianizing process is not Jesus but the Amer-European and Christian cultural value of individualism. The result of this Christianizing process is to further erode the Indian value of community and to bring us one step closer to the modern globalization of culture around Western values. The surface structures of our ceremonies may continue to look Indian, but the deep structure of meaning that undergirds the ceremony is slowly changing.

Most critically, the infestation of individualism that comes with the New Age invasion of Indian ceremonies means that there is a subtle degeneration in language that spreads the virus even among the teaching elders and spiritual leaders of a community as they struggle to translate their culture and the meaning of their ceremonies into language that can be accessed (often for money) by those with a radically different set of cultural behaviors and values. As I have already noted, it is very difficult for Indian people to say no. This is especially true when the white supplicant has greater economic resources than either the spiritual leader or the local Indian people in general. Even without engaging in the active marketing and selling of ceremonies, the spiritual leader may find himself or herself the recipient of some financial benefit. However small that benefit may be, it has a great impact in an environment of poverty. With the appearance of the first of these Amer-European supplicants, the degradation of language about the ceremony begins, as the spiritual elder changes the language of explanation to accommodate an outsider with money.

I am not arguing that these traditional spiritual leaders intend to change the meaning of the ceremony. Rather, I believe that their language about the ceremony changes gradually over time as each elder struggles to communicate with the outsider, struggles to translate from one culture into another. It seems to be a natural colonizing process whereby the colonized shift their language to accommodate the understanding of the colonizer. But I should clarify here that this "natural" process is really an unnatural process of oppression and conquest that has inherently logical and devastating effects on both the colonized and the colonizer. So it becomes a natural response on the part of the oppressed to accommodate power. As a result, the traditional elder may make small shifts in her or his language, so small that they may be imperceptible even to the speaker. Yet slowly, the meaning of the ceremony is Christianized toward the Western, Christian valorization of the individual. Eventually, even the young from the elder's own community pick up this new language, not knowing that it is new or that it represents a concession to the dearth of understanding on the part of colonizer participants, and the virus of individualism has gained a firmer foothold. And suddenly, it seems, the ceremony is performed to enhance one's personal spiritual well-being or power rather than the well-being of the community.

The net result is a tragic loss for both Indian peoples and Amer-Europeans. For the former, a way of life is changed forever. The latter have paid out bundles of dollars in return for the purchase of an illusion of Indianness, for a spiritual experience that they can wear with pride but that has little meaning in terms of what is actually claimed. For American Indian communities, it amounts to a loss of culture and the erosion of the system of values that has given indigenous traditions the strength to resist the full power of colonization until now. For Amer-Europeans and Europeans, the addiction to power and dominance is enhanced as they take the illusive surface structure of Indian ceremonies and colonize them into a new religious resource for the colonizer, a resource clothed with the appearance of righteousness, much as statutory rape can be clothed with the claim of consensuality.

What we are experiencing in the Indian world is the globalization of ourselves as a commodity and the concomitant transformation of our cultures into an emerging world culture marked by market symbols of global consumption such as McDonald's, Nike, Pizza Hut, and Sony billboards in every major Third World city. Perhaps technology will eventually provide for a new spirituality that will prove satisfying to the contemporary Star Trek mentality. Unfortunately, there may be no alternative as the globalized, Christianized indigenous religions of the world lose their antiquity and the cultural value base on which they have always been predicated.

NATIVE AMERICAN GENEROSITY
AND SPIRITUAL SCALP COLLECTING

At a deeply philosophical level, then, the question must be raised: Can and should non-Native Americans participate in the ceremonial spirituality of Native American peoples? This question seems ever present these days in my classroom, in discussions at lectures, and in the mail that comes across my desk. For the most part, the question is articulated by people whose sincerity I do not question. They voice, at least, a great respect for the ceremonies but also a deep-felt need for their individual participation in Pipe Ceremonies, "sweat lodge" purification rites, Sun Dances, and a variety of other events. Many of these non-Natives have come to see Native American ceremonial spirituality as somehow essential to their own well-being.

For their part, Native Americans have responded in a variety of ways across a spectrum of possibilities. Many, especially Lakota practitioners, have welcomed non-Native American participation and have increasingly come to see their spirituality as a human universal. Finding their knowledge eminently marketable, these spiritual salespersons have become virtual missionaries developing converts and followers in places as far removed from their own lands as Oregon and Germany. They have made the teaching of Native spirituality a for-profit industry servicing a spiritually starved Amer-European clientele. Although they inevitably alienate themselves from their own people, there are financial rewards that become especially lucrative in places like Malibu, Marin County, Boulder, Aspen, or Germany. There continue to be significant communities of people, however, who resist both these spirituality evangelists and the economic impetuses, who continue to see their ceremonial life as a community event closed to outsiders.[7]

Since opinion seems so divided among Native American practitioners themselves, a corollary question becomes even more important: Who are the appropriate spokespeople for giving an authoritative answer to the first question? Non-Natives who have participated in Native ceremonies invariably announce that they were, in fact, invited by Indian people to participate. The invitation, in a sense, becomes their passport into the spiritual world of Indian peoples. The actuality is that hospitality is one of the most important virtues in every Indian community. This makes it difficult for Indian people to say no, even when it means the invasion of ceremonial privacy, and sometimes even when we want to say no. Non-Indians seem, correspondingly, to have difficulty not taking advantage of Indian peoples in any context, even taking advantage of extreme generosity. It can be argued that Amer-European people are culturally good at taking what they want or think they need but have great difficulty receiving any gift, especially if understanding the boundaries of the gift is implicit in the giving; Amer-Europeans are best at imposing on others rather than offering their own gifts. Somehow, it is never quite clear that there are some things that we do not want to share.

Even in those cases when a non-Indian has a clear invitation from an Indian participant, the question must be raised whether the Indian person has the right to extend the invitation. In any Amer-European context, of course, the invitation of one individual to another individual can be taken at face value as a valid and authentic invitation that can be accepted or not, merely on the basis of personal preference. The complicating factor in the American Indian ceremonial context is the community. Since the ceremony is a community event and all participants affect the entire community, who has the right to invite a nonmember into the community's intimate and private ceremony? Although this complexity should be a warning to all of us in the Indian community in terms of our sense of generosity, it should also be taken seriously by our Amer-European relatives. Any non-Indian who is so invited needs to question seriously whether the invitation is even remotely valid and genuine—even if it comes from a high-status elder or leader. And perhaps the non-Indian should also question his or her own motives for having any interest in experiencing somebody else's intimate spiritual relationships.

GENEROSITY: A DYSFUNCTIONAL VIRTUE

I have already suggested that the enduring results of colonialism have left Indian people fighting with chronic levels of dysfunctionality that may lead to inappropriate invitations to intimacy, similar to many other abuse survivors in our modern world of violence. Indeed, the very values that our cultures have always lived by can actually enhance our dysfunctionality when they are lived too uncritically in our modern relationship with our colonizer. This is to say that even virtues can ultimately have a dysfunctional potential, especially in our contemporary world of colonial power and transition. The valorizing of the virtue of generosity is one example.

The missionaries who intended to civilize American Indian peoples found much to criticize in Indian cultures. The propensity for a family to periodically give away all or much of its accumulated wealth consistently came under missionary attack as diabolical. Since the church has always intended that people's generosity extend primarily to itself, one can see how generosity toward other people may have been perceived as a significant threat to the church. Be that as it may, generosity is counted as one of the cardinal virtues by nearly all Indian peoples.

In my own tribe, traditional leadership on the council of "little old ones," the $No^nho^nzhi^nga$, was contingent on proving oneself with regard to this virtue of generosity. For instance, a candidate for appointment to the council must have given away all that his (and occasionally her) family had on at least three occasions.[8] Along with bravery, intelligence, and community morality, generosity helped define those who were paradigmatic for the whole community. The open generosity of Indian peoples in New England upon the arrival of the first English colonizers is well known. Without the agricultural skill and generosity of the original inhabitants of the land, the colonists would have certainly perished during their first winters in North America.[9] To this day, to admire something in another's possession quite often means receiving it as a gift. Such an ethic proved to be foreign and alienating to the missionaries, even as it proved useful in building solid community existence and alliances within and among Indian nations.

Although the virtue of generosity as different Native American peoples practice it can be touted as superior to the values of civilization imposed on Indian peoples by the Europeans, it has also become susceptible to abuse, misappropriated by our white relatives and misdirected by Indian peoples themselves. The inability of Indian people to say no, for instance, to the white, New Age invasion of Indian spirituality leaves our communities extremely vulnerable. The ethic of generosity dictates that we share what we have with all those who come our way. Food is always shared with a guest who happens to drop by, and it is only natural that what we treasure most highly, our spirituality, is also so easily and generously offered to others. What we are dealing with today is a *spiritual* give-away in which Indian generosity has been pressed to an extreme of dysfunctionality. Moreover, as we seem to invite more and more white relatives to join us in our traditional ceremonial life, the very ceremonies that give us life are being changed before our eyes, even though we usually do not recognize the change.

The modern Indian context of conquest and colonization has resulted in significant levels of emotional and mental health dysfunctionality, from chronic, communitywide levels of depression to widespread alcoholism, high rates of teen suicide, serious alienation from the Amer-European culture of work and achievement, and an ongoing mental colonization. One result of this process is a pervasive codependency with our colonizer,[10] resulting in what I would characterize as a serious addiction to the color white. There is a constant need for the approval of white institutions (especially government and church), white authority figures, and white friends. Thus, when Amer-Europeans clamor for acceptance into our ceremonies, all too often we are flattered and feel a sense of affirmation for our culture and our religious traditions instead of being wary, guarded, suspicious, and distrusting.

The codependent need for approval on the part of the abused person is a common theme in contemporary mental health analysis. In the same way, Indian people, struggling with our own history of abuse under the paternalistic control of colonialism, seem to have an underlying need for white approval. Indian churches clamor for the approval of white bishops; Indian national government figures clamor for the approval of Washington, D.C., and its array of senators and congresspersons; employees of Indian community agencies all clamor to meet the approval of the U.S. government's Bureau of Indian Affairs or Indian Health Service bureaucracies. Always, we are susceptible to the well-meaning, liberal do-gooders who want so much to help us and tell us what is best for Indian peoples. White greed compounds this Indian dysfunctionality in the rape of our natural resources, in extraction contracts that are entirely too favorable to the multinational conglomerates that enrich themselves almost at will on many reservations.[11] Likewise, the New Age aficionados move into our world with approving words of affirmation about the spiritual treasures of Indian peoples and then proceed to steal those treasures, just as they stole the land a generation or two earlier.

Many kindhearted Indian persons respond in this codependent relationship out of a felt need to help our white relatives find their way spiritually. Yet it seems that there is an even stronger felt need to garner the approval and affirmation of these same spiritually impoverished white friends.

CONCLUDING CONCERNS

Only with some understanding of the complexity of late colonial relationships and the exotic appeal of Indian ceremonies in our contemporary world can we begin to raise and address some critical concerns. This chapter ends with a list of those concerns that seem most pertinent. These concerns focus on a simple question: Is the sharing of Indian ceremonial life helpful to either Indian or non-Indian people?

- Cross-cultural differences make it difficult for non-Indians to internalize Indian meanings relating to ceremonial acts. This makes it necessary for Indian structures to remodel themselves culturally around non-Indian structures in order to include non-Indian individuals.
- As a result, the Amer-European participant usually has only a surface structure participation in the ceremony. There is a deep structure significance, of course, for both Indian and non-Indian participants in a ceremony, but the deep structure significance is quite different in each case. The sense of individual spiritual self-enhancement that is so central to white New Age participants means that they experience only the illusion of Indianness and the illusion of spiritual power. The result is not at all real, or, to the extent that the experience is real, it is no longer in any way Indian because it has been radically individualized.
- Along with the community-individual cultural difference comes another significant difference regularly overlooked by New Age wanna-bes. Namely, American Indian national communities are modal social organizations, as opposed to sodal social organizations. That is, Indian nationality, and hence participation in the ceremonial spirituality of the community, is not a voluntary act like joining a church. Rather, the concept of modality signifies that membership in the community is a birthright. This means that New Agers who invite themselves into Indian ceremonies enjoy a privilege that we Indian people do not and can not. New Age Amer-Europeans are able to choose their tribe of presumed affiliation from among a wide range of choices, whereas Indian people are stuck, so to speak, with the tribe of their birth. For the New Ager, choosing Indian spirituality and choosing a particular Indian community to imitate is much like choosing a church denomination or congregation. That, of course, is the history of voluntary organization in the United States, dating especially from the eighteenth century on. Indian people choose neither tribe nor clan. We are what we are by birth.
- In many cultures, spiritual knowledge is not the universal right of all citizens in the national community; there is a division of labor according to clans and societies. In many cultures, different clans or societies have particular responsibilities for parts of a national ceremony and thus possess particular knowledge not necessarily shared by all in the community. The success of the ceremony in this case depends on each clan and society appropriately performing its discrete role in the ceremonial whole. Not only does the whole community depend on each

subgroup to do its part, but the knowledge associated with each part belongs to the particular clan or society responsible for performing it. Other clans, family members, or neighbors may have no right to "know" any part of that knowledge. The Hopi spokesperson Talayesva, for instance, declined to comment on such knowledge when pressed by Simmons, the anthropologist, on exactly such a basis.[12] The sentiment of having a "right to know" is an inherently white and Amer-European valorization of the individual, whether anthropologist–scientific scholar or New Age aficionado. This right to know is countered by the communitarian interest in the good of the whole. Pressing the individual's presumed right to know can violate the good of the whole, especially when that right to know is pressed by someone outside of the community itself.

- Essentially, I have argued that white participation in Indian community ceremonial actions contributes to the ongoing destruction of Indian culture, ceremonies, and communities.

Finally, white participation in Indian ceremonial life reinforces the notion of white privilege so prevalent and dominant in our larger societal whole. White involvement in Indian ceremonies is actually harmful to our white relatives, because it reinforces the inbred sense of white privilege that is the heritage of every white person in North America, just as male privilege is the heritage of every male. One can hear the appeal to white privilege in the seemingly neutral claim of many of our white relatives: "Spirituality does not belong to anyone." Yet the neutrality dissolves when one understands the claim to be a white claim on Indian spirituality and either the replication of our ceremonies or direct participation in them. "You must share" is a second claim, one that holds us to a dysfunctional valorization of our own cultural value of hospitality. Yet it needs to be emphasized that we hurt our white relatives and friends when we naively invite them into our private, community ceremonial life. We are only encouraging the final act of colonization and conquest. In an amazing but convenient turnaround, our ceremonies are no longer castigated as demonic, savage, and uncivilized; instead, with Indian land and natural resources already plundered, our ceremonies have become the new prize possession of the colonizer, and their theft is the ultimate act of postmodern colonialism. It is a new version of the colonizer's indulgence in colonial exoticism, a fetishization of Indian people and Indian traditions.[13] This becomes a primary reason for arguing that the inclusion of white folk in the community intimacy of our ceremonies is not healthy for those white relatives, especially if they really want to make a difference in the world and find creative ways to do things differently.

NOTES

1. See Paul Chaat Smith and Robert Allen Warrior, *Like a Hurricane: The Indian Movement from Alcatraz to Wounded Knee* (New York: New Press, 1996).

2. I make this argument for the community-centered nature of American Indian ceremonial structures in spite of the persistent attempt of white scholars (the recognized "experts" on Indians) to twist Indian cultural values into a more Euro-compatible form of individualism. See, for instance, Clyde Holler, *Black Elk's Religion: The Sun Dance and Lakota Catholicism* (Syracuse, N.Y.: Syracuse University Press, 1995); but also note Dale Stover's insightful critique in his review of Holler's book: "Eurocentrism and Native Americans," *Cross Currents* (1997), 390– 97. Stover particularly addresses the tendency of Holler and others to impose an individualist interpretive overlay on the Indian cultures they purport to describe with "old fashioned . . . scholarly objectivity" (Holler, xvi).

3. Perhaps there is a connection here between the Indian sense of *doing* and liberation theology's notion of *praxis.*

4. *National* is used here in reference to the traditional sovereign communities of Indian peoples. It is used in preference to the usual but derogatory words *tribe* and *tribal.* See Ward Churchill, "Naming Our Destiny: Towards a Language of Indian Liberation," in *Indigenous Autonomy and the Next Five Hundred Years,* ed. G. E. Tinker, a double issue of *Global Justice,* vol. 3, nos. 2, 3 (1992).

5. See Ward Churchill, "Carlos Castaneda: The Greatest Hoax since Piltdown Man," in *Fantasies of the Master Race: Literature, Cinema and the Colonization of American Indians* (Monroe, Me.: Common Courage Press, 1992), 43–64; and "Spiritual Hucksterism: The Rise of the Plastic Medicine Men," in ibid., 215–28. Also see Wendy Rose, "The Great Pretenders: Further Reflections on White Shamanism," in *The State of Native America: Genocide, Colonization and Resistance,* ed. M. Annette Jaimes (Boston: South End, 1992), 403–22.

6. See the essay on the "men's movement" by Ward Churchill in this regard: "Indians Are Us: Reflections on the Men's Movement," in *Indians Are Us: Culture and Genocide in Native North America* (Monroe, Me.: Common Courage Press, 1994), 207–77.

7. Many distinguish between open and closed ceremonies. The Pueblos of New Mexico, for instance, publish a calendar of ceremonies that are open to the public but also maintain their more critical ceremonies as private community events.

8. Louis F. Burns, *Osage Indian Customs and Myths* (Fallbrook, Calif.: Ciga Press, 1984), 3ff., discusses the qualifications of the No^{n}ho^{n}zhi^{n}ga, based on the extensive work of Francis LaFlesche.

9. See, e.g., Neal Salisbury, "Survivors and Pilgrims," in *Manitou and Providence: Indians, Europeans, and the Making of New England, 1500–1643* (New York: Oxford University Press, 1982), 110–40.

10. Already noted by Albert Memmi in the context of 1950s Africa in *The Colonizer and the Colonized,* trans. Howard Greenfeld (Boston: Beacon Press, 1967), and further described in the colonial context of India by Ashis Nandy, *The Intimate Enemy: Loss and Recovery of Self under Colonialism* (New York: Oxford University Press, 1983).

11. See Ward Churchill, *Struggle for the Land: Indigenous Resistance, Ecocide and Expropriation in Contemporary North America* (Toronto: Between the Lines, 1992).

12. D. Talayesva (Leo Simmons), *Sun Chief: The Autobiography of a Hopi* (New

Haven, Conn.: Yale University Press, 1942). See a similar ethnographic description for the Osage people: Garrick Bailey, *The Osage and the Invisible World from the Works of Francis La Flesche* (Norman: University of Oklahoma, 1995), 56.

13. See Anne McClintock, *Imperial Leather: Gender, Race and Sexuality in the Imperial Contest* (Delhi: Routledge, 1996).

PART IV: INDIAN INTELLECTUAL CULTURE AND RESISTANCE

There Is No Such Thing as a One-Way Land Bridge

Joy Harjo (Mvskoke)

I imagine someone walking through the ruins of my house, years later when I am gone and all who knew me and my family and nation are gone and there are only stories as to what happened to us. Did we flee from an enemy, or die of famine or floods?

The story depends on who is telling it. A colonizer will say that the people disappeared, though their descendants are still living in the same area and going to school with his or her children. The descendants of the Anasazi are my granddaughters and will be their children, yet they are catalogued as "disappeared." If it can be postulated that a people came to a natural end, that no one was there, that the land was abandoned, then the colonizer will assume a right of ownership.

For years, the predominant anthropological theory in the study of North American Indians was and still is the Bering Strait theory, that is, that North America was settled by a relatively late migration of peoples from Asia. This meant that prior rights of occupation were tentative, and the land claims of the indigenous peoples held less weight, for if we were recent immigrants too, who were we to make such claims?

The Bering Strait theory and so many others in the Western world hold that Indians are somehow less than human, or at least not as advanced as Western, European, cultured humans. We are constantly being defined from the point of view of the colonizer. We are human and live complex and meaningful lives. I like the response given to an anthropologist when he asked a teacher in a particular Asian culture about ideology and theory. "What ideology? We just dance."

When I am home in Oklahoma at the stomping grounds, we may talk about the complexities of meaning, but to comprehend it, to know it intimately, that intricate context of history and family, is to dance it, to be it.

I think back to the ruins of a house in Chaco Canyon, an Anasazi ruin near Crownpoint, New Mexico. The winds are cool and steady, and through the years they have eroded the adobe. There is no protection from the sun and rain. Tourists quickly pass through ruins. The clouds, too, walk on. Everything keeps moving—even me, moved by my thoughts through the house, through time. I converse with my own death, which will one day leave a track behind me, like the ruins of this house.

There was a woman here who was loved. She was good to look at because she was a quick and imaginative thinker. She liked the view of the peach orchard from the southern window and loved the turquoise earrings her mother had given her when she was married. Her life mattered, utterly, to herself, to her children, to the man she loved, to the birds she scattered crumbs to after the family had eaten. This was her house, and years later the house still remembers her, though it is almost gone and the woman's spirit has flown to the other side.

CHAPTER TEN

Contours of Enlightenment: Reflections on Science, Theology, Law, and the Alternative Vision of Vine Deloria, Jr.

Ward Churchill (Keetowah Band of Cherokee)

On the wings of synthesis one can fly to such a height that the blood turns to ice and the human body freezes, a height which no flyer has ever attained.

Valerian Maikov

It is a testament to the centrality of Vine Deloria, Jr., to the thinking of my generation of Native scholars, that many of us can scarcely recall a time when our opinions were formed without reference to his. It is as if, for us, he has somehow *always* been there, a kind of institutional presence whose major purpose has been to test the verisimilitude of taken-for-granted propositions, challenging the pat assumptions and assertions of orthodoxy, calling inconsistencies, hypocrisies, and sheer banalities by their right names. Many a balloon of pretension, both academic and official, he has punctured on our behalf, leaving those who would preside as emperors over our minds standing naked and exposed, red-faced, spluttering and without adequate retort, the eventual objects of ridicule or revulsion rather than reverence.

Such exercises have won Deloria few admirers among those thus humbled, of course. On the contrary, the number of those now bearing him a degree of professional animus has grown to the proportions of a legion. There were surely more personally comfortable and convenient ways in which he might have proceeded. Yet the result has, on the whole, been quite empowering, licensing the rest of us to engage our own inquisitiveness and critical faculties, coming thereby to actually understand something of what we think we know. And this, to be sure, has been his intention all along. From the outset, Deloria's project has been an implicitly "counterhegemonic" one.[1] It follows that his posture has been that of a consistently and explicitly liberatory figure.

All this I know to be true, and still I am aware that my sense of remembrance bears the unmistakable signature of retrospective apostasy. We did not "grow up on Deloria."[2] He was *not* "always there." In my own case, there is nothing at all to recollect until his first book, *Custer Died for*

Your Sins, came along in 1969.[3] By then I was twenty-two, working in a foundry while attending a community college, having already reached my "maturity" in the central highlands of Vietnam. Our "encounter," moreover, was no more direct than my reading of what he had written. For me, however, as with many of my peers, that experience alone prompted a resonance so profound as to cause our embrace of the author—or, rather, our imaginings of him—with all the presumptuous intimacy of those who believe they have found another speaking in their own voice and whom they therefore feel they have known forever.

It would be another decade and another half dozen books[4] before I actually met the man, and in the event, there seemed nothing especially cerebral or intellectually portentous about our rendezvous. Although he was awaiting the release of his *Metaphysics of Modern Existence,*[5] and I was collaborating on several essays for a volume of the *Smithsonian Handbook on North American Indians* that he was compiling (but which never appeared),[6] the fact is that I simply tagged along with Joe Bageant, a mutual friend and editor of the Boulder-based *Rocky Mountain Musical Express,* a pop periodical in which Deloria had published a short satire lampooning New Age filmmakers.[7]

Joe had it in mind to coax another such contribution, so we spent the afternoon chatting mostly about Vine's interactions with Marlon Brando,[8] the Denver Broncos' prospects for the coming season, and local country-western songwriter Michael Burton, whom we all knew and who had just finished a tune entitled "The Cowboy's Lament." Since Vine was in the process of packing for his move to Tucson, where he had recently accepted a professorship at the University of Arizona, no article for the *Express* was ever forthcoming. Bageant ended up putting together a riff about the Deloria-Brando connection himself.[9] The Broncos, typically, had a miserable year. As for Mike Burton, Jerry Jeff Walker acquired the rights to his song, pronouncing it "the greatest piece of cowboy music ever written."[10]

For myself, maybe it was because we both smoked the same brand of cigarette (and at about the same rate), or perhaps it was because I knew who played the Steve McQueen character's parents in *Junior Bonner,*[11] but for whatever reason, Vine took a liking to me. Thus began what would eventually add up to a close, fifteen-year relationship in which many an evening was spent watching NFL football and reruns of *Shane.* Others were passed in rambling discussions of everything from the influence of Gene Autry's 1930s recordings on the emergence of 1950s rock 'n' roll to questions such as whether dinosaurs were warm-blooded or cold and the likelihood that the universe functions primarily on electromagnetic rather than thermonuclear principles.[12] Almost never did our far-ranging conversations land directly within the subject matters on which either of us was working at any given moment.

I recount such things not as an indulgence in the vice of personal reminiscence but to illustrate the nature, or at least certain facets, of what Raymond DeMallie has aptly described as Deloria's "disconcertingly brilliant intellect."[13] Like Theodor Adorno (whose approach to understanding Vine's often reminds me of), his gaze is at once probing and virtually all-encompassing in its perpetual labor to apprehend meaning in its most subtle, nuanced, and thoroughly contextualized essence. Although he would undoubtedly resist being saddled with the label, Deloria is, as was Adorno, a master dialectician, insisting that the sum and substance of anything can be ascertained only in its intrinsic relationality to others.[14] Hence the abiding preoccupation of both men with situating the concreta on which they have focused—politics, law, or whatever—within the vastly broader ferment of sociocultural expression—art, music, and so forth—which both reflects and lends them their inherent shapes and trajectories.[15]

Unlike his counterpart's coldly ascetic preference for such rarified fare as Schoenberg's twelve-tone row,[16] however, Deloria's fascination has remained firmly ensconced within the framework of the very mass cultural idioms that Adorno's densely theoretical tracts were designed to critique (and, it is hoped, eventually negate altogether).[17] Both the orientation and the expository style it compels have left Deloria's texts, and consequently the reasoning underlying them, vastly more accessible than those of Adorno, their author far less tormented and self-isolating.[18] Whereas Adorno can rightly be said to have cast himself as an exemplar of elitist obscurity, Deloria has proceeded along the same lines but in a precisely opposite direction. This, I think, accounts for much—though certainly not all—of the resonance his work has mustered over the years.[19]

THE POLITICS

Like so many of my peers, I came to Deloria politically. The matter can be explained only in part by the explicitly political content of the criticisms of Congress, the Bureau of Indian Affairs (BIA), and other official institutions he advanced first in *Custer,* then in *We Talk, You Listen* (1970), and, most unequivocally, in *Behind the Trail of Broken Treaties* (1974).[20] His credibility, and thus his appeal, devolved in at least equal proportion from the sense that, although clearly an intellectual of the first order, he was also in some discernible sense an activist, involved at least indirectly in such watershed processes and events as the 1969–1971 occupation of Alcatraz Island,[21] the 1972 occupation of BIA headquarters in Washington, D.C.,[22] and the 1973 siege of Wounded Knee.[23]

Although such ideas had been present in his work all along, it was especially in the latter connection that Vine set forth with greatest clarity his conception of American Indian peoples' aboriginal and treaty-based right to the status of nations, separate and distinct from the United States.[24] Most forcefully, he summarized the thrust of his arguments in testimony challenging U.S. jurisdiction over Lakota territory, and thus the Wounded Knee defendants, during the "Sioux Sovereignty Hearings" of 1974.[25] It would not be until 1979 that this radical fecundation of Native legal standing was finalized and available in essay form.[26] Meanwhile, it had galvanized a successful effort by the American Indian Movement (AIM) to establish a formal presence in the United Nations (UN) for purposes of (re)asserting indigenous rights through available international mechanisms.[27]

On some levels, these developments and the logic underlying them dovetailed quite well with the principle of decolonization enshrined in the UN Charter and actualized on a global scale since the end of World War II.[28] AIM's "diplomatic arm," the International Indian Treaty Council (IITC), originally headed by Russell Means and Jimmie Durham, set on an agenda of forging what it hoped would be mutually supportive alliances with liberation movements and newly independent governments, most of them with a decidedly Marxian orientation, throughout the so-called Third World of colonized or formerly colonized countries.[29] Among the other early accomplishments of this strategy was the formation of the Working Group on Indigenous Populations, a subpart of the UN Economic and Social Council mandated to review the conditions affecting Native peoples around the world, assess the implications of their treaty relations with the various nation-states to which they were subordinated, recommend applications of extant international law where appropriate, and, ultimately, draft an entirely new Declaration of the Rights of Indigenous Peoples.[30]

Suffice it to say that the overt anti-imperialism of such ferment proved more than sufficient to draw me from the ranks of the mostly white Students for a Democratic Society, which I'd become rather heavily involved in after my stint in the army, and into AIM. From late 1972 onward, I was increasingly engaged with the latter, missing Wounded Knee altogether but winding up a decade later as codirector of the movement's Colorado chapter, a participant in the Yellow Thunder occupation in the Black Hills,[31] and an IITC delegate to Libya, Cuba, and the working group.

By 1983, the initial blush of optimism attending the admission of indigenous peoples to United Nations processes had waned considerably. The ascendant First World (capitalist) UN member-countries had already begun to make it clear that they would defend themselves against our claims to the right of self-determination by invoking a clause in the charter guaranteeing the territorial integrity of all states and defining a colony as being a country separated from its colonizer by at least thirty miles of open ocean.[32] Many of us set out to counter this "blue water thesis" by following the lead of Cherokee anthropologist Robert K. Thomas, who, during the mid-1960s, had undertaken to adapt the Gramscian theory of internal colonialism to the situation of American Indians.[33]

Despite the patent analytical and polemical utility of Gramsci's construction, our embrace of it served mainly to reveal the disjuncture between the objectives pursued by indigenous rights advocates and those acceptable to our Marxist "allies," virtually all of whom were busily working out their own variations of statist order squarely atop the territories—and using the resources—of whatever Native peoples were situated within their purported boundaries.[34] Although a number of examples might be cited, the nature of the problem was perhaps best illustrated by the campaign of Nicaragua's Sandinista regime during the 1980s to forcibly suppress the aspirations of the Miskito, Sumu, and Rama peoples to regain a genuinely self-determining status in a postrevolutionary context.[35]

The most noticeable outcome was the Sandinistas' failure to achieve the degree of stability necessary to fend off a U.S. low-intensity war waged to depose them. The dispute also led to the disintegration of AIM and IITC, as both groups split along the lines of those determined to align with anyone opposing the United States, no matter what, and those of us dedicated to supporting indigenous liberation struggles, irrespective of their oppressors' ideological persuasion.[36] The latter tendency has come to be referred to as "indigenism," and its adherents are known as "Fourth Worlders,"[37] those committed not to the revolutionary ideal of seizing state power but rather to dismantling the territorial and jurisdictional corpus of the state altogether.[38]

Although he contributed to the framing of our disavowal of Marxism as a remedy to the oppression suffered by Native people,[39] by the early 1980s, Deloria had already begun to look askance at the way things were shaping up. As he later explained, although conceding its descriptive accuracy, he had come to view the whole notion of internal colonialism as presenting at best a practical dead end in terms of realizing indigenous rights.[40] Consequently, his next two books, *American Indians, American Justice* and *The Nations Within,* both coauthored with Clifford M. Lytle, embodied a substantive departure from the explicit anticolonialism marking the earlier Deloria.[41] Instead, he advocated a "progressive" approach, working within the parameters of colonial legality to achieve limited but nevertheless tangible improvements in the dire material circumstances afflicting most of Native America.[42]

This sort of pragmatism, manifested most recently in *Tribes, Treaties, and Constitutional Tribulations,* Vine's 1999 collaboration with his protégé David Wilkins,[43] has caused many to view him as an aging sellout (accommodationist).[44] In actuality, although my own persistence in exploring indigenist thematics has led to our increasing estrangement over the past decade, I believe this to be a profound misreading of both the man and the nature of his endeavor. If anything, it seems to me that he has harnessed himself to a task far more subversive in its implications than any conceivable brand of purely political praxis. Indeed, like Adorno, he long ago came to the realization that alterations in the political status quo, irrespective of their extremity, accomplish little in terms of correcting the core problems that confront us all, oppressed and oppressor alike.[45]

Beneath the web of extant political relations lies a much deeper matrix of ostensibly "apolitical" (mis)perceptions, (dis)understandings, and imputed values that foster the illusion that the relations themselves, or some discernibly close approximation, are "natural" and therefore "inevitable." Thus, in Deloria's assessment, concentration on the superficialities of a mere political "fix" is at best diversionary. Worse, it tends to instill a false sense of resolution among those who accomplish it.[46] Absent an attendant reconsideration of the more fundamental aspects of consciousness that gave rise to the political conditions supposedly confronted and transformed, the confronters and transformers are doomed inevitably to replicate that which they sought to oppose.[47]

The object is therefore to engage in what Michel Foucault, in a celebrated turn of the phrase, once referred to as the "archaeology of knowledge," apprehending the codes and symbologies of domination at their sources, and, to borrow a term from Jacques Derrida, "deconstruct" them from start to finish.[48] Only then, freed from the conceptual blinders imposed by what Jean-François Lyotard called "the master narrative,"[49] can one—or an entire culture—hope to (re)envision a truly liberatory reordering of the polity. Outlined today, nearly twenty years after postmodernism became intellectually fashionable, such ideas sound almost clichéd. In the late 1960s, however, when Deloria first began to delve into them, the opposite was true.

Vine, moreover, has always wielded a decisive advantage over the great majority of postmodernists. Steeped during his upbringing in the traditional Lakota cosmology, yet formally trained in the canons of Western intellectualism (he was schooled in geology, theology, and law), he has been ideally positioned to assault paradigmatic Eurocentrism from a perspective that is, to borrow the nomenclature of anthropology, simultaneously emic and etic.[50] In philosophical terms, his critique has been uniquely both "immanent" and "transcendent."[51] Additionally, his lifelong immersion in the vocabularies of popular culture has precluded his ever sliding into the deliberate opacity marking virtually all postmodernist discourse, including that offered by such Native poseurs as Gerald Vizenor.[52]

EXCAVATIONS

"Long before anyone in anthropology had heard of Michel Foucault or Pierre Bourdieu," Thomas Biolsi and Larry Zimmerman point out, "Deloria had put his finger on what would later be called discursive formations, symbolic capital, and the micropolitics of the academy."[53] Deloria's initial critique, advanced most forcefully in *Custer*,[54] was openly political, assailing the sheer arrogance of anthropological practice and practitioners, as well as the function of resulting theory in casting a patina of rationalism and objectivity over the otherwise glaring irrationality in the formation of U.S. Indian policy.[55] Here, he shared a conclusion shortly enunciated by Jean Baudrillard that "the deepest racist avatar is to think that an error about [other] societies is politically or theoretically less serious than a misinterpretation of [one's] own world. Just as a people that oppresses another cannot be free, so a culture that is mistaken about another must also be mistaken about itself."[56]

Among other methodological observations offered in *Custer*, Deloria noted that while conducting fieldwork and other sorts of research, anthropologists invariably seemed to have predetermined what they would find and what it would mean. Their purpose could thus be seen as little more than an exercise designed to create the appearance—but hardly the reality—that their preconceptions had been verified.[57] It follows that the whole procedural thrust of anthropology stems from a fundamental violation of the very "scientific method" on which the discipline has based its claim to being a mode of understanding more accurate than, and therefore superior to, the modes prevailing among the mostly non-Western peoples it studies.[58]

In seeking to dig out the source of this dysfunction, Deloria unearthed a far broader and more disconcerting reality: although the colonially inspired enterprise of anthropology[59]—its brief history laden with such clear-cut illustrations of racist pseudoscience as craniometry, phrenology, eugenics,[60] social Darwinism,[61] and the Piltdown hoax[62]—represents a thoroughly sordid example, it is by no means uniquely so. Everywhere he turned, in the "hard" sciences such as physics, biology, and astronomy as much as among the pretenders of anthropology and the social sciences, Deloria encountered the same sorts of unscientific or even antiscientific claptrap passed off as the opposite of itself.[63]

As his excavations became deeper, he was more strongly drawn to the conclusion that the origins of Western science itself could be located not in an oppositional relationship to the mysticism of Judeo-Christian tradition—as the "scientific community" was wont to insist—but in an obsessive and usually subliminal desire to fulfill the biblical enjoinder, set forth on the first page of Genesis, for humans to dominate nature.[64] As a consequence, the very notion of scientific objectivity can best be understood as a myth designed to mask the underlying and utterly subjective motivations of those claiming allegiance to it.[65] The result is that science has been transposed into scientism—that is, a religion-like belief structure—and its adherents have been transformed from scientists into beings more accurately categorized as "scientians." As a matter of practicality, scientism may be said not to have supplanted but to have subsumed Christianity as the "faith of choice" in Western societies.[66]

Significant evidence of this, Deloria argued in his 1973 God Is Red, may be found in the fact that the scientific establishment has incorporated the essentially theological charge of "heresy," once deployed by the church against scientists such as Galileo, as a weapon in the arsenal with which it defends its own dogmas.[67] To illustrate, he offered the case of Immanuel Velikovsky, an interdisciplinary scholar of undeniable stature who had the audacity to demonstrate that a profound rethinking would be necessary to rectify the many substantial inadequacies, inconsistencies, and full-fledged logical impossibilities embodied in orthodox geological and astronomical theory.[68]

Correlating the traditional histories of the Mideast and elsewhere with available physical data, Velikovsky set out in a 1950 book entitled Worlds in Collision to offer what he called a "catastrophist" alternative to conventional explanatory paradigms.[69] As Deloria recounts, he was thereupon subjected to a modern scientian equivalent of the medieval Inquisition: "Worlds in Collision was attacked by 'respectable' scientists even before it was published. A concentrated effort was begun to force the Macmillan Company, Velikovsky's publisher, to stop the presses. Scholars began a boycott of Macmillan's textbook division, its most vulnerable place. Macmillan could not withstand the concerted attack and transferred the book's rights to Doubleday. A conspiracy of silence dropped over discussion of Velikovsky's works. He subsequently published Earth in Upheaval, which was an embarrassing revelation of geological shortcomings."[70]

Although Velikovsky would remain an intellectual pariah for the remainder of his life, several of his supposedly "wild-eyed" theories have been borne out. Indeed, his contention that the sun is an electrically charged body, and that the solar system must therefore function as a large, gravitating electromagnet, has been appropriated without attribution by some of the very scientists who were most scornful in their dismissals when Velikovsky first advanced the idea.[71] Similarly: "Velikovsky . . . suggested in a 1953 talk at Princeton that Jupiter was probably a dark star giving off radio signals. Less than two years later, two scientists discovered radio signals coming from Jupiter, and by 1965 Jupiter was declared a dark star. [He] also argued that Earth [had] a magnetosphere reach as far as the moon. In 1958 the Van Allen Belts were discovered, named after James Van Allen who had only measured them and not after Velikovsky who had predicted [their existence]."[72]

Deloria returned briefly to the "Velikovsky affair" in *The Metaphysics of Modern Existence*,[73] a 1979 book intended as the first in a trilogy of volumes devoted to exploring the problematic substitution of science for religion in the West. Opining that "Indians don't write books on philosophy," Harper and Row first tried to evade its contractual obligation to release it; then, failing that, it published only a small hardcover edition that was remaindered almost immediately.[74] Absent the other two volumes, fragments of which have appeared as commentaries and freestanding essays over the years,[75] Deloria was left with a somewhat unbalanced and largely unread critique of Heisenberg's physics and Jungian psychology, as well as the thinking of theologians such as Teilhard de Chardin and Paul Tillich.[76]

By then, having realized along with Paul Schmidt that the conception of sovereignty at issue in the indigenist liberation struggle amounted in important respects to a Christianesque expression of "political theology,"[77] Deloria had taken to calling for a refocusing of the movement's energy and attention. Our continuing investiture in the attainment of power in terms defined by the worldview of our oppressors, he reasoned, could, even if successful, serve only to complete their grip on our consciousness, thereby consummating rather than repudiating our subordination.[78] The imperative, as he saw it, was to reclaim the insights and understandings lodged within our own non-Western traditions, employing them first as a counter to the distortive outlooks imposed by the West and then as the basis on which to determine for ourselves the form and meaning of the relations we should pursue not just with other cultures but with the natural world in its totality.[79]

Deloria, for his part, more or less picked up where Velikovsky left off,[80] undertaking a protracted study in which he combined a broad selection of Native North American origin stories with elements of the same peoples' cosmologies and oral histories, comparing the resultant narrative overview with the continent's geological record. Additional comparisons to the fossil record completed the picture, allowing him to systematically demolish the factual-logical structures underpinning entire components of standard evolutionary theory and attendant chronologies, while validating much of what is contained in indigenous "lore" as the literal recapitulation of observed reality.[81]

Much of this was brought together in *Red Earth, White Lies*, a 1995 release subtitled *Native Americans and the Myth of Scientific Fact*.[82] Therein, it is demonstrated that the Hopi "legends" depicting a sequence of ages marked by fire, ice, and water might be interpreted as recountings of literal volcanic events, the last ice age, and the following period of glacial melt.[83] Similarly, it is shown that a traditional Klamath story perfectly describes the formation, violent eruption, and subsequent collapse of a volcanic cone. Other stories shared by the peoples of the Warm Springs Reservation account quite well for the formation of the mountains known as the "Three Sisters" in central Oregon.[84]

The "problem" with these and numerous other uncannily accurate Native depictions of geological events is that, according to scientian orthodoxy, they occurred far too long ago for humans to have witnessed them. People, after all, are decreed to have first entered the hemisphere across the Bering Strait land bridge not more than 15,000 years ago (until 1950, the official "truth" was that the migration occurred only 3,000 years ago), with only heretics and other "irresponsible" types suggesting otherwise.[85] This constraint, in turn, is necessitated by the requirements of conventional evolutionary theory, which has modern humans—*Homo sapiens sapiens,* the only variety of hominid known to have resided in the Americas—emerging somewhere in Africa about 100,000 years ago and slowly spreading across the planet.[86]

Noting that there is virtually nothing in traditional indigenous accounts that suggests a traverse of the Bering Strait—a major exception, the so-called Walam Olum of the Leni Lenapes (Delawares), turned out to be an outright fabrication[87]—Deloria proceeds to make mincemeat of the whole proposition. Juxtaposing the elements of geography, geology, meteorology, biology, and anthropology that bear on the Beringian migration hypothesis, he points out how each tends to contradict the other. For openers, while anthropologists posit pursuit of America's "megafauna"—mammoths, giant rhinos, and the like—as being the motive for Paleolithic hunters to cross the strait from Siberia to Alaska during the last ice age, biologists account for the appearance of these same species in Asia at about the same time by having them migrate in the opposite direction.[88]

Actually, neither of these mutually nullifying scenarios is especially plausible, given the geological barriers involved; to get to the fabled land bridge from either direction would have required migrants to traverse several of the more formidable mountain ranges on the planet.[89] Nor does the meteorological record conform to the requirements of anthropological orthodoxy; an "ice-free corridor" along the Mackenzie River, through which migrant humans are supposed to have moved southward from Alaska into the U.S. portion of North America, could not have existed during the period indicated (if it ever existed at all).[90] Even the conventional explanation of the weather patterns precipitating an ice age—on which the existence of the Bering land bridge itself depends—is found wanting.[91]

Other aspects of what passes for science fare no better. Even the technological "proofs" with which the discipline professes to have confirmed key elements of its theory are demonstrably faulty. With respect to the sophisticated potassium-argon tests that supposedly establish the dates of geological events with great precision, Deloria, following Cremo and Thompson, points out that "scientists have obtained dates ranging from 116 million to 2.96 billion years for Hawaiian lava flows that occurred in the year 1800."[92] Much the same pertains to radiocarbon dating, by which the antiquity of organic material is supposedly ascertained:

- In the *Atlantic Journal of the United States,* W. Dort wrote that freshly slaughtered seals, when subjected to radiocarbon analysis, were dated at 1,300 years old.
- In *Science,* M. Keith and G. Anderson wrote that shells of living mollusks were dated at 2,300 years old.
- In *The Physiology of Trees,* Bruno Haber wrote that wood from a growing tree was dated at 10,000 years old. [93]

Compounding such technological defects is the fact that "responsible" anthropologists have routinely suppressed radiocarbon datings that conflict with orthodoxy. Although test results from materials gathered at a number of sites as far south as Brazil have indicated human occupancy in the Americas for as long as forty millennia, they have invariably been dismissed—when they have been acknowledged at all—as "marred by serious questions of whether the material used for radiocarbon dating was contaminated by older carbon, or whether the dated material was really associated with human remains," and the like.[94]

Impossible standards have been assigned to the verification of evidence conflicting with the Bering Strait migration hypothesis, but the reverse does not hold true. Assessing the work of the late William Laughlin, Deloria observes that he provides "no evidence at all that any Paleo-Indians were within a thousand miles of Alaska during [the specified period]. No sites, trails, or signs of habitation are cited. . . . Laughlin is the acknowledged dean of American Bering Strait scholars, and yet he offered no concrete evidence whatsoever . . . in support of his theory.[95] Nonetheless, anthropologists all but invariably "begin with the *assumption* that the Bering Strait migration doctrine was proved a long time ago . . . and proceed without the slightest doubt" as to its validity, having "accepted the idea at face value on faith alone" and defending it ferociously against all challengers.[96]

A better illustration of how science has been diverted from its original purposes into service as "a secular but very powerful religion" would be hard to find.[97] Indeed, had he wished, Deloria could easily have demonstrated that the very notion of the Bering Strait crossing was given birth around 1580, not by scientists but by Jesuits eager to conjure up some means of reconciling the Christian version of how humanity was created with the recently discovered fact that there was an entire "New World" teeming with people who, to all appearances, could not have descended from Adam and Eve.[98] Since Judaism shares its origin story with Christianity, rabbinical scholars also had a stake in the issue. It is thus unsurprising that the next major contributor was a rabbi, Israel ben Mannasseh, who in 1650 published the thesis that people had found their way from the Old World to the New across what was then called the Strait of Anian, and he had tentatively identified the migrants as descendants of several "lost tribes" of Hebrews mentioned in the Bible.[99]

Mannasseh's speculation quickly took hold and was eventually adopted as an article of faith by the Church of Latter-Day Saints, which to this day maintains a lavishly funded New World Archaeological Institute at Brigham Young University, the primary mission of which is to locate physical evidence supporting its sponsor's unabashedly theological agenda.[100] Nor has non-Mormon anthropology proved itself one whit less doctrinally biased. Although the idea that Indians are Jews has long since been abandoned, the anthropological establishment has, from at least the publication of Thomas Jefferson's 1781 *Notes on the State of Virginia*, harnessed itself with astonishing single-mindedness to the task of proving the Judeo-Christian Old World origin story correct in its essentials.[101] In the process, anthropology has as a discipline proved itself quite insistent on ignoring or suppressing countervailing evidence while busily cooking the books to make its preferred postulations seem vastly more solidly based than they actually are. Thereby, it has forfeited whatever claim to scientific integrity it might ever have possessed.[102]

Insofar as it reduces in the end to nothing more than an elaborate advocacy of a given origin story (however much revised), there is no *rational* reason why interpretations of the world advanced via the scientian edifice of anthropology should be privileged over belief systems arising in conjunction with any other such story. By extension, much the same can be said of the other sectors of what is typically referred to as "scientific knowledge."[103] To say that scientism presently possesses the *power* to impose itself on other traditions at their expense—a power acquired largely through the sustained subterfuge of pretending that science and scientism are synonymous—is not to concede that it enjoys any *right* to do so. The principle is identical to that enshrined in international law that precludes any people, no matter how powerful, from legitimately preempting the self-determining prerogatives of another.[104] Although usually subtler than its physical counterpart, intellectual imperialism is, after all, imperialism nonetheless.[105]

From this standpoint, Deloria's laying bare the religious roots of scientism, his tracing of their outgrowths and consequent debunking of contemporary scientian pretension, as well as his concomitant (re)assertion of the validity of indigenous knowledge, can only be seen as integrally related components within an overarching and steadily expanding intellectual *anti*-imperialism. His is, in substance, a veritable frontal assault on the entire conceptual structure by which the system of Eurocentric global dominance has come to be rationalized, justified, and made to seem inevitable over the past five centuries. To this extent, if none other, the effects of his endeavor are potentially more radical and far-reaching than anything those of us locked into the trajectory of mere political activism ever aspired to achieve.[106]

TOWARDS A NEW SYNTHESIS OF UNDERSTANDING

For obvious reasons, none of this has gone unnoticed by the status quo. The response, predictably enough, has been a stream of invective from establishment attack dogs, who have branded Deloria everything from a "creationist" to an "ethnic pseudoscientist."[107] Although much of the spew has issued from dolts like H. David Brumble, representing the most openly reactionary elements of anthropology (those who find continuing appeal in the long-discredited doctrines of nineteenth-century "scientific racism"),[108] a more sophisticated approach has been adopted by liberals such as David Hurst Thomas, who, while readily admitting that the bulk of Deloria's argument is well-founded, nevertheless manage to conclude that the solution to the problem he presents can be found *only* within the problem itself. Deloria's, Thomas sums up, is a "stridently anti-science position" that must ultimately be discounted on that basis alone.[109] Far more "constructive," he implies, are the contributions of Indians such as novelist N. Scott Momaday, who are willing to confirm scientian "understandings" through such mystical devices as "genetic memory,"[110] and those imbued with the smugly subaltern mentality of Roger Echo-Hawk, who are prepared to offer all the proper genuflections to the sanctity of scientism even as they purportedly inject it with their dubiously "Native" voices.[111]

Although this systematic conflation of science and scientism has been mirrored to some extent in Deloria's own formulations—apparently in the not unreasonable belief that to the degree scientists have avoided an outright disavowal of scientism, they deserve to be tarred with the brush of the latter's improprieties—such criticisms are grossly and in all likelihood deliberately misleading. Were Deloria's critique accepted for what it is, and the paradigms of "scientific understanding" correspondingly purged of their present scientian pretensions,[112] science itself might at last have a chance to fulfill the revelatory promise with which it has been invested since the days of the Enlightenment.[113] By the same token, obfuscatory rejections like those advanced by Brumble and Thomas exhibit every probability of foreclosing such potential, consigning "science," for all the narrowly technological proficiency its adherents have amassed over the past two centuries,[114] to the realm of the most vulgar form of ideological existence imaginable.[115]

Divesting science of scientian religiosity might also serve to detach it from the deep teleological linkages with Judeo-Christian values that have all along undermined its quest for objectivity. By demoting Christianity to its legitimate standing as merely one among many spiritual appreciations of the world, neither inferior nor superior to any other, either in its own right or in its relationship to scientific inquiry, the door would be opened for the literal content of myriad other traditions to inform and immeasurably broaden both the context and the process of empirical research.[116] The result could only be that humanity as a whole would be better positioned to realize the goal of understanding all we think we know, even as we come to know with increasing accuracy the limits of what it is we are inherently capable of understanding.[117] As Deloria put it as far back as 1979:

> [As] we seek to expand our knowledge of the world, the signposts point to a reconciliation of the [various] approaches to experience. Western science must now reintegrate human emotions and institutions into its interpretation of phenomena; Eastern peoples must confront the physical world and technology. We shall understand as these traditionally opposing views seek a unity that the world of historical experiences is far more mysterious and eventful than we had previously suspected. In the re-creation of metaphysics as a continuing search for meaning which incorporates all aspects of science and historical experience, we can hasten a time when we will come to an integrated conception of how our species came to be, what it has accomplished, and where it can expect to go in the millennia ahead. Our next immediate task is the unification of human knowledge.[118]

To paraphrase Chardin,[119] Deloria was and still is in effect calling for and sketching out the parameters of a "new synthesis of understanding" in which *all* the constituent components of knowledge are brought together on a level playing field for the first time, their presumptive efficaciousness constrained only by the requirement that they not be phenomenologically self-contradictory, and then joined on the basis of their interactive logical consistencies into an unprecedentedly panoramic whole. In this sense, his project can and should be seen as an effort to achieve not only an immanent completion of the "old" Enlightenment but also its transcendence, a tracing of the contours of what would, if pursued and refined, constitute an entirely new and overarching dimension of intellectual possibility.[120]

Like dominoes, the toppling of any one of scientism's more cherished "truths" necessitates a fundamental rearrangement of the entire "field of knowledge" that attends it, and rearranging a given field necessitates a concomitant rearrangement of related fields; at each step along the way, the inherent plausibility of alternative explanations offered by "primitive" and "dissident" traditions is underscored. Eliminating the fraudulent Bering Strait migration theory, for example, elevates the credibility of American Indian origin stories holding that indigenous people have "always" been here. This, in turn, requires a fundamental rethinking of human dispersal patterns across the planet and, ultimately, of prevailing notions concerning human evolution.[121] Equally, it renders implausible scientian contention that the abrupt die-out of whole species of megafauna was precipitated by the initial influx of humans into North America some 12,000 to 15,000 years ago.[122]

If these so-called Pleistocene extinctions cannot be accounted for by an imaginary invasion of Paleolithic hunters, they must be explained in another, more reasonable fashion. Here, Velikovsky's theory of catastrophism, conforming as it does with the recollections of natural phenomena encompassed within the traditions of America's indigenous peoples, immediately presents itself as a viable candidate.[123] Any serious investigation of the meaning of such correlations would entail a foundational reassessment not only of the duration of human habitation in the New World but of its geological and meteorological chronologies as well.[124] Even the most tentative verification of the Velikovskian formulation would demand a reconsideration of the history and functioning of the solar system and, from there, of the universe as a whole.[125] The implications are, or should be, obvious.

Neither Deloria's deconstruction of the extant master narrative nor his efforts to forge a more tenable alternative has been confined to the masturbatory realm of petty postmodernist abstraction. Instead, he has been actively and consistently engaged in an attempt to communicate his alternative vision in terms of a viable grassroots pedagogy,[126] at least as concrete and potentially empowering as anything offered by Illich, Freire, Giroux, or McLaren.[127] If, as Martin Carnoy once famously observed, educational "mainstreaming" has served the purpose of cultural imperialism,[128] then Deloria's must be appreciated as one of the more explicitly *de*colonizing strategies yet conceived. Paradoxical as it may seem, the "antiscientific" arguments contained in *God Is Red, Metaphysics,* and *Red*

Earth, White Lies are revealed as one of the stronger attempts to salvage science from the ravages of its impersonators in recent years. Only thus can Deloria's desired "unification of human knowledge" be completed.

Though it is plainly true that there *was* life before Deloria, it is equally the case that things have not been—indeed, can never be—the same since his arrival on the intellectual scene. He has flown higher and farther on the wings of synthesis than anyone, or any three people, I can name. That he has dragged the rest of us along, despite our often strenuous kicks, screams, and general recalcitrance, is something for which we—his most bitter detractors above all—owe him an incalculable debt. If we as a species are to have a future, much less achieve liberation from the condition imposed by the collectivity of our blinders, it is because he has forced us to see things in new ways, equipping us with the minds to free ourselves from a fate that had come to seem preordained.

The conceptual seeds he has sown will undoubtedly continue to sprout decades hence, after the man himself and those of us who have been honored to know him personally are no longer present to savor the pleasures of their fruit. His, then, has been the bestowal of the gift of his very life on coming generations and, in perhaps greater denomination, the eternity of this land that is the mother of us all.[129] Irrespective of the cosmopolitanism that has marked his learning, he has remained first, foremost, and *always* an Indian, unshrinking from the responsibilities attending that identity, the pride of all who came before. He stands as the signpost of continuity between that which was, that which is, and that which may yet be (if only because he has done so much to make it so).

NOTES

1. For explication of the concept, see Walter L. Adamson, *Hegemony and Revolution: A Study of Antonio Gramsci's Political and Cultural Theory* (Berkeley: University of California Press, 1980), esp. 170–79.

2. Elizabeth S. Grobsmith, "Growing up on Deloria: His Impact on a New Generation of Anthropologists," in *Indians and Anthropologists: Vine Deloria, Jr., and the Critique of Anthropology*, ed. Thomas Biolsi and Larry J. Zimmerman (Tucson: University of Arizona Press, 1997), 35–49.

3. Vine Deloria, Jr., *Custer Died for Your Sins: An Indian Manifesto* (New York: Macmillan, 1969).

4. Vine Deloria, Jr., *We Talk, You Listen: New Tribes, New Turf* (New York: Macmillan, 1970); *Of Utmost Good Faith* (San Francisco: Straight Arrow Books, 1971); *God Is Red* (New York: Grosset and Dunlap, 1973); *Behind the Trail of Broken Treaties: An Indian Declaration of Independence* (New York: Delacorte, 1974); *The Indian Affair* (New York: Friendship Press, 1974); *The Indians of the Pacific Northwest: From the Coming of the White Man to the Present Day* (Garden City, N.Y.: Doubleday, 1977).

5. Vine Deloria, Jr., *The Metaphysics of Modern Existence* (New York: Harper and Row, 1979).

6. When the Smithsonian project derailed, Deloria arranged for my coauthors and me to publish our material in a now-defunct journal. See Ward Churchill, Mary Ann Hill, and Norbert S. Hill, Jr., "Media Stereotyping and the Native Response: An Historical Overview," *Indian Historian*, vol. 11, no. 4 (winter 1978–1979); Ward Churchill and Norbert S. Hill, Jr., "An Historical Survey of Tendencies in American Indian Education: Higher Education," *Indian Historian*, vol. 12, no. 1 (spring 1979); Ward Churchill, Norbert S. Hill, Jr., and Mary Jo Barlow, "An Historical Survey of Twentieth Century Native American Athletes," *Indian Historian*, vol. 12, no. 4 (winter 1979–1980).

7. Vine Deloria, Jr., "Why Me Tonto?" *Rocky Mountain Musical Express*, March 1977.

8. Deloria himself has never written about his relationship with Brando. It is, however, mentioned in Peter Manso's *Brando: The Biography* (New York: Hyperion, 1994) 797, 804, 817, 890.

9. Joe Bageant, "Cracks in the Bottom of the Brando Pool," *Denver Magazine*, September 1980.

10. The song is recorded on Walker's *Ridin' High* (MCA, 1975). Although he has never said so, Deloria may have played a key role in connecting the two men. In any event, he not only knew Burton but was familiar enough with Walker to have stood in on rhythm guitar with the Lost Gonzo Band during a 1977 concert at Red Rocks Amphitheater, outside Denver. A photo of him taken during that performance accompanies his interview in Studs Terkel's *American Dreams: Lost and Found* (New York: Pantheon, 1980).

11. Robert Preston and Ida Lupino. The 1972 film, directed by Sam Peckinpah, is one of Deloria's favorites.

12. As will be understood by anyone who has bothered to actually listen to Autry's bass lines, Deloria made his case. They are often identical to those utilized by rocker Bill Haley and his Comets. The point of departure for the dinosaur discourses was usually Adrian J. Desmond's *The Hot-Blooded Dinosaurs: A Revolution in Palaeontology* (New York: Dial Press, 1976). The thrust of the electromagnetic-thermonuclear queries derived from Deloria's ongoing preoccupation with Velikovsky, discussed later.

13. The characterization was offered in a 1990 letter submitted in support of Deloria's application to join the Ethnic Studies faculty at the University of Colorado at Boulder.

14. Max Horkheimer and Theodor W. Adorno, *The Dialectic of Enlightenment* (New York: Continuum, 1972). For explication, see Martin Jay, *Adorno* (Cambridge: Harvard University Press, 1984), esp. 51–54, 114–17, 150–52.

15. Theodor W. Adorno, *Prisms: Cultural Criticism and Society* (London: Neville Spearman, 1967). For methodological analysis, see the relevant sections in Fredric Jameson's *Marxism and Form: Twentieth-Century Dialectical Theories of Literature* (Princeton, N.J.: Princeton University Press, 1971).

16. Theodor W. Adorno, *Philosophy of Modern Music* (New York: Seabury Press, 1973); *Introduction to the Sociology of Music* (New York: Seabury Press, 1976).

17. Anyone who has broken their teeth on Adorno's *Negative Dialectics* (New York: Seabury Press, 1979), as I have, will know what I mean by "densely theoretical tracts." For an excellent effort at decipherment, see Susan Buck-Morss, *The Origin of Negative Dialectics: Theodor W. Adorno, Walter Benjamin and the Frankfurt Institute* (Brighton, U.K.: Harvester Press, 1977).

18. Theodor W. Adorno, *Minima Moralia: Reflections from a Damaged Life* (London: New Left Books, 1974). For analyses, see Gillian Rose, *The Melancholy*

Science: An Introduction to the Thought of Theodor W. Adorno (London: Macmillan, 1978); Edward Said, "Intellectual Exile: Expatriates and Marginals," in his *Representations of the Intellectual* (New York: Pantheon, 1994), 54–61.

19. Deloria once explained to me that he consciously restricts the vocabulary he uses in his writings for precisely this reason. As he articulated the trade-off, whatever might be sacrificed in terms of precision is more than recaptured by breadth of readership. "It doesn't matter how accurate you are," he contends, "if nobody is [or only a relatively few people are] able to understand what you're trying to say."

20. See note 4. Also of particular interest in this respect are Deloria's "Custer Died for Your Sins," *Playboy*, August 1969; "The War between the Redskins and the Feds," *New York Times Magazine*, 7 December 1969; "This Country Was a Lot Better off When the Indians Were Running It," *New York Times Magazine*, 8 March 1970; "Bureau of Indian Affairs: My Brother's Keeper," *Art in America*, July–August 1970; "It Is a Good Day to Die," *Katallagete*, vol. 4, nos. 2–3 (winter 1972); "Old Indian Refrain: Treachery on the Potomac," *New York Times*, 8 February 1973; "Federal Policy Still Victimizes and Exploits," *Los Angeles Times*, 17 August 1975.

21. For the best available overview, see Troy R. Johnson, *The Occupation of Alcatraz Island* (Urbana: University of Illinois Press, 1996). A more personal rendering, introduced by Deloria, is provided by a participant, Adam Fortunate Eagle (Nordwall), in his *Alcatraz! Alcatraz! The Indian Occupation of 1969–1971* (Berkeley, Calif.: Heyday Books, 1992).

22. The BIA takeover is probably best handled in Paul Chaat Smith and Robert Allen Warrior, *Like a Hurricane: The American Indian Movement from Alcatraz to Wounded Knee* (New York: New Press, 1996), 149–68. Also see Deloria, *Trail of Broken Treaties*; "The New Activism," *Dialogue*, vol. 6, no. 2 (1973).

23. There is a raft of material available on Wounded Knee and its backdrop. Among the better efforts is Peter Matthiessen's *In the Spirit of Crazy Horse*, 2nd ed. (New York: Viking, 1991). Also see Smith and Warrior, *Like a Hurricane*; Vine Deloria, Jr., "Wounded Knee," *Los Angeles Times*, 2 April 1973; "Final Reflections on Wounded Knee," *Black Politician*, vol. 4, no. 1 (summer 1973); "Beyond Wounded Knee," *Akwesasne Notes*, vol. 5, no. 4 (late summer 1973); "From Wounded Knee to Wounded Knee," in *The World of the American Indian*, ed. Jules Billard (Washington, D.C.: National Geographic Society, 1974), 355–83; "The Indian Movement: Out of Wounded Past," *Ramparts*, March 1975.

24. Deloria addressed not only the legal doctrines underlying such entitlement but also questions of the material viability of its exercise; see the chapter entitled "The Size and Status of Nations" in *Trail of Broken Treaties*, 161–86. Also see Vine Deloria, Jr., "The Basis of Indian Law," *American Airlines Magazine*, April 1972; "The Question of the 1868 Sioux Treaty: A Crucial Element in the Wounded Knee Trials," *Akwesasne Notes*, vol. 5, no. 2 (spring 1973); "The Significance of the 1868 Treaty," *Medicine Root Magazine*, vol. 1, no. 2 (1974); "Breaking the Treaty of Ruby Valley," *New Dimensions Magazine*, September 1975.

25. Two excerpts from Deloria's testimony, entitled "Sovereignty" and "The United States Has No Jurisdiction in Sioux Territory," are included in Roxanne Dunbar Ortiz, ed., *The Great Sioux Nation: Sitting in Judgement on America* (New York: American Indian Treaty Council/Moon Books, 1977), 16–18, 141–46.

26. Vine Deloria, Jr., "Self-Determination and the Concept of Sovereignty," in *Economic Development in American Indian Reservations*, ed. Roxanne Dunbar Ortiz (Albuquerque: University of New Mexico, Native American Studies Cen-

ter, 1979), 22–28. Relatedly, see "Sovereignty: Fact or Fiction? A Debate between Congressman Lloyd Meeds and Vine Deloria, Jr.," *La Confluencia,* vol. 2, nos. 2–3 (October 1978).

27. For Deloria's thinking on this initiative, see the second edition of *Behind the Trail of Broken Treaties* (Austin: University of Texas Press, 1985), 266–74.

28. The relevant portion of the charter can be found in Ian Brownlie, ed., *Basic Documents on Human Rights,* 3rd ed. (Oxford: Clarendon Press, 1992), 9–10. Amplification and a certain degree of clarification of the principle are embodied in the UN General Assembly's subsequent Resolution 1514 (XV), usually referred to as the "Declaration on the Granting of Independence to Colonial Countries and Peoples (1960)" (ibid., 28–30). On the postwar trend toward decolonization itself, see Franz Ansprenger, *The Dissolution of Colonial Empires* (New York: Routledge, 1989).

29. For Means's recollections on this score, see his autobiographical collaboration with Marvin J. Wolf, *Where White Men Fear to Tread* (New York: St. Martin's Press, 1995), 324–26, 356–57, 365. Durham has yet to produce so concise a recounting, although his views, or fragments of them, are scattered throughout his *Columbus Day* (Minneapolis, Minn.: West End Press, 1983) and *A Certain Lack of Coherence: Writings on Art and Cultural Politics* (London: Kala Press, 1993). Probably the best, or at least broadest, overview is in Roxanne Dunbar Ortiz, *Indians of the Americas: Human Rights and Self-Determination* (London: Zed Press, 1984).

30. Douglas Sanders, "The UN Working Group on Indigenous Populations," *Human Rights Quarterly,* no. 11 (1989). The global survey was completed early on; see José R. Martinez Cobo, *Study of the Problem of Discrimination against Indigenous Populations* (UN Doc. E/CN.4/Sub.2/1983/21/Add.83, September 1983). The treaty study has now been completed by working group special rapporteur Miguel Alfonso Martínez but has yet to be published. The Draft Declaration has also been completed but remains stalemated by the United States, which insists that it must be revised in a manner legitimating U.S. violations of indigenous rights; see, e.g., Glenn T. Morris, "Commentary: Further Motion by State Department to Railroad Indigenous Rights," *Fourth World Bulletin,* no. 6 (1998).

31. On Yellow Thunder, of which Deloria was an active supporter, see Means and Wolf, *White Men,* 407–36. Also see Rex Weyler, *Blood of the Land: The U.S. Government and Corporate War against the American Indian Movement,* 2nd ed. (Philadelphia: New Society, 1992), 241–54.

32. Brownlie, *Basic Documents,* 4. For analysis of the "blue water" interpretation and its implications, see Roxanne Dunbar Ortiz, "Protection of American Indian Territories in the United States: The Applicability of International Law," in *Irredeemable America: The Indians' Estate and Land Tenure,* ed. Imre Sutton (Albuquerque: University of New Mexico Press, 1985), 260–61.

33. Robert K. Thomas, "Colonialism: Classic and Internal," *New University Thought,* vol. 4, no. 4 (winter 1966–1967). For my own first attempt at applying the idea in a systematic way, see "Indigenous Peoples of the U.S.: A Struggle against Internal Colonialism," *Black Scholar,* vol. 16, no. 1 (February 1985). The concept was originally formulated by Antonio Gramsci in his 1920 essay "The Southern Question," included in *The Modern Prince and Other Writings* (New York: International, 1957), 28–51.

34. For an excellent and relatively comprehensive survey and analysis, see Walker Conner, *The National Question in Marxist-Leninist Theory and Strategy* (Princeton, N.J.: Princeton University Press, 1984).

35. See, generally, Glenn T. Morris and Ward Churchill, "Between a Rock

and a Hard Place: Left-Wing Revolution, Right-Wing Reaction, and the Destruction of Indigenous Peoples," *Cultural Survival Quarterly*, vol. 11, no. 3 (fall 1988).

36. An overview is provided in Means and Wolf, *White Men*, 459–88. To be fair, however, it should be noted that the split over Nicaragua represented the culmination rather than the precipitation of the process. Both AIM and IITC had been fragmenting for several years by that point; see Jimmie Durham's 1979 "Open Letter on Recent Developments in the American Indian Movement/International Indian Treaty Council," in *Lack of Coherence*, 46–56.

37. The term *indigenist* derives from the Spanish *indigenista*, as employed by Guillermo Bonfil Batalla in his *Utopia y Revolución: El Pensamiento Politico Contemporáneo de los Indios en América Latina* (Mexico City: Editorial Nueva Imagen, 1981). On the concept of an indigenous Fourth World underlying Mao Tse-tung's famous "three world" schematic, see George Manuel and Michael Posluns, *The Fourth World: An Indigenous Reality* (New York: Free Press, 1974); Weyler, *Blood of the Land*, 212–40. Anishnaabe activist Winona LaDuke has also described indigenous peoples as making up a "Host World" atop which the other three have been erected; see her "Natural to Synthetic to Back Again," in my *Marxism and Native Americans* (Boston: South End Press, 1983), i–ix.

38. In this, indigenism shares certain obvious commonalities with anarchism. See, e.g., Ulrike Heider, *Anarchism: Left, Right, and Green* (San Francisco: City Lights Books, 1994).

39. Vine Deloria, Jr., "Circling the Same Old Rock: The Coming of the Materialist Missionaries," in Churchill, *Marxism and Native Americans*, 113–36.

40. Vine Deloria, Jr., "Bob Thomas as Colleague," in *A Good Cherokee, a Good Anthropologist: Papers in Honor of Robert K. Thomas*, ed. Steve Pavlik (Los Angeles: UCLA American Indian Studies Center, 1998), 31.

41. Vine Deloria, Jr., and Clifford M. Lytle, *American Indians, American Justice* (Austin: University of Texas Press, 1983); *The Nations Within: The Past and Future of American Indian Sovereignty* (New York: Pantheon, 1984). Much the same can be said of *The Aggressions of Civilization: Federal Indian Policy since the 1880s* (Philadelphia: Temple University Press, 1984), which Deloria coedited with Sandra L. Cadwalader.

42. For a brief summary of these conditions, set forth in an argument not dissimilar to Deloria's own, see Rennard Strickland, "You Can't Rollerskate in a Buffalo Herd Even If You Have All the Medicine: American Indian Law and Policy," in his *Tonto's Revenge: Reflections on American Indian Culture and Policy* (Albuquerque: University of New Mexico Press, 1997), 53–54.

43. Vine Deloria, Jr., and David E. Wilkins, *Tribes, Treaties, and Constitutional Tribulations* (Austin: University of Texas Press, 1999).

44. As Vine recently put it, with decided understatement, the shift resulted in his receiving "several bad book reviews"; Deloria, "Bob Thomas," 31.

45. For Adorno, "reification was not merely a relationship among men, but also one entailing the domination of the otherness of the natural world. Through the kind of conceptual imperialism Adorno discerned in both positivism and idealism, the natural world was reified into fungible fields for human control and manipulation," a circumstance that, unless addressed at a foundational conceptual rather than political level, would result in the perpetuation of "a negative dialectics [that] played off nature against . . . society and vice versa chiasmically." Within this framework, reification of human relations would be unavoidable, regardless of political arrangements. Jay, *Adorno*, 69.

46. At issue here is essentially the conception of "false consciousness" first

articulated by Georg Lukács in his 1930 essay collection *History and Class Consciousness: Studies in Marxist Dialectics* (Cambridge, Mass.: MIT Press, 1971), and much refined by Herbert Marcuse in *An Essay on Liberation* (Boston: Beacon Press, 1969) and elsewhere. See, generally, Joseph Gabel, *False Consciousness: An Essay on Reification* (New York: Harper Torchbooks, 1978).

47. Hence, as has been amply demonstrated throughout the Third World since 1960, "postcolonial" regimes have demonstrated an all but uniform proclivity not only to maintain themselves on the basis of the internal colonial domination of indigenous peoples but also to submit themselves to the ravages of neocolonial subordination and exploitation. It should be noted that the recipe concocted by "scientific socialism" to combat the latter devolves upon an ever more virulent intensification of the former. See, e.g., Kwame Nkrumah, *Neo-Colonialism: The Last Stage of Imperialism* (New York: International Publishers, 1966); Elenga M'buyinga, *Pan Africanism or Neo-Colonialism: The Bankruptcy of the O.A.U.* (London: Zed Books, 1982).

48. Michel Foucault, *The Archaeology of Knowledge* (New York: Pantheon, 1972); Jacques Derrida, *Of Gramatology* (Baltimore: Johns Hopkins University Press, 1974).

49. Jean-François Lyotard, *The Postmodern Condition: A Report on Knowledge* (Minneapolis: University of Minnesota Press, 1984).

50. *Emic* refers to the view of a culture arising from within it; *etic* describes views arising from without. Born in 1933, Deloria spent his first sixteen years on the Pine Ridge Sioux Reservation, which afforded him a solid foundation in the conceptions of his own culture. However, his credentials include a diploma from the Kent School, an undergraduate education obtained at the Colorado School of Mines and Iowa State University, a graduate degree from the Lutheran Theological Seminary (1963), and a degree in law from the University of Colorado (1970). James Treat, "Introduction: An American View of Religion," in Vine Deloria, Jr., *For This Land: Writings on Religion in America* (New York: Routledge, 1999), 9–11.

51. "Immanent" critique is that which arises from within a philosophical tendency or tradition and is offered with the object of completing, perfecting, and thus surpassing it. "Transcendent" critique is usually advanced by those opposing the philosophy at issue and is intended to supplant it. See, generally, the chapter entitled "The Transformation of Critique" in John Rajchman, *Michel Foucault: The Freedom of Philosophy* (New York: Columbia University Press, 1985), 7–95; Dick Howard, *The Politics of Critique* (Minneapolis: University of Minnesota Press, 1988), 84–87.

52. Overall, see the chapter entitled "The Jargon of Postmodernity" in Alex Callinicos, *Against Postmodernism: A Marxist Critique* (New York: St. Martin's Press, 1989), 9–28. For samples of the pretentiously jargon-driven fare ladled up by Vizenor, see his *Manifest Manners: Postindian Warriors of Survivance* (Hanover, N.J.: Wesleyan University Press, 1994); *Fugitive Poses: Native American Scenes of Absence and Presence* (Lincoln: University of Nebraska Press, 1998); and, with A. Robert Lee, *Postindian Conversations* (Lincoln: University of Nebraska Press, 1999).

53. Thomas Biolsi and Larry J. Zimmerman, "What's Changed, What Hasn't," in *Indians and Anthropologists*, 4.

54. Deloria, "Anthropologists and Other Friends," in *Custer*, 78–100. Also see Vine Deloria, Jr., "Hobby Farm: On the Reservation," in *Defiance #2: A Radical Review*, ed. Dotson Rader (New York: Paperback Library, 1971), 22–42; "Some Criticisms and a Number of Suggestions," in *Anthropology and the American Indian: Report of a Symposium*, ed. Jeanette Henry (San Francisco: Indian Historian Press, 1973), 153–57.

55. See, e.g., the dissection of Peter Farb's *Man's Rise to Civilization as Shown by the Indians of North America from Primeval Times to the Coming of the Industrial Age* (New York: E. P. Dutton, 1968) in Deloria, *Custer*, 96–99.

56. Jean Baudrillard, *The Mirror of Production* (St. Louis: Telos Press, 1975), 107.

57. Deloria, *Custer*, 80.

58. In simplest terms, the scientific method requires that any hypothesis be subjected to empirical and logical interrogation designed to disprove it. The relative validity of the hypothesis is thus adduced by the extent to which it withstands such tests. Tailoring the tests to support the hypothesis nullifies the utility of the method itself. See, e.g., Karl Popper, *The Logic of Scientific Discovery* (1934; reprint, New York: Science Editions, 1961); *Conjectures and Refutations: The Growth of Scientific Knowledge*, 2nd ed. (New York: Harper Torchbooks, 1968).

59. On the origins and development of anthropology, see Asad Talal, ed., *Anthropology and the Colonial Encounter* (London: Ithaca Press, 1973); Nicholas Thomas, *Colonialism's Culture: Anthropology, Travel, and Government* (Princeton, N.J.: Princeton University Press, 1984).

60. For the best overview, see Stephen Jay Gould, *The Mismeasure of Man* (New York: W. W. Norton, 1981). Also see William Stanton, *The Leopard's Spots: Scientific Attitudes towards Race in America, 1815–1859* (Chicago: University of Chicago Press, 1960); Stefan Kühn, *The Nazi Connection: Eugenics, American Racism, and German National Socialism* (New York: Oxford University Press, 1994).

61. The concept of "social evolution" articulated by Lewis Henry Morgan in his *Ancient Society* (New York: World, 1877) served as "the backbone of American anthropology" during the late nineteenth century. Together with an entirely similar theory laid out in John Lubbock's *Pre-historic Times, as Illustrated by Ancient Remains, and the Manners and Customs of Modern Savages* (London, 1865), it has provided the foundation for the white supremacist doctrine known as "social Darwinism" right up to the present; David Hurst Thomas, *Skull Wars: Kennewick Man, Archaeology, and the Battle for Native American Identity* (New York: Basic Books, 2000), 44–51.

62. The Piltdown hoax began in 1912 with the purported discovery of a skull belonging to the "missing link" between man and ape in an English gravel quarry. It was actually a combination of a modern human cranium and an altered ape's jaw. Insofar as the "find" supposedly proved that the first true humans were Europeans, it served as the ultimate scientific confirmation of white supremacist dogma. Validated by several curators of the British Museum and carefully shielded from public scrutiny, the fabrication continued to serve this useful purpose until it was finally exposed as a fraud during the mid-1950s. Frank Spencer, *Piltdown: A Scientific Forgery* (New York: Oxford University Press, 1990).

63. One of Deloria's better articulations of this theme is in "Comfortable Fictions and the Struggle for Turf," *American Indian Quarterly*, vol. 16, no. 3 (summer 1992).

64. The theological dimension is covered quite well in Deloria's "Christianity and Indigenous Religion: Friends or Enemies?" in *Creation and Culture: The Challenge of Indigenous Spirituality and Culture to Western Creation Thought*, ed. David G. Burke (New York: Lutheran World Ministries, 1987), 31–43. It should be noted that, at least in terms of the secular enunciation of theological concept, Deloria's point was acknowledged by Western scientists themselves until rather recently; see, e.g., E. A. Burtt, *The Metaphysical Foundations of Natural Science* (1924; reprint, New York: Doubleday, 1954).

65. Vine Deloria, Jr., "Myth and the Origin of Religion," *Pensée,* vol. 4, no. 4 (fall 1974).

66. For a materialist critique that arrives at remarkably similar conclusions, see Stanley Aronowitz, *Science as Power: Discourse and Ideology in Modern Society* (Minneapolis: University of Minnesota Press, 1988).

67. This theme is most fully developed in Deloria's "The Fascination of Heresy," *Katallegete,* vol. 6, no. 4 (spring 1977). On Galileo's experience at the hands of the Inquisition, see Georgio De Santillana, *The Crime of Galileo* (New York: Heinemann, 1958).

68. Deloria, *God Is Red,* 123–34.

69. Immanuel Velikovsky, *Worlds in Collision* (Garden City, N.Y.: Doubleday, 1950). The ideas therein were developed with greater precision in Velikovsky's second book, *Ages in Chaos* (Garden City, N.Y.: Doubleday, 1952).

70. Deloria, *God Is Red,* 127–28. The second reference is to Immanuel Velikovsky, *Earth in Upheaval* (Garden City, N.Y.: Doubleday, 1955).

71. Deloria, *God Is Red,* 129.

72. Ibid., 129–30. For further details, see Alfred de Grazia, *The Velikovsky Affair: The War of Science and Scientism* (New Hyde Park, N.Y.: University Books, 1966); Editors of *Pensée, Velikovsky Reconsidered* (Garden City, N.Y.: Doubleday, 1976).

73. Deloria, *Metaphysics,* 167–74.

74. These circumstances were summarized in my review, "A Critique of Vine Deloria, Jr.'s *The Metaphysics of Modern Existence," American Indian Culture and Research Journal,* vol. 5, no. 3 (fall 1981).

75. See, as examples, Deloria's "The Traditional Western Answers Offer No Solution to Me," in *Stories of Survival: Conversations with Native North Americans,* ed. Remmelt Hummelen and Ruth Hummelen (New York: Friendship Press, 1985), 13–15; "American Indian Metaphysics," *Winds of Change,* vol. 1, no. 2 (June 1986); "Ethnoscience and Indian Realities," *Winds of Change,* vol. 7, no. 3 (summer 1992); "Relativity, Relatedness and Reality," *Winds of Change,* vol. 7, no. 4 (fall 1992); "If You Think About It, You Will See That It Is True," *Noetic Sciences Review,* no. 27 (autumn 1993).

76. Harper and Row did not bother to have *Metaphysics* indexed. On Heisenberg, see esp. 33–45; on Jung, 90–101; on Chardin, 52–69; on Tillich, 25–32.

77. Deloria, "Self-Determination and the Concept of Sovereignty," 22; "Law and Theology III: The Theme," *Church and Society,* no. 79 (September/October 1988); Paul Schmidt, *Political Theology: Four Chapters on the Concept of Sovereignty* (1922; trans., Cambridge, Mass.: MIT Press, 1985). Interestingly, Schmidt emerges from the Hegelian philosophical tradition, which Deloria has by and large ignored in his interrogations.

78. See, e.g., "From Reservation to Global Society: American Culture, Liberation and the Native American—An Interview with Vine Deloria, Jr., by Michael McKale," *Radical Religion,* vol. 2, no. 4 (fall 1976); "A Native American Perspective on Liberation," *Occasional Bulletin of Missionary Research,* vol. 1, no. 3 (July 1977).

79. Aside from the relevant sections of *God Is Red* and *Metaphysics,* the more important articulations offered during the period include "The Theological Dimension of the Indian Protest Movement," *Christian Century,* 19 September 1973; "Religion and Revolution among American Indians," *Worldview,* vol. 17, no. 1 (January 1974); "Religion and the Modern American Indian," *Current History,* vol. 67, no. 400 (December 1974); "The Desperate Need for Understanding," *Cross Talk,*.vol. 3, no. 4 (February 1975); "God Is Also Red: An Interview with Vine Delo-

ria by James R. McGraw," *Christianity and Crisis,* 15 September 1975; "Native American Spirituality," *Gamaliel,* vol. 13, no. 1 (spring 1977); "Kinship and the World," *Journal of Current Social Issues,* vol. 15, no. 3 (fall 1978).

80. Velikovsky's last book, *Peoples of the Sea,* was published by Doubleday in 1977. Therein, he attempted a comprehensive restructuring of Mideastern historical chronology corresponding to the sequence of physical phenomena he had outlined in his earlier works. That Deloria was in some sense consciously adopting Velikovsky's task as his own is made clear in his essay "Catastrophism and Planetary History," *Kronos,* vol. 3, no. 4 (1978).

81. Deloria has always evidenced a strong inclination in the latter direction. See, e.g., his "Revision and Reversion," in *American Indians and the Problem of History,* ed. Calvin Martin (New York: Oxford University Press, 1987), 84–90.

82. Vine Deloria, Jr., *Red Earth, White Lies: Native Americans and the Myth of Scientific Fact* (New York: Scribner, 1995).

83. Ibid., 99, 184, 203–4. During the early 1980s, Deloria's interest in the Hopi origin story led him into a brief association with independent archaeologist Jeffrey Goodman, who attempted to confirm it by conducting a dig at the location indicated. Although the results were ambiguous, Goodman may have unearthed the oldest humanly inscribed stone yet recovered in North America. Jeffrey Goodman, *American Genesis* (New York: Summit Books, 1981), 193–216.

84. Deloria, *Red Earth, White Lies,* 194–202.

85. The 3,000-year limit, which makes no geological sense at all, was proclaimed and defended by Smithsonian curator Ales Hrdlicka throughout the first half of the twentieth century. In 1953 Alfred Kroeber, who succeeded Hrdlicka as "dean" of Americanist anthropology, acknowledged the cumulative weight of evidence embodied in the discovery of Clovis culture, as well as the geological chronology of Beringia, by announcing that the limit had been revised to 12,000 to 15,000 years. Presently, it appears that the accumulation of linguistic, genetic, and other evidence is on the verge of precipitating a revision to about 30,000 years, a dating that comes much closer to what Native people have been saying all along. At each step along the way, however, archaeologists like the late George Carter, who have argued that the human occupancy of America was much older than what was admitted by anthropological orthodoxy, have been subjected to ridicule, marginalized, and often driven from the profession altogether. For a detailed examination of the record and its implications, see "About that Bering Strait Land Bridge . . . On the Falsity of 'Scientific Truth,'" in my *In the Alternative: Studies in Indigenist Pedagogy* (San Francisco: City Lights, forthcoming).

86. Rather instructively, this is referred to as the "Eve hypothesis." Deloria recommends William Fix's *The Bone Peddlers* (New York: Macmillan, 1984) as an effective antidote to the belief that it has been proved.

87. The forgery, first published in 1836, was put together by an amateur naturalist named Samuel de Rafinesque. Although it had long since been discredited as a fraud by linguists, its contents were supposedly "verified" by an archaeological team funded by the Lilly Foundation during the 1950s. As recently as 1987, it was still being cited by "reputable" scholars such as historian C. A. Weslager as corroborating the Bering Strait migration hypothesis; see, generally, David M. Oestreicher, "Unraveling the *Walam Olum,*" *Natural History,* October 1996.

88. Deloria, *Red Earth, White Lies,* 86–90, 100–4. On animal migrations, he relies in large part on L. Taylor Hansen, *The Ancient Atlantic* (Amherst, Wis.: Amherst Press, 1969).

89. From a starting point on the Kolmya River in eastern Siberia, these

would have included the daunting Khrebet Gydan and Chukotskoye ranges. To get to the strait from the American side would have entailed scaling Kaiyuh, Kuskokwim, and Richardson ranges from the south or the Ogilvie, Mackenzie, and Franklin ranges from the southeast. Deloria, *Red Earth, White Lies*, 88.

90. Ibid., 96–97. For the particulars of the meteorological data, see Reid Bryson, *Radiocarbon Isochrones of the Laurentian Tide Sheet* (Madison: University of Wisconsin Technical Report no. 35, 1967). For implications to anthropological theory, see Alan Bryan, "Early Man in the Late Pleistocene Chronology of Western Canada and Alaska," *Current Anthropology*, vol. 10, no. 4 (fall 1969).

91. They would require a prevailing south-to-north wind direction, whereas east-west is the actual planetary norm. Deloria, *Red Earth, White Lies*, 92–93.

92. Ibid., 203, quoting Michael Cremo and Richard Thompson, *Forbidden Archaeology* (San Francisco: Bhaktivedanta Institute, 1993), 694.

93. Deloria, *Red Earth, White Lies*, 247, referencing Charles Ginenthal, "Scientific Dating Methods in Ruins," *Velikovskian*, vol. 2, no. 4 (1994), 53.

94. Deloria, *Red Earth, White Lies*, 250, quoting Jared Diamond, "American Blitzkrieg: A Mammoth Undertaking," *Discover*, June 1987, 84. On the denial and suppression of inconvenient evidence, see Goodman, *American Genesis*, 81–87. Also see George F. Carter, *Earlier than You Think: A Personal View of Man in America* (College Station: Texas A&M University Press, 1980).

95. Deloria, *Red Earth, White Lies*, 87. His reference is to William S. Laughlin, "Human Migration and Permanent Occupation in the Bering Sea Area," in *The Bering Land Bridge*, ed. David M. Hopkins (Stanford, Calif.: Stanford University Press, 1967), 409–50. Although Deloria does not mention it, I can attest that no better evidence is assembled in the more recent and reputedly definitive collection of specialist essays edited by Frederick Hadleigh West under the title *American Beginnings: The Prehistory and Paleontology of Beringia* (Chicago: University of Chicago Press, 1996).

96. Deloria, *Red Earth, White Lies*, 84–85, 87.

97. Ibid., 87.

98. The first recorded articulation of the idea is attributed to Father Acosta, a Spanish priest; Carter, *Earlier than You Think*, 7. For further background, see Lee H. Huddleston, *Origins of the American Indians, European Concepts, 1492–1729* (Austin: University of Texas Press, 1969).

99. Ronald Sanders, *Lost Tribes and Promised Lands: The Origins of American Racism*, 2nd ed. (New York: HarperPerennial, 1992), 370.

100. In 1683 Quaker leader William Penn, for example, went on record to assert that he was "ready to believe [Indians] to be of the Jewish race—I mean of the stock of the ten tribes"; quoted in Goodman, *American Genesis*, 25. The Puritan leader Cotton Mather also professed such beliefs in his 1702 book *Magnali Christiani Americana*. On Mormon beliefs, see Milton R. Hunter and Thomas Stuart Ferguson, *Ancient America and the Book of Mormon* (Oakland, Calif.: Kolob Books, 1950). On the New World Archaeological Institute, see Goodman, *American Genesis*, 28.

101. Thomas Jefferson, *Notes on the State of Virginia* (1781; reprint, Chapel Hill: University of North Carolina Press, 1982), 101. Actually, the inception of the "scientific" process should probably be dated from 1775, when amateur linguist James Adair first published a lengthy set of phonetic "proofs" that American Indian languages derive from ancient Hebrew. James Adair, *The History of the American Indians* (London: E. and C. Dilly, 1775).

102. This has been at least as true—and in some ways more so—after Franz Boas's supposedly rigorous scientific footing during the first decade of the twentieth century as it was at any earlier point. On the Boasian "revolution"—which is sometimes referred to as being a manifestation of anthropology's "physics envy"—see Thomas, *Skull Wars*, 97–98.

103. A comparable, if entirely secular, conclusion is drawn in Aronowitz, *Science as Power*.

104. As the matter is framed in UN General Assembly Resolution 1514, it is a fundamental legal requirement that "the principle of equal rights and self-determination of all peoples" be respected. Brownlie, *Basic Documents*, 28.

105. See, generally, John Tomlinson, *Cultural Imperialism* (Baltimore: Johns Hopkins University Press, 1991). For an example of Deloria consciously working the same theme, see his "Education and Imperialism," *Integrateducation*, vol. 19, nos. 1–2 (January 1982).

106. The term *radical* is used here in accordance with its actual meaning—to "go to the root"—rather than its colloquially corrupted form of serving as a synonym for "extreme," "extremist," or "revolutionary."

107. H. David Brumble, "Vine Deloria, Jr., Creationism and Ethnic Pseudoscience," *Reports of the National Center for Science Education*, vol. 18, no. 6 (1998).

108. Alan Goodman, "Resurrecting Race: The Concept of Race in Physical Anthropology in the 1990s," in *Race and Other Misadventures: Essays in Honor of Ashley Montague in His Ninetieth Year*, ed. L. T. Reynolds and L. Lieberman (Dix Hills, N.Y.: General Hall, 1996), 174–86; Yolanda Moses, "An Idea Whose Time Has Come Again: Anthropology Reclaims 'Race,'" *Anthropology Newsletter*, vol. 38, no. 7 (1998).

109. Thomas, *Skull Wars*, 251.

110. Momaday, a Kiowa, professes a vague "genetic recollection" of a time when his ancestors resided in Asia. N. Scott Momaday, "Disturbing the Spirits: The Bones Must Stay in the Ground," *New York Times*, 2 November 1996. Deloria publicly demanded that Momaday provide some—any—form of material corroboration of his "memory." Vine Deloria, Jr., "OK, Scott, Where's the Beef?" *News from Indian Country*, late December 1996. Momaday declined to attempt such substantiation, but Thomas—a self-professed scientist—plainly sides with him, even to the extent of reproducing a photo to illustrate how "Asiatic" Momaday appeared as a child. Thomas, *Skull Wars*, 256–57.

111. Like every good colonialist author since Kipling wrote "Gunga Din," Thomas makes a fetish of showcasing the statements of "right-thinking wogs" who are willing, in exchange for preferential treatment by their colonizers, to endorse colonialism as desirable. Echo-Hawk, a Pawnee, is a University of Colorado–trained anthropologist who has denounced *Red Earth, White Lies* as "fringe literature" while championing a "partnership ecology" between Indians and the archaeological establishment on which his livelihood and status depend. Thomas, *Skull Wars*, 252.

112. The idea here, although it is advanced in a far deeper and more sweeping fashion, is not altogether different from that put forth by Thomas Kuhn in his acclaimed but poorly understood *The Structure of Scientific Revolutions* (Chicago: University of Chicago Press, 1962).

113. For a good overview of the expectations at issue, see Ernst Cassirer, *The Philosophy of the Enlightenment* (Princeton, N.J.: Princeton University Press, 1951). My own view is that Deloria's position shares much in common with Marcuse's contention that, although long derailed by its context, fulfillment of the more

hopeful aspects of the Enlightenment remained a "possibility" in the late twentieth century. Herbert Marcuse, *One Dimensional Man* (Boston: Beacon Press, 1964), 234–35.

114. One indication of the degree to which scientism has supplanted science is the ubiquitous belief that technology and science are synonymous, the former being simply the "application" of the latter. For a powerful and insightful delineation of the reasons why science, to be science, must function in a manner that is entirely autonomous from considerations of technological applicability, see David Landes, *Unbounded Prometheus* (London: Cambridge University Press, 1969). Also see Jacques Ellul, *The Technological Bluff* (Grand Rapids, Mich.: Wm. B. Eerdmans, 1990).

115. See, e.g., Alvin W. Gouldner, *The Dialectic of Ideology and Technology: The Origins, Grammar, and Future of Ideology* (New York: Continuum, 1976). Related arguments can be found in Jacques Ellul, *The Technological Society* (New York: Alfred A. Knopf, 1964); J. G. Merquoir, *The Veil and the Mask: Essays on Culture and Ideology* (London: Routledge and Keegan Paul, 1979); Jürgen Habermas, "Technology and Science as 'Ideology,'" in his *Towards a Rational Society* (Boston: Beacon Press, 1970), 81–122.

116. For a somewhat garbled enunciation of a similar thesis, see Jerry Mander, *In the Absence of the Sacred: The Failure of Technology and the Survival of the Indian Nations* (San Francisco: Sierra Club, 1991). The book's main strength is its survey of Western theorists whose thinking is taking them in the same direction.

117. Vine Deloria, Jr., "Knowing and Understanding: Traditional Education in the Modern World," *Winds of Change*, vol. 5, no. 1 (winter 1990). For a much denser but nonetheless comparable Western articulation, see Noam Chomsky's discussions of accessible and inaccessible knowledge in the chapters entitled "A Philosophy of Language?" and "Empiricism and Rationalism," in *Language and Responsibility: An Interview by Mitsou Ronat* (New York: Pantheon Books, 1977).

118. Deloria, *Metaphysics*, 212–13.

119. Teilhard de Chardin, *A New Synthesis of Evolution* (Glen Rock, N.J.: Deus Books, 1964).

120. This is again not inconsistent with the dynamic described by Horkheimer and Adorno in *The Dialectic of Enlightenment*. Taken from a somewhat different angle, it dovetails quite neatly with the thinking of Jürgen Habermas, especially in his essay "Modernism—An Incomplete Project," in *Postmodern Culture*, ed. Hal Foster (London: Routledge, 1985), and, more broadly, his *Knowledge and Human Interests* (Boston: Beacon Press, 1971).

121. For elaboration, see Nelson Eldredge and Ian Tattersal, *The Myths of Human Evolution* (New York: Columbia University Press, 1982).

122. The idea is that small groups of Paleolithic hunters rapidly exterminated the woolly mammoth and other similarly daunting types of prey, apparently by alternately beating them to death with sticks or somehow driving them off cliffs in huge numbers. Diamond, "American Blitzkrieg." More comprehensively, see the collections of essays in Paul S. Martin and H. E. Wright, eds., *Pleistocene Extinctions: The Search for a Cause* (New Haven, Conn.: Yale University Press, 1967); Paul S. Martin and Richard G. Klein, eds., *Quaternary Extinctions* (Tucson: University of Arizona Press, 1984). An even more absurdist variation on the theme was offered by Sheperd Krech III in *The Ecological Indian: Myth and History* (New York: W. W. Norton, 1999), wherein Indians are depicted as doing essentially the same thing with the buffalo during the nineteenth century.

123. For what may be the best overview of the evolution of Velikovskian

thinking over the past twenty years, see Derek Ager, *The New Catastrophism* (London: Cambridge University Press, 1993).

124. Deloria's thesis, expressed most compellingly in *Red Earth, White Lies*, is that while the chronology of human occupancy in the Americas has been arbitrarily rendered in far too shallow a manner, the geological chronology has been rendered in a manner that is in many cases far too deep. For elaboration on the problems attending the scientian depiction of geological chronology, see Derek Ager, *The Nature of the Stratigraphic Record* (New York: John Wiley and Sons, 1973).

125. Vine Deloria, Jr., "Conclusion: Anthros, Indians, and Planetary Reality," in Biolsi and Zimmerman, *Indians and Anthropologists*, 209–21.

126. See Vine Deloria, Jr., "The Rise and Fall of Ethnic Studies," in *In Search of a Future for Education: Readings in Foundations*, ed. Steven A. Margaritis (Columbus, Ohio: Charles E. Merrill, 1973), 153–57; "Integrity before Education," *Integrateducation*, vol. 7, no. 3 (May–June 1974); "The Place of Indians in Contemporary Education," *American Indian Journal*, no. 2 (February 1976); "Token Indian, Token Education," *Four Winds*, no. 1 (winter 1980); "Out of Chaos," *Parabola*, vol. 10, no. 2 (spring 1985); "Indian Studies: The Orphan of Academia," *Wicazo Sa Review*, vol. 2, no. 2 (summer 1986); "Transitional Education," *Winds of Change*, vol. 5, no. 3 (summer 1990); "Research, Redskins and Reality," *American Indian Quarterly*, vol. 15, no. 4 (fall 1991); "Tribal Colleges and Traditional Knowledge," *Tribal College*, vol. 5, no. 2 (autumn 1993); "Redefining the Path of Indian Education," *The Circle*, vol. 16, no. 9 (September 1995). Also see the entire section entitled "Education" in Barbara Deloria, Kristen Foehner, and Sam Scinta, eds., *Spirit and Reason: The Vine Deloria, Jr., Reader* (Golden, Colo.: Fulcrum, 1999), 129–86.

127. Ivan Illich, *Deschooling Society* (New York: Harper and Row, 1970); Paulo Freire, *Pedagogy of the Oppressed* (New York: Herder and Herder, 1970), and *Education for Critical Consciousness* (New York: Continuum, 1983); Paulo Freire and Antonio Faundez, *Learning to Question: A Pedagogy of Liberation* (New York: Continuum, 1989); Henry A. Giroux, *Ideology, Culture and the Process of Schooling* (Philadelphia: Temple University Press, 1981); Henry A. Giroux and Peter McLaren, eds., *Critical Pedagogy, the State and Cultural Struggle* (Albany: State University of New York Press, 1989).

128. Martin Carnoy, *Education as Cultural Imperialism* (New York: David McKay, 1974). Deloria's interpretation and application of the same theme can be found in his "Education and Imperialism."

129. The connection is not lost on Deloria; see his *For This Land: Writings on Religion in America*, ed. James Treat (New York: Routledge, 1999).

CHAPTER ELEVEN

Transforming American Conceptions about Native America: Vine Deloria, Jr., Critic and Coyote

Inés Talamantez (Apache/Chicana)

We live in time and space and receive most of our signals about proper behavior from each other and the environment around us. Under these circumstances, the individual and the group must both have some kind of sanctity if we are to have a social order at all. By recognizing the various aspects of the sacredness of lands as we have described, we place ourselves in a realistic context in which the individual and the group can cultivate and enhance the sacred experience.

Vine Deloria, Jr., *Spirit and Reason*

In a recent book, *Singing for a Spirit: A Portrait of the Dakota Sioux,* Deloria recounts stories of his great-grandfather, Saswe, through the memory of his grandfather, Tipi Sapa (Philip Deloria). In more than a dozen books, Deloria's work has functioned to mark the persistence of American Indian peoples, the importance of our cultures, and the struggle for survival, sovereignty, and religious freedom. Yet it is this little volume that gives us new insight into what has driven the sharp, critical edge that is this celebrated Native American scholar's particular gift. In this personal history derived from the oral tradition of a Native community, we are reminded of the wisdom and the imagination of our Native ancestors. Through patient and prolonged observation of the natural world, they acquired the knowledge necessary to survive genocide and religious conversion throughout these centuries of colonial conquest and then passed that knowledge on to succeeding generations with an oral exactitude. Central to the diversity of beliefs among the various Native American nations are elaborate explanations of how the cosmos came into being and what our corresponding responsibilities are to the world of nature that surrounds us and connects us. Implied are our instructions in reciprocity for all the gifts we receive from nature, especially from the land, and our obligation to sustainability.

The impact of Deloria's insightful and provocative scholarship on the emerging academic discipline of Native American studies has probably surpassed even his own expectations. His work continues to deeply influence the scholarship of a new cadre of American Indian scholars. Deloria's work has touched me profoundly, at times angered me, always motivated me to continue, and shaped my own work as a critical thinker. He has enriched me and countless others with new ways of thinking about the world we live in, enabling us to begin to free our minds of colonialism and missionization and to return to respecting the way our ancestors lived, with reverence toward people, nature, the land, and community. *Singing for a Spirit* underscores Deloria's own rootedness in the traditions of his people and nudges all of us to reaffirm our own connections with our Native communities.

Today, Native American ways of knowing still reflect the ethical, aesthetic, religious, and social concepts of appropriate behavior with regard to the self and our responsibilities to our relations in both the human and nonhuman worlds. It is well known that in many of our ceremonial and mythological teachings, cleansing of the mind, spirit, and body is essential before it is possible to arrive at a sacred state of being. Once this is accomplished, it is implied that we are obligated to connect in a respectful way with our kin, our sense of place, that is, where we belong on the earth, and with all living entities of that place. This is also how children acquire a sense of security. Later they learn to use the senses in observation of the nonhuman worlds, that is, how to observe and nurture the plant world, how to understand and learn from the patterns of animal behavior and migrations, and how to understand the atmosphere and the sky. This leads to exceptional and sustainable living.

"Indians" has been defined by whites for many years. Always they have been outside observers looking into Indian society from a self made pedestal of preconceived ideas coupled with an innate superior attitude toward those different from themselves.
                                   Vine Deloria, Jr., *Custer Died for Your Sins*

Other scholars studying Native Americans for the past century have indulged in a self-enthrallment with their own interpretations and understandings of our ritual practices and accompanying symbolism. Anthropologists, historians, linguists, folklorists, and literary critics have made intriguing suggestions, but always from their own outside cultural and intellectual perspectives. As we enter into this new century, these exogenous interpretations represent three overlapping perspectives about Native Americans that continue to shape scholarship in the United States. First, some anthropologists continue to study Native Americans as a phenomenon of the past, as having long since vanished because of government policies of conquest, programmed assimilation, and Manifest Destiny—without acknowledging the genocide inflicted on Native

American nations by the colonial invasion. They then conclude self-right-eously that there are no "real" Indians anymore, but only Indians that have been assimilated.[1] Even these Indians, according to them, must meet the anthropologists' or federal government's criteria for legitimacy by revealing their Bureau of Indian Affairs credentials or by submitting to DNA testing and genealogical documentation. Needless to say, no other Americans experience such violations of their civil rights and religious freedom. No other Americans need to show proof of their racial-ethnic identity.

Second, historians, with a few notable exceptions, have failed to write an American history that represents the role of Native Americans in shaping American history. These historians seem to think that Indians stood mute among the trees, helplessly watching the invasion and occupation of their lands, unable to think or act. Our oral traditions, especially mythologies, that record this complex history reveal otherwise. Since most of our past is recorded in long oral narratives, which require an understanding of the language, it is easy to understand why it is so difficult for historians to find their bearings or to discover primary sources other than the colonizer's own legitimizing rationalizations. Unless they spend considerable time in the field and take the time to learn the language of the indigenous nation under study, they will always fail to comprehend the complete historical reality. There are scholars, of course, who do take the time and put in the effort to learn the language, are captivated by those they hope to know more about, and do the long-term, slow, and pedantic field research. Such scholars often prove more capable of preserving the dignity and reality of Native Americans in their studies, but they are a minority of voices.

Finally, too many scholars rely on the trendy theories of the moment to presume to interpret Indian realities.[2] Sometimes they go so far as to claim that they understand Native American culture, histories, oral traditions, and contemporary literature better than Native Americans themselves.[3] They often overlook the fact that much of contemporary Native American literature, for example, is produced by a complex transformation from diverse oral traditions to written text. Knowledge of language is key if one is to move beyond the "ethnopoetics perspectives" of reworking so-called primitive texts into new narratives or modern poetry. Likewise, images that focus on the exotic curiosity of earlier works or the erotic violence in Hollywood films need to be challenged.

The chapters in this volume, all written by Native American scholars influenced by the groundbreaking work of Deloria, represent a Native reaction to the continuing crisis in Native American scholarship, which too often persists in misinterpreting Indian cultural realities. Like Deloria, our commitment to our communities and our intellectual posture of resistance put us distinctly at odds with the bulk of white scholarship produced by white academics over the past century and more. Above all else, these chapters should mostly be understood as reactions to a persistent crisis in American scholarship that fails to recognize and appreciate the efforts of Native and non-Native scholars of academic integrity who expose the irrational political ideologies that continue to permeate and plague scholarly disciplines and the education system in America.

> *The nature of tribal religion brings contemporary America a new kind of legal problem. Religious freedom has existed as a matter of course in America only when religion has been conceived as a set of objective beliefs. This condition is actually not freedom at all, because it would be exceedingly difficult to read minds and determine what ideas were being entertained at the time. So far in American History religious freedom has not involved the consecration and setting aside of lands for religious purposes or allowing sincere but highly divergent behavior by individuals and groups.*
> Vine Deloria, Jr., *Spirit and Reason*

The religious philosophical expressions and belief systems of Native Americans are much more profound than the way they are depicted and "preserved" in the ethnographic record. For the most part, much of the scholarship on Native American beliefs reflects premature generalizations, and information is misinterpreted, though often with good intentions. Fortunately, the future holds more promise. An approach and a methodology that integrate the distinct Native American religious belief systems, each with its own cultural characteristics emerging from and responding to historical experience, are finally being developed and published. The specific social and mythological environment, with regard to the language of the past as well as the present, is integrated and approached by concern for the necessity of a land base. In each case, one must refer to a diversity of traditions rather than a single one. Since the colonial historical experience of most Native Americans has been one of military, religious, and political oppression, combined with assimilation, it is critical to recognize that what is happening to these religious traditions today is as important as what happened to them in the past. In other words, continuity and change should be seen as equally valid elements of preservation, adaptation, and renewal. Representations of our past in our oral traditions have facilitated the resurgence and transformation of indigenous memory. As we attempt to rationalize, in terms of our own logic, how colonialism and its invasion destroyed everything that had been good, balanced, and sacred, we are confronted with a catastrophe of enormous proportions.

Even though the First Amendment guarantees religious freedom to all Americans, Supreme Court decisions over the past century have consistently denied the religious and scientific claims of Native Americans. Rather, the courts have constantly focused on the importance of missionization and have demonstrated their ignorance with regard to Native American religious and cultural diversity and concerns for survival. American jurisprudence needs to come to terms with Native Americans in all our cultural diversity in order to understand the bond between our cultures and religious-scientific realities. Finally, these assumptions imply that Native American religious traditions (to my knowledge, no one has written a Native American religious history) have not been carefully understood. The spiritual and aesthetic dimensions of these diverse belief systems illustrate in detail the importance of sustained observation; the interconnectedness of the social, cultural, and mythological categories of each of these distinct nations; and their interdependence on the natural world for survival.

> One of the major problems for Indian people is the missionary. It has been said that when they arrived they had only the Book and we had the land; now we have the Book and they have the land. An old Indian once told me that when the missionaries arrived they fell on their knees and prayed. Then they got up fell on the Indians and preyed.
>
> Vine Deloria, Jr., *Custer Died for Your Sins*

Although American Indian belief systems have been observed and studied since the seventeenth century, it is only with relatively recent published works that they have finally begun to come into their own and are gaining a long overdue and justly deserved recognition in the study of religion and science in America. As early as 1887, Washington Matthews, a medical officer in the U.S. Army, published the first major work on a Navajo ceremony. Yet fifty years later, Franc J. Newcomb and Gladys A. Reichard expressed their surprise that Matthews's work had not inspired investigators to exert greater efforts in obtaining more complete information on Navajo ritual. Reichard's *Navajo Religion: A Study of Symbolism* (1950) widened the horizon through her ethnography, complemented by her experiences living with the Navajo—or *Diné*, as they prefer to call themselves. She learned to speak their language and made the frames of meaning of Diné religious traditions intelligible to non-Diné. More recently, Gary Witherspoon (13–150) provided an important linguistic analysis of the Diné language and worldview. Many of the earlier introductions to Native American religious traditions provide only superficial descriptions, with the project of interpretation and meaning being left to the reader. The exegesis, when not provided by "the Native point of view," is left to the eyes and hands of future researchers. In view of such an impossibly diverse amount of material, one wonders where to start. What is the intellectual fabric that illuminates studies of American Indian belief systems? Are we forever bound to missionary misinterpretations?

Today a conceptual dilemma confronts us when we ask why there remains such a lack of understanding about indigenous peoples in both America and elsewhere. Yet there is so much interest that it is time to point out that religious pluralism in America requires that we try to understand and respect one another's religious preferences. The basic methodological and epistemological questions need to be asked and answered within an appropriate framework. What is a religious reality? What do we mean by religious behavior? Although scholars of religion have attempted to answer these and other questions about religion in America, we have until now understood only some aspects of the larger religious cultures in this country, and even less about Native American religious traditions. We still struggle to respect religious preferences. The Protestant religion of the English colonists and the Catholic beliefs of European immigrants were for a long time the most influential religious forces in most of America's communities. Other diverse groups of peoples who have settled in America more recently also affirm their distinct religious traditions. To mention only a few, the European, Latino, Mexican, Asian, Muslim, and African immigrants, like the peoples who are native to this land, must also be recognized as the core and substance of religious America. Moreover, the collisions of cultures and misunderstandings among the different groups of immigrants form a political-historical change that is problematic. In the past, one of the strongest points of cultural collision between Indians and others was the conflict and contradiction that occurred between their respective sacred stories, methods of healing, and daily rituals. Euro-American Christians argued that their religion was the universal truth for all. Even though missionaries spread the values of European culture—both explicitly and implicitly—along with Christian ideology, in theory, at least, they seemed to think that Christianity transcended culture and that Indians were without culture, religion, languages, or approaches to science.

> When one examines the history of American society one notices the great weakness inherent in it. The country was founded in violence. It worships violence and it will continue to live violently. Anyone who tries to meet violence with love is crushed, but violence used to meet violence also ends abruptly with meaningless destruction.
> Vine Deloria, Jr., *Custer Died for Your Sins*

In doing research for three decades, I have found that any study of this violent and problematic dilemma should seriously consider Roy Pearce

(3–49). His succinct thesis takes the initiative by providing an analysis of the dominant Euro-American attitudes and ideas toward American Indians from 1609 to 1851. In his work on the immigrant American mind, Pearce reveals a seminal American belief: the progress of civilization over savagism. This belief came to life in the immigrants' idea of the American wilderness. The ideas about Indians and land formed by European philosophers, explorers, travelers, colonial officials, missionaries, and later Indian agents coalesced with everyday frontier experiences and created the historical complex of ideas that shaped the thinking and perceptions of nineteenth-century Euro-Americans in America. This period of hostilities and tension produced enduring racist suppositions, such as those indelibly popularized by James Fenimore Cooper. "The Indian" was a noble and virtuous hunter, a brave warrior, possessor of freedom to roam unhindered, and a simple and childlike predecessor of a civilized America. As a savage and pagan, "the Indian" was to be feared for his cunning and cruelty, disdained for resisting civilization and Christianity, pitied for the inevitable loss of his land and culture and his probable extinction. Robert Sayre (6) described these attitudes toward "the Indian" as follows: "He was, according to these stereotypes, solitary and ancient, simple and heroic, and doomed by a fate he could but rarely see." This prophesied extinction went hand in hand with what was considered the Pilgrims' progress: the God-given idea of taming the land through conquest (i.e., genocide) and saving souls through forced conversion.

> *When the two religious movements came into conflict, the Christian religion was able to overcome tribal beliefs because of its ability to differentiate life into segments which were unrelated.*
>
> Vine Deloria, Jr., *Custer Died for Your Sins*

Another aspect taken up in the literature and pertinent to the attitudes of non-Indians toward Indians is the misunderstanding of the indigenous relationship of humans and nature and the Western idea that land and natural resources can be owned. Through his reinterpretation of American history and its empire building, as well as the metaphysics of Indian hating, Richard Drinnon (xvii–xviii) made the argument that in the twentieth century the Western presumption that one may freely expropriate land and natural resources has been carried out even beyond the boundaries of this country. Following this line of thinking today, many students of Native American religious studies, ecology, and environmental studies, as well as people working on these issues in the community, express concerns for the ecological and spiritual dimensions of our symbiotic relationship to the cosmos. Continual development of landownership without regard for sustainability in our highly productive technological society is the prevailing concern of these groups as they work for a balanced alignment of the earth as ecosystem by using an integrated approach that looks at the entire picture without compartmentalization.

Anthropologists and other researchers have for many years asserted that, with few exceptions, the Euro-American colonists did not understand Native American worldviews. The tense situation created by the colonizers' ambition, fear, misunderstanding, and lack of respect for Native American cultural, ecological, and sacred boundaries is still a major problem for many Native Americans today. For evidence of these concerns, we have only to look at the recent examples of the struggle to regain control of the Black Hills by the Seven Council Fires of the Lakota, the struggle to retain Black Mesa in Arizona, or the struggle in Arizona by the Apache to keep telescopes off their sacred mountain (to mention only a few). Government policy and Christian missionary strategies continue to create an atmosphere in which control, assimilation, and cultural extinction are still being carried out. Native American responses to these policies are manifest in the struggle that continues today in the effort to stop the destruction and exploitation of the land and natural resources and to correct insensitive and disrespectful attitudes toward Native American religious traditions that are rooted in tribal histories, mythologies, and reverence for nature. Acquiring knowledge, participating in ritual and ceremony, and prolonged observational skills are usually considered ways of gaining wisdom and power to be used in one's life and for helping others. But the informing objective is the maintenance of the ecological balance in nature. Native American attempts at survival over the past two centuries have been, and continue to be, a struggle to preserve these traditional sacred values even while living on reservations or in urban areas.

As Native people, what we need now is precisely what Deloria proposed in *Custer Died for Your Sins*. We need to take the time to reflect. As scholars, we are very much aware of the centuries of colonization, assimilation, and missionization and the ongoing damage this has done to our nations. In our communities, this manifests itself as existentialist anger. There is a need for leaders who can guide us into self-awareness and healing. Tragically, there are limited federal resources that address or promote research on the effects of the Native American holocaust. Many have adopted the ways of the oppressor, often because survival is seen as connected to an alliance with Christianity and mainstream society. Because of American media, many young Native people no longer respect knowledgeable elders or see them as viable sources of cultural wisdom. Many of the elders have been subjugated into believing that they are not important. This has to change, because we are losing many of these keepers of our traditions at an alarming rate, and our young people are suffering.

On a positive note, some of our languages are being revived, with people working on language preservation in local communities with their Native speakers as well as in universities. This is beginning to promote a positive perspective on Native American language education and social justice issues. We are now beginning to see Native scholars studying and teaching their own languages in universities. These new linguists often collaborate with elders in the effort to continue the progressive vision for the preservation of America's indigenous languages.

In the areas of culture, health, sexuality, and disease, first there is a need to recognize that we come from a diversity of cultures and religious traditions, and there is much work to be done before our nations are freed from colonialism.

Indian societies, long before the coming of Europeans to America, were in the process of significant development in the areas of cultural religious practices, economic production, and artistic and material achievements. These were hardly simple or primitive peoples. Archaeological records as well as oral traditions attest to the development of new ideas and their diffusion to other geographic areas, where they were often exchanged or elaborated and adapted by a new group of people in a different environment. Ceremonial exchange such as burial practices, rites of passages, and ritual transformations; concepts of healing and the diagnosis of illness; and the order and structure of bioregional ecological relationships were already a part of the life experiences of these societies. The ordering of spatial-temporal relationships was powerful enough to persist in the geographic and spiritual or sacred boundaries, and most Native people still have a strong sense of belonging to a specific land that was given to them by the Creator. On these American lands, the sacred histories of their religious lives have taken place. The people are obligated to protect the ecological balances of the plant and animal life in these areas. Destroying these delicate balances means destroying what is held to be sacred and disrupting indigenous societies.

Again, my own thinking has been influenced deeply by Deloria. Freeing the indigenous mind to go back to the thinking modalities of our ancestors and to respect the way we were raised is the first step in freeing our minds from the shackles of colonialism (academic as well as political and social) and becoming aware once again of our indigenous heritage. This is a difficult task, because there is still so much pressure to follow the ways of Euro-American culture and scholarship. This creates major problems for our youth, who are caught between knowing they are Indians and knowing they are also Americans. We come from diverse communities and recognize our identities as central to our humanity and integral to our spirituality. I feel the need to speak out against this oppressive loss of meaning that many experience in the struggle to find their identity. The pain and fracturing that assimilation and missionization continue to impose on our youth are genocidal. Native American oral traditions continue to celebrate the goodness of the universe, and diverse creative narratives continue to teach respect for the body, sexuality, health, spiritual development, and restored relationships. Our cultures need to be more focused on personal and communal consciousness-raising.

> But hopefully, enough Indian people will take the time to reflect on their situation, on the things going on around them both in the cities and on the reservation, and will choose the proper points of leverage by which Indian renewal can be fully realized.
>
> Vine Deloria, Jr., *Custer Died for Your Sins*

Another contribution of Deloria's mentorship has been my development of a translation theory. After thirty years of field research, I developed lines of inquiry and adjusted my methods of field observation to fit what the community expected of me. I observed ceremony in as regularized a way as possible and continued to develop my theory by which this completed ritual could be studied. I recorded and translated the content of songs sung at the girls' initiation ceremony at the request of several singers and used this work as one unit of understanding. The analysis of the songs provided a style of intellectual thought as seen in performance and ritual behavior. I observed what happened before the songs of the ceremony were performed and what happened during and afterward. My "scientific" training and my own intuition and observation allowed me to develop a hypothesis of the structure for behavior in the Mescalero environment. I realized that this behavior had significant meaning and that it related to my approach to field research on my theory of translation. Some of the data I collected revealed interesting and heretofore neglected questions on the nature of adolescence in Mescalero society. From observation and conversations with Mescalero adolescent girls, I gathered that adolescence is similar yet different from that experienced in mainstream society. This can be observed behaviorally as well. Menarche is very special; it marks the time for a sacred rite announcing a young, marriageable woman. In American society, menarche appears to be unimportant and certainly is not very significant in the lives of young girls. It usually takes at least another ten years before an American girl is considered to be of a marriageable age; yet today, teenage pregnancy is a major problem in both societies. A synthesis of what I have learned can be sketched in the following manner:

Field observation and participation in order to reciprocate for knowledge received.

Development of a method that replicates an indigenous approach to gaining knowledge.

Refinement of a method for control of what I was observing.

Development of a framework for studying the ritual practices and locating who controls them.

Creative use of the song text with proper ritual attention to language.

Gaining and maintaining a relationship with medicine women or sponsor and medicine men or singers (chanters).

Awareness of ritual structures as they relate to participants.

With this approach, I realized that the most powerful elements of Mescalero society, those that would explain what was really going on in the ceremony, would take years of study. I became aware that the answers were embedded in the song texts and that the values of the culture could best be explained by analysis of the song texts themselves within the ceremonial framework. A more detailed analysis and other topics related to the girls' puberty rite required a long-term qualitative study. I first wanted to understand the Mescalero viewpoint from the inside, and this I found in mythological sacred narratives and religious aspects of the song texts. These texts contain the most elegant and refined rules for behavior; an aesthetic component, what the Mescalero call *bikehozhoni* (its power is good); a condensed form of all the history; and appropriate behaviors and attitudes that are relevant to the society. These songs are sung year after year for the continuation of the culture.

After thirty years of research and participation, I have found that the song-prayers, chants, music, dances, and dramatic portrayals in Mescalero ceremonies are a multidimensional performance-communication situated in ritual. The performance must be properly carried out according to Mescalero tradition in order to establish communication between the supernaturals and the community. To understand the transcendent qualities of the performance and to gauge its effectiveness within the matrix of the ceremony, it is necessary to know the nuances of the language, as well as the ceremonial and ritual components of the culture.

Harry Hoijer's *Chiricahua and Mescalero Apache Texts* are an important contribution to Apachean studies. He enriched the linguistic interpretation of the song texts and, more than any other scholar, untangled some of the linguistic complexity of the Mescalero Apache language. His parallel translations of Mescalero and Chiricahua Apache texts with corresponding idiomatic English are the only written ones available, and for them I am grateful. His texts were collected in the summers of 1930 and 1931 and the spring of 1934. The sample texts from the girls' puberty ceremony were collected originally by Dr. Jules Henry from David Fatty, a Chiricahua medicine man. Later they were supplied with ethnological notes by Dr. Morris Opler.

The oral texts common to Mescalero Apache ceremonial discourses are in the form of poetic song-prayers usually referred to as chants. The experience intrinsic to their performance is lost in a prose translation without placing them in a cultural-mythological context.

To interpret the intricacies of the symbolism of Mescalero song, which is also the model for cultural behavior penetrating just about every aspect of Mescalero life, we need a new style of translation, one that considers the elements of language, cultural reality, ritual, and performance. Ideally, a translation from which we could gain knowledge would produce a performable text, incorporating all translatable and correspondent meanings inherent in the oral tradition. Such a translation would do more than deal with a succession of linguistic entities; it would reflect care taken to incorporate an awareness of the substantial elements of the entire Mescalero ceremonial system. Mescalero ceremonial rules of conduct explicitly require attention to the sacred traditions of the performance. Because such sacred traditions have become embedded into the structure of ritual, they force on the performers obligations and expectations. Traditional observance of these obligations produces the matrix of the culture.

That which has been efficacious in the maintenance or restoration of equilibrium among personality, mythology, culture, and environment for the Mescalero becomes codified over time and often ceremonialized. In its most pristine form, Mescalero ceremonial art is powerful, the evocation of skillful engagement with the supernatural and nonhuman world. It follows that the text should be treated with the same respect we accord the ceremony itself. Both are instructive and sacred to the people from whose culture they have evolved. The relationship between the traditional function of the oral rendition of the ceremonial texts and their contemporary function becomes a vehicle for communication and understanding, eliciting a response from the supernatural powers invoked by the participants and from the observers.

If translation produces only a word-for-word rendering, the logic and aesthetic uniqueness of the traditional text are lost, leaving a gap between the language and ritual experience. To gain insight into the Native belief system, the translator must also attend to the verbal conventions that indicate the elements of performance as they define the imagery—silences, rhythm, phrasing, pauses, volume, music, and movement. Repetition in the chanting establishes the atmosphere of ritual and demonstrates the power of language. Through careful attention, a translator learns to listen to vocal qualities, loudness, silences, repetitions, emphasis, and much more than just literal translations.

Translation requires an integrated experience: the study of language, translation theory, oral tradition, culture, and ceremonialism and an appreciation of the mood and content of the performative complex. The singers or chanters of these texts function as religious practitioners. Because of the highly developed nature of the ritual song texts, it is necessary to understand their integration into the Native belief system to fully appreciate them. Dennis Tedlock explains this from a different perspective—the Zuni culture, where he has done considerable work—remembering the insights he received in small doses from Zuni interpreters. On his first visit to the Zuni, Tedlock learned dramatically about orality and storytelling when one of his interpreters announced, "You don't know the time when you're telling stories; it's not like working at a desk." He was working tediously on a word-for-word literal translation of a Zuni tape with another local interpreter-storyteller, who asked a leading question. In the middle of all this laborious work where "I was madly scribbling down what he had just said, Joe said, 'When I tell these stories, do you picture it? Or do you just write down?'" Even the countryside must be experienced as part of the hearing and learning of traditional stories, as Tedlock discovered. Repeatedly, as he traveled the reservation area with one of his storyteller informants, he was directed to one location after another as actual sites where stories had occurred. "You're going along with a Zuni and the Zuni says, 'That's the cave, you remember that story about the Astoshle ogress? That's the cave where she lived when that little girl wandered into her cave to spend the night.'" Even in the telling of stories, spatiality, the miming of directionality, the facing of the appropriate direction, and the appropriate gesturing in the correct direction all become part of the telling itself. As Tedlock concludes, "The sense of being in place also exists at the same moment the story is actually being told. Even if you're telling it in Milwaukee you've at least got the directions. And you always have to know before you can tell one of these stories which way east is" (708).

Tedlock's concern with the properties of Zuni oral narrative and its social context is exemplified and made clear on his printed page. He has demonstrated that oral narratives elicited in the field and oral discourse have historical validity as well as religious poetic qualities. This is also exemplified in the following Mescalero text: "When the earth had been made, Killer of Enemies put us down right here in the vicinity of White Mountain. 'That which lies on this mountain will be the land of the Mescalero' (he said). Then Killer of Enemies put us down right here. We are still here. . . . It is true that right here will be the land of the

Mescalero."[4] On one level, this text appears to be a sacred narrative relating to the traditional Mescalero homeland and the Mescalero Apache creation myth. White Mountain *is* the sacred home of Isanaklesh, the female deity, and the home of the Mountain Spirits, or Gahe. The text itself verifies the geographic references as the place of origin: "It is true that right here will be the land of the Mescalero." What we know about the Mescalero's past is delineated and given an added dimension by the study of this myth, which is both historically and aesthetically enriching. There can be no doubt that a study of oral traditions is a source of knowledge about the past, especially for a people that have no written language or history. This myth is designed to instruct, to explain the origin of the Mescalero spatially and temporally within a religious framework.

Since tradition is passed on orally, it is impossible to determine the actual moment of creative insight, nor is it necessary. The structure and connotations of the myth are religious and are passed on with great care; they have overtones that cannot be doubted. Taking this body of oral traditions apart and translating them analytically will never be the same as actually experiencing them in real life. In his provocative essay "The Man Made of Words," N. Scott Momaday exemplifies his concern with the religious, moral, and verbal dimensions in which we live. Through the creative process, his work as a Native American writer and storyteller, Momaday once again connects us with the past and makes sense of the present. He was struggling to write, and to write as a Kiowa man with some sense of authenticity, when he suddenly remembered a very old Kiowa grandmother by the name of Ko-sahn who had been his teacher and a teacher of his grandparents. At that moment, writing coalesced around orality, the story traditions of his own people. It gave his writing sudden and new power: "The living memory," writes Momaday, "and the verbal tradition which transcends it, were brought together for me once and for all in the person of Ko-sahn." As he remembered that she had spoken and sung to him on a summer afternoon long ago in Oklahoma, he pictured her again: "An old whimsy, a delight in language and in remembrance, shone in her one good eye. She conjured up the past, imagining perfectly the long continuity of her being." Her name seemed "to humanize the whole complexity of language." When repeating her name aloud startlingly results in her appearance before him, Momaday struggles to explain to himself the occurrence—in dialogue with the old woman, in terms of mental imagination or dreaming. The woman responds, calling Momaday to carefulness in his choice of words even as he protests that her appearance is not real. "You imagine that I am here in this room, do you not? That is worth something. You see, I have existence, whole being, to be sure, but it is perhaps the best of all kinds. If I am not here in this room, grandson, then surely neither are you."

Martin Heidegger, the German existential philosopher, affirms life lived in the same poetic spaces claimed by Momaday: "Language tells us: to be a human being is to be on the earth as a mortal, to dwell, doing the 'building' that belongs to dwelling: cultivating growing things, constructing things that are built, and doing all this in the context of mortals who living on earth and cherishing it, look to the sky and to the gods to find the measure of their dwelling. If man's being is dwelling, and if man must look to the way the world fits together to find the measure by which he can determine his dwelling life, then man must dwell poetically" (xiv). Heidegger's concern with living poetically reaffirms Momaday's realization that our most essential being consists in language and understanding how the world fits together.

> *The most memorable event of my early childhood was visiting Wounded Knee where 200 Sioux, including women and children, were slaughtered in 1890 by troopers of the Seventh Calvary in what is believed to have been a delayed act of vengeance for Custer's defeat. The people were simply lined up and shot down much as was allegedly done, according to newspaper reports, at Songmy. The wounded were left to die in a three-day Dakota blizzard, and when the soldiers returned to the scene after the storm some were still alive and were saved. The massacre was vividly etched in the minds of many of the older reservation people, but it was difficult to find anyone who wanted to talk about it.*
>
> Vine Deloria, Jr., *Red Power: The American Indians' Fight for Freedom*

For me, my most memorable recollection as a child was watching my grandfather plant corn. In the process he explained why it was our most important food if we were to survive. Studying the origins of corn later led me to an interest in indigenous religions. At the University of California–Santa Barbara, I have spent the last two decades developing this field of study on the doctoral level. My own vision was indeed inspired by Vine Deloria's work. As we enter this new century, we are both inspired by the work of the students we have trained and their dedication to the field.

NOTES

1. A particularly egregious example of this is James Clifton's edited volume *The Invented Indian;* only slightly less offensive is Sam Gill's *Mother Earth.* For an incisive critique of both, see Ward Churchill, "A Little Matter of Genocide: Sam Gill's *Mother Earth* and the Expropriation of Indigenous Spiritual Traditions in Academia," in *Fantasies of the Master Race: Literature, Cinema and the Colonization of American Indians* (Monroe, Me.: Common Courage Press, 1992), 187–213. Gill, it should be noted, also has an essay in the Clifton volume.

2. See, e.g., Irwin's attempt to explain visions gained in Rites of Vigil in terms of current psychological and neurological theories of dreams in *Dream Seekers*.

3. See, again, *Mother Earth*, where Gill presumes to know that the identification of the earth as "mother" was invented by Amer-Europeans, imputed to Indian peoples, and later adopted by Indians as tribal doctrine.

4. Personal communication with Willetto Antonio, Mescalero, N.M., 1980.

REFERENCES

Clifton, James, ed. *The Invented Indian: Cultural Fictions and Government Policies.* New Brunswick, N.J.: Transaction Publishers, 1990.

Cooper, James Fennimore. *The Leatherstocking Saga,* ed. Allan Nevins. New York: Pantheon Books, 1954.

Deloria, Vine Jr. *Behind the Trail of Broken Treaties: An Indian Declaration of Independence.* New York: Delacorte Press, 1974.

———. *Custer Died for Your Sins: An Indian Manifesto.* New York: Macmillan, 1969.

———. *God Is Red: A Native View of Religion.* Golden, Colo.: Fulcrum Publishing, 1994.

———. *The Metaphysics of Modern Existence.* San Francisco: Harper and Row, 1979.

———. *Of Utmost Good Faith.* San Francisco: Straight Arrow Books, 1971.

———. *Red Earth, White Lies: Native Americans and the Myth of Scientific Fact.* New York: Scribner, 1995.

———. *Singing for a Spirit: A Portrait of the Dakota Sioux.* Santa Fe, N.M.: Clear Light Publishers, 1999.

———. *We Talk, You Listen: New Tribes, New Turf.* New York: Macmillan, 1970.

———, ed. *Spirit and Reason: The Vine Deloria, Jr. Reader.* Golden, Colo.: Fulcrum Publishing, 1999.

Drinnon, Richard. *Facing West: The Metaphysics of Indian-Hating and Empire-Building.* Minneapolis: University of Minnesota Press, 1980.

Gill, Sam. *Mother Earth: An American Story.* Chicago: University of Chicago Press, 1987.

Heidegger, Martin. *Poetry, Language, Thought,* trans. Albert Hofstadter. New York: Harper Colophon Books, 1971.

Hoijer, Harry. *Chiricahua and Mescalero Apache Texts.* Chicago: University of Chicago Press, 1939.

Irwin, Lee. *The Dream Seekers: Native American Visionary Traditions of the Great Plains.* Norman: University of Oklahoma Press, 1994.

Josephy, Alvin M. *Red Power: The American Indian Fight for Freedom.* New Haven, Conn.: Yale University Press, 1970.

Matthews, Washington. "The Mountain Chant." Annual Report of the Bureau of American Ethnology, 1887, vol. 5, pp. 385–467.

Momaday, N. Scott. "The Man Made of Words." In *Indian Voices: The First Convocation of American Indian Scholars.* Princeton, N.J.: Princeton University Press, 1970.

Newcomb, Franc, and Gladys Reichard. *Sandpaintings of the Navajo Shooting Chant.* New York: Dover Publishing, 1937.

Pearce, Roy. *The Savages of America: A Study of the Indian and the Idea of Civilization.* Baltimore: Johns Hopkins University Press, 1953.

Reichard, Gladys. *Navajo Religion: A Study of Symbolism.* New York: Pantheon Books, 1950.

Sayre, Robert. *Thoreau and the American Indians.* Princeton, N.J.: Princeton University Press, 1977.

Tedlock, Dennis. "Learning to Listen: Oral History as Poetry." *Boundary,* vol. 2, no. 3 (spring 1975).

Witherspoon, Gary. *Language and Art in the Navajo Universe.* Ann Arbor: University of Michigan Press, 1977.

CHAPTER TWELVE

Yuchi Travels: Up and Down the Academic "Road to Disappearance"
Richard A. Grounds (Yuchi/Seminole)

While a graduate student in Princeton, New Jersey, I happened onto a 110-year-old encyclopedic volume on the history of the United States. This tome, which had been cut from the university library stacks, included a brief chapter on the "Uchee" and made the following statement: "In the pleasant country extending from the Savannah River, at Augusta, westward to Milledgeville, and along the banks of the Oconee and the head waters of the Ogeechee and Chattahooche, the Europeans found a remnant of the once powerful nation of the UCHEES. . . . They, too, have been driven beyond the Mississippi by the pressure of civilization, and have become partially absorbed by the Creeks, with whom less than 800 souls yet remain. They are, in fact, an extinct nation, and their language is almost forgotten" (Lossing, 28). As a Yuchi tribal member, I was stunned to read the century-old report that my people were, "in fact," extinct. Yet I felt a sense of relief that this volume had finally been removed from the Princeton University library shelves (even if no one had used it for decades). I managed a knowing smile, realizing that the book was the product of the same benighted nineteenth-century "civilization" that the quotation itself referenced. This "civilization" had depended heavily on the all-the-Indians-are-doomed-to-disappear-any-way myth to justify its brutal actions in dispossessing aboriginal peoples from their ancestral lands.

However, as a graduate student attempting to keep abreast of what academics were writing about our community, I was even less prepared for the current "fact" that I found listed in the reference section at Princeton University's Firestone Library. In *A Concise Dictionary of Indian Tribes of North America*, edited by Barbara Leitch and published in 1979, the entry on the Yuchi (also often spelled Euchee) begins with the following statement:

> YUCHI: an extinct agricultural and hunting tribe living in eastern Tennessee and northern Georgia at the time of the 1539 De Soto expedition to this region.

With increasing consternation I read on. The final paragraph of the over 400-word article concluded: "The Yuchi bands were essentially dispersed by the mid-19th century, some settling with the Cherokee, some among the Upper Creek and others joining the Seminole in Florida. Many of these, following the removal of the Indians to the West, settled in Indian Territory (now Oklahoma) along with their adopted tribes. In the late 1970s, the Yuchi were extinct as a tribe" (Leitch, 536–38). There it was again—repeated twice in this authoritative article. A hundred years had passed, and my people were still being declared extinct. I—we—supposedly did not exist. I doubt that I can effectively communicate to nontribal persons what it feels like to read that your people are extinct.

The immediacy of experiencing the concept of extinction does not fall within the realm of possibility for the majority of people. Nontribal persons are not at risk for a malady that seems to be reserved for Native Americans and, perhaps, dinosaurs. Even the various groups from antiquity in Europe and Asia have somehow avoided the deadly ascription, despite their long absence, and are usually denoted as the "ancient peoples," with the connotation that they are "venerable" because they were older, predecessor "civilizations." Modern dictionaries typically indicate that the adjective *extinct* is most commonly used in terms of animals, volcanoes, or species. The human species is obviously not extinct. Yet the connotations of this word as applied to a particular group of humans, Native Americans, are disturbing and point to a long-standing Amer-European predisposition.

Most strikingly, this special use of the term for Native Americans has finally been recognized by *Webster's Third New International Dictionary* (1986), which provides a new definition for *extinct*. Moving beyond the original meaning of dying out altogether, the dictionary has distilled the essence of one special use of the adjective. The new meaning registered in the dictionary refers to something "that no longer exists in its original form." Without this adjusted definition, breaking from the commonsense and etymological meanings of the word *extinct*, the example the dictionary provides would be incomprehensible: "members of an extinct Indian people now living on a reservation." How could a major reference work of the English language include such semantically twisted phrasing? Members of an "extinct" Indian people "now living" on a reservation? This inverted definition of the word *extinct* can be accounted for only by the enormous internal pressures created through the illogics of American conquest and domination. These illogics demand the urgent erasure of our presence, at least in our original forms. Only Indigenous people on this continent are privileged to experience what it means to be both extinct and living. The inclusion of such convoluted language in the dictionary is merely a reflection of the widespread pattern within English language usage. This new definition, now formally registered in this authoritative dictionary, attempts to make sense out of the otherwise nonsensical use of the term *extinct* to describe people who are not extinct.

The use of the term *extinct* as a special marker became attached, over time, like a dark shadow to the predominating image of Native Americans. Beginning early in American history, the uncoordinated efforts toward physical genocide were followed by the concomitant efforts to achieve a kind of intellectual extinction of Indigenous peoples. Though foreshadowed in the colonial period (see examples in Porter, 5), the growth of this specialized employment of extinction seems to correspond to the rise of the American Republic in the late eighteenth century (cf. Sheehan, in which the notion of extinction—despite the title—is considered only obliquely and largely metaphorically). During the Jacksonian era in the early nineteenth century, when the Yuchi, along with other peoples, were forcibly removed from their homes in what is now the southeastern United States, the expectation of Native demise reached a high point. The mood was crisply summarized by Senator Thomas Hart Benton: "Civilization or extinction has been the fate of all people who have found themselves in the track of advancing whites" (cited in Rogin, 210). It was of paramount importance during this period to obtain a signed treaty (however fraudulently) to justify the coerced land cessions. Even so, the notion of extinction, like a signed death certificate, was intended to release American society from a multitude of obligations, including political and economic commitments, but above all from the guilt and moral concerns associated with dispossessing the recognized owners of the land (Rogin, 210–15, 243–48). The best way to ensure an extinct title for a Native land claim is to have an extinct Native tribe—even if the people themselves are still persisting.[1]

The idea that Native peoples were teetering on the edge of extinction continued throughout the nineteenth century (see Mitchell; Limerick) and remains a popular romantic image today. The notion has been purveyed by Hollywood so effectively, if unwittingly, that Native Americans traveling internationally are repeatedly confronted by people who are shocked to find that there are still living Native Americans. Such encounters are mutual surprises—both for local people around the globe, who have been acquiring their ideas from Hollywood films, and for those members of extinct nations who do not realize that they are extinct. This idea has had tremendous staying power. When the $35 million film *Last of the Mohicans* opened in 1992 it grossed $11 million in its first weekend. The film featured Russell Means, prominent American Indian Movement (AIM) leader and outspoken critic of such films as *Dances with Wolves* and *Black Robe*. Means plays the adoptive father of the film's hero, the Caucasian Hawkeye, and utters the final line of the film: that he is Chingachgook, the "last of the Mohicans." By so doing, Means is caught in the unenviable position of mouthing—on the everlasting medium of celluloid—one of the bottom lines of the Amer-European justification for continental conquest: that Indians are disappearing. And how much more effective it was to have a Native spokesperson to repeat and reinforce this favorite rationalization. Of course, the Mohegan people themselves continue to live and to maintain their identity, as they have over the last century and a half since James Fenimore Cooper wrote his romantic frontier classic, curiously titled *The Last of the Mohicans*. But perhaps more amazingly, the expectation of an imminent extinction continues to inform a significant portion of present-day academic discussion.

In moving beyond these general observations, I offer in this chapter a closer examination of these notions of Native extinction as they relate to the particular case of the Yuchi community. To have an opportunity to comment on reports of your own personal demise could be an occasion for ironic humor, as when Samuel Clemens remarked that the reports of his death had been "greatly exaggerated." But to respond to the pronouncement that your people are "extinct" creates a problem of another order. What follows is a reaction to scholarly assertions of Yuchi extinction. The first part of this chapter responds by baring an insistent orientation on the past, which is here taken as a pervasive malaise enervating much of the literature about Native Americans. I point out the difficulties of such a pattern of published negation not only for students searching for reliable information but also, and more importantly, for members of the community who are faced with such blatant affronts to their families, cultures, and communities. The economic and political impact of what might otherwise be considered value-neutral research is underscored, and I take note of the difficulties that can be created for tribal people when published results feed back into tribal awareness. In the conclusion of the chapter I reference more recent developments that reflect the complexities of community choices as Yuchis increasingly come to the attention of scholars. Instead of being denied, the Yuchi community is now being courted. This new attention is creating a series of unprecedented and difficult trade-offs as the group is asked to participate in its own public representation in ways that clearly have value to the external society in which the Yuchi community is immersed but may portend bleak prospects for the community's desired cultural continuity. Throughout the entirety of this discussion I emphasize the built-in, elemental rub between the academic enterprise and the "subjects" of scholarly investigation.

DOWN THE ACADEMIC "ROAD TO DISAPPEARANCE"

Historiography of Extinction

The path toward scholarly oblivion for the Yuchi people can be traced over a surprisingly long period. As early as 1821, J. A. Peniere, subagent for Indian Affairs, wrote in a report on the Native American population, "There are, besides, some remains of ancient tribes, known by the names of Outchis [Yuchis], Chiaas Cana-acké, &c. but they consist of only a few straggling families" (Peniere, 7). In an 1838 book from the period of so-called removal from the Southeast, the writer reported that his work was "drawn from a very interesting legendary account of the slaughter and almost total extinction of the Uchee tribe of Indians, which was related to the author . . . where the awful catastrophe occurred" (Ransom, 3). By the late nineteenth century, the Yuchi were being declared "an extinct nation" (Lossing).

In 1910 a report from the governmental agency working directly in the region, the Five Civilized Tribes Agency, erroneously listed only seventy-eight Yuchi (Wright, 265). The prevailing attitude is well represented by the phrase used to entitle Angie Debo's standard history of the Creek and Yuchi people, which was called *The Road to Disappearance* (1941).[2] Another book burdened with an unfortunate title that contains a central chapter on the Yuchi is Lewis and Kneberg's *Tribes that Slumber: Indian Times in the Tennessee Region* (1958). In typical funereal tones, the final sentence of Lewis and Kneberg's presentation states, "By 1930, census returns showed *only* 216 Yuchi *still surviving*" (emphasis added to underscore the authors' underlying expectations). Not only did they use twenty-eight-year-old information for their population figure; they also had failed to notice the already published count of 1,216 Yuchi tribal members (Wright, 265). Of course, this same information could have been obtained by contacting tribal leaders in Oklahoma.[3] The stance betrayed by these titles might be expected for works originally published in the 1940s and 1950s. However, these books remain in print and retain their appeal.[4]

It appears that there may be a variety of alternative routes along this academic "road to disappearance." One of the enduring favorites is the scenic route of romantic indulgence. In 1983 Joseph Mahan—the primary scholar then active in the study of Yuchian traditions—published a work that developed broad schemes of transoceanic contacts prior to the activities of Columbus. Mahan casts the Yuchi as central figures in this study, which lavishes in the glorification of an ancient Yuchi past, a depiction that has not been accepted by some members of the present-day Yuchi community. Mahan concludes: "We now know that the American Yuchis and the Asian Yueh-chih were once the same people; and we know that they comprised the governing element of an elaborate socio-religious organization based on a religion acclaiming the union of the Earth and Sky. We know that this organization was, in fact, a league or alliance among the leaders of such diverse peoples as the original 'Mediterraneans,' the Semites and the Aryans" (Mahan, *The Secret,* 188; cf. Gordon).[5]

The work of Mahan inspired the poetic sensibilities of William Keith Overstreet, who wrote of the demise of Yuchi people and their ceremonial traditions. In the poem "Where Are the Children of Earth and Sky?" Overstreet laments the darkening of the light from the Yuchi sacred fires as the traditions have been abandoned and the people seem to have been lost:

> Life Ruler speaks
> "Where are the children?"
> I, Cohantoney, search for them
> Where are the Tali, the Listeners?
> Where are the Hak-aha, the Seers?
> Where are the Haia, the Knowers?
> Where are . . ."
>
> Long ago, the Old Ones, Yudjiha
> Took care of Cohantoney's Gift
> In mid-summer, they came . . .
> To celebrate the Marriage
> Of Earth and Sky . . .
>
> Long ago, the Old Ones
> Listened to each other . . .
> They loved each other
> And drank the Good Medicine of life, Zoti
>
> Now, I seek them, but where?
> They do not take care of the Light
> They grow weak
> They do not burn the Sacred Fire . . .
>
> . . . Where is the Sacred Fire?
> Where are the Tsoyaha?
> The Sun weakens . . .
>
> Life Ruler speaks
> "Where are the children of Earth and Sky?"

In this poem, Overstreet employs the term *Tsoyaha,* the word used by Yuchi people (or "Yudjiha") to identify themselves. Tsoyaha has often been glossed as "children of the Sun." Strikingly, in this portrayal, even the Life Ruler (rendered from the Yuchi language as "Cohantoney") is left wondering where the missing children are. Perhaps it should be no surprise that earthbound academics are also having a hard time locating Yuchi people.[6]

The persistence of the backward focus of the literature can be found in the article on the Yuchi written by James Crawford in 1972[7] for the *Handbook of North American Indians,* a multivolume reference source in an ongoing process of publication by the Smithsonian. Although written in the 1970s for inclusion in the yet-to-come volume on the Southeast, and now likely to undergo major revision or replacement prior to publication, the article models the backward cast of the academic perspective, which incessantly nudges people along the road toward "extinction." The article is based almost completely based on Frank Speck's work, which was the source for the Yuchi entry in the last handbook published in 1910. The grossly underestimated population figures (600 as opposed to approximately 2,000), along with the rearward orientation, give the original article a decided tone of a memorial to things past rather than a description that recognizes present-day tribal vitality.

How large is the impact of a reference dictionary (Leitch) that has sold 8,000 volumes primarily to university and college libraries in which Yuchi extinction appears as a fact to be learned by untold numbers of students? There is, of course, a multiplication effect resulting from errors originally printed in reference works. The repetition of the *fact* of Yuchi extinction is easily extended to the World Wide Web, where, for example, South Carolina's Information Highway site (http://sciway.net/hist/indians) lists information on South Carolina Indians:

> Name: Yuchi.
> Meaning: From far away.
> Current Status: Extinct.

Not surprisingly, the short bibliography attached to this posting on the web site lists Leitch's volume as a source for further information on the Yuchi.

Even subsequent published reference materials have apparently been influenced by Leitch's erroneous assertion of Yuchi extinction. In the more recent *Encyclopedia of Native American Tribes* by Carl Waldman, the error has been given further life. This volume, intended for a juvenile audience, was published in 1988 by *Facts* on File (emphasis added) and has also found its way into many depositories of learning. In this article on the Yuchi, which focuses on the sixteenth and seventeenth centuries, the Yuchis seem to disappear among neighboring tribal groups in the early nineteenth century, even before the period of removal from the

Southeast.[8] In a softened version of the extinction theme, Waldman states, "The Yuchi eventually lost their tribal identity" (259). With this choice of words, Waldman moves the literary demise of Yuchi people beyond mere passive victimization by external actors. They are not simply absented from the stage of active history. Here they become—like the Ten Little Indians of popular lyric—the authors of their own demise. It is they who have lost their identity, and an outside researcher who pretends to know the inner state of the community's self-awareness.

By 1994, the denial of Yuchi existence could be published without qualification. In an ironic twist of educational publishing efforts, Josephine Paterek wrote about the Yuchi in her *Encyclopedia of American Indian Costume*. The careful documentation of Yuchi clothing and adornment, which includes the categories of men's and women's basic dress, footwear, outerwear, hairstyles, headgear, accessories, jewelry, garment decoration, face and body embellishment, and transitional dress, is coupled with the blunt statement that "they seem to have disappeared from the records in the nineteenth century" (35). The strangeness of this particular statement is amplified by the meticulous description of Yuchi *costume* while the living bodies of the people animating and creating those clothing styles are somehow lost from view.

In the most recent published negation of the Yuchi community (of which I am aware), a conservative columnist does not directly confront the existence of the community. Rather, he voices what I take to be a broadly held if half-articulated notion of the utter futility of indigenous cultural continuity as expressed in Native languages. The attitude of relegating our rich Indigenous languages to the level of useless antiquarian relics has had enormous staying power in American popular culture.[9] The nationally syndicated columnist James J. Kilpatrick wrote that the loss of the Yuchi language, long identified as a language isolate, was "a cause for cultural antiquarians. . . . As a specimen of linguistic paleontology, Yuchi will interest experts in the field." He dismissed the importance of our language in terms that resonated with the attitudes from over a century before that had led to the false claim that the Yuchi language was "almost forgotten" (Lossing, 28). Kilpatrick's bottom line reinforces the long-standing social injunction to relinquish our invaluable language: "Yuchi is a rare stamp, meant for a collector's album. Make some recordings. Let it go."

Consequences of Extinction

The use of the term *extinct* in reference to the Yuchi may be an extreme instance of misinformation, but it is entirely consistent with a major thrust of published literature about tribal groups across the breadth of the continent. These issues are familiar to the Wampanoag on the shores of the Northeast and to the Chumash on the Southern California coast.[10] This is not to deny that tribal groups were decimated by disease, war, and the like. Nor is it to suggest that Yuchi identity and recognition hinge on the same issues as for the Chumash or Wampanoag. Each tribal group has a particular history and a unique set of challenges. Nor can it be said that having a sense of one's own tribal identity correlates well with having a political relationship with the federal government as a formally recognized tribe. As Porter (4) has commented on the over 100 recognizable groups that remain officially nonrecognized: "Failure by the Federal Government to recognize certain tribes has usually been the product of long-forgotten historical accidents, or of the belief that many tribes became extinct. Whatever the reasons for the nonrecognized status of many Indian groups, one thing is certain: they have not vanished!" However, lethal results—an occasional erroneous extinction—are to be expected in scholarly reports, given the nature of the approach and the underlying attitude in much of what is published and presented.[11]

There is a deep strain within the academic literature on Native Americans that persists in the mummification of living people by a morbid focus on the past. This problem is evident within the theoretical assumptions about the "assimilation" of aboriginal cultures—even though, for example, scholars now generally avoid the tendentious appellation the "Five Civilized Tribes," preferring the less obviously colonialist designation "Five Tribes." It can be seen in the search for "ideal types" and the quest for "real" Indians and the implicit measuring of present-day people against a "static" past. It can be sensed in the unconsidered classist suppositions of "deprivation" studies. Its effects are demonstrated, negatively, by the limited attention to Native American Christians (as if these people were no longer worthy of academic consideration as "authentic" Indians). And it is often exhibited in an excessive dependence on eighteenth- and nineteenth-century ethnographic materials in scholarly articles that ignore input from contemporary members of living traditions.

Thus, I am suggesting that the predilection toward assuming extinction in academic circles results in a curious gravitational pull on the corpus of academic publications, skewing them away from a true reflection of Native American cultural existence. But beyond the limitations implied by the assumptions of extinction for the realm of scholarly publications, such an embedded approach has an impact on Native communities. Although the existence of our culture is not dependent on scholarly publications, there are important consequences to all such studies. They have a political, economic, and social impact.[12]

One of the consequences of academic work is that it feeds back into tribal self-conceptions. This is clear in the experience of the Yuchi artist

Richard Ray Whitman, who sat through a scholarly lecture in Columbus, Georgia, entitled "Who Were the Yuchi?" which was delivered as if there were no remaining Yuchis who could respond to the question.[13] The artist responded on canvas, depicting a dramatic correction of the lecture title, changing it to the present tense. Two Yuchi elders who attended the conference where the lecture was given were overheard commenting to each other in the Yuchi language: "How come we exist for them to write about us, but we don't exist for ourselves?"

Of course, the obverse of direct or implicit denial of Yuchi existence is the simple omission of acknowledging the historical or present Yuchi existence. How can we measure the consequences for community members who repeatedly fail to find themselves in the history books?[14] The Yuchi nation is often omitted from popular publications and guides to Indian country. A recent exhibition on Native arts at one of the local museums displayed a map of Oklahoma's Native American groups *sans* Yuchi. In such cases it is what is missing or subtly altered that betrays the profundity of the assumptions of Native demise. The Indigenous presence simply is not important enough to register in many instances. In the town of Sapulpa, Oklahoma, where a main thoroughfare once passed the Euchee Mission Boarding School, the busy avenue has long been called simply Mission Street. The problem of Yuchi invisibility had become such a commonplace that a popular article honoring Yuchi elder Sadie Skeeter was entitled, "Invisible Too Long: A Yuchi Woman Who Would Not Let Her Tribe Be Forgotten" (Pearson).

There are, it seems, a range of reasons behind the sundry manifestations of denial of the existence of the Yuchi nation. Odd alignments of interests may be detected behind the resistance to acknowledging Yuchi existence. Occasionally the published academic and popular literature can have a curious consonance with diffuse social pressures that would deny or limit Indigenous existence. The notion of Native disappearance can be seen permeating local educational and publishing efforts in the production of a public school textbook on tribal history and traditions (*Oklahoma Indian and Nature Guide*). Yuchi contributions were subjected to significant alterations in the final stages of publication under a Title IX federal grant. The editors made drastic changes in the drafts, which had been composed in the present tense and submitted by a team of Yuchi elders. Although the overall text retained its original present-tense form, all those verbs in the section on Yuchi religious traditions were changed to the moribund past tense—as if the members of the three Yuchi ceremonial grounds were no longer keeping their fires and taking medicine. Efforts of elders to use this locally produced publication to pass on community history to younger community members were seriously impaired when editors of the final version of the manuscript expurgated the vivid accounts of the unbelievably cruel removal trek. And most significantly, the editors dropped from the published version of the book the statement by Yuchi elders that read: "But what remains for the Yuchi of today is a struggle to regain their rights as an independent tribe."[15]

Denials forced on the Yuchi people may be born of administrative prerogatives as expressions of underlying interests. This has been registered at the levels of city, tribal, and federal government. In 1980 town officials in Sapulpa, Oklahoma, denied a proposed and already funded $3.7 million retirement project for housing elderly people with low income. The Indian Village proposal, which was spearheaded by Yuchi leaders (see Martin), was denied due to pressure from a large group of organized home owners who were ostensibly concerned about the effect of the project on the city's water supply but whose underlying motivation clearly seemed to be concern about the creation in their neighborhood of "an Indian ghetto" (as some were heard to say; August 1990 interview with Mose Cahwee, president of the Indian Village project). In the mid-1970s the Creek Nation forced the Yuchi Community Center in Sapulpa to be renamed with a Creek designation. And back in 1955 the independent case brought on behalf of the Yuchi people to the Indian Claims Commission was denied consideration because the commission preferred to continue to operate within the familiar bounds of the long-standing relationship between the federal government and the Creek Nation, where the Yuchi as a group have long been sublimated in political terms (cf. Moore).

The political realities for Native American nations are heavily influenced by academic discourse, one of the consequences of which may be the formal denial of claims for federal recognition. This is clear in the case of the Yuchi bid for tribal independence through the processes of federal recognition, which require demonstration of tribal continuity from the time of white contact. This is difficult to do when the records required for validation are spotted with denials of your existence and, in particular, with denials of your corporate or governmental existence. However, the continuation of Yuchi culture itself is not dependent on federal recognition. Yuchis would reject the implication that the government can bureaucratically define the existence of a people or, conversely, that it can administratively deny the existence of a tribe (see "Policy Gives Bush Administration Power"). Yuchis know who they are, and federal recognition is merely a political expedient to aid in furthering group goals.

It is ironic that precisely at the time Yuchi obituary notices were multiplying, the tribe was, in fact, pursuing a historic bid for federal recognition. The petition submitted under the Yuchi Tribal Organization (YTO) in Sapulpa, Oklahoma, for the purpose of obtaining independent tribal status was denied in 1995. At least at the surface level, there may be a welter of technical reasons for denying Yuchi existence that cover over the deeper tectonic movements of Amer-European culture incessantly pushing Native Americans toward some form of extinction. In the "Summary under the Criteria and Evidence for Proposed Finding against Federal Acknowledgment of the Yuchi Tribal Organization, Inc.: Prepared in response to a petition submitted to the Assistant Secretary of the Interior–Indian Affairs that this group exists as an Indian tribe," the logic of the ruling was crisp: "There was clear evidence, based on the preliminary technical assistance review, that the YTO did not meet the criterion in section 83.7(f). . . . Section 83.7(f), in brief, requires that a petitioner not be principally composed of members of another, already acknowledged tribe" (Deer, 4).

Fortunately, most Yuchis are not reading the scholarly publications about themselves. Therefore, they are not aware that they do not exist, and they do not assume that the tribal ceremonies they participate in have ceased. They do not know that their tribal identity has been lost. Indeed, they are actively struggling to retain their ancient language and promoting their independent political existence. In the face of these many printed statements of Yuchi extinction and the innumerable omissions of recognizing Yuchi presence, Yuchi people continue to speak their existence. As community leader Mose Cahwee says at the beginning of his prayers to the Creator, "yUdjEhanAnô s'ôKAnAnô" [we, the Yuchi people, we are still here]. Meanwhile, the stiffened Native American figures created through the language of an academic past tense—those false figures, securely bound in the old clothing woven by the mentality of a salvage anthropology—continue to live in the annals of the academy. As Vine Deloria, Jr., wrote in *God Is Red*, "The tragedy of America's Indians—that is, the Indians that America loves and loves to read about—is that they no longer exist, except in the pages of books" (49). For Yuchis, however, it is the pages of books that have repeatedly insisted that they no longer exist.

Interpretations of Extinction

The question becomes what is to be made of this propensity toward the premature labeling of Native communities as extinct? How might we interpret such a curious expression within the published literature about Native Americans? Could it be that I am unnecessarily conflating types of extinction?[16] That is, am I not being careful enough about recognizing the difference between saying a culture or some particular expression of it has disappeared and saying that all the descendants of a specific tribal nation have expired? (Might this be a way to defend some of the published statements?)

Although there may be some technical distinction between the demise of a political structure and the cessation of the existence of community members, the fact remains that it is the language of extinction that is being used to refer to these changes. This is a very strange language indeed. I can think of no instance where such language would be applied to Amer-European political or social structures that have stopped functioning, but it is readily applied in reference to Native Americans. It even goes unquestioned. It appears to be based on the underlying premise that whereas Amer-European political entities may change or cease functioning, they will be followed by newer political institutions as expressions of the ongoing vitality of Amer-European society. Native nations, in contrast, are presumed to be vanishing or decaying, and the language of extinction is unthinkingly taken to be an appropriate marker, even when community members are clearly acknowledged to be still living.

The language of extinction carries twin advantages. It at once communicates a perception of a situation that appears to be the result of some passive change of state—that is, there is no implied reference to the active and destructive processes of colonial assault on Native nations' political structures, land base, economic viability, and so forth—while at the same time it carries the weight of an apparent and unquestionable fact. However, such a statement could not possibly constitute a statement of fact. It cannot be known whether a particular community may regenerate its political structures at some point in the future, even from a very small membership (witness the political and economic recrudescence of the Pequots of Mashantucket, Connecticut). Rather than being a statement of fact or representing a scholarly analysis, the language of extinction is an expression of a social idea. This is the language of social Darwinism. It carries the idea that Native peoples, or at least their social and political structures, have been superseded by stronger, better-adapted European institutions in some presumed grand developmental pattern among human societies. It is a carryover from the nineteenth century and is not a useful descriptive device for current scholarship. And it is certainly, for community members, one of the most offensive statements that can be published. But even if a community's governance is no longer being carried out in a public sphere, who would possibly have the recognized authority to make such a pronouncement that a group has become extinct? Who would have the competence, with all the requisite information concerning the vital signs of a community, to reach a conclusion of such finality, to declare that a Native body politic is dead on arrival?

Am I overreacting to the statements of extinction? Are these publishing errors simply the surface results, the inadvertent and occasional by-products of the techniques of the publication processes and therefore something to be expected? It seems to me that the language of extinction is itself an artifact of colonialist mentality. Only out of an extreme and deeply embedded position of colonialist domination is it possible to arrogate to oneself the authority to define peoples out of existence. This represents not just an error of omission or a mistaken statement born of a confusion of facts. Rather, to publish that a community is extinct requires an active assertion. The default stance seems to be that in the absence of readily available hard evidence to the contrary, the existence of the community will be denied. This is not the result of some secret pact or hidden publishers' code; the pattern of denial simply comes into play when the demanding mechanisms of the publishing industry fail. Such a publishing travesty is possible only in a situation of nearly complete colonialist domination of the conceptual framework out of which members of the society operate. This suggests an advanced, internalized state of colonialist control of ideational resources in which writers and publishers accept and replicate the mythic self-representations of a colonial power seeking legitimation.

To follow the case of the Yuchi as a specific instance, the question is how modern reference works (Leitch; Waldman; Paterek) could commit errors of such proportions about a people's very existence. It could be argued that the repeated and recent mistaken evaluations of Yuchi existence stem in part from what was then a lack of academic attention to the group. The published literature on the Yuchi from all fields of scholarship, until the mid-1990s, would consist of only about a half dozen substantial pieces supplemented by a number of brief treatments.[17]

However, a more comprehensive explanation is surely to be found through an examination of linkages with the patterns of physical genocide and the history of so-called removal from the Southeast. It is these larger historical movements that demarcate the fundamental nature of Amer-European society in relation to Indigenous peoples. The intellectual erasure of Yuchi and other so-called southeastern peoples corresponds directly to these processes of physical destruction and societal removal. Taken together, these constitute the intermittent waves that characterize the historical assault on Indigenous peoples and properties. The fact that the publishing industry and the academic enterprise reflect the popular notions of Native disappearance is not particularly surprising, as these fields are expressions of the larger society of which they are a part.

This overall pattern of interrelated obscuring, destroying, and denying of Indigenous peoples appears to result from the strange pressures of the illogic of American colonial domination. Indeed, if a society is genocidal, the "disappearance" of targeted peoples may represent a basic solution to the moral, ethical, and political consequences of such extreme actions. As Beral Lang has characterized the Nazi genocide, which was conducted without a formal announcement of the final solution:

> It is clear that an essential part of the policy of the Nazi genocide was precisely the opposite of this, that is, concealment (from Germans

themselves as well as from others). It was an ideal here that, in Himmler's words, the Jews should "disappear," and the implication of this and the other evidence cited is that they should also *seem* to have disappeared, that is, impalpably and mysteriously to have dropped out of existence. (This was evidently also a premise on which the Nazi plan for building a Jewish museum in Prague was based: a museum that was being developed for the study of the history and ways of an extinct group at the same time and by the same people, that the process of making that group extinct was being carried on.) (26)

Although the overall processes of destroying and denying Native Americans were not carried out through a formal plan, the eliminating of peoples and cultures and the minimizing of the assault's realities were being done at the same time that the artifacts of material culture from the disappearing peoples were being amassed into large collections. And now a major collecting effort has focused on obtaining DNA from Indigenous peoples. The Yuchi community was the first group contacted in the United States by the Human Genome Diversity Project (HGDP). This project targeted groups considered at high risk, those for which a final opportunity to collect genetic data carried by "full-blood" community members might be imminent. It is the context of denial of the existence of the Yuchi community that generates such extreme irony in the quest for Yuchi genetic codes. The history of genocide is the key to understanding the resistance to HGDP (see Grounds). Likewise, this larger context of genocide is essential for understanding and interpreting the recurring language of extinction found scattered throughout the published literature. Developing a more complete interpretation of the consequences of cascading colonial extinction requires appreciating the responses to extinction discussed in the closing section.

UP THE ACADEMIC "ROAD TO DISAPPEARANCE"

At the American Anthropological Association's annual meeting (November 1999), I sat in a small, crowded room at the Chicago Hilton and Towers and hesitantly looked over the stapled handout that was being distributed for the next academic presentation. As part of the panel, I knew that the presentation was to be a scholarly report on the Yuchi community, but I was ill prepared for the impact of those few sheets of paper. In my hands were "choreographic diagrams" of one of the special dances that is part of the annual Yuchi Green Corn ceremonial cycle. It felt strangely alienating to see the sixteen individual computer-generated schematic diagrams. Somehow I was failing to get caught up in the expected fascination with the intrigues of scholarly analysis. Instead I had a churning, draining feeling in my abdomen as I listened to this aspect of Yuchi tradition "treated as a cultural artifact," as the presenter remarked. Disconcerted by my visceral reaction and the surreal atmosphere of the panel, I attempted to find an appropriate response. At the end of the presentation I raised the question of the impact of such academic discourse on the Yuchi community and other so-called southeastern peoples. What was meant by the term *social dances*, and does it in any way reflect the terminology used in the actual languages of the Yuchi, Shawnee, Cherokee, or Muskogee Creek peoples? More important, how might such terminology—which is academically useful, providing entree for public discourse—affect those communities whose ceremonial traditions were being categorized, in this case, as mere "social" activities?

Although this had a different feel than sitting in Princeton's Firestone Library and reading that your people are extinct, it was not clear that this situation was much of an improvement. In reality, this was the flip side of published extinction. It represented part of one general mode of response to repeated denials of the Yuchi community. It was also continuous with the long-standing substructure for doing anthropology as the study of the other, although with more of a contemporary surface texture. Somehow I could not entirely avoid the suspicion that this professional meeting, this awkward eventuality was, to some extent, a product of my own doing, some sort of miscarriage of my earlier efforts to spur community members toward greater action in preserving cultural traditions. By pointing out the bizarre published statements of Yuchi extinction, I had hoped to encourage the planning of concrete actions that would belie such pronouncements and result in more intentional efforts to pass the rich Yuchi language and cultural heritage on to younger generations within the community. On the contrary, it seemed that the majority of the collective energy from the community had gone into supporting projects external to the life of the community itself, or worse, that the life of the community was increasingly shaping itself around the interests of the external society even as the community became increasingly targeted for scholarly analysis. Museum and scholarly projects may seem almost irresistible, with their offers of newfound respectability and supposed immortality.

But such community choices seem understandable. Such reactions might be expected from community members who grew up in rural Oklahoma long before the state adopted the slogan "Oklahoma: Native America," at a time when anti-Indian racism often took palpable form. After years of felt pressure toward disappearance, many community members are anxious to have the social standing of the community raised, the heritage proclaimed, and the existence of the Yuchi community affirmed. These desired ends, along with perceived political and economic advantages, have driven the push for formal federal acknowledgment. These overall goals have fostered the development of interrelated strategies for placing the Yuchi community on the road map of public discourse.

Thus, it is within a larger colonial frame that these community concerns have led toward an alignment with the interests of the academic enterprise, resulting in a strange set of trade-offs for the community. On the one hand, a majority group of culturally active Yuchi members has participated in a growing range of museum projects in which the religious traditions of the community are the primary attraction for public display. On the other hand, there has been an increasing involvement with sundry academic research projects with varying degrees of potential benefit for community goals. This willing participation in such projects represents a reversal of attitudes from those of previous generations, toward engaging outsiders by the bearers of traditional knowledge within the community.[18] The result is that the new generation of scholars working on traditional academic themes not only find the needed raw materials for their chosen careers but also receive a strong moral mandate as part of the overcoming of past slights toward the Yuchi nation, and this work may contribute toward a hoped-for federal acknowledgment.

Now no longer moving toward disappearance, the Yuchi community is, as it were, moving in the opposite direction, on a return trip from published oblivion. Once a vanishing, occasionally lamented people, Yuchis are now lauded as a persistent and distinctive cultural subgroup noted by more recent scholarship. The change of direction may have been signaled by an arcane 1989 journal article by Thomas Buckley, which was theoretically creative but offered a strained interpretation, since it was based on the scant available academic publications. It was written without any direct engagement of the community and instead relied on communication with a linguist who had worked in the Yuchi community twenty years earlier. Since that time, a small corps of graduate students has produced three dissertations and at least one master's thesis based on fieldwork with the Yuchi community.

The more recent scholarly publications include discussions that touch on the ceremonial life of the community. Some of this recent discussion deals with marginally sensitive material, such as the publication of "Calling in the Members" (Jackson and Linn 2000). This publication offers two complete dance call "texts," along with linguistic and cultural analysis. It is notable that this information, the "texts" of the dance calls, is presented to a public audience. By contrast, I would not feel free to include this same information on the computer-based Yuchi language materials we are developing for the use of community members. This contrast appears to reflect different sensibilities about what is appropriate for public discourse.

At the more extreme end of the scale on the question of appropriate subject matter are public disclosures of highly sensitive material that is at the heart of Yuchi sacred beliefs. The most shocking and disturbing is the published account of the origin of the unique songs of the Yuchi ceremonial day dances openly discussed by Jackson in a 1999 article. This sensitive material was disclosed without any direct sanction from the community. The reproduced text articulating these sacred beliefs is now posted on the World Wide Web and available at the click of a button to non–community members from any point on the globe. Perhaps equally disturbing is the attempt to identify the academic project with community concerns; hence the title "Indians and Scholars Join Forces to Document the Dance Music of Oklahoma's Yuchi Tribe."[19] Surprisingly, there seems to be no recognition of the distinction between effectively passing traditional knowledge to younger community members and the process of participating in museum and academic projects: "For younger tribal members, these projects have helped to pass on the traditions most valued by community elders" (Jackson, Indians and Scholars, 4). This convenient blurring of the differences between academic ways of knowing and community epistemologies is further represented in a 2000 article Jackson wrote for Southern Folklore. This piece repeatedly makes a direct link between the formal academic process and the activities of community members, who themselves can even be identified as "ethnographers": "The Yuchi ceremonial leaders who have taught me about the richness of their own world are, simultaneously, curious ethnographers when it comes to the beliefs and practices of their native friends and neighbors" (47). By blurring the boundaries between the motivations, goals, and outcomes of the anthropological project and the immediate and long-range goals of the community, certain advantages accrue to those engaged in scholarly investigation. It provides a sanction for the analytical work in the eyes of those doing the research and their academic audience. At the same time, it clouds the critical issue of how best to maintain traditional continuity within the community, thereby facilitating the ongoing participation of community members in the academic research.

Though I would not expect wide agreement with the fullness of my critical stance toward the scholarly project vis-à-vis Indigenous peoples, which I view as a clear extension of acquisitive, deep-rooted colonial patterns, the consequences of engaging in museum and scholarly enterprise seem fairly obvious. If the new goal of current scholarship is to protect and preserve traditional culture, it seems that the greater its involvement with traditional communities, the greater the corrosive influence on the core traditional beliefs and practices. That is, the current scholarship on the Yuchi community poses an even greater threat to cultural continuity than the earlier published denials of the existence of the community. The increasing academic attention calls on community members to accede to external definitions of the traditional beliefs and practices as something exotic, socially untenable, and, ultimately, serving the interests of the larger society. To engage in the processes of public performance and display is to adopt a distanced stance toward one's own cultural heritage. Rather than continuing to hold a direct grasp of that heritage, the embrace of those traditions increasingly becomes mediated through the perceptions and significance accorded by Amer-European society. I can think of little that would be a greater threat to the beating heart of Yuchi sacred traditions.

In making these observations, I am not attempting to minimize the hermeneutical problem intrinsic to any attempt at cross-cultural communication or the increasingly self-critical stance evident in the fields of anthropology, history, and religious studies (which was brought to wider attention with the 1986 work by Clifford and Marcus). Nor am I ignoring the benefits of some of the scholarly work for Native peoples who may mine it for their own purposes.[20] What I am most struck with is the inherent violence of academic inquiry itself—a violence that comes with presuming to expose and analyze Native "cultures." The process becomes like exploratory surgery and is always traumatic for those who come under the academic scalpel. It places the flesh of living communities on theoretical stretchers and involves the vivisection and exposure of the tissues of real individuals and communities. Yet it must be borne in mind who stands to gain the most from such a procedure. Unlike conventional surgery, the aim is not to heal the patient but to benefit the surgeons themselves and those in the operating theater silently nodding approval. Such operations advance the goals of an acquisitive culture, perhaps carrying out a further conquest.

Yuchi people can little afford to support the academic enterprise with the substance of their lives. There is no right of inquiry that automatically opens the way for scholarly investigation. Better to learn the secret, along with Beatrice Medicine (285–86), that there are things we may never write about, privileged information we may never divulge. The reporting of results at academic meetings is no longer a closed-door affair that excludes tribal representatives. Nor is academic work value-neutral (as is still widely believed). There are risks involved in any such exercise, regardless of the intentions of the researchers.

I am not attempting to impugn the good intentions of individuals involved in academic research (see Deloria's positive and hopeful comments in the introduction to the misinformed dictionary noted earlier; Leitch, 17–21). The nature of the study, especially how closely it approaches the core beliefs of the culture, and the particular social situation of a community, such as the size of the population, the strength of the cultural resources within the community, and the standing attitudes toward disclosing cultural information to outsiders, have a bearing on the publication's potential impact on the community under investigation. Rather, I am calling attention to pervasive approaches toward the study of Native American peoples, which seems to have a death of its own and creeps into academic fields that are themselves the peculiar products of the dynamics of a Western culture that has not been overly kind to aboriginal Americans.

The game of ferreting cultural secrets from traditional societies has mostly been done with a few willing informants who felt that cooperation was for the best. By offering this chapter for publication, I fall subject to all the issues of cultural representation. In fact, as a Native American, rather than rising above or being immune to the concerns voiced here, all the issues take on an even greater poignancy precisely because it is my own community involved in my engagement of public discourse. As an interpreter I face the problem of fair and adequate communication. As an informer I bear the risks of cultural betrayal. It is much dicier for me to consider conscripting the lives of my own kinfolk into the service of some arcane theory about the origin of religion or about social transformation among inheritors of "primal" cultures. This ontological root positions me quite differently from, say, the formalistic and heavily theoretical stance espoused by Gill in his 1994 diatribe against Native scholarship.[21]

My fear is that in the inevitable alchemy of the academy, both directions along the academic road to disappearance lead toward the same final destination, albeit by different routes. The pressure is toward disappearance, whether moving up or down. But traversing back up the road seems more dangerous than the original path down the road toward disappearance, since the return trip poses numerous and unforeseen threats to the cultural continuity of the community. In my view, this threatens the existence of the community in a way that the earlier paper denial, though feeding into official denial, social negation, and community isolation, could only begin to anticipate. Whereas the earlier period of academic cloaking primarily challenged the community's relationship to outsiders and posed questions about the self-confidence of the group's identity, the newer period of academic discovery and subsequent cultural mapping forces a realignment of the community in relation to its own internal values and cultural self-understanding. It appeals to community members to become participants in the mining of their own limited cultural resources. Or, to use a more community-oriented metaphor, the community members themselves are being conscripted into the harvesting of a delicate line of rich cultural life that is in danger of being lost instead of regenerated and perpetuated.

Like all discoveries in the context of colonial inequalities, the consequences of being brought into the colonial exchange can be lethal. Community members are asked to participate in processes that are dominated and defined by the needs of colonial society. The fact that these are academic needs does not mean that they are any less important to fulfill. The trade-off is that this means, in some fundamental way, acceptance of the colonial project's definition of your community, yourselves, your heritage. To construe the meaning and significance of ceremonial life in terms of museum display and public performance seems to me to be an inherently dangerous enterprise, one that works against the hope that, somehow, the received self-understandings of traditional ceremonies will survive. Surely this also works against the long-term goals and best intentions of scholars. The seduction for community members is to begin to look at their own community as it is viewed by outsiders, to begin to internalize the perspectives and attitudes about their own traditions, beliefs, convictions, and knowledge. Underlying this shift in community self-deportment is the colonized conception that it has now become okay to hold forth traditional expressions, since they clearly have demonstrable value to a powerful outside society.

With partial support generated from the larger museum project in which Yuchi community members were participating, three Yuchi artists collaborated in "The Solar Fires Exhibition" in downtown Tulsa, Oklahoma. One of the insightful pieces was an installation of a mock Yuchi house by Richard Ray Whitman. On the outside of the tar-paper structure he wrote with chalk: "What did the Yuchis used to eat?" On the inside, viewers found shelves stocked with government-issued commodities. The most insightful remark scrawled in chalk by the artist, whose first language is Yuchi, was expressed in these English words: "From the earliest contact with Europeans, we (the people) have been the object-subject of intense scrutiny. First by adventurers & missionaries seeking to exploit our lands & souls; and more recently by anthropologists & sociologists, filmmakers, literature experts . . . looking for 'mythic' themes or 'exotic' research projects. Despite all this, white culture has consistently failed to perceive all but the more superficial aspects of Indigenous cultures; or worse, it has mistaken the outward consequences of colonialization for 'innate' attributes."

My concern is that through the more recent encroachments by concerned academics, *our community* will begin to mistake participation in the dialectics of colonization for our authentic traditions, the traditional meanings displaced by performance activities for outsiders.

NOTES

1. So the Massachusetts jury ruled in denying the Wampanoag land claim in the 1977 case *Mashpee Tribe v. New Seabury, et al.* when it refused to acknowledge the tribe's continuous existence according to court-stipulated definitions.

2. This work focuses on the story of the Creeks, which is intertwined with that of the Yuchis. Though Yuchis share some similarities with their Creek neighbors in terms of social customs, they speak an entirely unrelated and unique language and have always maintained their independent identity. However, the federal government has officially considered the Yuchis part of the Creek confederacy since the time of removal. Thus, traces of the Yuchi past are sometimes clouded in historical records, as in the case of the documents from the Euchee Mission boarding school, which operated for half a century after opening in 1894 (Foreman, 489).

3. An incomplete tribal roll begun in the late 1940s as part of the Yuchi case presented to the Indian Claims Commission lists the names of 1,300 Yuchi tribal members as of 1956. An updated tribal census is presently under way by the Yuchi Tribal Organization.

4. In fact, I was only recently informed by a colleague who grew up in Yuchi country of her experience with an otherwise well-informed and successful woman who ran a shop in the state of Tennessee, where she not only sold the volume *Tribes that Slumber* but adamantly insisted that Yuchi people were extinct, apparently based on the content of the book.

5. The use of this reference is not to say that historical or archaeological work cannot have some merit. However, here I am focusing on the trajectory of the available literature on the Yuchi people in its excessive emphasis on the past.

6. It should be noted that since writing these poems, Overstreet has found his way to the Yuchi ceremonial grounds and, presumably, a more current perspective.

7. Crawford's papers, along with tape recordings and an extensive lexical file on the Yuchi language, are now found at the American Philosophical Society in Philadelphia. These materials represent the great effort he exerted toward the preservation of the Yuchi language.

8. It should be acknowledged, however, that the entry in Waldman's encyclopedia on the Mohegans makes it clear that despite the erroneous indications of Cooper's *Last of the Mohicans,* the Mohegan people are still around.

9. In an 1848 discussion of "Uchees" and other southeastern nations, it was expressed that "the only vestiges" left of these peoples would soon be "the books of missionaries printed in their idioms, and vocabularies, unsatisfactory but invaluable to science. Too much honor and praise cannot be accorded to those enlightened men, who have devoted themselves to the preservation of these vestiges which are to become the fossil, organic remains of intellectual humanity" (W. B. Hodgson's introduction to Benjamin Hawkin, "Sketch of the Creek Country," in *Collections of the Georgia Historical Society,* vol. 3 [1848]).

10. Francis Jennings pointed out the incredible shift in census figures for the population of the Wampanoag town of Mashpee, Massachusetts, between 1860 and 1870 as it changed from 305 whites and 17 "Coloreds" to 39 whites and 307 "Coloreds." The difference between these sets of figures was the reassignment of the Indian population from one wrong column to another. By the 1970s, the Mashpee and Gay Head Wampanoag groups were forced to go to court to seek acknowledgment of their existence (cf. Tamarin). The Chumash, on the opposite

coast, have felt the impact of arguments that their ethnicity is the by-product of outside resources. They have dealt with the insinuations of scholarly statements such as: "no one is likely to dedicate a long term project to the contemporary 'Chumash,' simply because they are so few and there are few, if any, cultural elements left"; "The case of the Chumash demonstrates the power of outside resources to actually construct an ethnic entity where there had been none before. . . . in fact they learned of these cultural elements as adults from anthropologists" (O'Conner, 11). I take it that O'Conner's statements were intended as an "in-house" commentary that was published in a trade bulletin and therefore was not expected to reach the Chumash themselves. The article completely ignores any need to document the presumed Chumash cultural extinction, which is instead taken as a known "fact" delivered in a kind of wink-and-nudge manner. The problem with this kind of discourse is illustrated by the young Chumash girl who told her mother after returning from school, "I just had to let them know that we're still here. They always talk about us as if we don't exist anymore" (Gorman, 6). Compare also Bernard Fontana's "Savage Anthropologists and Unvanishing Indians of the American Southwest."

11. Indeed, the slighting of the existence of Native American communities is a recurring oversight. I had the awkward experience of responding to a paper presented at the American Academy of Religion's annual meeting that mistakenly spoke of the Mandan as a vanished group: "And I want to talk about them during an earlier time period because today, the Mandan have been wiped out due to early Euro-American smallpox plagues along the upper Missouri River in the early 1800s" (Irwin, 2).

12. Hicks and Handler have effectively contended that anthropological work, generally reflecting attitudes in the larger "American society," has had little effect on public policy concerning Native Americans. Given the dismal record of these governmental policies, Hicks and Handler's conclusions offer little consolation to anthropologists. However, I am concerned here with the effect of published academic perspectives on the specific application of policies to individual tribal groups.

13. Beyond the strictly academic sphere, the realm of art is cluttered with images such as that of the lonely, slump-shouldered brave atop a worn horse called "End of the Trail," which often appears on mantels in Native American homes in eastern Oklahoma. On a broader scale across American society, one must ask, for example, what messages are being projected about Native Americans by the perennially popular image of the wooden (unchanging) Indian found in shops scattered from coast to coast?

14. It is these concerns that motivated Takaki to write A Different Mirror.

15. Prepublished version of manuscript obtained from Mose Cahwee, committee member on Yuchi traditions instructional project.

16. As the well-known anthropologist Raymond Fogelson seemed to insist in a reaction to my presentation on this theme at the American Society of Ethnohistory annual meeting in Kalamazoo, Michigan, in 1995.

17. Since the ethnographic work by Frank Speck (1909, 1911) after the turn of the twentieth century, most of the publications have arisen from the riddle of Yuchi as an isolate language (Ballard 1975; Crawford 1973, 1979; Elmendorf 1964; Haas 1951, 1964; Wolff 1948, 1951). The study of the Yuchi language was the initial reason for Speck's traveling to Oklahoma in 1904 (his linguistic notebooks are presently in the National Anthropological Archives), though nothing significant was published on the language until the work of Günter Wagner (1931, 1934).

Even the ethnographic work of Crawford (1972) and Ballard (1978) was inspired through their linguistic interests. Another theoretical problem that has generated literature on the Yuchi has to do with their identification and their place in colonial history (Swanton 1919, 1922, 1952; Crane 1918; Juricek 1964; Mason 1963). The Yuchi have also been studied as the greeters of Columbus (Hollander 1951) and identified as prime bearers of pre-Columbian, transoceanic high culture, as noted earlier (Mahan 1983; cf. Mahan 1970; Gordon 1971). Beyond references in regional or general studies (Swanton 1925, 1946; Milling 1940; Debo 1941; Lewis and Kneberg 1958; Hudson 1976), there had been only one brief article (Foreman 1960) on Yuchi history per se, which was motivated by a desire to acquire for the Oklahoma Historical Society the materials collected by Yuchi leader S. W. Brown, Jr. (letter from Carolyn Thomas Foreman in Grant Foreman Collection, Oklahoma Historical Society, Oklahoma City).

18. This shift in stance toward the demands of Amer-European society runs parallel to the more well-known pattern of eventual compliance with the conversion efforts of missionaries. It was only after economic, military, and spatial oppression and assault had been carried out under classic colonialism that communities became willing to adopt such major cultural changes (e.g., Salisbury, 35). For Yuchis in the contemporary context, it is no longer the material interests required by colonial domination that define relations with Amer-European society; rather, it is the eccentricities of Yuchi cultural production that are most desired in the public market.

19. Simply recording the songs has little value to community members, who could, of course, record the songs on their own if making tapes was a chosen instrument for teaching. However, such recordings do have enormous value for scholars who are seeking to develop academic analyses of such materials.

20. Frank Speck's field techniques among the Yuchi were often tactless. For example, at the 1905 Green Corn Ceremony at Sand Creek, he discharged a flash in the night to take photographs of the opening dance without giving any warning or seeking permission for his intrusive activity (Speck, *Ethnology*, 118). His coarse efforts often met with resistance. As Speck complained in a letter from Oklahoma back to Pennsylvania about the Yuchi's refusal to make pottery samples for him: "They ridicule the idea at this season [winter] and persist in referring me to an old lady who died" (letter dated 21 February 1908, Speck Files, American Philosophical Society, Philadelphia). Yet his work has had the benefit of registering certain aspects of the Yuchi past that continue to be of interest to tribal members.

21. As a summarizing illustration of the issues intrinsic to scholarly work among Native peoples, I turn to an incident with James Mooney. In 1891 he unceremoniously unearthed two Yuchis who had been buried near Tahlequah, Oklahoma (*Fort Smith Weekly Elevator*, 3 April 1891) and shipped the remains along with accompanying "artifacts" back to the Smithsonian in order to preserve these "relics" of the Yuchi past for scientific investigation. The Yuchi had only arrived in Indian Territory during the lifetime of the prior generation, and these burials of 1840 (Mooney, 385) were only fifty years old. Close family members were likely still living, but Mooney was intent on salvaging the bones of a Yuchi past and ignored the living community. By removing the remains from their ritually fashioned human context, Mooney was effectively translating them into the idiom of his own meaning structure in the service of an imagined immortality found in the higher goals embodied in Western science. For many of us, such ethnocentric actions grate on our present sensitivities. Yet I am convinced that much of our

current work merely reflects a greater subtlety gained over the past hundred years for fossilizing living people in their past. We have developed a greater sophistication for detaching fragments from ongoing communities to store them on their assigned shelf in our academic mausoleums.

REFERENCES

Ballard, William L[ewis]. "Aspects of Yuchi Morphonology." In *Studies in Southeastern Indian Languages*, ed. James M. Crawford. Athens: University of Georgia Press, 1975.
———. *Yuchi Green Corn Ceremonial: Form and Meaning*. Los Angeles: UCLA American Indian Studies Center, 1978.
Buckley, Thomas. "The Articulation of Gender Symmetry in Yuchi Culture." *Semiotica*, vol. 74 (1989), 3–4, 289–311.
Clifford, James, and George E. Marcus, eds. *Writing Culture: The Poetics and Politics of Ethnography*. Los Angeles: University of California Press, 1986.
Crane, Verner W. "An Historical Note on the Westo Indians." *American Anthropologist*, new ser., vol. 20 (1918), 331–37.
Crawford, James M. Manuscript, 1972. Crawford Papers, American Philosophical Society, Philadelphia.
———. "Timucua and Yuchi: Two Language Isolates of the Southeast." In *The Languages of Native America: Historical and Comparative Assessment*, ed. Lyle Campbell and Marianne Mithun. Austin: University of Texas Press, 1979.
———. "Yuchi Phonology." *International Journal of American Linguistics*, vol. 29 (1973), 173–79.
Debo, Angie. *The Road to Disappearance*. Norman: University of Oklahoma Press, 1941.
Deer, Ada E. "Summary under the Criteria and Evidence for Proposed Finding against Federal Acknowledgment of the Yuchi Tribal Organization, Inc.: Prepared in response to a petition submitted to the Assistant Secretary of the Interior–Indian Affairs that this group exists as an Indian tribe." Approved 11 July 1995.
Deloria, Vine Jr. *God Is Red*. New York: Dell, 1973.
Elmendorf, William W. "Item and Set Comparison in Yuchi, Siouan, and Yukian." *International Journal of American Linguistics*, vol. 30 (1964), 328–40.
Fontana, Bernard L. "Savage Anthropologists and Unvanishing Indians of the American Southwest." *Indian Historian*, vol. 6 (winter 1973), 5–8, 32.
Foreman, Carolyn Thomas. "The Yuchi: Children of the Sun." *Chronicles of Oklahoma*, vol. 37 (1960), 480–96.
Gill, Sam D. "The Academic Study of Religion." *Journal of the American Academy of Religion*, vol. 62 (1994), 965–75.
Gordon, Cyrus H. *Before Columbus: Pre-Columbian Links Between the Old World and America*. New York: Crown Publishers, 1971.
Gorman, Gary. "New Age Chumash." *Los Angeles Times*, 10 June 1990, B1, 6.
Grounds, Richard A. "The Yuchi Community and the Human Genome Diversity Project." *Cultural Survival Quarterly* (summer 1996), 64–68.
Haas, Mary R. "Athapaskan, Tlingit, Yuchi, and Siouan." *Congreso Internacional de Americanistas*, 35th (1962), Mexico. *Actas y Memorias*, Tomo 2. Mexico, 1964.
———. "The Proto-Gulf Word for Water (with Notes on Siouan-Yuchi)." *International Journal of American Linguistics*, vol. 17 (1951), 71–79.

Hicks, George L., and Mark J. Handler. "Ethnicity, Public Policy, and Anthropologists." In *Applied Anthropology in America*, 2nd ed., ed. Elizabeth M. Eddy and William L. Partridge. New York: Columbia University Press, 1987.

Hollander, Herbert. "Greeters of Columbus May Be Oklahomans." *Seattle Times*, 7 October 1951, 10.

Hudson, Charles. *The Southeastern Indians*. Knoxville: University of Tennessee Press, 1976.

Irwin, Lee. "Native American Epistemology: Traditions of the High Plains and River-Valleys." Paper presented at American Academy of Religion annual meeting, Chicago, 1994.

Jackson, Jason B. "Indians and Scholars Join Forces to Document the Dance Music of Oklahoma's Yuchi Tribe." *American Folk Life Center News*, vol. 21 (spring 1999), 1–5.

———. "Signaling the Creator: Indian Football as Ritual Performance among the Yuchi and their Neighbors." *Southern Folklore*, vol. 57 (2000), 33–64.

Jackson, Jason B., and Mary S. Linn. "Calling in the Members: Linguistic Form and Cultural Context in a Yuchi Ritual Speech Genre." *Anthropological Linguistics*, vol. 42 (2000), 61–80.

Jennings, Francis. "A Growing Partnership: Historians, Anthropologists, and American Indian History." *Ethnohistory*, vol. 29 (1982), 21–34.

Juricek, John T. "The Westo Indians." *Ethnohistory*, vol. 11 (1964), 134–73.

Kilpatrick, James J. "The Writer's Art." *Seattle Times*, 22 August 1999, L4.

Lang, Berel. *Act and Idea in the Nazi Genocide*. Chicago: University of Chicago Press, 1990.

Leitch, Barbara A. *A Concise Dictionary of Indian Tribes of North America*. Algonac, Mich.: Reference Publications, 1979.

Lewis, Thomas M. N., and Madeline Kneberg. *Tribes That Slumber: Indian Times in the Tennessee Region*. Knoxville: University of Tennessee Press, 1958.

Limerick, Patricia Nelson. *The Legacy of Conquest: The Unbroken Past of the American West*. New York: W. W. Norton, 1987.

Lossing, Benson J. *Lossing's New History of the United States, from the Discovery of the American Continent to the Present Time*. New York: Gay Brothers & Co., 1881.

Mahan, Joseph Buford Jr. "Identification of the Tsoyaha Waeno, Builders of Temple Mounds." Ph.D. diss., University of North Carolina–Chapel Hill, 1970.

———. *The Secret: America in World History before Columbus*. Columbus, Ga.: Author, 1983.

Martin, Bill. "Housing Project Bid Suffers Narrow Loss." *Sapulpa Herald*, 9 December 1980, 1, 2.

Mason, Carol Irwin. "A Reconsideration of Westo-Yuchi Identification." *American Anthropologist*, vol. 65 (1963), 550–51.

Medicine, Beatrice. "Learning to Be an Anthropologist and Remaining 'Native.'" In *Applied Anthropology in America*, 2nd ed., ed. Elizabeth M. Eddy and William L. Partridge. New York: Columbia University Press, 1987.

Milling, Chapman J. *Red Carolinians*. Chapel Hill: University of North Carolina Press, 1940.

Mitchell, Lee Clark. *Witnesses to a Banishing America: The Nineteenth-Century Response*. Princeton, N.J.: Princeton University Press, 1981.

Mooney, James. "Myths of the Cherokee." *Nineteenth Annual Report of the Bureau of American Ethnology*. Washington, D.C.: Government Printing Office, 1900.

Moore, John H. "The MVSKOKE National Question in Oklahoma." *Science and Society*, vol. 52 (1988), 163–90.

O'Conner, Mary L. "Environmental Impact Review and the Construction of Contemporary Chumash Ethnicity." *NAPA* [National Association for the Practice of Anthropology] *Bulletin,* no. 8, *Negotiating Ethnicity: The Impact of Anthropological Theory and Practice,* ed. Susan Emley Keefe, 1989.

The Oklahoma Indian and Nature Guide. Southwest Center for Human Relations Studies, University of Oklahoma, with the Oklahoma Curriculum Improvement Commission, 1977.

Overstreet, William Keith. "'Marriage of Earth and Sky': A Collection of Poems." Manuscript, 1990.

Paterek, Josephine. *Encyclopedia of American Indian Costume.* Santa Barbara, Calif.: ABC-CLIO, 1994.

Pearson, Julie. "Invisible Too Long: A Yuchi Woman Who Would Not Let Her Tribe Be Forgotten." *Oklahoma Today* (May–June 1992), 23–26.

Peniere, J. A. Extract of letter to General Jackson, dated 15 July 1821, in *Letter from the Secretary of War, to the Chairman of the Committee on Indian Affairs, Transmitting Sundry Documents and Correspondences in Relation to the Indians of Florida.* Washington, D.C.: Gales and Seaton, 1823.

"Policy Gives Bush Administration Power to Declare Tribes Extinct." *Tulsa World,* 3 July 1992, A-14.

Porter, Frank W. III. "An Historical Perspective on Nonrecognized American Indian Tribes." In *Nonrecognized American Indian Tribes: An Historical and Legal Perspective,* ed. Frank W. Porter III. Occasional Papers Series, no. 7. Chicago: Newberry Library, 1983.

[Ransom, James Birchett]. *Osceola; Or, Fact and Fiction: A Tale of the Seminole War. By a Southerner.* New York: Harper and Brothers, 1838.

Rogin, Michael Paul. *Fathers and Children: Andrew Jackson and the Subjugation of the American Indian.* New York: Alfred A. Knopf, 1975.

Salisbury, Neal. "Red Puritans: The 'Praying Indians' of Massachusetts Bay and John Eliot." *William and Mary Quarterly,* 3rd ser., vol. 31 (1974), 27–54.

Sheehan, Bernard W. *Seeds of Extinction: Jeffersonian Philanthropy and the American Indian.* Chapel Hill: University of North Carolina Press, 1973.

Speck, F. G. *Ceremonial Songs of the Creek and Yuchi Indians,* with music transcribed by Jacob D. Sapir. University of Pennsylvania Museum Anthropological Publications, vol. 1. Philadelphia: University Museum, 1911.

———. *Ethnology of the Yuchi Indians.* University of Pennsylvania Museum Anthropological Publications, vol. 1. Philadelphia: University Museum, 1909.

———. "Yuchi." In *Handbook of North American Indians North of Mexico,* U.S. Bureau of American Ethnology *Bulletin,* no. 73, pt. 2. Washington, D.C.: Government Printing Office, 1910.

Swanton, John R. *Early History of the Creek Indians and Their Neighbors.* U.S. Bureau of American Ethnology *Bulletin,* no. 73 (1922), 184–91, 286–312.

———. "Identity of the Westo Indians." *American Anthropologist,* new ser., vol. 21 (1919), 213–16.

———. *The Indian Tribes of North America.* U.S. Bureau of American Ethnology *Bulletin,* no. 145 (1952), 103–4, 116–20 (main entry), 152, 174, 229, 307.

———. *The Indians of the Southeastern United States.* U.S. Bureau of American Ethnology *Bulletin,* no. 137 (1946).

———. *Social Organization and Social Usages of the Indians of the Creek Confederacy.* U.S. Bureau of American Ethnology *Annual Report,* vol. 42 (1925), 23–472.

Takaki, Ronald. *A Different Mirror: A History of Multicultural America.* New York: Little, Brown, 1993.

Tamarin, Alfred H. *We Have Not Vanished: Eastern Indians of the United States.* Chicago: Follett Publishing, 1974.

Wagner, Günter. "Yuchi." In *Handbook of American Indian Languages,* ed. Franz Boas, pt. 3. New York: Columbia University Press, 1934.

———. *Yuchi Tales.* Publications of the American Ethnological Society, ed. Franz Boas, vol. 13. New York: G. E. Stechert, 1931.

Waldman, Carl. *Encyclopedia of Native American Tribes.* New York: Facts on File, 1988.

Wolff, Hans. "Yuchi Phonemes and Morphemes, with Special Reference to Person Markers." *International Journal of American Linguistics,* vol. 14 (1948), 240–43.

———. "Yuchi Text with Analysis." *International Journal of American Linguistics,* vol. 17 (1951), 48–53.

Wright, Muriel H. *A Guide to the Indian Tribes of Oklahoma.* Norman: University of Oklahoma Press, 1951.

The Passage of Generations
Vine Deloria, Jr. (Standing Rock Sioux)

When my father died in 1990 at age eighty-eight, I spent some quiet moments contemplating his life. It occurred to me that he represented a generation so remote from my upbringing as to be almost prehistoric. Sitting Bull had been killed eleven years before his birth, and there were still highly volatile feelings at Standing Rock between the traditional people and those Indians who recognized the radical changes occurring and were trying to adjust to them. No cars, telephones, or refrigerators existed in that part of South Dakota, and store-bought clothes were just making their appearance in many places on the reservation. Most important, it seemed to me, my father was of that generation of Indians who were not U.S. citizens until they were adults. He had been classified as a noncitizen until he was twenty-three years old.

In the closing decades of the twentieth century, generations seemed to change with the increasing complexity of our technology, so that several complete changes in society separate me from my children, and even more differences exist between me and my grandchildren. Although I feel close to many people who contributed to this collection, I recognize that they represent several new generations whose point of view and motivations I can barely understand. All of them are capable of offering significant intellectual leadership for Indian people in the years ahead, and most of them have already made important contributions. I thank them for the compliments, most of which are not deserved, and for helping me hide the quirks in my personality and the many failures I have experienced along the way.

When I entered Indian affairs, the Indian world was very simple. Two organizations represented Indians—the National Congress of American Indians and the National Indian Youth Council. The League of Nations—Pan-American Indians was in its final phase, although I tried my best, in the afterword in *Custer*, to boost its status. The Association of American Indian Affairs and the older Indian Rights Association were the dominant non-Indian organizations that, along with several churches, controlled Indian affairs. Today we have a multitude of Indian organizations, one for each interest or profession in which there are a significant number of people. We now have spokespeople in buffalo raising, psychology, museums, law, the environment, and a bewildering number of educational groups. Massive forests are leveled annually to provide paper for the memos and position papers needed to fuel this large beehive of activity.

Indian affairs can now be said to consist of several networks in which energies are being channeled. Gaming consumes the time and energy of many small tribes located near urban areas and has become a complicated area of its own. Another network is the bevy of professional groups that are working nationally on problems in their interest areas, primarily educators of all kinds and the professional groups. A third specialized area consists of the Indians within the Beltway who incessantly seek contracts to represent tribes in Washington and work for a variety of government agencies. They form a society with virtually no relationship to the people in Indian communities, and their names appear frequently as candidates for federal jobs at the beginning of each new administration. Finally, there are the reservation people and the lands they live on. During most of the past century, these people were the focus of all federal legislation; today, they are beneficiaries and victims of the activities of the other networks in Indian affairs.

When I came into national Indian affairs, I was fortunate to know some of the outstanding Indian leaders of the century who were building new economies and institutions in spite of the sporadic efforts of Congress and various administrations to terminate Indian rights and benefits. Although hardly any of them had more than a high school education, they had spent countless hours devouring Cohen's *Handbook of Federal Indian Law,* and they knew it almost word for word. Although they could not easily articulate complex doctrines of law, they were skilled politicians and used legal concepts in their political activities in sophisticated ways. They shared a common belief that when any tribe or right was in peril, all the tribes were in danger. That sentiment seems not to have descended to the present generation.

Litigation and legislation in those days were simple in comparison with what we have today. Look at the Indian Reorganization Act—it was written in simple language, short paragraphs for the most part, and with sufficient ambiguity to enable Indians and the bureaucrats a larger undefined arena in which they could struggle to develop consensus on interpretations and confirm the rights and benefits of the tribes. Today, a simple statement of purpose and a few definitions take up the same amount of space. Litigation today often emphasizes the interpretation of the fictional intent of Congress that courts read into complex sections and subsections. With tribes eligible for many federal programs that are available to other citizens through state, county, and city programs, we have a difficult time tiptoeing through the mass of authorizing provisions to determine exactly how a political entity like a tribe stands in the constitutional framework.

I wonder if those old chairmen could have handled the complexity of today. I certainly cannot do so. They always sought to understand the underlying principles of policy and could quickly cut through bureaucratic rhetoric to gain their objectives. Their melding of legal concepts and political necessities was superb. Most impressive, however, were the close ties they had with reservation people. They could afford to take chances because they understood what their people wanted. It was not a case of simply getting grants funded and money flowing to the reservations.

In a fundamental way, those old people were also artists of a high caliber. They sought to find a symmetry and logic in law and were puzzled at the inconsistencies in decisions of the state and federal courts that did not fall within the boundaries of precedent and logic. So committed were they to understanding legal nuances that they permanently turned my attention to the quest to find a consistent logical format in which federal Indian law might be understood by the rank-and-file Indian people who will someday be serving on tribal councils or making policy decisions regarding Indian rights and programs. For several decades I have more or less nibbled at the edges of some of the doctrines of federal Indian law, continually searching for a format in which I could articulate a view of law that could be used by Indians as a means of correcting the tendencies of the courts to reach ad hoc conclusions.

The most successful efforts to bring consistency to Indian law in my lifetime have been the activities surrounding treaties. I refer primarily to the fishing rights struggle in the Pacific Northwest, followed by the same struggle in the Great Lakes area, and then followed by tribes seeking to confirm water rights on some of the western rivers. Unfortunately, this movement has too often depended on the small tribes and, within them, a few families who were determined to exercise their treaty rights. I often wonder what Indian affairs would be like if the large land-based tribes had been aggressive about treaty provisions in the past four decades. Would we have a much different perspective on self-government and the inherent powers of Indian tribes?

Federal Indian law should be tightly embraced by and subject to the critiques of historians. Federal courts in particular pay little attention to the historical context in which they decide cases. The most casual remarks become definitive statements about American and Indian history, and determining congressional "intent" has become an exercise in fiction writing. For the Supreme Court to suggest that Congress has always had plenary power over Indian tribes is quite a distance from the actual historical events in the federal-Indian relationship. Many tribes were completely independent from the United States politically until late in the nineteenth century. Certainly the 1854–1857 series of treaties in the Pacific Northwest made by Isaac Stevens partially sought to restrict the Indian trade with

Vancouver Island, which was a British possession. Some of the Choctaws, when told that their governments were being abolished and their schools closed, proposed to migrate to Nicaragua as a nation.

Treaties have always been more than a backdrop against which other federal policy provisions were to be understood. When the Seven Major Crimes Act became law, the language clearly stated that it was applicable to all Indians. It was never enforced or cited with respect to the Five Civilized Tribes, however, indicating that general legislation probably could not override specific treaty provisions. One can study the various treaty provisions and find that each tribe has been treated as a nation not subject to anything more than is ceded in their treaties and agreements. Yet the notion persists that a decision unfavorable to one tribe is applicable to all other tribes, whereas a favorable decision is not taken to have the same applicability.

In spite of horrendous departures from precedent based on temporary notions of reform, such as the allotment act and the termination movement, the principle of consent of the governed has generally been held to describe the continuing relationship of Indians and the United States. Today, tribes are consulted on all proposed legislation that would affect them. Granted, often the motive is to escape a discussion of the legislation in the media, but there is a genuine effort to reach agreement with tribal governments on changes in their rights and status.

Unfortunately, we have taken as a given the belief that the United States must obtain our consent for legislation affecting us. Few people realize that this attitude comes out of the poverty program era, when the slogan was that poor people knew better than anyone how to solve poverty. Thus consent is more a habit than a legal necessity. Until we develop the scholarly literature that can transform consent into a legal requirement, we will not have made much progress in Indian law. Contemporary Indian leaders must understand the necessity of producing a large body of literature that will inform law clerks, judges, and justices of the Indian side of the story. We cannot continue to tell our story piecemeal as legal briefs give us the opportunity to do so.

Indian religions have become one of the most popular topics in contemporary life. Lacking any serious emotional experiences in mainstream Christianity, many people have embarked on spiritual quests of their own, examining and adopting a wide variety of rituals, beliefs, and practices. Although Eastern religions have gathered numerous converts or appropriators, tribal religions seem to provide religious novelty *and* a sense of personal authenticity that people feel they need. We therefore see efforts on a wide scale to incorporate tribal religious ceremonies into the lives of interested individuals. This practice is regarded by many Indians as a theft, while others believe that Indian religions should be available to everyone. Therein lies the intellectual dilemma of the future for Indians.

Far too many people view religion as a set of beliefs and ceremonial practices handed down through generations. In today's world, most of the beliefs have become outmoded, and the ceremonies have become habits with considerable accommodation to secularism. Thus we say that Western religions are linear, while Indian traditions emphasize the circle or spiral. But these figures are merely convenient frameworks to enable us to illustrate the underlying realities in a comprehensible format. As I have grown older, I have come to realize that the powers possessed by the great spiritual leaders stand on a much more fundamental foundation than mere historical practices. They give us a glimpse of a more complex and yet ultimately simpler reality than we face in our daily lives. The old people understood that; we moderns do not understand.

Now I always refer my thoughts to some of the recorded stories about the powers of medicine men. These stories record sacred events that certainly violate the laws of physics and raise questions about the nature of time and space. But ultimately those ideas must be seen as another convenience we use to make sense of our daily routines and relationships. I think here of Last Horse's ability to split a threatening thunderstorm to allow his people to continue their dance. Or Black Elk lost in a snowstorm, hearing the coyote telling him where he could find game to feed his people. I think of Roman Nose riding casually back and forth in front of the soldiers, encouraging them to fire at him until the breaches of their rifles were too hot to handle cartridges properly, so that his warriors could charge them.

Any particular anecdote can be turned aside by claiming that it was a misunderstanding, that the oral tradition had changed the story to make it more spectacular, or that the event, while accurate, represented a happy coincidence. But calling something a coincidence does not explain it; it simply classifies the event to make it a harmless thing we can avoid understanding. Once a number of these things are collected and analyzed, coincidence vanishes, the oral tradition is seen as the carrier of important data, and we are confronted with the reality of the fact that these old people knew a greatly expanded universe filled with entities that we presently deny.

In science we are faced with some revolutionary and perhaps unpleasant facts. Everyday heresy grows closer to the establishment with regard to evolution. Reasonably bright thinkers are now challenging parts of the Darwinian paradigm from different angles and pointing out that Darwinism does not deal with the empirical facts as we have uncovered them. It is increasingly looking like our planet has had several blossoms of life, with at least eight major catastrophes followed by biotic systems that were complete and had an integrity to themselves. Absent the discovery of some new mechanism, we seem to have little choice but to abandon the Western-Christian idea of a single creation or evolution and opt instead for sporadic events in which the earth itself brings forth a whole new complex of organic life.

Indian traditions may become an important part of the new scientific paradigm that will seek to give a better explanation of the history of our planet. Here, even the star migrations told by some tribes may play an important role in our thinking. Sadly, we have only fragments of the knowledge our people once possessed, so it will take an alert and aggressive generation of Indians who can articulate tribal traditions and refuse to surrender our heritage, who can make Indian knowledge important to others. I now take seriously the beliefs of some tribes that a time existed when you could change your body shape and experience what the birds and animals experience in their bodies. Perhaps each time the earth renews itself we have "plastic" conditions in which life takes its shapes and relationships.

I wish I had another twenty years of work ahead of me, since the coming decades will be filled with the opportunity to do some great things. I have never believed that I could do the proper scholarly work to make permanent changes in our body of knowledge. Consequently, my books should be regarded as simple sketches of general areas and topics that might serve as frameworks for others coming after me to fill in with footnotes and statistics. I have most often seen my work as merely clearing away some of the silly ideas and leaving a better landscape for future development.

Today we have thousands of educated young people who can make a great difference in how our species understands itself. I am convinced that the world and everything we have are ultimately spiritual, manifested briefly as matter, but subject to directives having greater cosmic significance than we have ever dreamed. It is truly ironic, and infinitely sad, that in little more than a century, the Great Plains is now emptying out and is best suited for a massive buffalo-wildlife pasture. So why did so many people have to suffer, starve, and die to play out a doomed scenario? What other things have been done that, after the passage of time, will be seen as equally futile? Will the great cities of the Southwest become ruins of a contemporary Anasazi?

I do appreciate my colleagues and friends putting this book together as a way of honoring me. It is a bit like a prolonged dialogue and a bit like a testimonial. We are all carriers of ideas, and we have a responsibility to always move forward with whatever the previous generation has given us to use. In that sense, I hope I have contributed something toward the success and accomplishments of future generations of Indian people.

United Nations Draft Declaration on the Rights of Indigenous Peoples

36th Meeting

26 August 1994

Affirming that indigenous peoples are equal in dignity and rights to all other peoples, while recognizing the right of all peoples to be different, to consider themselves different, and to be respected as such,

Affirming also that all peoples contribute to the diversity and richness of civilizations and cultures, which constitute the common heritage of humankind,

Affirming further that all doctrines, policies and practices based on or advocating superiority of peoples or individuals on the basis of national origin, racial, religious, ethnic or cultural differences are racist, scientifically false, legally invalid, morally condemnable and socially unjust,

Reaffirming also that indigenous peoples, in the exercise of their rights, should be free from discrimination of any kind,

Concerned that indigenous peoples have been deprived of their human rights and fundamental freedoms, resulting, *inter alia*, in their colonization and dispossession of their lands, territories and resources, thus preventing them from exercising, in particular, their right to development in accordance with their own needs and interests,

Recognizing the urgent need to respect and promote the inherent rights and characteristics of indigenous peoples, especially their rights to their lands, territories and resources, which derive from their political, economic and social structures and from their cultures, spiritual traditions, histories and philosophies,

Welcoming the fact that indigenous peoples are organizing themselves for political, economic, social and cultural enhancement and in order to bring an end to all forms of discrimination and oppression wherever they occur,

Convinced that control by indigenous peoples over developments affecting them and their lands, territories and resources will enable them to maintain and strengthen their institutions, cultures and traditions, and to promote their development in accordance with their aspirations and needs,

Recognizing also that respect for indigenous knowledge, cultures and traditional practices contributes to sustainable and equitable development and proper management of the environment,

Emphasizing the need for demilitarization of the lands and territories of indigenous peoples, which will contribute to peace, economic and social progress and development, understanding and friendly relations among nations and peoples of the world,

Recognizing in particular the right of indigenous families and communities to retain shared responsibility for the upbringing, training, education and wellbeing of their children,

Recognizing also that indigenous peoples have the right freely to determine their relationships with States in a spirit of coexistence, mutual benefit and full respect,
Considering that treaties, agreements and other arrangements between States and indigenous peoples are properly matters of international concern and responsibility,
Acknowledging that the Charter of the United Nations, the International Covenant on Economic, Social and Cultural Rights and the International Covenant on Civil and Political Rights affirm the fundamental importance of the right of self-determination of all peoples, by virtue of which they freely determine their political status and freely pursue their economic, social and cultural development,
Bearing in mind that nothing in this Declaration may be used to deny any peoples their right of self-determination,
Encouraging States to comply with and effectively implement all international instruments, in particular those related to human rights, as they apply to indigenous peoples, in consultation and cooperation with the peoples concerned,
Emphasizing that the United Nations has an important and continuing role to play in promoting and protecting the rights of indigenous peoples,
Believing that this Declaration is a further important step forward for the recognition, promotion and protection of the rights and freedoms of indigenous peoples and in the development of relevant activities of the United Nations system in this field,
Solemnly proclaims the following United Nations Declaration on the Rights of Indigenous Peoples:

PART I
Article 1
Indigenous peoples have the right to the full and effective enjoyment of all human rights and fundamental freedoms recognized in the Charter of the United Nations, the Universal Declaration of Human Rights and international human rights law.

Article 2
Indigenous individuals and peoples are free and equal to all other individuals and peoples in dignity and rights, and have the right to be free from any kind of adverse discrimination, in particular that based on their indigenous origin or identity.

Article 3
Indigenous peoples have the right of self-determination. By virtue of that right they freely determine their political status and freely pursue their economic, social and cultural development.

Article 4
Indigenous peoples have the right to maintain and strengthen their distinct political, economic, social and cultural characteristics, as well as their legal systems, while retaining their rights to participate fully, if they so choose, in the political, economic, social and cultural life of the State.

Article 5
Every indigenous individual has the right to a nationality.

PART II
Article 6
Indigenous peoples have the collective right to live in freedom, peace and security as distinct peoples and to full guarantees against genocide or any other act
of violence, including the removal of indigenous children from their families
and communities under any pretext.
In addition, they have the individual rights to life, physical and mental
integrity, liberty and security of person.

Article 7
Indigenous peoples have the collective and individual right not to be subjected
to ethnocide and cultural genocide, including prevention of and redress for:
(a) Any action which has the aim or effect of depriving them of their integrity as
distinct peoples, or of their cultural values or ethnic identities;
(b) Any action which has the aim or effect of dispossessing them of their lands,
territories or resources;
(c) Any form of population transfer which has the aim or effect of violating or
undermining any of their rights;
(d) Any form of assimilation or integration by other cultures or ways of life
imposed on them by legislative, administrative or other measures;
(e) Any form of propaganda directed against them.

Article 8
Indigenous peoples have the collective and individual right to maintain and
develop their distinct identities and characteristics, including the right to identify themselves as indigenous and to be recognized as such.

Article 9
Indigenous peoples and individuals have the right to belong to an indigenous
community or nation, in accordance with the traditions and customs of the community or nation concerned. No disadvantage of any kind may arise from the
exercise of such a right.

Article 10
Indigenous peoples shall not be forcibly removed from their lands or territories.
No relocation shall take place without the free and informed consent of the
indigenous peoples concerned and after agreement on just and fair compensation and, where possible, with the option of return.

Article 11
Indigenous peoples have the right to special protection and security in periods
of armed conflict.
States shall observe international standards, in particular the Fourth Geneva
Convention of 1949, for the protection of civilian populations in circumstances
of emergency and armed conflict, and shall not:
(a) Recruit indigenous individuals against their will into the armed forces and,
in particular, for use against other indigenous peoples;
(b) Recruit indigenous children into the armed forces under any circumstances;
(c) Force indigenous individuals to abandon their lands, territories or means of
subsistence, or relocate them in special centres for military purposes;
(d) Force indigenous individuals to work for military purposes under any discriminatory conditions.

PART III
Article 12
Indigenous peoples have the right to practise and revitalize their cultural traditions and customs. This includes the right to maintain, protect and develop the past, present and future manifestations of their cultures, such as archaeological and historical sites, artifacts, designs, ceremonies, technologies and visual and performing arts and literature, as well as the right to the restitution of cultural, intellectual, religious and spiritual property taken without their free and informed consent or in violation of their laws, traditions and customs.

Article 13
Indigenous peoples have the right to manifest, practise, develop and teach their spiritual and religious traditions, customs and ceremonies; the right to maintain, protect, and have access in privacy to their religious and cultural sites; the right to the use and control of ceremonial objects; and the right to the repatriation of human remains.
States shall take effective measures, in conjunction with the indigenous peoples concerned, to ensure that indigenous sacred places, including burial sites, be preserved, respected and protected.

Article 14
Indigenous peoples have the right to revitalize, use, develop and transmit to future generations their histories, languages, oral traditions, philosophies, writing systems and literatures, and to designate and retain their own names for communities, places and persons.
States shall take effective measures, whenever any right of indigenous peoples may be threatened, to ensure this right is protected and also to ensure that they can understand and be understood in political, legal and administrative proceedings, where necessary through the provision of interpretation or by other appropriate means.

PART IV
Article 15
Indigenous children have the right to all levels and forms of education of the State. All indigenous peoples also have this right and the right to establish and control their educational systems and institutions providing education in their own languages, in a manner appropriate to their cultural methods of teaching and learning.
Indigenous children living outside their communities have the right to be provided access to education in their own culture and language.
States shall take effective measures to provide appropriate resources for these purposes.

Article 16
Indigenous peoples have the right to have the dignity and diversity of their cultures, traditions, histories and aspirations appropriately reflected in all forms of education and public information.
States shall take effective measures, in consultation with the indigenous peoples concerned, to eliminate prejudice and discrimination and to promote tolerance, understanding and good relations among indigenous peoples and all segments of society.

Article 17
Indigenous peoples have the right to establish their own media in their own languages. They also have the right to equal access to all forms of non-indigenous media.
States shall take effective measures to ensure that State-owned media duly reflect indigenous cultural diversity.

Article 18
Indigenous peoples have the right to enjoy fully all rights established under international labour law and national labour legislation.
Indigenous individuals have the right not to be subjected to any discriminatory conditions of labour, employment or salary.

PART V
Article 19
Indigenous peoples have the right to participate fully, if they so choose, at all levels of decision-making in matters which may affect their rights, lives and destinies through representatives chosen by themselves in accordance with their own procedures, as well as to maintain and develop their own indigenous decision-making institutions.

Article 20
Indigenous peoples have the right to participate fully, if they so choose, through procedures determined by them, in devising legislative or administrative measures that may affect them.
States shall obtain the free and informed consent of the peoples concerned before adopting and implementing such measures.

Article 21
Indigenous peoples have the right to maintain and develop their political, economic and social systems, to be secure in the enjoyment of their own means of subsistence and development, and to engage freely in all their traditional and other economic activities. Indigenous peoples who have been deprived of their means of subsistence and development are entitled to just and fair compensation.

Article 22
Indigenous peoples have the right to special measures for the immediate, effective and continuing improvement of their economic and social conditions, including in the areas of employment, vocational training and retraining, housing, sanitation, health and social security.
Particular attention shall be paid to the rights and special needs of indigenous elders, women, youth, children and disabled persons.

Article 23
Indigenous peoples have the right to determine and develop priorities and strategies for exercising their right to development. In particular, indigenous peoples have the right to determine and develop all health, housing and other economic and social programmes affecting them and, as far as possible, to administer such programmes through their own institutions.

Article 24
Indigenous peoples have the right to their traditional medicines and health practices, including the right to the protection of vital medicinal plants, animals and minerals.
They also have the right to access, without any discrimination, to all medical institutions, health services and medical care.

PART VI
Article 25
Indigenous peoples have the right to maintain and strengthen their distinctive spiritual and material relationship with the lands, territories, waters and coastal seas and other resources which they have traditionally owned or otherwise occupied or used, and to uphold their responsibilities to future generations in this regard.

Article 26
Indigenous peoples have the right to own, develop, control and use the lands and territories, including the total environment of the lands, air, waters, coastal seas, sea-ice, flora and fauna and other resources which they have traditionally owned or otherwise occupied or used. This includes the right to the full recognition of their laws, traditions and customs, land-tenure systems and institutions for the development and management of resources, and the right to effective measures by States to prevent any interference with, alienation of or encroachment upon these rights.

Article 27
Indigenous peoples have the right to the restitution of the lands, territories and resources which they have traditionally owned or otherwise occupied or used, and which have been confiscated, occupied, used or damaged without their free and informed consent. Where this is not possible, they have the right to just and fair compensation. Unless otherwise freely agreed upon by the peoples concerned, compensation shall take the form of lands, territories and resources equal in quality, size and legal status.

Article 28
Indigenous peoples have the right to the conservation, restoration and protection of the total environment and the productive capacity of their lands, territories and resources, as well as to assistance for this purpose from States and through international cooperation. Military activities shall not take place in the lands and territories of indigenous peoples, unless otherwise freely agreed upon by the peoples concerned.
States shall take effective measures to ensure that no storage or disposal of hazardous materials shall take place in the lands and territories of indigenous peoples. States shall also take effective measures to ensure, as needed, that programmes for monitoring, maintaining and restoring the health of indigenous peoples, as developed and implemented by the peoples affected by such materials, are duly implemented.

Article 29
Indigenous peoples are entitled to the recognition of the full ownership, control and protection of their cultural and intellectual property.

They have the right to special measures to control, develop and protect their sciences, technologies and cultural manifestations, including human and other genetic resources, seeds, medicines, knowledge of the properties of fauna and flora, oral traditions, literatures, designs and visual and performing arts.

Article 30
Indigenous peoples have the right to determine and develop priorities and strategies for the development or use of their lands, territories and other resources, including the right to require that States obtain their free and informed consent prior to the approval of any project affecting their lands, territories and other resources, particularly in connection with the development, utilization or exploitation of mineral, water or other resources. Pursuant to agreement with the indigenous peoples concerned, just and fair compensation shall be provided for any such activities and measures taken to mitigate adverse environmental, economic, social, cultural or spiritual impact.

PART VII
Article 31
Indigenous peoples, as a specific form of exercising their right to self-determination, have the right to autonomy or self-government in matters relating to their internal and local affairs, including culture, religion, education, information, media, health, housing, employment, social welfare, economic activities, land and resources management, environment and entry by non-members, as well as ways and means for financing these autonomous functions.

Article 32
Indigenous peoples have the collective right to determine their own citizenship in accordance with their customs and traditions. Indigenous citizenship does not impair the right of indigenous individuals to obtain citizenship of the States in which they live.
Indigenous peoples have the right to determine the structures and to select the membership of their institutions in accordance with their own procedures.

Article 33
Indigenous peoples have the right to promote, develop and maintain their institutional structures and their distinctive juridical customs, traditions, procedures and practices, in accordance with internationally recognized human rights standards.

Article 34
Indigenous peoples have the collective right to determine the responsibilities of individuals to their communities.

Article 35
Indigenous peoples, in particular those divided by international borders, have the right to maintain and develop contacts, relations and cooperation, including activities for spiritual, cultural, political, economic and social purposes, with other peoples across borders.
States shall take effective measures to ensure the exercise and implementation of this right.

Article 36
Indigenous peoples have the right to the recognition, observance and enforcement of treaties, agreements and other constructive arrangements concluded
with States or their successors, according to their original spirit and intent, and
to have States honour and respect such treaties, agreements and other constructive arrangements. Conflicts and disputes which cannot otherwise be settled
should be submitted to competent international bodies agreed to by all parties
concerned.

PART VIII
Article 37
States shall take effective and appropriate measures, in consultation with the
indigenous peoples concerned, to give full effect to the provisions of this Declaration. The rights recognized herein shall be adopted and included in national
legislation in such a manner that indigenous peoples can avail themselves of
such rights in practice.

Article 38
Indigenous peoples have the right to have access to adequate financial and
technical assistance, from States and through international cooperation, to
pursue freely their political, economic, social, cultural and spiritual development and for the enjoyment of the rights and freedoms recognized in this
Declaration.

Article 39
Indigenous peoples have the right to have access to and prompt decision
through mutually acceptable and fair procedures for the resolution of conflicts
and disputes with States, as well as to effective remedies for all infringements of
their individual and collective rights. Such a decision shall take into consideration the customs, traditions, rules and legal systems of the indigenous peoples
concerned.

Article 40
The organs and specialized agencies of the United Nations system and other
intergovernmental organizations shall contribute to the full realization of the
provisions of this Declaration through the mobilization, *inter alia*, of financial
cooperation and technical assistance. Ways and means of ensuring participation
of indigenous peoples on issues affecting them shall be established.

Article 41
The United Nations shall take the necessary steps to ensure the implementation
of this Declaration including the creation of a body at the highest level with special competence in this field and with the direct participation of indigenous peoples. All United Nations bodies shall promote respect for and full application of
the provisions of this Declaration.

PART IX
Article 42
The rights recognized herein constitute the minimum standards for the survival,
dignity and well-being of the indigenous peoples of the world.

Article 43
All the rights and freedoms recognized herein are equally guaranteed to male and female indigenous individuals.

Article 44
Nothing in this Declaration may be construed as diminishing or extinguishing existing or future rights indigenous peoples may have or acquire.

Article 45
Nothing in this Declaration may be interpreted as implying for any State, group or person any right to engage in any activity or to perform any act contrary to the Charter of the United Nations.

Contributors

S. JAMES ANAYA (Purepecha/Apache) is professor of law at the University of Arizona in Tucson. He has written widely on the development of indigenous law at the international level. He is the author of *Indigenous Peoples in International Law* (1996).

WARD CHURCHILL (Keetowah Band of Cherokee) is professor of Native American studies at the University of Colorado–Boulder, where he is chair of the Ethnic Studies Department. His research has focused on indigenous political history and political activism. His numerous books include *A Little Matter of Genocide: Holocaust and Denial in the Americas, 1492 to the Present* (1997).

CECIL CORBETT (Nez Percé) served for over twenty-five years as president of Cook College and Theological School, and he is now director of the Native American Training Resource Center in Phoenix, Arizona.

VINE DELORIA, JR. (Standing Rock Sioux), retired from his teaching position as professor of history at the University of Colorado–Boulder in 2000. His research and writing interests continue to expand and encompass philosophy, theology, psychology, education, natural science, law, political theory, history, archaeology, and anthropology. His publications include *Spirit and Reason: The Vine Deloria Jr. Reader* (1999) and, most recently, *Evolution, Creationism, and Other Modern Myths: A Critical Inquiry* (2002).

RICHARD A. GROUNDS (Yuchi/Seminole) is director of the Euchee Language Project in Oklahoma. His research has focused on Native language preservation and indigenous religious traditions.

JOY HARJO (Mvskoke) is a poet, filmmaker, and musical artist. She has received numerous awards and has published several novels and many works of poetry.

INÉS HERNÁNDEZ-ÁVILA (Nez Percé/Chicana) is professor of Native American studies at the University of California–Davis. Her research interests include Native American religious traditions, Native American women's literature (particularly poetry and performance), Native American and Chicana studies, Native American and Chicana feminism, and early-twentieth-century Texas-Mexican women's literature.

M. A. JAIMES-GUERRERO (Juaneño/Yaqui) is associate professor of women's studies at San Francisco State University. Her research has concentrated on Native political activism, indigenous feminism, and biocolonialism. She is the editor of *The State of Native America: Genocide, Colonization, and Resistance* (1992).

CLARA SUE KIDWELL (Choctaw/Ojibwe) is professor and chair of the American Indian Studies Department at the University of Oklahoma. Her publications include *Choctaws and Missionaries in Mississippi, 1818–1918* (1997).

HENRIETTA MANN (Cheyenne) is the endowed chair in Native American studies at Montana State University–Bozeman. She sits on the Council of Elders for the American Indian Science and Engineering Society. In 1991, *Rolling Stone Magazine* ranked her as one of the top ten professors in the United States.

JOHN MOHAWK (Seneca) is associate professor of American studies at the State University of New York–Buffalo. His research includes indigenous law and nationalism. He is currently director of the Center for the Americas. He is the author of *Utopian Legacies: A History of Conquest and Oppression in the Western World* (1999).

GLENN T. MORRIS (Shawnee) is associate professor of political science at the University of Colorado–Denver. His research examines indigenous political activism both in the United States and internationally. He is also director of the Fourth World Center, a research center focusing on indigenous issues locally, regionally, and globally.

MICHELENE E. PESANTUBBEE (Choctaw) is associate professor in the Religious Studies Department at the University of Colorado–Boulder. Her research has focused on Native American religious traditions.

INÉS TALAMANTEZ (Apache/Chicana) is associate professor of Native American religious studies in the Department of Religious Studies at the University of California–Santa Barbara. Her research interests include Native American female initiation ceremonies and indigenous attitudes toward the environment. She directs the Society for the Study of Native American Religious Traditions.

GEORGE E. "TINK" TINKER (Osage/Cherokee) is professor of American Indian cultures and religious traditions at Iliff School of Theology. His research interests focus on Native American religious traditions. He has written on the history of missionaries among American Indian communities and is the author of *Missionary Conquest: The Gospel and Native American Cultural Genocide* (1993).

DAVID E. WILKINS (Lumbee) is professor of American Indian studies and adjunct professor of political science, law, and American studies at the University of Minnesota. His research interests include federal Indian policy and law, comparative indigenous peoples, tribal governments, judicial politics, and tribal-state relations. His publications include *American Indian Politics and the American Political System* (2002).

Index

Aboriginal rights, 91, 110
"Aboriginal title," 96, 110, 193
Aborigines (Australian), 138
Acculturation, 23, 54, 55
Acosta, Father, 269
Acquisition and Government of Backward Territory in International Law, The, 159
"Action Required Internationally to Provide Effective Protection for Indigenous Peoples," 169
Adair, James, 269
Adley-SantaMaria, Bernadette, 62
Adorno, Theodor, 247, 250, 261, 264
Advocates for Indigenous California Language Survival (AICLS), 46
Affirmative action, 171, 172
Africa, 138, 144, 179, 238, 254
African Americans, 97, 98
Agreements, of San Andrés, 48
Agriculture, 23. *See also* Farming/planting
Aguilar-Amat, Anna, 55, 60, 71
Alaska, 91, 254, 255
Albright, Madeleine, 139
Alcatraz, 99, 137, 247
Aleut, 196
Alfred, Taiaiake, 129–34, 136, 154; "colonization of the mind" and, 125; facts about, 152
Allen, Paula Gunn, 20, 21
Allman, T. D., 141
Allomorphism, 39
Allotment, 87, 163, 179, 321
Amazon area, 40
Amer-European settlers. *See* Euro-American culture
American Anthropological Association, 304
American Declaration of the Rights and Duties of Man, 128
American Indian Movement (AIM), 97, 116–17, 180, 248; Churchill and, 248; disintegration of, 249, 264; Means of, 135, 138, 146, 151, 292; Peltier of, 100; resistance and, 224; sovereignty and, 135; Trudell of, 129; UN and, 248; Wounded

Knee and, 99, 146
American Indian Politics and the American Political System, 337
American Indian Religious Freedom Act (AIRFA), 196–97, 198, 204; amendments to, 201–2; sacred sites and, 200
American Indians: as "barbarians/savages," 108, 126, 140, 142, 148, 158, 279; citizenship conferred on, 163; as codependents, 235; as college students, 99; DNA testing of, 275, 304; dysfunction among, 233–35; as hunter-gatherers, 88; as "infidels," 107, 109, 126, 148; intellectual/scholarly thought among (*see* Indigenous scholars); as Jews, 256, 269; mythology about (*see* Mythology, about indigenous peoples); organizations for, 318–19; "real," 275, 298; as scientists, 6, 7, 16 (*see also* Ethnoastronomy; Science); stereotypes of, 279; trade by, 320–21; tribes/clans of, 236–37 (*see also specific ones*). *See also entries beginning* Native Americans; Native/Indian
American Indians, American Justice, x, 249
American Indian Science and Engineering Society, 336
American Revolution, 20, 21, 22, 31
Amoco Production Co. v. Southern Ute Indian Tribe, 93
Anarchism, 264
Anasazi, 243, 323
Anaya, S. James, 77, 136, 152, 153, 155, 335
Anderson, G., 255
Andrews, Lynn, 228
Anishnaabe, 264
Anthropology, 126, 256, 312; activism and, 180; archaeology and, 268, 270; biology versus, 254; Deloria and, 191, 250–57; emic/etic aproaches in, 209–10, 250, 265; exogenous interpretations from, 274; geology and, 268; Gramscian theory in, 249; "Kennewick Man" and, 77, 192–93; physics and, 270; radiocardon datings suppressed by, 255; "real"

Haskell Indian Nations University, 202
Haskew, Derek C., 150
Hassler, Peter, 141
Haudenosaunee, 127
Haw, Dora Luz, 49
Hawaii, 138, 185, 196, 205; lava flows in, 255; sacred sites in, 196, 205
Hawkeye, 292
Health services, 174–75, 185
Heidegger, Martin, 287
Heisenberg, Werner, 253
Henry, Jules, 284
Henry VII (England), 109
Hernández, Francisco, 17
Hernández, Natalio, 36, 39–43, 45, 49–50, 68, 70; Bonfil Batalla and, 68; Chiapas and, 44; leadership of, 53–54, 68; Mexican languages and, 53
Hernández-Ávila, Inés, 35, 335–36
Heron Clan, 152
Hewitt, J. N. B., 34
Hicks, George L., 312
Hierarchical global ideology, 132
"Hierarchies of knowledge," 124
Hispaniola, 141
History, 105, 127, 140, 253; collective amnesia about, 129–30; colonialism's effect on indigenous economic, 124; Deloria and, x, 210–11; exogenous interpretations and, 274; federal Indian law and, 320–21; interpreting, 145, 210–11, 216; oral narratives and, 285–86; religion as part of, 209; role of Native Americans in American, 275; sacred sites and, 198, 199
Hitchcock, Peter, 217
Hobbes, Thomas, 131–32
Hochschild, Adam, 138
Hoijer, Harry, 283
Holler, Clyde, 238
Homogenization, 49, 101, 133
Hopi, 8, 9, 11, 237; language of, 10; origin story of, 253–54, 268; Soyal ceremony of, 6, 11
"Host World," 264
House of Writers in Indigenous Languages, 36, 42
Howard, Dick, 265
Hrdlicka, Ales, 268
Huasteco, 41
Huichol, 41, 55, 56, 57
Huicholes, 41
Hultkrantz, Ake, 210, 211
Human Genome Diversity Project (HGDP), 304

Human rights, 43, 100, 102, 122–23, 128; IITC and, 146; indigenous rights movement and, 165; Native languages and, 66; special-duty doctrine and, 155; UN and, 147, 151, 161; World Conference on, 169–70. *See also* International human rights forums
Human Rights—Indian Rights, 180
Human sacrifice, 13, 14, 141
Hunting rights, 81, 84; of Chippewa, 93; off-reservation, 91; Public Law 280 and, 90; state law and, 93; Termination Act and, 90–91; today, 90
Huron, 25, 33

"Ice-free corridor," 254
Ideologies, 243; hierarchical global, 132; Marxist, 249; religious studies and, 215; scholarship and, 276; semantics and, 120, 123, 127; statist, 132, 249
Illich, Ivan, 138, 139, 259
Illinois, 13
ILO Convention No. 107, 162–63, 166, 182; Kickingbird and, 136; regarded as "outdated," 181
ILO Convention No. 169, 122, 165–67, 181, 182; Draft Declaration of UN compared with, 168; ELIAC and, 50; votes for and against, 183
Immigrants, 278, 279
Imperialism, 32, 33; cultural, 259; intellectual, 256; semantic, 104
Inca, 7, 11–12
India, 238
Indian Child Welfare Act (ICWA), 174, 185
Indian Claims Commission, 100, 128, 300, 311
Indian Financing Act, 173
Indian Health Care Improvement Act, 174–75, 185
Indian Health Service, 174, 184, 185
Indian Job Corps, 218
Indian Law Resource Center (ILRC), 114, 117, 127, 136, 151, 180
"Indian problem," 112
Indian Religious Freedom Act, 175
Indian Reorganization Act, 81, 89, 131, 163–64; congressional debate about, 179; Deloria and, 100, 319
Indian Rights Association, 318
Indian Self-Determination and Education Assistance Act, 173, 174
Indian Tribal Government Tax Status Act, 174

NATIVE VOICES